eat fresh, stay healthy

eat fresh, stay healthy

Tony Tantillo
and Sam Gugino

Macmillan * USA

MACMILLAN
A Simon & Schuster Macmillan Company
1633 Broadway
New York, NY 10019-6785

Copyright © 1997 by Tony Tantillo and Sam Gugino

MACMILLAN is a registered trademark of Macmillan, Inc.

Library of Congress Cataloging-in-Publication Data
Tantillo, Tony
Eat fresh, stay healthy / Tony Tantillo and Sam Gugino.
    p.   cm.
Includes bibliographical references and index.
ISBN 0-02-860383-4 (alk. paper)
1. Cookery (Vegetables) 2. Vegetables. 3. Cookery (Fruit)
4. Fruit. I. Gugino, Sam. II. Title.
TX801.T37 1997   96-29178
641.6'5—dc20   CIP

ISBN: 0-02-860383-4

Manufactured in the United States of America

10 9 8 7 6 5 4 3 2 1

Book design by Nick Anderson

To Giovanni Tantillo,
who taught me
about the produce business
and about love and respect for family and life
—TT

To Anna Gugino,
whose love of family and cooking
has always been an inspiration
—SG

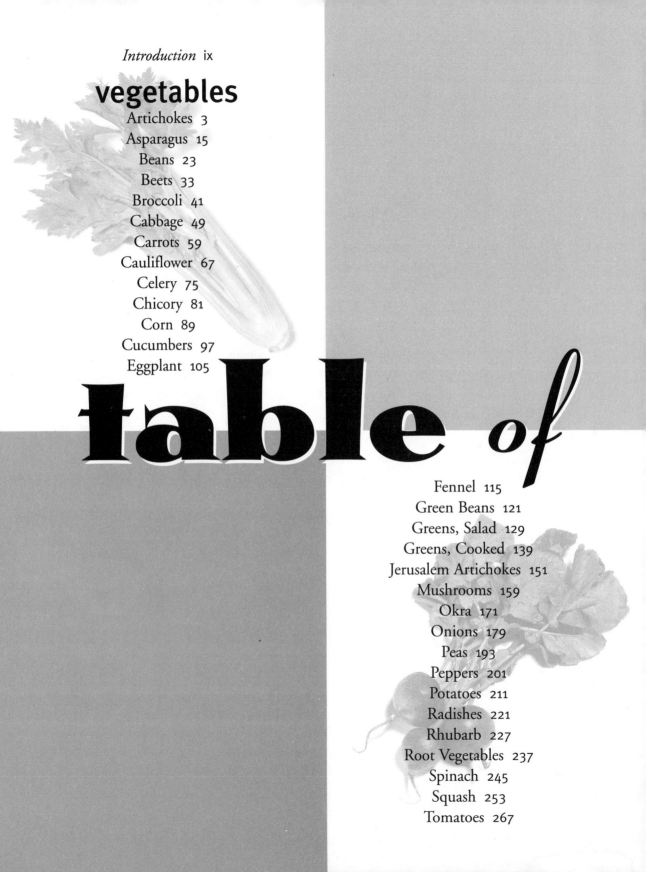

table of

contents

fruits

introduction

Americans are constantly being told by health educators, nutritionists, and food writers to eat more fruits and vegetables. But research shows that while many would like to eat more fruits and vegetables, they don't. There are a number of reasons for this, but the obvious ones are that most people don't know how to choose produce properly or how to cook it for maximum flavor and nutritional retention. So they stay with the tried and true. By limiting the kinds of fruits and vegetables that are eaten and how they are eaten, Americans necessarily limit their total consumption of produce. After all, how many baked potatoes or ears of corn can you eat?

One such average American is Bud Polley, the superintendent of an apartment building where Sam used to live. He loves to cook but admits, "When I go into the produce section, I see a lot of fruits and vegetables that look interesting. But I have no idea about how to choose or cook with them. I could sure use a book that gives me that information."

For the past three years on his daily radio and television spots, Tony has been telling people throughout Northern California to "Eat Fresh and Stay Healthy!" Logically, Tony's television and radio audience—not to mention the hundreds of supermarkets who sponsor his segments—have been asking, "Hey Tony, when are you going to put all those great produce tips you give us together in a book?"

Well, we've finally done it. We think *Eat Fresh, Stay Healthy* will please Bud Polley, Tony's listeners, and thousands of other Americans. With this book you can not only feel confident in choosing the best produce and storing it under optimum conditions, you can also select from 250 recipes that will make it taste great.

It's not our aim to turn everyone into vegetarians. Though both of us frequently make entire meals of nothing but vegetables and fruit, particularly in late summer, we do eat meat, but in much smaller amounts than we used to. Indeed, while the recipes in the book are healthful, quite a few do contain meat or meat stocks.

Rather, our point is to help more Americans enjoy the abundance of fruits and vegetables available to us. The variety of produce and overall quality far surpasses what any other country has. So why shouldn't we take advantage of it?

And not just because expanding our horizons makes eating more interesting. Eating more fruits and vegetables makes us all healthier. A diet rich in produce helps us to maintain or lose weight more easily and helps us cut down on excess fats that can lead to numerous diseases. But more than that, fruits and vegetables have been shown in recent years to contain an abundance of compounds that can prevent and fight a wide range of diseases and degenerative conditions, from high cholesterol to colon cancer to osteoporosis.

Most of the recipes in the book are Mediterranean, but with the fats and calories pared away. Why Mediterranean? The Mediterranean diet has been shown to add years to people's lives. In addition to reliance on fruits and vegetables, the Mediterranean diet includes a lot of grains and the primary fat is olive oil. (There will be some obvious exceptions to Mediterranean recipes. For example, tropical fruits aren't used extensively in Mediterranean cooking.)

Although we often substitute olive oil for butter, we don't pour it on like pancake syrup. Despite the fact that olive oil has been shown to be more heart healthy than butter, even "good" fat has to be limited because in the end, it's the overall fat in our diet as well as the kind of fat that counts. And what's the point of eating more fruits and vegetables if they're larded down with fat?

However, though we've tried to keep the fats down, this isn't a low-fat cookbook, but a lower fat cookbook. A certain amount of fat is necessary for flavor. And frankly, most of the truly low-fat cookbooks and recipes we've seen leave us cold. We've always followed the dictum that it doesn't matter how low the fat is if people don't eat it.

Our recipes strive for 10 grams of fat or less per serving, or a total amount of fat that is less than 30 percent of overall calories, or both. Nutritionists tell us that the ideal is a diet that is less than 30 percent fat, preferably one that is between 20 and 25 percent. But merely following the 30 percent rule can be misleading. What if a dish, such as the fennel and blood orange salad, has only 100 calories but has 8 grams of fat? That translates into 72 fat calories, or 72 percent fat. But is this out of line? We don't think so given its context and the total amount of fat.

Essentially, what we're saying, in addition to "Eat fresh, stay healthy," is to "Eat sensibly, stay healthy." Part of eating sensibly also means not playing games with portion sizes. It's easy to say your food is low fat if your portions would be sufficient for hummingbirds but not humans. We think you'll be satisfied with the portion sizes in all our recipes. More importantly, you'll love the way the food tastes.

Eat Fresh, Stay Healthy is divided into two main parts: vegetables and fruits. In each section we list common fruits and vegetables and their varieties. And we have a few out of the ordinary ones (or exotic, depending on your tastes) like persimmons and broccoli raab. But even these are now readily available in most parts of the country.

We don't have too many of the truly exotic fruits or vegetables like cherimoya or cardoons. For the most part, we wanted to stick with mainstream produce. There is plenty of that when you count all the varieties. And some of what we consider mainstream used to be exotic a mere decade or so ago, like the kiwifruit.

We think the more you use the produce in that broad grouping, the more likely you'll begin to seek out new and different fruits and vegetables. And by then, we'll have written our sequel!

For each fruit and vegetable, we list where it is grown, varieties, seasonal availability, selection, handling and storage information, nutritional information, yields, and preparation instructions. Tony will give his famous tips. And Sam will give cooking tips as well as recipes.

Where possible we've gotten our nutritional information from the most recent (August, 1996) nutrition labels approved by the Food and Drug Administration. But not all produce has an FDA nutrition label, only the top twenty fruits and twenty vegetables, plus a few arcane ones like the guava, whose manufacturers conduct their own nutrient testing. Produce like dandelion, Jerusalem artichokes, and mangoes, however, doesn't have labels. So we've had to scour nutrition books (which weren't always in agreement) to come up with the numbers.

Also, FDA serving sizes can be pretty strange and inconsistent. For example, the serving size for green cabbage is $\frac{1}{12}$ of a medium head (84 grams). But for red cabbage it's 1 cup, shredded (70 grams). For a green bell pepper it's 148 grams but for a red bell pepper it's 68 grams. When we relied on sources other than the FDA, serving sizes for nutritional purposes are generally 100 grams, about 3.5 ounces.

In revising the nutrition labels, the FDA changed the recommended daily allowance for vitamins and minerals (RDAs) to reference daily intakes (RDIs) for vitamins and minerals and daily reference values (DRVs) for macronutrients such as protein and fiber. The combined term for the RDIs and DRVs is the daily value or DV. And DV is the term used in this book.

While we think the information contained in this book is comprehensive, there is still much to be learned by all of us. We invite consumers to ask questions of produce managers in supermarkets or wherever they buy the bulk of their fruits and vegetables. Where did this come from? How long has it been stored? And so on.

We urge that you be demanding about quality. That's the only way produce will improve. If you've ever seen a French housewife dress down a produce merchant who has tried to foist less than perfect fruits or vegetables on her, you know what we're talking about. Americans are far too timid in accepting what's out there, perhaps because our produce has been so cheap for so long. It's not that way in other countries.

We also implore you to patronize farmer's markets wherever they may be in your area. And if there aren't any, find out why. Even in New York City, farmer's markets have been a boon to consumers in providing quality produce and a reconnection to the land that we've been lacking for so many years.

Finally, while we think it's important to eat more fruits and vegetables regardless of how they are grown, we want to put in a plug for produce that is raised organically, that is, without synthetic fertilizers, herbicides, or pesticides. We believe in organic produce for two reasons. First, because it preserves the land and is safer for farm workers and consumers. Second, we often, but not always, think organic produce tastes better.

You can help the whole organic movement by buying from local farmers who grow organically and by asking your retailers to carry more (or start carrying) organic produce.

When we start eating more fruits and vegetables, especially those in season, grown by local farmers, and in particular farmers who are judicious in using chemicals, then we will all truly be able to "Eat fresh, stay healthy."

artichokes

Ever wonder how our ancestors first discovered if a plant was edible? We think about that every time we see an artichoke. It's lovely to look at, especially the way it's harvested in Italy. Artichokes there have more of a purplish hue, and that familiar closed crown is attached to a longer stem than we see in the United States, sometimes a foot or more.

But the artichoke also looks menacing and impenetrable, like the pineapple. But unlike the pineapple, the meat of the artichoke is harder to find—and there's a lot less of it. We can just imagine our bearskin-robed forebears picking off leaves, chewing the wrong parts, then getting to the choke and gagging before arriving at the center or heart—if they lasted long enough to get there.

Centuries later, artichokes still require some effort one way or another. We like to say artichokes are like car oil filters. Remember the Fram oil-filter commercial? A mechanic, having just finished a complete engine overhaul on a car, advises the preventative maintenance of using a clean oil filter by admonishing "pay me now, or pay me later." With artichokes you have to spend time cleaning and paring them down before you cook them. If you don't, you have to eat around those inedible parts after you cook them. Fortunately, if you decide to do the latter, it won't cost you a new engine.

Artichokes are members of the small thistle family that contains only one other cultivated species, the cardoon. In fact, some believe that the artichoke is a cultivated version of the cardoon. Wild versions of both abound in the Mediterranean and to a lesser extent in the United States. Neither, however, is related to the Jerusalem artichoke, which is not a true artichoke at all.

WHERE GROWN

The artichoke flourishes in Mediterranean climates. Italy is the largest artichoke-producing nation, followed by Spain (where most artichokes are canned), France, Argentina, Egypt, and the United States. In warmer areas of the Mediterranean artichokes tend to be tough.

Thus, when they are raised commercially in these spots, they are usually a spring crop.

The central coast of California with its cool summers, mild winters, higher humidity, and lower evening temperatures is an ideal climate for an almost constant supply of artichokes. California produces virtually 100 percent of domestic artichokes and consumes about half of that as well. The major growing area stretches from San Mateo to Monterey. Smaller amounts are grown in Ventura and Riverside counties and the Imperial Valley in the south and in the south-central coastal areas of San Luis Obispo and Santa Barbara. The small town of Castroville in Monterey County is America's artichoke capital. You can easily recognize it by the giant artichoke towering above the downtown area, the symbol for a restaurant and produce stand called the Giant Artichoke.

VARIETIES

There are more than 140 artichoke varieties, but less than 40 are grown commercially. Italy produces more artichoke varieties than any other country. The United States and most other countries cultivate only a few.

The Green Globe variety accounts for about 90 percent of the artichokes produced domestically. It is a clone of the original Green Globe, developed by the California artichoke industry. The Desert Globe is similar to the Green Globe in shape and size but has a more compact appearance with a more uniform green color on the outside and less prominent thorns on the tips of the leaves. As the name implies, it was developed to grow in the desert areas of California. A third variety is called the Big Heart because it has a wide heart. Somewhat larger than the other two artichokes, the Big Heart is also thornless and has a more pronounced purple hue, especially in the summer.

Baby artichokes are not a separate variety but merely smaller versions of larger artichokes. Their size comes from their location on the artichoke plant. Baby artichokes are picked from the lower parts of the artichoke plant where the plant fronds protect them from sun, in effect stunting their growth. But unlike other baby vegetables, the baby artichoke is picked when fully mature so it has the same full flavor as a larger artichoke.

SEASONS

The Green Globe is available almost year-round with some shortages in the hot summer months, particularly August. The peak period for availability and low price is March, April, and May. In the Castroville area, artichokes are harvested as often as every five days or as infrequently as every two weeks. There may be as many as thirty harvests in a single year.

The Big Heart is also a year-round variety with peaks in early and late spring and in the fall. The Desert Globe is available from December to March. Small amounts of Chilean artichokes (primarily the Green Globe) are imported in October, November, and December.

Baby artichokes have the same availability as larger artichokes.

SELECTION, HANDLING & STORAGE

Artichokes are cut from stalks by hand using a small, stubby knife called a fruit knife. They are then flung into large backpacks slung over the pickers' shoulders. In peak season, pickers use two knives and two hands at once.

Under optimum conditions, artichokes are picked before their leaves, or bracts, begin to separate and with a stem end about 3 to 4 inches long.

Artichokes range in size from small or baby artichokes—2 or 3 ounces each—to jumbo artichokes that can weigh as much as twenty ounces each. Look for artichokes that are firm and compact and heavy for their size. In the spring and summer, artichokes should have an even green color. In summer and fall the leaves of artichokes tend to be flared rather than tightly closed. And in the fall and winter, artichokes may show some frost damage in the form of some light bronze to brown coloring on the outer leaves. But this "winter kiss" as the industry calls it is actually a good thing. Artichokes so affected are considered to have superior flavor.

Baby artichokes can range in size from as small as a walnut to as large as a goose egg. Size is no indication of age or quality, however. Use the same criteria for baby artichokes as you would for regular ones.

Artichokes dehydrate rapidly so it is important to put them in plastic bags and store them in the vegetable bin of the refrigerator as soon as you get home. A little sprinkle of water before you bag them wouldn't hurt. Artichoke growers tell retailers to keep artichokes on ice or gently mist them to keep them from drying out. (But not too much water or the artichokes will get moldy.) So if you see a produce manager doing this, he's probably taking good care of his chokes.

To refresh an artichoke that looks a little dehydrated, cut the brown part off the bottom of the stem and put the artichoke in a bowl of water. Cooked or raw artichokes will keep about a week in the high-humidity bin of your refrigerator.

NUTRITION

Considering that a 12-ounce artichoke has only 2 edible ounces, it is a pretty good source of nutrients. A single serving also contains 25 calories, 6g of carbohydrates, 2g of protein, 3g of dietary fiber, 10% of the DV for vitamin C, and 2% each for vitamin A, iron, and calcium. Artichokes also contain a decent amount of folic acid, potassium, and magnesium.

YIELD

One medium to large artichoke—about 12 ounces—yields about 2 ounces of edible flesh.

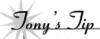

Tony's Tip

Artichokes are known as an appetite stimulator. In fact there is an Italian aperetivo called Cynar (pronounced CHEE-nawr, named after the word for the artichoke genus). It has a rather medicinal taste for the uninitiated, something like Campari. Try it over ice with tonic, club soda, or bitter lemon as a cocktail.

PREPARATION

Artichokes can be the most arduous of vegetables to prepare, depending on what you want to do with them and your level of patience. At the simplest level, one merely needs to lop off the stem so the artichoke sits upright, then cut an inch or so off the top. Thus prepared, the artichoke can be boiled, steamed, or microwaved, and the eater can do the rest of the work, eating around the inedible parts. Like broccoli stems, artichoke stems are often needlessly discarded. Peel and steam them with the rest of the artichoke. The stems can then be eaten as is or chopped and put into stuffing (to go inside the prepared artichokes).

To prepare artichokes for stuffing, remove the stem as explained above. Pull back the leaves to uncover the inedible center portion. Scrape out the very inner leaves (called the cone) and the fuzzy choke. (This can be done while the artichoke is raw but it's much more difficult that way.)

An added but simple step involves trimming $1/2$ inch or so from the tops of the outer leaves using scissors. This makes for a better appearance and eliminates the prickly needles that protrude from the tops of the leaves. Stuff the center of the cooked artichokes with such things as bread crumbs or sausage, and put some stuffing in between the leaves as well. Then bake them. Steamed or boiled artichokes can be served cold, stuffed with the likes of shrimp or crab salad.

For preparations such as deep frying or salads, the artichoke needs to be completely edible. Remove the very bottom leaves and slice off $1/2$ inch from the bottom of the stem. Hold the artichoke in one hand with the thumb positioned on the bottom portion of each leaf. Then bend back each leaf until it snaps naturally. Tear off the top part. What remains is the edible portion.

As you get closer to the center of the artichoke, only pale green and yellow inner portions will show and the edible portion of each leaf will be larger. Be scrupulous about the bottom portion of the artichoke, removing anything that looks like it might be tough. Taste if you're not sure and trim any dark green portions, particularly from the bottom, with a sharp paring knife. Rub cut portions with a cut lemon to prevent discoloration. Halve the artichoke lengthwise and remove the inner cone and choke with a spoon. At this point you can use the artichoke as is, cut it into quarters, or slice thinly.

Baby artichokes require less manipulation. Most have no fuzzy choke. And fewer outside leaves need to be removed to get to the pale green and yellow inner portion. Follow the same procedure as with large artichokes and soon you'll get to a smaller, completely edible version. Then leave whole, halve, or quarter for whatever type of dish you prefer.

We've always cooked artichokes in a fairly large pot of highly seasoned water (see Artichokes à la Grecque, page 8) but recently we've found that they can be nicely steamed, upside down, in an inch of boiling water, with or without a steaming rack.

Mayonnaise and hollandaise sauces, or variations of either, have been mainstays as artichoke dips. So too have vinaigrettes. A concession to healthfulness might involve well-seasoned yogurt or a compromise of yogurt and mayonnaise in equal portions. The seasonings could be any of those used in the Artichoke à la Grecque preparation.

ARTICHOKE ETIQUETTE

It amazes us that so many people still don't know how to eat an artichoke—but then we've been eating them all our lives. Sam remembers giving a dinner party in which the first course was an artichoke half. As he and his wife were returning the dishes to the kitchen, they noticed all the plates had the inedible parts of the leaves piled on them except one plate. It was completely clean. After the guests left, Sam and Mary checked under the rug, behind the curtain and in the bathroom. Nothing. Had the person eaten every portion of the leaves? Had she (they eventually figured out who it was) stuffed them into her pocket?

So, for all of you who dread being served artichokes because you never learned how to eat them, here is some artichoke etiquette.

- It is perfectly proper to pluck and eat artichoke leaves with your fingers. No utensils are necessary.
- To eat the leaves, pull off a leaf by grabbing the pointed end. At the other, wider end is a thin layer of edible flesh. Put about half of the edible end of the leaf into your mouth and scrape off the flesh with your teeth. Repeat with the remaining leaves. The edible portion of the leaves becomes greater as you get closer to the center of the artichoke.

- Just before you get to the very center, the leaves will become almost white with purple tips. Be careful of these leaves because their ends are prickly.

- Guarding the heart of the artichoke, which most consider the best part, is a fuzzy patch or choke. Scrape it off with a spoon or cut the heart away from it with a butter knife (though a properly prepared artichoke will already have the choke removed).

- If you're provided with a dip such as a vinaigrette or mayonnaise, put a small part of the edible portion of the leaf in the dip and scrape as directed above. Don't overdo it on the dip or you won't taste the artichoke.

- One last bit of etiquette involves wine with artichokes. The long-held axiom has been that artichokes and wine don't mix. But that's not necessarily true as wine writers David Rosengarten and Joshua Wesson have pointed out in *Red Wine with Fish* (Simon and Schuster, 1989). Artichokes do have a way of making wines taste sweeter, however. So choose very dry wines with high acidity. Rosengarten and Wesson recommend ultra *brut* or *brut sauvage* nonvintage champagnes and, especially if a tomato sauce is involved, high acid, fruity Italian red wines such as a Barbera. Dry rose wines such as French roses are a good choice as well.

Artichokes à la Grecque

Artichokes cooked in this fashion don't really need any further embellishment to make a delicious and healthful dish.

Makes 4 servings

1 teaspoon kosher salt

$3/4$ teaspoon each black peppercorns, coriander seeds, and fennel seeds

2 bay leaves

A few branches of fresh thyme or $1/2$ teaspoon dried

1 whole chile pepper or a pinch of hot pepper flakes

3 cloves garlic, crushed

6 fresh parsley stems

2 tablespoons extra-virgin olive oil

1 cup dry white wine or dry vermouth

4 large artichokes

1 lemon, washed thoroughly and halved

1. Combine all ingredients, except artichokes and lemon, in a small kettle with 3 quarts of water. Bring to a boil. Lower the heat and simmer 10 minutes, longer for a more flavorful broth.

2. Meanwhile, peel artichoke stems, detach them from the base of the artichokes, and remove $1/2$ inch from the end of each stem. Cut about 1 inch off the top of each artichoke. Remove the withered leaves at the base of the artichoke. With scissors, trim $1/2$ inch or so from the tops of the other leaves. Rub the cut portions of the artichokes with cut lemon to prevent discoloration.

3. Squeeze the juice of the lemons into the flavored water and toss in the lemons. Add the artichokes and stems. Cover with a plate to keep submerged and cook about 25 minutes. You should be able to easily pierce the base of an artichoke with a knife. (If the artichokes are to be cooked further, as in Artichokes Stuffed with Duxelles, page 10, there should be a bit more resistance.) Remove artichokes, squeeze gently to remove excess moisture, and cool upside down. Eat as is (warm or at room temperature), roast, or stuff and bake.

Sam's Cooking Tip

If you don't want the loose herbs and spices to get stuck inside the artichoke leaves, put all the herbs and spices in a tea ball or wrap them in cheesecloth. Speaking of seasonings, I use kosher salt because it has the purest, least adulterated salt flavor.

Baked Artichokes with Garlic

This preparation gives the artichokes a rustic flavor.

Makes 4 servings

4 medium to large artichokes	Kosher salt and freshly ground black
1/2 lemon	pepper to taste
4 large cloves garlic, chopped	1/2 cup Chicken Stock (recipe follows)
3 tablespoons olive oil	1/2 cup white wine

1. Remove the artichoke stems and save for another recipe. Trim the artichoke top and leaves as directed in Preparation (page 6), rubbing the cut surfaces with the lemon to prevent discoloration. Scoop out the center choke and inedible purple tinged leaves. Preheat oven to 350°F.

2. Mix garlic with olive oil, salt, and pepper. Spread artichoke leaves and, with a teaspoon, put some of the mixture in between the leaves of each artichoke as well as in the scooped out center. Put in a baking dish, add stock and wine to the bottom, and cover securely with foil. Bake about 1 hour. Serve warm or at room temperature.

Sam's Cooking Tip

You can bend many a teaspoon trying to scoop out the inner choke of an artichoke. Instead, use a melon baller, one of those miniature versions of an ice-cream scoop.

Chicken Stock

Makes about 2 quarts

4 pounds of any combination of chicken parts, giblets, or bones, including skin but excluding the liver	2 ribs celery (including leaves), cut into 1-inch pieces
2 medium carrots, scrubbed and cut into 1-inch chunks	10 parsley stems, cut into 1-inch pieces
	10 whole black peppercorns
2 medium onions, peeled and cut into quarters	2 bay leaves
	2 sprigs fresh thyme or 1/2 teaspoon dried thyme

1. Put chicken and vegetables in a pot with 4 quarts of cold water. Bring to boil over moderate heat. Before it reaches a full boil, skim off the scum that forms on the top with a ladle or large, deep spoon.

2. Reduce heat to simmer, add seasonings, stir and cook 3 hours at a bare simmer, stirring occasionally.

3. Line a colander or large sieve with a double thickness of cheesecloth. Strain stock through cheesecloth, pressing out as much juice as possible from solids with the back of a ladle or spoon. Refrigerate until cold and skim off any fat that has risen to the top.

Artichokes Stuffed with Duxelles

As was the case with many Italian Americans, we grew up eating artichokes as a Friday meat substitution and as a mainstay during the Lenten season. But you don't have to give up anything for Lent to enjoy this dish.

Makes 4 servings

4 large artichokes, cooked à la Grecque (see Artichokes à la Grecque, page 8), cooking liquid reserved

1 pound white mushrooms, quartered

1 tablespoon butter

3 large shallots, minced

2 teaspoons fresh thyme or 1 teaspoon dried

Kosher salt and freshly ground black pepper to taste

Olive oil cooking spray

1. Chop the cooked artichoke stems and put them in a mixing bowl. Remove the center cone and fibrous chokes from the center of each artichoke by pulling back the center leaves and scooping out the inedible portion with a teaspoon. Set artichokes aside.

2. Preheat oven to 400°F. Put mushrooms in a food processor and pulse until finely chopped but not mushy—or chop by hand. In a large skillet or wok, melt butter over medium-high heat. When foam subsides, add shallots and cook until just soft but not browned, about 2 minutes. Add mushrooms, increase heat to high, and cook, stirring. Continue to cook until virtually all the moisture has evaporated from the mushrooms, about 10 minutes. Add thyme and salt and pepper to taste. Cool slightly, then mix with chopped artichoke stems.

3. Stuff the center of each artichoke with the duxelle mixture. Open some of the outer leaves and put some stuffing in between the leaves as well. Put in a shallow baking pan with about 1/2 cup of reserved cooking liquid. Spray top with olive oil cooking spray and cook, uncovered, 15 minutes.

Sam's Cooking Tip

Duxelles (pronounced dook-SEHL), the finely chopped mixture of mushrooms, shallots, and herbs cooked in butter, is a common flavor enhancement in many French dishes from soups to stews and sauces. It's also delicious in omelets and scrambled eggs.

Artichokes Stuffed with Herbed Bread Crumbs

This is a favorite stuffing for many Italians. You can also vary it with plumped raisins or toasted pine nuts, for example.

Makes 4 servings

1 tablespoon olive oil

2 shallots, minced

2 cups bread crumbs (preferably home-made from quality Italian or French bread)

1/4 cup fresh mint, chopped

1/4 cup fresh Italian parsley, chopped

Pinch of cayenne pepper or hot pepper flakes

Kosher salt and freshly ground black pepper to taste

2 tablespoons freshly grated Parmesan cheese

4 large artichokes cooked and prepared as in Step 1 of Artichokes Stuffed with Duxelles (page 10) with cooking liquid reserved

Olive oil cooking spray

1. Heat oil in a large skillet or wok. Cook shallots over medium heat, stirring occasionally, until soft. Add bread crumbs and cook, stirring, until bread crumbs are lightly toasted, about 5 minutes. Put in a mixing bowl with the chopped artichoke stems, mint, parsley, hot pepper, salt, and pepper to taste.

2. Stuff artichokes as in Step 3 of Artichokes Stuffed with Duxelles (page 10). Spray with olive oil cooking spray and bake as in previous recipe.

Roasted Artichokes

The following recipe was inspired by a dish Sam had at the Buckeye Roadhouse in Mill Valley, California. To get an extra dimension of flavor, you can also cook the artichokes on a charcoal grill over a low flame.

Makes 2 servings as part of a light luncheon;
4 servings when used as a first course or part of an antipasto plate

2 large artichokes, prepared à la Grecque (page 8)
$1/4$ cup olive oil
2 cloves garlic, chopped
Kosher salt and freshly ground black pepper to taste

1.   While the artichokes cook, heat the oil and garlic in a microwave oven for 2 minutes on high. Or gently steep in a small saucepan on the stove over low heat about 10 minutes. Set aside.

2.   Preheat oven to 500°F. Remove stems from artichokes for another use. Halve the artichokes lengthwise, and remove choke and inedible inner cone. Put artichoke halves in a small roasting pan, making sure they are not crowded together. Brush with flavored olive oil. Season with salt and pepper. Roast 17 to 20 minutes, turning once and basting as you do. When done, artichokes should be nicely browned around the edges.

Artichoke Salad

Since artichokes stimulate the appetite, it is best that this salad be served as a first or middle course rather than as a side salad with the main course.

Makes 4 to 6 servings

1 lemon	3 medium shiitake mushrooms, stems
2 tablespoons olive oil	removed
2 tablespoons balsamic vinegar	1 ounce thinly sliced prosciutto, cut into
Kosher salt and freshly ground black	julienne strips
pepper to taste	1/3 cup shaved Parmesan cheese
3 medium artichokes	2 tablespoons fresh chives

1. Grate lemon rind and mix with oil, vinegar, salt, and pepper. Halve the lemon and set aside.

2. Trim the artichokes as directed in Preparation (page 6) so that the entire artichoke is edible. Rub the cut portions of the artichoke with one of the lemon halves as you go to prevent discoloration. Squeeze the other lemon half into a bowl of cold water and put the artichoke halves into the water to prevent discoloration as you work on them.

3. Put artichoke halves onto a cutting board, cut side down. Then cut into thin, lengthwise slices.

4. Put the artichoke slices in a bowl. Grate the mushrooms on their sides using the second-largest holes of a four-sided grater. Add to the artichokes along with the prosciutto. Add the dressing and toss. Top with shaved Parmesan and sprinkle with chives.

Sam's Cooking Tip

Lemons tend to be more heavily sprayed than other fruits. So when using the rind, for grating or any other purpose, make sure you wash the skin thoroughly.

asparagus

Life used to be a lot simpler and more predictable. Christmas decorations didn't go up until after Thanksgiving, the Colts played in Baltimore, and asparagus was a sure sign of spring.

The first asparagus would arrive from California in late March. By Easter we were practically bathing in asparagus. Then the short season of local asparagus came in late May and early June. And by the end of June asparagus was gone until next year, like pumpkins and Halloween.

Then, several years ago, our world became more complicated and less predictable. We were shopping one day at Fairway, a famous produce market on the West Side of New York City. It was mid-September, time to be thinking of apples, pomegranates, and persimmons. We noticed those familiar wooden crates that asparagus comes in; you know, the kind that look like they could double as shoe-shine boxes. Asparagus? September? Couldn't be.

Then we got closer and recognized those familiar green spears. But where in the world is asparagus coming from in September? The answer was stamped on the outside of the box: Product of Peru. Peru? Talk about your global village!

So now asparagus is a year-round vegetable like broccoli and zucchini. Is this a good thing? Yes and no. On the one hand, simple logic says that ideal asparagus weather is occurring somewhere in the world all the time, especially in the Southern Hemisphere where seasons are the reverse of those in the United States. So why not grow asparagus and take advantage of advanced transportation and handling techniques?

On the other hand, we're reminded of something legendary chef Fredy Girardet once said to us when he was bemoaning the pressure to have fresh raspberries on the menu all year long. "There is a reason why we have seasons and we should respect that," he said.

WHERE GROWN

Asparagus grows in a fairly wide range of climates. For example, in North America alone it is grown from Michigan to Guatemala. However, it thrives in Mediterranean-style regions such as California, Mexico, and, of course, its homeland, the Mediterranean basin.

California produces 70 to 80 percent of the nation's asparagus crop. Washington is second. Other producing states include Arizona, Oregon, New Jersey, Michigan, and Illinois.

The United States imports a huge quantity of asparagus from Mexico. Peru (the number-two world producer) and Chile are the second and third largest importers to the United States, which also receives some asparagus from Guatemala, Colombia, and Argentina.

VARIETIES

The vast majority of asparagus we eat is green. And the distinction among the most common varieties—UC 157, Jersey Giant, Ida Lee, and Brock—is not terribly significant.

White asparagus is the same as green asparagus. The difference is that it is picked while most of it is still underground, before the stalk below the crowned tip is exposed to sunlight.

SEASONS

The harvest season for asparagus is less than three months. But the numerous microclimates in California enable that state to provide asparagus from January through May with small amounts harvested in September and October. Peak supplies from California are available in March, April, and May, and from Washington in April, May, and June. Varieties from cooler regions such as New Jersey and Michigan begin in May and run through June.

Peru's peak season is September though December. Mexico begins exporting large quantities in January with peak supplies being available in February and March.

SELECTION, HANDLING & STORAGE

Asparagus is harvested when spears reach a length of 10 to 12 inches, which are then trimmed to about 9 inches. Spears should be very firm. The tips should be tight and compact, like the tip of a detail brush dipped in paint. Color should be a good, medium green with purple highlights. The white and woody bottom should be less than 15 percent of the total length.

Over-the-hill asparagus contains tips that are opened, stems that are wrinkled and withered, and often an odor that indicates deterioration or rotting.

Asparagus spears normally come in four sizes. Small spears, 31 to 35 per pound, are about $3/16$ inch in diameter at the base. Standard, 21 to 30 per pound, are $5/16$ inch. Large, 11 to 20 per pound, are $7/16$ inch. And jumbo, 7 to 10 per pound, are $13/16$ inch. (On occasion you will also see extra-large spears, which are $10/16$ inch in diameter.) Spears are sold in bunches, weighing 1 to $1^1/2$ pounds.

Many have the mistaken belief that thin, so-called pencil asparagus is more tender and more flavorful than fatter asparagus, which some mistake for older asparagus. Actually, the reverse is true. The younger the plant, the greater amount of jumbo asparagus it produces. Rarely have we found jumbo asparagus anything but juicy and tender. And usually we think they're more flavorful than pencil asparagus.

White asparagus will have the same qualities as green asparagus, including purple highlights, except that the color will be white instead of green.

Asparagus is shipped at temperatures between 34°F and 37°F with bottoms touching a moist pad to prevent spears from drying out. Cool temperatures—between 37°F and 41°F—should be maintained at home. Wrap bunches in plastic bags and put them in the high-humidity crisper drawer of the refrigerator. By cutting off an inch from the bottoms and wrapping fresh-cut areas in wet paper toweling, you can increase storage life beyond the normal recommended storage time of three or four days, though flavor will gradually deteriorate.

NUTRITION

A serving of five asparagus spears (93g, about 3.3 ounces) has only 25 calories and contains 4g of carbohydrates and 2g each of dietary fiber and protein. It contains 10% of the DV for vitamin A, 15% for vitamin C, and 2% each for iron and calcium. Asparagus also has decent amounts of potassium, about 230mg per serving.

Women contemplating pregnancy should know that a serving of asparagus contains about a third of the recommended daily amount (.4mg) of folic acid, a B vitamin that has been shown in recent years to minimize birth defects. And for prospective dads, asparagus also contains glutathione, an important antioxidant that helps to maintain healthy sperm.

Glutathione also helps prevent the progression of cataracts and has strong cancer-fighting properties.

YIELD

Yields of cut asparagus depend on the size of the stalks. But since most recipes don't call for cups of asparagus, it's best to look at how the asparagus will be used in a recipe. As a side vegetable, generally $1/4$ to $1/3$ pound per person is acceptable.

Tony's Tip

By storing at a temperature as low as possible, just above 32°F, asparagus will retain more than half its sugar for as long as fourteen days.

PREPARATION

"To peel or not to peel?" That is the question with asparagus. Our answer is "not." Peeling asparagus—actually the bottom 25 percent or so—is tedious and unnecessary. Our method: Hold the top half of one spear in one hand and the bottom half with the thumb and forefinger of the other hand. Bend each spear until it snaps. It will snap naturally where the toughest part meets the tender part. Save the bottoms and cooking water for stock, if you like, or discard them.

As to those special asparagus cookers—the tall cylinders where the spears stand straight up, and are three-fourths covered by water—we say you should put your money in more important kitchen tools like good knives and pots and pans.

Asparagus can be boiled in salted water, like green beans or broccoli, or steamed or microwaved. A pound of trimmed, boiled asparagus will be ready in 5 to 7 minutes, less if it is to be cooked ahead and reheated (see Sautéed Asparagus with Morels and Thyme, page 19). Microwaving (using higher wattage ovens and a few tablespoons of water) takes about the same amount of time. Steaming takes a little longer, 6 to 11 minutes, plus standing time of 3 to 5 minutes.

If you choose the boiling method, you don't need a large pot of water, unless you're cooking large quantities of asparagus (more than $1\frac{1}{2}$ pounds). An inch or two of water in a skillet will do. Bring the water to a boil with a teaspoon of salt, then add the asparagus and cook. Asparagus should be tender but quite firm.

Standard or small asparagus is the best size for stir-fries. Pieces need not be precooked and should be cut no longer than 2 inches.

Asparagus on the grill is a real treat, especially when you use the jumbo size. Boil, steam, or microwave halfway, brush with olive oil, and grill over medium heat.

Sautéed Asparagus with Morels and Thyme

Makes 4 servings

Kosher salt
1 pound asparagus, trimmed
1¹/₂ tablespoons butter
1 teaspoon olive oil

2 ounces fresh morels, sliced
1 teaspoon fresh thyme, chopped,
 or ¹/₂ teaspoon dried
Freshly ground black pepper to taste

1. Bring an inch or two of water in a skillet to a boil with a teaspoon of salt. Have a large bowl of ice water standing by in the sink.

2. Add the asparagus to the boiling the water and cook 4 to 5 minutes or until barely tender but still quite firm. With a skimmer or tongs, remove the spears to the ice water. When the asparagus has cooled, drain and set aside until you're ready to finish the dish. (Up to several hours later. Refrigerate if more than an hour.)

3. Heat butter and oil in a large skillet or wok over medium-high heat until butter stops foaming. Add morels, asparagus, thyme, and salt and pepper to taste. Stir until the morels are wilted and the asparagus is just heated through, about 3 or 4 minutes.

Asparagus and Soft-Shell Crab Sandwiches

In the spring and summer, you can find soft-shell crab sandwiches served in doughy hot dog-like rolls in taverns and luncheonettes all around the Chesapeake Bay. Don't skimp on the cayenne pepper for this recipe; it's a nice counterpoint to the crab flavor.

Makes 2 servings

2 tablespoons low-fat mayonnaise (preferably Hellman's or Best Foods)

2 teaspoons chopped capers

1 tablespoon minced scallion

3 tablespoons all-purpose flour

Kosher salt and freshly ground black pepper to taste

Healthy pinch cayenne pepper

2 soft-shell crabs, cleaned (see tip)

1 tablespoon clarified butter (page 284) or regular butter

6 to 8 asparagus spears, blanched and chilled (see Step 1 of Sautéed Asparagus with Morels and Thyme, page 19)

2 sesame seed hamburger rolls or other soft rolls

1. Combine mayonnaise, capers, and scallion in a small bowl. Set aside.

2. Combine flour with salt, pepper, and cayenne pepper. Dredge crabs in flour and shake off excess. Heat clarified butter in a large, heavy skillet over moderate heat.

3. Add crabs and cook 3 minutes on one side. Add the asparagus to the skillet, turn over the crab, and cook another 3 minutes, seasoning the asparagus with salt and pepper. Drain asparagus and crabs briefly on paper towels.

4. Spread the mayonnaise mixture on the rolls, and top with crab and asparagus.

Sam's Cooking Tip

To clean the crabs, slice off the eyes and mouth (they're small but easily recognizable) with a kitchen scissors. Lift up the two flaps on either side of the top of the crab and scrape off the fibrous gills underneath. Flip the crab over and remove the apron flap on the bottom.

Roasted Asparagus with Rosemary Oil

If you can resist dunking your bread in the rosemary oil, you'll have a delicious, low-fat vegetable dish. But it won't be easy!

Makes 3 to 4 servings

2 large sprigs of fresh rosemary
$1/4$ cup olive oil
1 pound asparagus, trimmed
Kosher salt and freshly ground black pepper to taste

1. Preheat oven to 500°F. Snap rosemary sprigs in half. Put in a micowaveable dish with oil and cook on half power for a minute. Then put oil, rosemary, and asparagus in a cast iron or other ovenproof skillet. Rub or brush asparagus thoroughly with oil. Let marinate 30 minutes at room temperature.

2. Put skillet in the oven and cook 10 minutes, shaking a few times to coat spears with oil and cook evenly. Drain oil and serve.

Asparagus Vinaigrette

This makes a nice side vegetable for a cold meal and an excellent buffet item.

Makes 3 servings

1 pound asparagus
Kosher salt
2 tablespoons extra-virgin olive oil
1 tablespoon lemon juice
1 tablespoon dry vermouth or light
  vinegar such as rice wine or cider

2 scallions, white and $2/3$ of the green,
  minced
$1/2$ teaspoon *herbes de Provence*
  (page 208)
Freshly ground black pepper

1. Trim, blanch, and chill asparagus as in Step 1 of Sautéed Asparagus with Morels and Thyme (page 19).

2. Meanwhile, combine remaining ingredients with salt to taste in a shallow dish. Add asparagus and toss to coat. Cover and marinate 3 hours at room temperature or refrigerate up to 24 hours. Bring to room temperature before serving. Toss a few times while marinating.

Risotto with Asparagus and Clams

The hot pepper and lemon offer a good contrast to each other in this dish. Notice the absence of cheese. Italians don't add it to pasta or risotto where seafood is involved.

**Makes 4 to 6 servings as a main course
or 6 to 8 as an appetizer**

30 littleneck clams, scrubbed

3 cups water mixed with 3 cups Chicken Stock (page 9)

1 tablespoon butter

$^1/_2$ cup finely chopped onion

3 teaspoons minced garlic

1 jalapeño pepper, seeded and minced

2 cups arborio rice

$^2/_3$ cup dry white wine

2 cups asparagus spears, trimmed of tough bottom ends and cut into 1-inch sections (10 to 12 medium spears)

2 tablespoons fresh parsley, chopped

$^1/_2$ teaspoon grated lemon rind

Kosher salt and freshly ground white pepper to taste

1. Put clams in a large covered skillet over medium-high heat, shaking a few times. Remove clams from heat as soon as they open. As soon as they are cool enough to handle, remove clams from shells, halve (unless very small), and reserve any liquid. Strain clam liquid through cheesecloth and into a large saucepan with Chicken Stock and water. Bring to a boil and reduce to a simmer.

2. Put butter in a heavy-bottomed saucepan over medium-low heat. Add onion, garlic, and jalapeño pepper. Cover and cook gently until soft, about 3 minutes. Add rice and stir to coat. Add wine, increase heat to medium, and bring to a boil.

3. Begin adding stock, a cup or so at a time, stirring occasionally while risotto is at a simmer. After the second cup, add the asparagus. Continue adding stock as the rice absorbs the previous amount of liquid.

4. When the last cup of stock has been added, stir in reserved clams, parsley, lemon rind, and salt and pepper to taste. When risotto is tender, but still firm, remove from heat. (You may not need to use up all the liquid.) Keep tasting to see when the risotto is just right. It should take about 25 to 30 minutes.

Sam's Cooking Tip

Though any dry white wine can be used in this dish, it's always a nice touch to use one that fits the ethnic makeup of the dish and especially one you can drink with it. In this case, I'd recommend an Italian white such as a Pinot Grigio or Verdicchio.

beans

Beans have often been thought of as poor people's food. If you couldn't afford meat, you ate beans. Some variation on beans and rice has long been a staple of many cultures whose income per capita was a fraction of ours in the United States. And as many immigrant Americans gained a level of affluence, they eschewed beans, a symbol of poverty, for larger amounts of meat that symbolized higher levels of affluence, if not wealth.

But a funny thing happened on the way to the butcher shop. A lot of Americans developed heart disease. And a major contributor was too much fat in our diet. And a good deal of that fat came from red meat.

So Americans started turning to, uh, beans. And many have since discovered that not only do beans provide a much leaner way to get protein, but that "they are one of nature's cheapest, most widely available, fastest-acting and safest cholesterol fighting drugs," according to Jean Carper, author of *Food: Your Miracle Medicine* (HarperCollins, 1993).

Not only do beans lower levels of blood cholesterol, they increase the level of "good" cholesterol known as high density lipoproteins (HDL, for short). Over time, a cup of beans a day can raise HDL about 9 percent.

Excluding green snap beans (which are dealt with in another chapter, page 121), most of the beans people eat today are canned or dried. But more and more fresh beans have been appearing, particularly with the increase in farmer's markets across the country.

And restaurants have taken up the banner of fresh beans. In fact, in the past several years, fresh beans have become chic. Trendy restaurants from New York to San Francisco have menus littered with beans of every persuasion. Ragouts with fava beans. Chowders with cranberry beans. Purees with lima beans.

Members of the legume family, beans are plants that contain several seeds in a pod and grow on bushes or vines. Though we eat them as such, beans are not vegetables from a botanical standpoint, but fruits. They are the reproductive part of the plant.

Beans can be divided into two broad groups, even though they can belong to any number of plant species. Fresh-shelled beans will be discussed in this chapter. Edible-pod beans (such as snap beans and snow peas) will be dealt with in another chapter (page 121).

WHERE GROWN

One reason why beans are such an integral part of so many ethnic diets is that they grow almost everywhere. China is the largest producer of fava beans, with the remainder coming from Egypt, Italy, Great Britain, Morocco, Spain, Denmark, and Brazil. Black-eyed peas come primarily from Africa, India, China, the West Indies, and the southeastern United States. Within the United States, California is the major producer of shell beans.

VARIETIES

New varieties seem to crop up every year, thanks to organizations such as Seed Savers Exchange, an organization dedicated to saving endangered varieties of vegetables like Montezuma Red beans. You might find some of the more obscure bean varieties in your local farmer's market (and more certainly by mail in dried form), but here are the more common varieties.

Black-eyed peas have many aliases: field peas, cowpeas, cream peas, Jerusalem peas, Tonkin peas, crowder peas, and marble peas. But despite the name, they're related to the yard-long bean common in Asia. Small and kidney shaped, these creamy beans have a black patch or eye on the inner portion.

Cranberry beans have no relationship to real cranberries except for the red color that streaks and speckles the pods, which look like deflated balloons, and the beans inside.

Fava beans look as if they are packed and ready for a long trip. The long (sometimes as much as 18 inches) puffy, green pods have a kind of insulation reminiscent of foam rubber. The pale green beans inside have a second skin to go through before getting to the edible bean (which may not be necessary if the beans are very young). Fava beans, also known as broad beans, horse beans, and Windsor beans, are native to Africa and are most often associated with the cuisines of the Mediterranean rim, particularly Italy and the countries of North Africa.

Lima beans, named after the capital of Peru, were brought to the United States from that city in 1824 by Captain John Harris of the U.S. Navy. The dark green, broad, and somewhat flat pods reveal a light green bean that can be small with a thin skin, known as baby limas, or large, known as Fordhook limas. When mottled with purple, lima beans are called calico or speckled butter beans. Lima beans are also known as sieva beans, butter beans, Civet beans, Seewee beans, Carolina beans, Buffin beans, and sugar beans.

Soybeans are probably the most versatile and widely used beans in the world. They are dried and ground into flour, turned into milk and cooking oil, and pressed into curd form as tofu, a mainstay of meatless protein by itself and in products such as hot dogs and burgers. But soybeans are less known as a fresh vegetable than they are as a processed food that uses a different type of bean. The cooking or vegetable soybean has a fuzzy, bright green pod that, when plump, contains about two beans.

SEASONS

Though technically available year-round, black-eyed peas are more obtainable from June through December, but even then supplies are sporadic. Frieda's, the specialty produce company in California, sells what look like fresh black-eyed peas but are, in reality, dried beans that have been presoaked, which makes them as perishable as the fresh ones. The season for cranberry beans is August through October. Spring and early summer are usually the seasons for fava beans, though we've seen supplies into September. Lima beans are generally available from July though September. However, the season can sometimes stretch into November in southern states like Georgia. Soybeans, when available, come in late summer or early fall.

SELECTION, HANDLING & STORAGE

In general, look for beans with pods that are plump and well filled but not cracked, bulging, or bursting. Pods should have good color and not be withered, brown, or dried. If the beans are already shelled, they should be plump and fresh looking.

Refrigerated in plastic bags, the unwashed beans—shelled or left in their pods—can last several days.

NUTRITION

Fresh-shelled beans have comparable nutritional profiles. For example, a quarter cup of raw large lima beans (45g, about 1.6 ounces) contains 140 calories, 24g of carbohydrates, 9g of protein, and 5g of dietary fiber. Limas are an excellent source of potassium (780mg, 22% of the DV), folic acid (40% of the DV), and magnesium (25% of the DV) and contain 15% of the DV for iron and 2% for calcium.

In addition to their positive effects on cholesterol, beans can help regulate blood sugar levels. Thus, they are an excellent food for diabetics.

The consumption of regular amounts of beans has been linked to lower rates of certain cancers. For example, some studies indicate that beans, particularly soybeans, have compounds that reduce the incidence of breast cancer. The fiber in beans may be effective in the inhibition of colon cancer. A compound in beans called protease may be the link to lower incidence of pancreatic cancer. Beans also have high levels of folic acid, which inhibits lung cancer and certain types of birth defects.

YIELD

The general rule of thumb with fresh-shelled beans is that a pound of beans in the pod will yield about 1 cup of beans. Because of their bulky pods, fava beans yield somewhat less than other beans, requiring about $1^{1}/_{2}$ to $1^{3}/_{4}$ pounds in the pod for 1 cup of beans. Soybeans yield somewhat more, with each pound of beans in the shell providing about $1^{2}/_{3}$ cups of beans.

Tony's Tip

Beans are a major source of flatulence or intestinal gas, which can be irritating and embarrassing. Small amounts of garlic and ginger have been shown to reduce gas. But don't use a lot of garlic because large amounts can also produce gas. We've also found the product Beano to be an effective antiflatulent.

PREPARATION

Fresh beans need only to be popped out of their pods before being boiled in salted water to be eaten simply with salt, pepper, and butter, or added to a more complex dish.

Most beans can be shelled by opening the casing at the seam. Sometimes, tearing off one end of the pod with a sharp paring knife facilitates this.

Fava beans are the most complex because of their double casing. Getting out the beans is easy enough, though superchef Daniel Boulud suggests in *Trucs of the Trade* by Frank Ball and Arlene Feltman (HarperPerennial, 1992) that you push out the beans at the seam, working down the pod from one end to the other.

That leaves the inner casing, which can be removed by first boiling the beans in salted water for 30 to 60 seconds. Then, after being refreshed in cold water, the beans can be squirted out of their inner skin, facilitated if need be by breaking the skin with a fingernail.

Garlic, onion, fresh herbs, and judicious amounts of cured pork bring out the best in most beans. Olive oil and Mediterranean or Middle Eastern spices like cumin are good with fava beans. Light ragouts are a wonderful way to enjoy beans, often with fresh tomatoes, which are at their peak when beans appear. And don't forget salads, with other vegetables, and with grains such as rice or couscous.

Seafood Salad with Lima Beans

Makes 4 servings as a main course, 6 as an appetizer

2 cups shelled lima beans
Kosher salt
1 cup white wine
1 bay leaf
4 ounces bay or sea scallops
8 ounces medium shrimp, shelled
8 ounces cleaned squid
1 small red onion
$^1/_2$ cup pimiento-stuffed green olives,
  halved lengthwise

3 tablespoons each olive oil and fresh
  lemon juice
$1^1/_2$ to 2 teaspoons fresh marjoram or
  fresh oregano, chopped, or 1 teaspoon
  dried
Kosher salt and freshly ground black
  pepper to taste

1. Put shelled lima beans in a saucepan with 3 cups water and 1 teaspoon salt. Bring to a boil, reduce to a simmer, and cook until tender, about 15 minutes, depending on size and freshness. Drain and cool.

2. Meanwhile, put wine, bay leaf, $^1/_2$ teaspoon salt, and 2 cups water in another saucepan. Bring to a boil and reduce to a bare simmer. If using sea scallops, halve to a size of about $^1/_2$- to $^3/_4$-inch square. Poach scallops for about 2 minutes. Remove and put in a mixing bowl to cool. Add shrimp to pan and cook about 3 minutes. Halve and add to the scallops. Cut squid sacs into $^1/_4$-inch-wide rings and halve the tentacles. Cook about 3 minutes and add to scallops and shrimp.

3. Halve onion lengthwise and cut into very thin crescents. Add to seafood along with olives and lima beans.

4. In a small bowl, combine olive oil, lemon juice, marjoram, and salt and pepper to taste. Pour over seafood and bean mixture. Toss well and cover for 20 minutes before serving. Refrigerate if waiting more than 1 hour.

Fresh Bean Chowder with Pistou

This dish can be made with any combination of fresh beans and any kind of all-purpose potato (not a baking or Idaho potato).

Makes 4 servings

2 ounces pancetta, cut into small dice

1/2 cup chopped onion

2 cups any combination of shelled cranberry, lima, or other fresh beans

4 cups defatted Chicken Stock (page 9)

2 cups cubed all-purpose potatoes (1/2-inch dice, peeled if desired)

Kosher salt and freshly ground black pepper to taste

1 clove garlic

1 tablespoon toasted pine nuts (see tip)

1 cup fresh basil leaves

2 tablespoons olive oil

1. Put pancetta in a large saucepan or small, heavy-bottomed kettle over medium heat. Cook, covered, until pancetta becomes crisp, about 10 minutes. Remove pancetta to paper towels and drain all fat except a thin haze, less than a teaspoon.

2. Cook onion, covered, over medium-low heat until just soft. Add cranberry beans and stock. Bring to a boil, then reduce to a simmer and cook, covered, 10 minutes. Add lima beans and potatoes and simmer, covered, 15 to 20 minutes more, just until beans and potatoes are tender. Season to taste with salt and pepper.

3. Meanwhile, with the motor running, put garlic down feed tube of a food processor. Scrape down sides, turn on again and add pine nuts. Scrape down, add basil, 1/2 teaspoon salt, and the oil. Puree until the pistou is smooth.

4. When beans and potatoes are tender, add about 1/2 cup of the broth to the pistou just until it starts to become runny.

5. Put soup into each of 4 bowls and drizzle a few tablespoons of the pistou on top. Sprinkle with crisped pancetta.

Sam's Cooking Tip

As you may have guessed, pistou *is another word for pesto, in this case in French. This version is considerably slimmed down by adding stock instead of oil. Flavor is enhanced by toasting the pine nuts.*

To toast pine nuts, put them in a pie plate so the nuts do not crowd each other. Toast in a preheated 350°F oven for 7 to 8 minutes (for 1/2 cup nuts). An equal amount of walnut pieces takes the same amount of time. One-half cup of sliced almonds takes about 6 minutes; one-half cup of sesame seeds, 12 minutes. Shake once during toasting to brown evenly.

Succotash Salad

The combination of beans and corn predates Columbus. Early American Indians used more than just limas to mix with their corn. And New Englanders prefer cranberry beans.

Makes 8 servings

1³/₄ to 2 pounds fresh lima beans

Kosher salt

3 cups fresh corn kernels (cut from
  4 medium ears of corn)

1 large tomato, diced (about 1 cup)

1 small Vidalia or other sweet onion,
  diced (about ³/₄ cup)

¹/₄ cup chopped basil

2 tablespoons chopped chives

2 tablespoons cider vinegar

3 tablespoons peanut or canola oil

Freshly ground black pepper to taste

1. Press down on the seam of the rounded side of each lima bean with your thumbs and pop open the pods, exposing the beans. Or, with the rounded side of the pod facing you, tear a piece off the top with a sharp paring knife. Pull down, removing the string and splitting open the pod. Discard any pods that are discolored or blemished. You should have about 2 cups.

2. Bring 3 cups water and ¹/₂ teaspoon salt to boil in a saucepan. Add lima beans, cover and cook over medium-low heat just until tender, about 15 minutes. Drain and cool.

3. If corn is very fresh and tender, do not cook. Otherwise cook in 3 cups of boiling water with ¹/₂ teaspoon salt for 2 or 3 minutes. Drain and cool.

4. Combine corn, tomato, onion, and basil in a mixing bowl. Mix chives, vinegar, oil, salt, and pepper. Add to corn mixture and toss.

Sam's Cooking Tip

To keep basil two weeks or longer, cut ¹/₂ inch from the bottoms of the stems and remove whatever ties the bunch together. Stick the stems in an inch or two of water in a small plastic bucket. Cover the top with plastic wrap and refrigerate.

Crostini with Spicy Cranberry Bean Puree

This hors d'oeuvre is a lot more healthful with drinks before dinner than cheese and crackers. And your guests will enjoy it just as much.

Makes 6 servings

1 pound cranberry beans
1 tablespoon olive oil
1 small onion, chopped (about $1/2$ cup)
3 cloves garlic, minced
$1/4$ teaspoon hot pepper flakes
$1/4$ teaspoon freshly ground black pepper

1 cup Chicken Stock (page 9)
Kosher salt and freshly ground black
  pepper to taste
1 French baguette, 12 to 14 inches long
Olive oil cooking spray
30 Italian parsley leaves, approximately

1. Pry apart bean pods with your fingers to expose the cranberry beans. If difficult, tear off a piece from the stem end of each bean pod with a paring knife. Pull down on the string, opening the pod. Discard any beans that are discolored. You should have about 1 cup.

2. Put oil in a large saucepan over medium heat. Add onion and garlic and cook, stirring, until onion is soft, about 5 minutes. Add beans, hot and black peppers, and $7/8$ cup of the Chicken Stock. Bring to a boil, reduce to a simmer, and cook, covered, until beans are very tender, about 30 minutes. Season with salt and pepper.

3. Meanwhile, preheat oven to 400°F. Cut bread into $1/4$-inch slices (25 to 30 slices). Spray a cookie sheet or baking pan with olive oil cooking spray. Arrange slices on sheet and spray tops. Bake until browned on both sides, about 10 minutes, turning slices over about halfway through.

4. Puree bean mixture in a food processor, but not too smooth. Add a little more Chicken Stock if too thick to spread. Check seasonings and add more hot pepper flakes if desired.

5. Spread a few teaspoons of puree on each crostini and top each with a parsley leaf.

Sam's Cooking Tip

In a pinch, you can make a quick version of this with canned beans (cannellini beans would be my choice). Just make sure to rinse the beans thoroughly first.

Bulgur Pilaf with Fava Beans

Fava beans can be daunting for some because their goodness is protected by two coverings. But once you get the hang of it, you'll understand why more and more chefs are cooking with fresh fava beans.

Makes 6 servings as side or buffet dish, 4 as a main dish

2 pounds fava beans
$^1/_2$ tablespoon olive oil
$^1/_2$ teaspoon butter
3 medium onions, halved and thinly
   sliced
2$^1/_2$ cups Lamb Stock (recipe follows), or
   Chicken Stock (page 9)
1$^1/_2$ cups medium-grain bulgur

1 cup chopped, cooked lean lamb (ideally
   from the lamb used to make the lamb
   stock)
1 tablespoon chopped fresh thyme or
   $^1/_2$ tablespoon dried
Kosher salt and freshly ground black
   pepper to taste
1 tablespoon each chopped chives and
   fresh mint, mixed together

1. Remove beans from their pods and put shelled beans in a quart of boiling, salted water for 1 minute. Drain and run under cool water. When cooled, remove beans from their inner shells by tearing off a small piece from the rounded end with your fingernail. Squirt the beans out by pinching the opposite ends.

2. Meanwhile, put oil and butter in a large, heavy-bottomed skillet over medium heat. Add onions and cover. Cook, stirring periodically, about 20 minutes, uncovering for the last 5 minutes, until lightly browned. Set aside.

3. Bring stock to a boil in a large saucepan and add bulgur. Bring to a boil again, reduce to a simmer, and cover. Cook about 8 to 10 minutes. Add beans, lamb, thyme, salt, and pepper. Stir and cook 3 to 5 minutes more. Remove from heat and let steam 10 minutes.

4. Fluff with a fork and pour onto a platter. Top with onions, then chives and mint.

Lamb Stock

Makes about 1 quart

1 large, meaty lamb shank,
   cut in 3 pieces
1 carrot, chopped
1 onion, chopped

1 celery rib
6 parsley stems, chopped
10 peppercorns
1 bay leaf

1. Put all ingredients in a pot with 3 quarts water. Bring to a boil, skim scum from the top, reduce heat, and simmer 2 hours.

2. Strain, reserving meat. Refrigerate broth to cool completely. Skim grease from the top. Chop lean lamb meat.

beets

The list of vegetables that kids hate is a long one. But we think beets are a good candidate for the top of the list. (We also think a lot of adults never outgrew their disdain for beets either.)

Why? First, most of the beets we got as kids came from a can. And even though canned beets are a decent substitute for fresh in some dishes (like the cold beet soup [page 37]), in many dishes they aren't.

Second, many people just don't know what to do with beets except dump some sugar and orange juice on them and heat them up. No wonder most beet presentations look as if they came from the high school cafeteria line.

Then there's the stain factor. Who wants to have the beet version of the Scarlet Letter all over the kitchen—for a vegetable they don't even like?

Yes, beets have a tough row to hoe. But we think they're worth spending some time on, especially when they're accompanied by their highly nutritious greens.

One way to start is to allow beets' natural sugar, as high as 10 percent, to come through without being masked. Roasting does this nicely. And speaking of roasting, beets make a delicious companion to roasted meats, especially pork and duck. Onion or a touch of garlic helps to accent the sweetness if you're looking for a contrast.

And about those red stains? In *Trucs of the Trade,* Daniel Boulud says the best way of removing them is not to get them in the first place. He covers his work surfaces with wax paper (plastic wrap would also probably work), and he wears disposable rubber gloves. Failing that, Rosalind Creasy, author of *Cooking from the Garden* (Sierra Club Books, 1988), suggests trying yellow or white varieties. If you can't find them, try growing them on your own. Look for Burpee's Golden or Albino White Beet.

WHERE GROWN

Beets are grown commercially in thirty-one states. California, New Jersey, Ohio, and Texas are the main producers. Beets are also imported from Mexico and Canada.

VARIETIES

If you're wondering why chard leaves, the red-ribbed ones in particular, look so much like beet greens, it's because beets, sugar beets, and chard are in the same family.

The Detroit or Detroit Dark Red is the primary commercial red beet. It has a kind of dusty red exterior and deep red flesh inside. Other varieties are the Ruby Queen, Crosby, and Early Wonder. All are round or have slightly flattened ends.

You'll need to seek out local farmer's markets and specialty produce retailers for less common varieties of beets. The *chioggia,* for example, is a bright red Italian beet on the outside with white inside flesh marked by red rings. Golden beets are more orange than gold and are a favorite of home gardeners, though small farmers will also grow them. They tend to be sweeter than red beets.

Beet greens are often discarded in favor of the bulbs to which they are attached, which is unfortunate because they contain a wonderful, earthy flavor. When small they can be put in a salad mix. If larger, they should be braised, stewed, or boiled like other hearty greens.

SEASONS

For the most part, beets are available all year long. But the peak period, particularly for local and more exotic varieties, is June through October. It's also the time of year when beet greens should be at their best.

SELECTION, HANDLING & STORAGE

Beets should be relatively smooth and firm. Small- to medium-size ones are best. Large ones may be tough. Leaves should be bright, dark green, and fresh looking without withering or slime.

To store, separate the leaves from the root, leaving an inch or two of the stems attached to the root. Remove any leaves that are damaged before storing the tops in a plastic bag, preferably one that is perforated, in the high-humidity crisper section of the refrigerator for no more than a few days. Don't peel or clean the root since the skins will slip off easily during cooking. Put roots in a plastic bag and put them in the refrigerator where they will keep at least a week.

NUTRITION

A 100g serving of beets (1 medium beet, about 3 ounces) has 50 calories, .5g fat, 11g carbohydrates, 2g dietary fiber, and 1g protein. Beets are also a good source of potassium (about 290mg per serving), a decent source of folic acid (15% of the DV), and a fair source of vitamin A (4% of the DV).

Beet greens are more nutritious than the beets themselves. They have almost twice the potassium of beets and high amounts of beta-carotene, an important antioxidant that helps to fight numerous diseases. Beet greens contain high levels of folic acid, which can help ward off certain birth defects and lung cancer. And speaking of lungs, some studies indicate that beet greens can dampen cravings for nicotine, which may help smokers kick the habit.

YIELD

A pound of trimmed beets will yield about 2 cups, chopped. A good-size bunch of beet greens will yield about 4 cups chopped.

Tony's Tip

If you've got some leftover roast beef from Sunday or holiday dinner, try making an old-fashioned dish called red-flannel hash. All you do is combine diced beets with cubes of cooked beef, cooked potato, and chopped onion, and fry in a large skillet until crisp and delicious.

PREPARATION

Many recipes, particularly older ones, call for boiling beets. But this promotes bleeding as well as loss of nutrients. We like steaming them in their skins, which takes about 35 to 40 minutes, depending on size. The jackets slip off easily, and beets are ready for salads and other preparations.

Microwaving with a small amount of water takes about half that time.

Baking and roasting have become more popular with vegetable preparations, and beets are a natural for these methods. (Baking implies more moderate temperatures and roasting higher.) This can be done in a covered or uncovered container, in a low (300°F) or higher (375°F or more) oven, but always with skins left on. Cooking times, of course, will vary depending on the method chosen, but figure an hour unless the beets are very small.

Beet greens should be handled like cooking greens. For preparation and recipe ideas, see the chapter titled "Greens, Cooked," (page 139).

Red and Yellow Beet Salad with Orange Vinaigrette

This recipe was inspired by a dish we had at the now defunct Symphony Cafe in New York. The contrast with warm beets and goat or blue cheese is marvelous.

Makes 6 servings

1 small bunch each orange and red beets with greens attached

1 tablespoon minced shallots

$1/4$ teaspoon ground cloves

$1/4$ cup fresh orange juice

$1/4$ cup cider vinegar

2 tablespoons canola oil

Kosher salt and freshly ground white pepper to taste

1 orange, peeled and thinly sliced

4 ounces crumbled low-fat goat or blue cheese

4 or 5 strands of fresh chives, roughly chopped

1.   Clean and steam beets as explained in Preparation (page 35). As soon as beets are cool enough to handle, but still quite warm, remove skins and cut beets into $1/4$-inch slices.

2.   Meanwhile, combine shallots, cloves, orange juice, vinegar, oil, salt, and pepper.

3.   Line a platter with cleaned beet greens. Layer beets, alternating orange and red. Pour dressing over. Garnish outside with orange slices. Sprinkle top with crumbled goat or blue cheese. Top with chives.

Cold Beet Soup

Unless you're Eastern European, the idea of beet soup—and cold beet soup at that—may not sound too appetizing. But this soup is easy to make, lovely to look at, and very refreshing on a hot day.

Makes 6 servings

2 bunches beets with green tops attached
4 teaspoons capers, drained
1 small cucumber, peeled, seeded and chopped
1 small dill pickle, seeded and chopped
3 tablespoons chopped fresh dill

1 tablespoon cider or wine vinegar
Zest of 1 lemon
1 small potato, cooked, peeled and cubed
Kosher salt and freshly ground black pepper to taste
1 pint nonfat sour cream

1. Remove beets from greens, leaving about 1 inch of stem on each beet. Use greens for another dish. You should have about 1½ pounds of beets. Wash beets thoroughly. Put 1 inch of water in a saucepan and add a steamer basket. Steam beets 30 to 45 minutes, depending on size, until a knife easily pierces them. Reserve steaming water.

2. Cool beets under running water and slip off the skins. Dice 1 cup of the beets and set aside with 2 teaspoons of the capers. Cut remaining beets into chunks and put into a food processor with remaining ingredients except sour cream and reserved capers and beets. Puree until smooth. Add a little of the cooking water if too thick.

3. Fold in reserved capers and diced beets and sour cream. Refrigerate several hours. Adjust seasonings as necessary.

Sam's Cooking Tip

Since canned beets are one of the better canned vegetables, you won't lose too much if you use them instead of fresh. I like to keep canned beets around for quick antipasto platters and salads as well.

Beets and Beet Greens Gratin

Makes 8 servings

2 small bunches beets with greens, about
 3 pounds total
2 tablespoons butter
2 tablespoons flour
1¹/₂ cups skim milk

3 large cloves garlic, minced
Kosher salt and freshly ground black
 pepper to taste
Butter-flavored cooking spray
¹/₂ cup flavored bread crumbs

1. Separate greens from beets, leaving about 1 inch of stems on the top of the beets. Steam as described in Preparation (page 35). Save the cooking pot with the water. Cool beets and peel off skins.

2. Meanwhile, trim stalks from greens unless they are very tender. Stack greens and roll like a fat cigar. Cut crosswise into ¹/₂-inch-wide ribbons. Wash thoroughly and drain. Add to the same pot that steamed the beets, with more water if needed, and steam over moderate heat just until wilted, about 7 minutes.

3. While greens steam, heat butter in a medium-size saucepan until it foams. Add flour and stir over moderate heat until well blended, about 2 minutes. Add milk, stirring constantly, until the sauce comes to a boil. Reduce to a simmer, add garlic, salt, and pepper, and stir as it thickens to the consistency of a light cream sauce. Turn off heat.

4. Preheat oven to 400°F. Cut beets into ¹/₂-inch cubes and add to saucepan with cream sauce. Squeeze out any excess moisture from the beet greens and add to the cream sauce, combining well. Season with more salt and pepper. Pour into a 2-quart gratin dish that has been sprayed with butter-flavored cooking spray.

5. Sprinkle with bread crumbs and bake 25 minutes or until top browns nicely and cream sauce bubbles up.

Raw Beet Salad with Apples and Raisins

To those who don't even like the thought of cooked beets, eating raw beets may sound like punishment. But this salad may change your mind forever about beets, raw or cooked. Try it with cold, leftover roasted or grilled meats.

Makes 4 servings

$^1/_4$ cup low- or nonfat sour cream
1 teaspoon Dijon mustard
1 tablespoon cider vinegar
Small bunch beets, about $^3/_4$ pound, trimmed and peeled
1 sweet and crisp apple such as a Fuji
2 tablespoons sultana raisins

1 tablespoon chopped toasted hazelnuts (page 346)
1 tablespoon chopped chives
Kosher salt and freshly ground black pepper to taste
Handful of watercress

1. In a small bowl, combine sour cream, mustard, and vinegar. Set aside.

2. Grate beets by hand using the second-largest hole on a four-sided grater or using the grating attachment on a food processor. Put in a mixing bowl.

3. Core apple but do not peel. Cut into $^1/_2$-inch cubes and add to beets. Add raisins, hazelnuts, and chives. Season with salt and pepper. Add sour cream dressing and mix well. Taste for seasonings.

4. To serve, put watercress at the end of a small oval platter and spoon out salad onto the platter.

broccoli

Remember a few years ago when former President Bush said he didn't like broccoli? And that he preferred such nutritious wonders as Butterfinger candy bars and pork rinds? Broccoli immediately came under scrutiny. The Broccoli Growers of America sent the White House cases of the stuff (which the president promptly donated to a good cause). Television commentators talked about broccoli. Comedians made jokes about it. And food editors wrote stories about it.

Suddenly we realized two things. First, despite Mr. Bush's disdain, broccoli was and remains one of America's favorite vegetables, ranking eighth in a 1995 study by the Produce Marketing Association of the best-selling vegetables sold in supermarkets.

Second, many Americans who ate broccoli simply because they liked it, or because their mother told them to, found out that broccoli is one of the most nutritious of all vegetables. As Jean Carper put it in *Food: Your Miracle Medicine* (HarperCollins, 1992), broccoli is "a spectacular and unique package of versatile disease fighters."

But as a member of the cruciferous family, broccoli contains sulfurous compounds that can emit odors that are off-putting to many people (see "Cauliflower," page 67). So scientists have been busy trying to come up with products that use broccoli for its nutrients but not for its flavor, such as sweetened broccoli-based vegetable juices and broccoli-flavored salsa. Ugh!

We think broccoli is just fine the way it is. Don't overcook it or it will stink up the joint. And don't undercook it because, well, we think raw or undercooked broccoli just doesn't taste very good.

And to former President Bush we say, even if you have to sprinkle it with crushed pork rinds or candy bars, eat your broccoli!

WHERE GROWN

California produces about 95 percent of the broccoli grown commercially in the United States. Arizona is the number-two producer, followed by Washington and Maine.

Mexico exports to the United States about as much broccoli as Arizona produces; Canada about as much as Washington.

VARIETIES

The word *broccoli* comes from the Latin *brachium,* meaning "arm" or "branch." Early settlers in the United States apparently knew it as brockala. And Italian Americans often referred to it as broccali.

The Calabrese is the primary commercial variety of broccoli, named for the Italian province of Calabria. Others are the Patriot, Marathon, Green Belt, Arcadia, Green Duke, Emperor, Cruiser, 458, Shogun, and Premium.

Packaged broccoli cuts are also becoming popular as a convenience item. Stalks, whether diced, sliced into "coins," or shredded, and florets (the small individual "flowers" that make up the larger head) can be used in stir-fries and salads. Trimmed broccoli spears are ready for steaming. And broccoli coleslaw (with red cabbage and carrots) is an alternative to the standard cabbage slaw.

SEASONS

Broccoli is a year-round vegetable, though there may be less availability in the summer months when quality may also wane due to the heat. The peak period for broccoli is January through March.

SELECTION, HANDLING & STORAGE

Fresh and well-kept broccoli will have a firm head with compact clusters. The clusters should be dark green and may have purple highlights. Leaves should be crisp. Yellowed clusters or yellow flowers showing on the inside are signs of poor quality. Avoid bunches with stems that are thick and tough, or broccoli that has a strong smell. It should smell clean and fresh.

Store broccoli in the high-humidity vegetable crisper of your refrigerator for up to three days.

NUTRITION

If there is a more healthful vegetable than broccoli, we don't know it. A serving of one medium stalk (148g, about 5.3 ounces) contains 45 calories, .5g of fat, 5g each of fiber and protein, and 8g of carbohydrates. You can get 220% of the DV for vitamin C in a serving, 15% for vitamin A, and 6% each for calcium and iron. Broccoli also has 15% of the DV for potassium (540mg) and 25% for folic acid.

That's just for starters. As a member of the cruciferous family, broccoli has enormous cancer-fighting properties. It is loaded with antioxidants such as beta-carotene and folic acid as well as lutein, a lesser known antioxidant that some scientists think may be as strong a cancer inhibitor as beta-carotene. Broccoli's high fiber helps keep cholesterol in check. It has antiviral and antiulcer properties. And it helps regulate insulin and blood sugar.

Message: Take three broccoli spears and call us in the morning.

YIELD

A good-size bunch of broccoli weighs about 1½ to 2 pounds and should serve four as a side vegetable, more if combined with other ingredients. One pound of broccoli yields about 2 cups chopped.

Tony's Tip

To enjoy broccoli's true flavor, do what the Italians do and keep preparations simple. I like broccoli with just some chopped garlic, lightly sautéed in olive oil, salt, and pepper.

PREPARATION

Separate the florets from the stalk by cutting them off where they naturally attach to the stalk. Peel the stalk and cut into thin rounds or matchsticks. Generally it's not necessary to peel the base of the florets.

By cutting the stalk into small enough pieces, it will cook in about the same time as the florets. Otherwise you should start cooking the stem pieces a few minutes before you add the florets.

As with many vegetables, nutrients are best preserved with microwave cooking. But we prefer steaming. (Call us old-fashioned.)

A head of broccoli cut into pieces will cook by boiling in about 5 minutes, by steaming in about 7 or 8 minutes, and by microwaving in about 5 minutes.

As with most green vegetables, keeping cooking time to a maximum of 7 minutes, and refreshing the broccoli in ice water, if you're not using it right away or are making a cold presentation, help to maintain the bright green color.

Broccoli, like its cousin broccoli raab (see "Greens, Cooked," page 139), goes well in Italian preparations such as pasta dishes, beans, potatoes, or polenta with garlic, olive oil, olives, balsamic vinegar, anchovies, and pork meats such as sausage and pancetta. Broccoli also works nicely with freshly grated nutmeg.

Broccoli with Bagna Cauda Sauce

Normally, bagna cauda is a nutritionist's nightmare, what with loads of oil and cream. But this version uses only a small amount of oil and evaporated skim milk instead of cream.

Makes 4 servings

1 large head broccoli
1 tablespoon extra-virgin olive oil
4 cloves garlic, minced

4 anchovy filets, minced
One 12-ounce can evaporated skim milk
Kosher salt to taste

1. Trim broccoli into florets. Peel stem and cut into rounds about ³/₈ inch thick. Set aside.

2. Heat oil in a small saucepan over very low heat. Add garlic and anchovy filets. Cook gently until garlic just barely turns golden, being careful not to let it burn. Meanwhile, heat skim milk in a saucepan over moderate heat, until volume of skim milk is reduced by half, stirring frequently with a wire whisk, about 8 minutes.

3. Add garlic-anchovy mixture to milk and continue to cook, stirring with a wooden spoon or whisk until the sauce forms streaks and you can begin to see the bottom of the pan when the sauce is stirred. Keep warm.

4. Steam broccoli until just tender, about 7 minutes. Pour sauce over and serve. Salt to taste.

Sam's Cooking Tip

Though it's not an exact duplication, you can sometimes simulate the texture of cream by using evaporated milk or evaporated skim milk.

Broccoli with Roasted Shallots and Mushrooms

Roasted shallots and mushrooms add another dimension to steamed broccoli.

Makes 4 servings

Olive oil cooking spray	1$\frac{1}{2}$ tablespoons olive oil
4 large shallots, peeled and halved	$\frac{1}{4}$ to $\frac{1}{3}$ teaspoon ground nutmeg
4 ounces whole mushrooms	Kosher salt and freshly ground black
1 large bunch broccoli, about 1$\frac{1}{2}$ pounds	pepper to taste

1. Turn oven to 500°F. Spray a small baking pan or cast-iron skillet with olive oil cooking spray and add shallots and mushrooms. Spray the tops and put in the oven. Cook about 15 minutes, shaking the pan a few times during cooking. Remove when nicely browned all over. Coarsely chop shallots and slice mushrooms.

2. Meanwhile, cut broccoli into florets, peel stalk, and cut into rounds $\frac{1}{4}$ inch thick. Put stalk slices in the bottom of a steamer basket in a large saucepan with about $\frac{1}{2}$ inch of water. Add florets on top. Cover and steam over medium-high heat for 7 minutes.

3. Put oil in a wok or large skillet over medium-high heat. Add broccoli, shallots, and mushrooms. Season with nutmeg, salt, and pepper. Stir a few times until heated through.

Broccoli Soufflé

Unlike normal soufflés that have a cream sauce base with egg yolks, this soufflé uses only egg whites.

Makes 4 servings

1 large bunch broccoli, about 1¹/₂ pounds
Kosher salt
Butter-flavored cooking spray
3 tablespoons plain bread crumbs
¹/₂ red bell pepper, roasted, seeded, and
  peeled as in Hot and Sweet Pepper
  Sauce (page 207), and diced

1 clove garlic, minced
3 tablespoons crumbled blue cheese
Freshly ground black pepper to taste
7 egg whites

1. Peel broccoli stems and coarsely chop as close to the buds of the florets as possible. Break florets into pieces as small as possible.

2. Put just enough water in a large skillet to cover broccoli. Add 1 teaspoon kosher salt and bring to a boil. Add broccoli and cook, covered, 7 minutes or until tender. Drain and refresh in a colander under cold water. Drain well and puree in a food processor.

3. Preheat oven to 400°F. Spray a 2-quart soufflé dish with butter-flavored cooking spray. Dust with bread crumbs.

4. In a large bowl, combine broccoli, bell pepper, garlic, cheese, salt, and pepper. Put egg whites into the bowl of an electric mixer with a pinch of salt and beat until stiff but not dry.

5. Stir ¹/₄ of the egg whites into the broccoli mixture. Then fold in the rest in three stages. Don't overmix. Spoon into the soufflé dish and bake 25 to 30 minutes or until the soufflé has risen and is nicely browned.

Quick Broccoli with Pasta

Serve this fast and healthful dish with crusty Italian bread and a simple, light red wine such as a dolcetto or a barbera.

Makes 4 servings

1 large bunch broccoli, about 1¹/₂ pounds
2¹/₂ teaspoons kosher salt
¹/₂ teaspoon freshly ground black pepper
1 pound ziti or other short pasta
2 ounces sun-dried tomatoes
  (not oil-packed variety)
20 black olives (oil-cured preferred),
  pitted and quartered

2 tablespoons olive oil
¹/₄ teaspoon hot pepper flakes
¹/₂ teaspoon grated lemon rind
¹/₂ cup freshly grated Romano cheese
  plus more for passing at the table

1. Put on a pot with at least 4 quarts of water and a teaspoon of salt to boil. Peel broccoli stems and cut sticks about 2 inches long, ¹/₄ inch thick. Separate heads into florets. Rinse in a colander. When water comes to a boil, add broccoli and cook, covered, about 5 minutes or until just tender.

2. Using a skimmer or strainer, remove broccoli to a wok or large skillet. Season with ¹/₄ teaspoon each salt and pepper. Cover and keep warm. Add another teaspoon of salt to the pot of water and return to a boil. Cook pasta 5 minutes, add tomatoes and cook about 3 or 4 minutes more or until pasta is al dente. Drain well, reserving a few tablespoons of cooking water, and add to the broccoli.

3. Heat wok over low flame and add olives, oil, hot pepper flakes, lemon rind, remaining ¹/₄ teaspoon each of salt and pepper, and reserved cooking water. Toss well but gently. After a few minutes, toss with cheese and spoon onto individual soup plates. Pass additional cheese at the table.

Sam's Cooking Tip

Use the above method for cooking other vegetables that will be mixed with pasta, such as asparagus and hearty greens like kale.

cabbage

One of our most vivid food memories involves cabbage and Alsace, the French region along the Rhine border with Germany. France is not known as a cabbage-eating country like Germany. But Alsace has been part of Germany at various times over the centuries, as a result of wars or annexations.

As we drove through Alsace in early September, we saw what seemed like an endless succession of cabbage fields. And in the fields farmers with long pitchforks were hoisting cabbage after cabbage over their shoulders into large, open wooden wagons just as they had been doing for hundreds of years. Not a machine in sight.

Then, when we arrived at one of the several charming small towns of Alsace, we ordered a plate of *choucroute garnie,* the signature dish of Alsace. Literally, it means "garnished sauerkraut." It's a huge platter (depending on how many are to be served) with freshly made sauerkraut in the center. The sauerkraut tasted nothing like the sour stuff that comes in cans or bags in the United States. Flavored with juniper berries and local Riesling wine, this was fresh, sweet, and delicious with a pleasant tang. And surrounding the sauerkraut was every kind of pork you could think of—sausages, bacon, hams, and pork loin.

What is interesting is that all that meat is the *garnie* or garnish. The center of attention is the sauerkraut. A lot of people think it's the other way around because they confuse the word *choucroute* with *charcuterie,* which are prepared meats like pâté and sausages (as well as the place that sells them). And after all, some might reason, how could sauerkraut be the focus of the dish? We think the Alsatians have it right and that Americans ought to have the same kind of respect for cabbage, especially now that we know how nutritious it is.

We also know that people are cutting back on fat and pork in particular. But there are lots of lean hams out there. Pork tenderloin is leaner than dark meat chicken. And some of the turkey kielbasa sausages are just terrific. (We use both the turkey kielbasa and pork

tenderloin in several recipes.) So try your own *choucroute garnie* and wash it down with a good Alsatian Riesling or pinot blanc.

WHERE GROWN

More than thirty states grow cabbage commercially. Major producers are California, New York, Texas, Florida, and Georgia. Cabbage is also imported from Canada and Mexico. Most of the nation's brussels sprouts come from California, especially the cool and foggy central coast areas of Monterey, Santa Cruz, and San Mateo counties. Florida, Texas, and California are the main kohlrabi-producing states.

VARIETIES

There are basically four types of cabbage, or head cabbage to be specific, since the extended cabbage family is bigger than the Kennedy clan. The most common cabbage is the **green cabbage,** with pale green outer leaves leading to an almost white center. The two main varieties of green cabbage are domestic and Danish. The medium-size domestic is sweeter and used more for coleslaw. The larger Danish is somewhat more spicy and is preferred in cooking.

Red cabbage is exactly the same as green cabbage except for color. **Savoy cabbage** has color similar to green cabbage, but the leaves are crinkled. Its mild flavor and tender texture is adaptable to cooking and salads. Salad savoy is really more of an ornamental kale (which is also in the cabbage family) than a true cabbage.

The fourth main cabbage type is **napa cabbage,** also called Chinese or celery cabbage. It is oblong rather than round with a white base and pale green tops on the leaves. The flavor is sweet and mild.

There are five common varieties of **brussels sprouts:** Oliver, Valiant, Content, Rowena, and Rampart. Each one stakes out a different time of the fall and winter to appear, but the average consumer wouldn't know the difference among any of them in appearance or taste.

Kohlrabi always reminds us of vegetables from outer space, those green balls with thin stalks shooting out from them like appendages. As with head cabbage, there is a red version with essentially the same flavor.

The name kohlrabi literally means "cabbage turnip" in German, which is logical because its hearty flavor is very much like turnips and turnip greens. In fact, it is sometimes referred to as a Hungarian turnip, probably by the Hungarians.

SEASONS

All head cabbages are available year-round. Brussels sprouts run from August through April, with supplies from Mexico coming in during the winter and spring; peak season is September through February. Kohlrabi season is from June through October.

SELECTION, HANDLING & STORAGE

Look for head cabbage that is firm and heavy for its size; lightweight cabbage has lost a lot of moisture, which can sometimes result from overly trimmed butt ends. Heads should not look puffy or have any blemishes or withered leaves. With newer green cabbage you'll often see large deep gray-green outer leaves that almost look like elephant ears. As green cabbage gets older in storage, it whitens.

Red cabbage is really more of a purple or a magenta than a red. Otherwise, its characteristics are the same as green cabbage. For napa cabbage, avoid especially large heads that may taste too strong. Like green cabbage it should feel heavy with moisture and be free of blemishes.

Brussels sprouts look like knobs growing in rows on stalks, attached by what looks like wooden pegs. Sections of these stalks, about 2 to 3 feet, with the sprouts attached, are occasionally sold in better produce and retail stores. Otherwise, most of the brussels sprouts sold come in plastic canisters weighing about 10 ounces. The individual sprouts should have a bright green color and fresh appearance. The head should have no black spots, holes, or yellowed leaves. They should also smell fresh, so take off the plastic that covers sprouts in those canisters and take a whiff. Younger and smaller brussels sprouts will have a less "cabaggey" flavor.

Kohlrabi is usually sold in bunches of three or four. Choose kohlrabi with bulbs or globes that are bright, pale green (or purple red), free of blemishes, and no more than 2½ inches in diameter. Larger globes will be tough and woody. Leaves should be bright and fresh looking.

Head cabbage will last a week or more wrapped in a plastic bag in the high-humidity crisper section of the refrigerator. Savoy and napa cabbages should be consumed within three or four days. Brussels sprouts, trimmed of any blemished leaves, should be stored (unwashed) in a plastic bag in the crisper section of the refrigerator and consumed within two to three days.

Kohlrabi globes will last a few weeks in the refrigerator, but the leaves are more perishable and should be used within a few days.

NUTRITION

Three ounces or 84g (¹⁄₁₂ of a head) of green cabbage has 25 calories, 1g of protein, 2g of dietary fiber, and 5g of carbohydrates. It also contains about 70% of the DV for vitamin C, 4% for calcium, and 2% for iron. Red cabbage has a comparable nutritional profile.

A serving of four brussels sprouts contains 40 calories, .5g fat, 3g dietary fiber, 2g protein, 6g carbohydrates, 8% of the DV for vitamin A, 120% for vitamin C, and 2% for calcium. Brussels sprouts are also a decent source of potassium (290mg, 8% of the DV).

A serving of 3.5 ounces of kohlrabi (100g) contains 29 calories, 2g protein, about 7g carbohydrates, 1g of dietary fiber, 110% of the DV for vitamin C, 3% for iron, and 4% for calcium. Kohlrabi is also a good source of potassium.

Cabbage is a major league cancer fighter, particularly against colon, breast, and stomach cancers, though some of its effectiveness is lost in cooking. It has strong antibacterial and antiviral properties. And cabbage juice has been found to be an effective remedy for ulcers.

YIELD

A 1½-pound cabbage yields between 6 and 8 cups of shredded cabbage. Four ounces or a little more than 1½ cups is about a serving. Figure on 4 to 5 ounces of brussels sprouts per serving and one small to medium kohlrabi bulb.

Tony's Tip

Try shredded cabbage in a taco instead of lettuce. That's what they do in San Diego for their famous fish tacos. Cabbage holds up better, particularly in hot weather. And it's a lot more nutritious than iceberg lettuce.

PREPARATION

A simple preparation for head cabbage is to core the head and cut it into wedges that can then be put in braised or baked dishes or steamed on its own. Microwaving is also a good method. In either case, however, take pains not to overcook the vegetable for both nutritious and aesthetic reasons as well as taste.

Shredding is the most common method of dealing with cabbage. This can be accomplished with the shredder attachment of a food processor, the large holes of a four-sided grater, or a mandoline. Hand shredding is the simplest method but difficult for some. Here's a way to make it easier.

Remove the leaves of the cabbage and flatten them on a work surface, one on top of the other. (Don't wantonly discard those outer leaves; they're very nutritious.) When you get a half dozen or so leaves stacked, cut them into strips.

Soaking the shredded cabbage in cold water makes for a crisper coleslaw. Dry it in a salad spinner to remove all the moisture.

For brussels sprouts, remove damaged outer leaves, trim the stem end and cut an **X** about $1/16$ of an inch into the stem end to ensure faster and more even cooking. Microwaving in a small amount of water in a covered dish takes the least amount of time, about 7 minutes at full power for 1 to 1½ pounds. Boiling takes a few minutes more, and steaming takes about 10 to 12 minutes. To reduce steaming time (which helps keep the color bright), halve the sprouts. Refreshing them in ice water, if you're not using them immediately, will also keep the color green.

For kohlrabi, separate the leaves and the bulb. Steam or stir-fry the leaves as you would spinach or chard. After peeling, the bulb can be cubed or sliced and used in stir-fries, stews, and gratins, or as a vegetable by itself.

Braised Cabbage in Saffron Tomato Sauce

Saffron adds an exotic touch to the plain-Jane image of cabbage.

Makes 6 servings

1 tablespoon olive oil

1 small onion, chopped

1 small leek, chopped

$1/4$ teaspoon saffron threads soaked in $1/3$ cup white wine

One 16-ounce can whole tomatoes, seeded and chopped with juice

Kosher salt and freshly ground black pepper to taste

Hot pepper flakes to taste

1 small cabbage, about $1^1/2$ pounds

1 tablespoon chopped fresh parsley

1. Put oil in a medium saucepan over medium heat. Add onion and leek and cook, stirring, until soft, about 5 minutes. Add saffron and wine. Cook 1 minute. Then add tomatoes, salt and pepper to taste, and hot pepper flakes, as desired. Simmer 15 to 20 minutes. Adjust seasonings as needed.

2. Meanwhile, preheat oven to 375°F. Core cabbage and cut into 6 wedges. Put a small amount of sauce on the bottom of an oval baking dish. Add cabbage, cut side down, in a staggered fashion. Season cabbage with salt and pepper. Then add remaining sauce. Cover and put in the oven. Cook about 45 minutes or until just tender. Remove from oven halfway through and baste cabbage with tomato sauce. Top with parsley and serve.

Braised Cabbage with Chestnuts and Apples

Duck or goose fat isn't all bad. Here, a little of either goes a long way. Since duck or goose fat isn't normally sold separately, trim a few ounces of fat from any duck or goose you're preparing to cook, or ask your butcher for some fat scraps. Then freeze it until you're ready to cook this or another dish. (It's great for frying potatoes.)

Makes 6 to 8 servings

12 chestnuts
1 tablespoon rendered duck or goose fat, or olive oil
1/2 cup chopped onion
2 pounds red cabbage, shredded
1 cup fruity, off-dry wine such as gewürztraminer

2 tart apples such as Granny Smith, peeled and cored
3 tablespoons brown sugar
1/2 teaspoon ground allspice
1/2 teaspoon ground ginger
Kosher salt and freshly ground black pepper to taste

1. Using a sharp knife, make an **X** on both sides of the chestnuts, put them in a saucepan, and cover with water. Boil 10 minutes, then, when cool enough to handle, remove chestnuts one by one. (Wearing rubber gloves helps speed the process.) Peel, removing the inner lining as well, and set aside.

2. Preheat oven to 350°F. Melt fat or heat oil in a small Dutch oven or heavy-bottomed casserole. Add onion and cook over medium heat until onion is soft but not browned. Add cabbage and wine. Stir and raise heat slightly. Halve and cut apples into 1/4-inch slices. Add with remaining ingredients, including chestnuts.

3. Bring to a boil, stir well, cover, and bake 1 hour. Taste for seasonings. Adjust and serve.

Sam's Cooking Tip

Peeling chestnuts is a major pain and most methods don't work. But the one above, which was developed after countless hours of experimentation, does. Regardless of the method, prepare more than you need in case some chestnuts are bad.

Braised Kohlrabi

The assertive flavor of kohlrabi holds up well to spicy preparations.

Makes 8 servings

A good-size bunch kohlrabi with greens attached, about 3 pounds

1 tablespoon peanut oil

1/2 teaspoon each cumin and yellow mustard seeds

1 tablespoon chopped garlic

1 small jalapeño or other hot pepper, seeded and minced

1/2 cup Chicken Stock (page 9) or water

Kosher salt and freshly ground black pepper to taste

1. Discard any yellowed or badly withered greens from the kohlrabi and cut off most of each stem. Stack the leaves, then roll them in cigarlike fashion and cut across into thin strips 1/4 to 1/2 inch wide. Put greens in a basin of cool water to remove grit. Drain in a colander. Peel and cut kohlrabi into 1/2-inch dice and add to the greens.

2. Put oil in a wok over medium heat. Add cumin and mustard seeds and stir a few seconds until mustard seeds begin to pop. Add garlic and jalapeño and stir a minute or two until garlic turns light golden.

3. Add diced kohlrabi, greens, stock, and salt and black pepper to taste. Toss, cover, and reduce heat to medium-low. Cook, tossing once or twice, about 20 to 25 minutes or until kohlrabi is tender. Add a bit more liquid if needed.

Brussels Sprouts with Morels

This is a "winter meets spring" dish. The brussels sprouts are the last vestiges of winter and the morels let you know spring is here. Use shiitake or other wild mushrooms in place of the morels if you can't find them or if they're just too expensive.

Makes 2 to 3 servings

1 pint brussels sprouts, about 10 ounces
Kosher salt
1 tablespoon butter
1 ounce morels (or 2 ounces of other
  mushrooms), thinly sliced

2 teaspoons chopped fresh savory, or
  fresh thyme
Freshly ground black pepper to taste

1. Halve the brussels sprouts and put in a pot with 2 quarts of boiling water and a teaspoon of salt. Cook 7 minutes. Drain and put in a small pan of ice water until they cool completely. Drain. (Refrigerate if not using within an hour.)

2. Melt butter in a large skillet or wok over medium heat. When the foam subsides, add morels and cook 1 minute. (If using shiitake or other wild mushrooms, cook 2 to 3 minutes.) Add brussels sprouts, savory, and salt and pepper to taste. Cook, stirring, until the brussels sprouts are heated through, about 3 minutes.

Stuffed Cabbage with Couscous

Cabbage leaves are logical candidates for stuffing. Try other grains as well, like basmati rice and bulgur.

Makes 12 servings as a side dish, or 6 as a main course

$1/2$ cup raisins

1 tablespoon butter

1 tablespoon olive oil

1 large onion, thinly sliced

Kosher salt

$1/2$ teaspoon cinnamon

4 cups cooked couscous (instant couscous cooked according to package directions)

1 cup canned chickpeas, rinsed and drained

$1/3$ cup coarsely chopped toasted walnuts (page 28)

1 teaspoon ground ginger

Freshly ground black pepper to taste

12 large cabbage leaves

2 cups defatted Chicken Stock (page 9)

2 tablespoons chopped fresh mint or parsley

1. Soak raisins in warm water for 30 minutes. Heat butter and oil in a skillet and cook onion over medium heat, stirring, until lightly browned, 5 to 7 minutes. Add salt to taste and cinnamon, stir and cook a few minutes more. Put in a mixing bowl.

2. Add couscous, chickpeas, walnuts, and drained raisins to onion mixture. Season with salt and pepper. Set aside. Preheat oven to 350°F.

3. Drop cabbage leaves, 4 at a time, in a few quarts of boiling water and cook until just tender, about 3 to 4 minutes. Drain and pat dry. Lay cabbage leaves flat on a work surface and put $1/2$ cup of filling into the center of each one. Roll halfway, fold in sides so that stuffing can't fall out, and continue to roll each filled leaf.

4. Put stuffed rolls, seam side down, in a shallow baking dish. Add Chicken Stock, cover tightly, and bake about 40 minutes. Allow to cool about 10 minutes and sprinkle with mint.

carrots

When our moms told us to eat carrots because they were good for our eyesight, they were right (as usual). Adults who lack vitamin A, which is provided by the beta-carotene in carrots, may suffer from night blindness. Carrots also help prevent susceptibility to some eye infections and may reduce the risk of cataracts.

It would be worth eating a carrot a day for all that. But we've found in recent years that carrots are even more healthful than we thought previously—much more. The reason is the emergence of beta-carotene as a powerful antioxidant with wide-ranging powers. And carrots are loaded with beta-carotene.

How powerful are carrots? Eating carrots can reduce the incidence of heart disease and strokes among women. It cuts the lung cancer rate among smokers. It lowers blood cholesterol. It helps treat diarrhea. And carrots build up the immune system to protect us against a variety of infections and diseases.

An apple a day used to be the slogan for good health. And while we have nothing against apples, we think a carrot a day makes a lot more sense.

Carrots belong to a very large family that includes celery, parsnips, parsley, and fennel.

WHERE GROWN

California is the nation's largest carrot producer, growing more than ten times the amount of number-two Florida. Michigan is third. Canada is the biggest importer, followed by Mexico. In terms of quality, California consistently produces the sweetest carrots.

VARIETIES

The varieties of carrots aren't really significant in terms of what most Americans see, though Imperator is the most widely used. It's the variety most of us are familiar with, sold in 1-pound cellophane bags.

Carrots are shipped by grade—U.S. Extra No. 1, U.S. No.1, U.S. No. 1 Jumbo, and U.S. No. 2—and size, anywhere from $4\frac{1}{2}$ to $5\frac{1}{2}$ inches to almost a foot.

Baby whole peeled carrots are about 2 to 3 inches long and less than $\frac{3}{4}$ inch wide and are usually sweeter than larger carrots. These carrots are commonly referred to as Belgian or French carrots, and they come in plastic bags.

As far as mainstream produce goes, you'll probably see more organic carrots than other commodities, though it is far from a significant portion of carrot sales, about 2 percent of what is produced in California.

SEASONS

Carrots are available year-round from California. There is no significant peak season, though you may find an upsurge in supply during April and May. The majority of carrots from Canada and states east of the Mississippi come in summer and fall.

SELECTION, STORAGE & HANDLING

Bigger is not better when it comes to carrots. Choose carrots that are less than 8 inches long and relatively uniform. They should be well shaped, firm, and smooth with no cracks. Carrots should be bright orange to orange red—the deeper the color, the more beta-carotene—with bright green tops, if possible. While the green tops don't guarantee that the carrots attached to them are fresher than the ones in plastic bags, there's no way that plastic (or "cello") bagged carrots are fresher than ones with tops.

Whether loose or in plastic bags, reject carrots with green shoots sprouting out, yellowed tips, and soft spots or withering. All are a sign of age. Also pass by carrots with large green areas at the tops. They indicate sunburn.

If the carrots have tops, remove and discard them. Then rinse, drain, and put the carrots in plastic bags and store them in the coldest part of the refrigerator (as close to 32°F as possible) with the highest humidity. They'll last several months this way. But, of course, you should be eating them regularly, so that won't be necessary, right?

Carrots should be stored away from fruits such as apples and pears, which release ethylene gas that causes carrots to become bitter.

NUTRITION

Though there isn't a recommended daily allowance for it, beta-carotene is converted into vitamin A. And a single carrot has 270% of the DV for vitamin A. A serving of one carrot (78g, 2.8 ounces) also contains 35 calories, 8g of carbohydrates, 2g of dietary fiber, 1g of protein, 10% of the DV for vitamin C, and 2% for calcium. Carrots are also a fairly good source of potassium, with 280g.

A lot of people think that carrots are most healthful when eaten raw. But carrots are actually better when at least lightly cooked. It helps the body to more easily absorb the beta-carotene.

YIELD

One large carrot (slightly more than the DV serving size) will yield about 1 cup, shredded. Figure on serving four people with a pound of carrots.

Tony's Tip

> You can firm up limp carrots by cutting off one of the ends and sticking the carrots in ice water, cut side down.

PREPARATION

We like to buy organic carrots whenever possible, either from California in plastic bags, or loose from local farmers. That way we don't have to peel them, just trim the ends and scrub them well before slicing, shredding, or dicing. For peeling, we like the swivel action peelers that have fat handles, which put less strain on hands and wrists.

Raw carrots are a staple on so many vegetable platters—crudités if you're French or fancy. Instead of the usual strips, however, try this method. Cut the carrot crosswise into two or three pieces, each about 3 inches or so. Then, with the cut side down, steady the carrot with one hand on the top and slice down, cutting the carrot into wide, thin "planks." This is especially good for scooping up dip. These planks can also be stacked and cut into julienne or matchstick strips.

Don't forget that carrots form the basis of many sauces and stocks, so keep plenty on hand for those purposes. Carrots are even good for some spaghetti sauces along with diced onion and celery. Though baby carrots look nice and are time savers, cutting your own regular carrots for stews and braised dishes is a lot cheaper.

Favorite things we like with carrots are mint, dill, ginger, cardamom, coriander, cumin, nutmeg, and brown sugar.

Parsnip and Carrot Soup with Cardamom

We think of cardamom and coriander seeds as sweet spices, which is why they seem to go so well with vegetables that have a natural sweetness, such as carrots and parsnips.

Makes 4 to 6 servings

1 tablespoon butter
1 medium onion, finely chopped
1 pound parsnips, peeled and cut into
  1-inch chunks
1 pound carrots, peeled and cut into
  $1/2$-inch chunks
$5^{1}/_{2}$ cups defatted Chicken Stock
  (page 9)

$^{3}/_{4}$ teaspoon ground cardamom
1 teaspoon ground coriander
Kosher salt and freshly ground black
  pepper to taste
1 cup skim milk

1. In a large saucepan, melt butter over moderate heat and add onion. Cook until softened, about 5 minutes.

2. Add parsnips, carrots, and 5 cups of the stock. Bring to a boil, reduce heat, and simmer 20 minutes or until vegetables are soft.

3. Remove to a food processor to puree and return to saucepan, adding seasonings and milk. Heat to a bare simmer, thinning with remaining stock and adjusting seasonings as necessary. Serve hot.

Sam's Cooking Tip

When pureeing soup in a food processor, make sure you have a balance of solids and liquids before pureeing to get a smooth texture. Also, don't try to puree too much at once or liquid will begin to seep out the sides of the bowl.

Carrot and Cabbage Salad

Makes 6 servings

3$\frac{1}{2}$ tablespoons walnut oil
3 tablespoons fresh lemon juice
2 teaspoons honey
Kosher salt and freshly ground black
  pepper to taste

$\frac{1}{2}$ pound medium carrots, shredded
1 pound red cabbage, shredded
$\frac{1}{4}$ cup fresh parsley, chopped

1. Combine oil, lemon juice, honey, salt and pepper in a small cup.

2. Put carrots, cabbage, and parsley in a mixing bowl. Add dressing and toss well. Refrigerate 1 hour. Toss, adjust seasonings if needed.

Oven-Roasted Carrots and Sweet Potatoes

A perfect side dish for roast chicken or turkey.

Makes 4 servings

Butter-flavored cooking spray

1 pound carrots, peeled and cut into 1-inch chunks

1 pound sweet potatoes, peeled and cut into 1-inch chunks

2 tablespoons defatted Chicken Stock (page 9) or Vegetable Stock (recipe follows)

1¹⁄₂ tablespoons melted butter

Kosher salt and freshly ground black pepper to taste

1 teaspoon ground mace

1. Preheat oven to 500°F. Spray a shallow roasting pan with cooking spray.

2. Put carrots and sweet potatoes in the roasting pan. Combine stock, butter, salt, pepper, and mace in a cup. Pour over carrots and sweet potatoes and toss.

3. Roast about 25 minutes (tossing twice) or until tender.

Vegetable Stock

Makes about 1¹⁄₂ quarts

1 tablespoon olive oil

1 cup each diced carrot, celery (including leaves), and onion

¹⁄₂ cup chopped fresh parsley stems

4 cups of any other coarsely chopped vegetables or vegetable scraps such as mushroom stems, potato peelings, trimmings from greens, etc.

5 cloves garlic, coarsely chopped

2 sprigs fresh thyme or ¹⁄₂ teaspoon dried thyme

10 whole black peppercorns

2 bay leaves

1. Put oil in a 5-quart pot over low heat. Add carrot, celery, and onion, cover and cook gently 5 to 10 minutes or until soft but not brown.

2. Add remaining ingredients along with 3 quarts of water and bring to a boil. Reduce heat to a simmer and cook 2 hours, stirring occasionally.

3. Line a colander or large sieve with a double thickness of cheesecloth. Strain stock through cheesecloth, pressing out as much juice as possible from solids with the back of a ladle or spoon.

Carrots with Honey-Mustard Glaze

The butter, honey, and mustard all work together to both accent and complement the carrots in this easy and delicious dish.

Makes 4 servings

1½ tablespoons butter
2 tablespoons minced shallots
1 pound carrots, peeled and sliced
 ⅜ inch thick
Kosher salt and freshly ground black
 pepper to taste

3 tablespoons fresh orange juice
1 tablespoon honey mustard or
 2 teaspoons Dijon mustard and
 1 teaspoon honey

1. Put butter in a nonstick skillet over medium-low heat. Add shallots and cook, stirring, until soft, about 3 minutes. Add carrots, salt, and pepper, stir and cover. Cook 10 minutes.

2. Combine orange juice, mustard, and 3 tablespoons water. Add to carrots, stir well, cover, and cook until carrots are tender, about 10 minutes.

cauliflower

In addition to fish and cabbage, what other food stunk up the house when Mom cooked it? Cauliflower, of course. Is it any wonder, therefore, that the only way people eat cauliflower these days is raw as part of a vegetable platter?

Unfortunately, we don't think raw cauliflower is very appetizing. Yes, it's crunchy, but so are raw potatoes. About the only thing that's less appetizing is the way Mom cooked it: to death. Bring on the extra-strength Glade and Air-Wick.

In addition to the smell, overcooking also diminishes the nutrients significantly. In fact, you can reduce the levels of some vitamins by cooking with one method over another. A while back, food writer Mark Bittman quoted a Cornell University study in an article in *The New York Times*. It stated that 100 grams of cauliflower had 55 milligrams of vitamin C after boiling, 70 milligrams after steaming, and 82 milligrams after being cooked in the microwave oven.

The problem is chemical. Cauliflower, like broccoli and cabbage, belongs to the cruciferous family of vegetables, which has been shown to be effective in fighting certain forms of cancer. But cauliflower also contains sulfur compounds that can smell pretty bad. If you ever made hydrogen sulfide in high school chemistry class, you know what we're talking about.

The best way to guard against these compounds turning your kitchen into a chemistry lab is to cook cauliflower minimally. And instead of using raw cauliflower on your vegetable tray, try cooking it about half as long as you would for a side vegetable. Then refresh the cauliflower in ice water to stop the cooking and keep it from turning gray.

Cauliflower is a member of the cabbage family. However, despite its name, which literally means cabbage flower, it is not the flower of the cabbage. Unlike broccoli, another member of the cabbage family, cauliflower hasn't yet caught on as a popular vegetable. Part of this may be price. A head of cauliflower is rarely as cheap as broccoli. And part of it may be the color, or absence of color. That may be remedied as purple and green varieties are more widely available.

WHERE GROWN

Cauliflower likes cool, moist areas. So the foggy coastal climates of the California central coast and the coastal areas of New York are prime cauliflower growing areas.

Not surprisingly, California is the leading supplier followed by Arizona. New York, Michigan, Oregon, and Texas also produce cauliflower. Cauliflower is imported from Canada and Mexico as well.

VARIETIES

Ninety percent of the cauliflower in markets is the familiar pure-white type. Cauliflower varieties differ mainly by when they are grown. For example, Early Snowball and Super Snowball are the earliest varieties of the year. In mid-season, we see Snowdrift and Danish Giant cauliflower. And later in the year, it's the Veitch Autumn Giant.

Most cauliflower comes packed by size: six, nine, twelve, or sixteen per case, with the size sixteen about 5 inches across. Occasionally size will be as small as twenty per case. This size is especially favored by the Japanese. Baby cauliflower, as the name implies, is a miniature version of regular cauliflower, about 2 inches in diameter. But it is rare, more likely seen at four-star restaurants than at retail markets, even upscale ones.

Romanesco is a yellow-green cauliflower variety with spiraled florets that make it look like a headdress for a Siamese princess. It has a milder flavor than regular cauliflower. Look for it in specialty markets.

Broccoflower is the brand name of a mutant strain of cauliflower that was developed commercially about nine years ago by Tanimura and Antle, a Salinas, California, grower that brought seeds to the United States from Holland. Broccoflower has the green color of broccoli all the way through, but it tastes like cauliflower, though somewhat sweeter. There are other versions of green cauliflower, sometimes incorrectly called Broccoflower the way tissues are sometimes called Kleenex. Some of these other versions may not have green color all the way through but may just have a green head.

SEASONS

Cauliflower is grown year-round, but the best time for uniform quality and price is late fall. The worst time to buy cauliflower is in the middle of the summer. Broccoflower is also available year-round, but in far lower quantities. Romanesco is available from September to December.

SELECTION, STORAGE & HANDLING

Choose cauliflower with white or creamy white, tightly packed heads (also called curds) and no loose or spreading florets. Heads may have a purplish tint but it will not affect flavor. Avoid any heads with black specks, browning, or other blemishes. (Though in a pinch, these defects can sometimes be trimmed off if the rest of the cauliflower looks okay.)

Size has nothing to do with quality. Sometimes heads will display a slightly granular appearance but, again, this is not a sign of quality.

Since most cauliflower is packed in plastic wrap, you'll have to work a little bit to inspect what are called the jacket leaves, the greens that wrap the underneath and sides of the cauliflower like giant hands. They should be green and fresh looking without yellowing or withering.

Another indicator is the firmness of the bottom. If it is soft, the cauliflower is over-the-hill.

Wrapped in a plastic bag and stored in the crisper section of the refrigerator, cauliflower will last about five days but should be used within three.

NUTRITION

Most of the same great nutritional benefits found in cabbage and broccoli are contained in cauliflower. In addition, a 99g (about 3.5 ounces, or $\frac{1}{6}$ of a head) serving of cauliflower has 25 calories, 5g carbohydrates, 2g each of dietary fiber and protein, 100% of the DV for vitamin C, and 2% each for calcium and iron. Cauliflower is also a good source of potassium. Broccoflower or green cauliflower has roughly the same profile as white cauliflower. Cauliflower is also a fairly good source of potassium (270mg).

YIELD

One medium-size head (about $1\frac{1}{2}$ pounds) will serve four people.

Tony's Tip

This tip actually comes from Craig Claiborne's The New York Times Food Encyclopedia. *If you're having a problem with cooked cauliflower turning dark, Claiborne suggests adding a cup of milk to the cooking water.*

PREPARATION

Remove the jacket leaves, which can be cooked by themselves like a hearty green such as collards (see "Greens, Cooked," page 147). Core out the stem. Then cut the cauliflower into florets, much like broccoli, though the stem is less usable than the broccoli stem.

The florets can be steamed, which takes between 12 and 15 minutes, or microwaved for about 8 to 10 minutes. Remember, shorter cooking is better for nutrients and the smell of your kitchen.

For stir-fries and in salads, cook the cauliflower about halfway, then refresh in cold water. Cauliflower tends to get mucked up in cheese sauces and the like. We prefer lighter sauces such as lemon butter with chives. In addition to putting florets in omelets (see Cauliflower Frittata, page 71), try them in quiches. And if you can spare the calories, breaded and fried cauliflower can be delicious.

Cauliflower Frittata

This was a staple in the Gugino household on Fridays and especially during Lent. Other vegetables such as asparagus, broccoli, and dandelion can be substituted.

Makes 4 servings

5 whole eggs plus 3 egg whites

3 tablespoons grated Parmesan cheese

1 tablespoon chopped fresh mint, or
  1 teaspoon dried

1 tablespoon chopped fresh oregano, or
  1 teaspoon dried

Kosher salt and freshly ground black
  pepper to taste

3 cups steamed cauliflower florets
  (see Cauliflower with Caramelized Red
  Onions, page 73)

2 teaspoons butter

1. Combine eggs, egg whites, cheese, and seasonings in a mixing bowl. Mix well and stir in cauliflower. Turn oven to broil.

2. Put butter in an ovenproof nonstick skillet over medium-low heat until hot—when it stops sizzling. Add egg mixture and reduce heat to as low as possible. When the eggs are set on the bottom, but the top is still slightly runny, put the pan under the broiler. Cook about 60 to 90 seconds, rotating the pan to cook evenly. When just set—be careful not to overcook—remove and slide onto a plate. Let cool until warm or room temperature and cut into 4 wedges.

Giardiniera Salad with Shrimp

Giardiniera is a pickled vegetable mélange familiar to Italian Americans. This is a salad variation of that dish. You can leave out the shrimp and make this a side vegetable salad for six people.

Makes 4 servings

1 small to medium head cauliflower, about 1¹/₄ pounds, separated into small florets

1 pound peeled and trimmed carrots, cut into ¹/₄-inch slices

24 pearl onions, peeled

1 red bell pepper, cored and cut into thin strips

12 ounces shrimp, peeled (deveined if desired)

Kosher salt

¹/₄ cup chopped fresh parsley

2 tablespoons rice vinegar

2 tablespoons extra-virgin olive oil

1 clove garlic, finely chopped

1 teaspoon fennel seeds, ground

1 teaspoon ground coriander

Freshly ground black pepper to taste

Hot pepper flakes to taste

Pinch sugar

1. Steam cauliflower, carrots, onions, and pepper in ¹/₂ inch of water over a steamer basket in a covered large saucepan or small kettle until vegetables are tender but still firm, about 15 to 20 minutes. Refresh briefly under cold water (the vegetables should not be completely cooled). Drain.

2. Meanwhile, cook shrimp in 1 quart of boiling water and 1 teaspoon of salt for 3 or 4 minutes. Drain, let cool slightly, and cut into ¹/₂- to 1-inch pieces.

3. Put vegetables in a bowl with shrimp and parsley. Combine remaining ingredients with salt to taste. Pour over mixture and toss well. Serve at room temperature or refrigerate. Bring to room temperature to serve.

Cauliflower with Caramelized Red Onions

The onions add a natural sweetness and the toasted pine nuts give richness without lots of fat. Oh, if only Mom had cooked cauliflower this way.

Makes 4 to 6 servings

1¹/₂ tablespoons butter

2 large red onions, about 1 pound, thinly sliced

1 teaspoon balsamic vinegar

Kosher salt and freshly ground black pepper to taste

1 head cauliflower, about 1¹/₂ pounds, separated into florets

2 tablespoons toasted pine nuts (page 28)

1. Put butter in a heavy-bottomed skillet over medium heat. Add onions and cook, stirring periodically, until the onions are a deep golden color, about 20 minutes. (The longer the onions cook, the more frequently they need to be stirred.) Add balsamic vinegar, salt, and pepper. Cook until most of the moisture evaporates and onions are deep brown, about 5 minutes.

2. Meanwhile, steam (12 to 15 minutes) or microwave (8 to 10 minutes) cauliflower until tender but still firm.

3. Put cauliflower on a platter and top with caramelized onions. Sprinkle with pine nuts.

Pasta con le Sarde

One of the essential Sicilian dishes for Lent, and particularly St. Joseph's Day, March 19, is Pasta con le Sarde (pasta with sardines), the signature dish of Sicily. In many Italian American households, Pasta con le Sarde (often without the le) is made with a mix that is sold in cans at Italian specialty shops. But these are too heavy and too strongly flavored. Pasta con le Sarde should be delicate with a multitude of flavors and textures.

Makes 6 servings

1 pound fresh sardines

3 fennel bulbs with fronds

3 cups cauliflower florets

1 tablespoon tomato paste

$^1/_2$ teaspoon saffron threads, dissolved in $^3/_4$ cup hot water

$^1/_4$ cup currants, soaked 30 minutes in warm water

1 pound hollow-type spaghetti such as bucatini or perciatelli

1 tablespoon extra-virgin olive oil

1 medium onion, chopped

2 cloves garlic, minced

6 anchovy fillets, chopped

$^1/_4$ cup pine nuts, lightly toasted (page 28)

Kosher salt, freshly ground black pepper, and hot pepper flakes to taste

1 cup lightly toasted bread crumbs (10 minutes at 350°F)

1. Clean sardines by removing heads, innards, fins, and tails. Open each sardine with your hand and remove the backbone. Trim and cut each sardine into 2 fillets, or have your fishmonger do it. Wash with cool water. Pat dry.

2. Separate fronds from fennel stalks. Wash, dry, and chop the fronds. Discard the stalks. You should have about 1 cup. In a pot of salted water large enough for the spaghetti, blanch one fennel bulb about 10 minutes; save the others for another use. Remove bulb with a strainer, chop, and set aside. Blanch cauliflower until just tender, 5 to 7 minutes. Set aside. Keep water hot.

3. Add tomato paste to saffron water. Blend thoroughly. Add currants and set aside. Cook the spaghetti in the fennel water until firm but tender. Meanwhile, in a wok or large skillet, heat oil gently. Cook onion and fennel bulb, stirring, until onion is translucent, 5 to 7 minutes. And garlic and anchovies, mashing the anchovies with the back of a spoon. Add sardines and cook a few minutes on each side, or until they lose color. Add tomato paste and saffron mixture, fennel fronds, pine nuts, and cauliflower. Blend well but gently so as not to break up sardines. Cook just until sauce begins to thicken.

4. When spaghetti is cooked, drain thoroughly and add to sauce. Add salt, pepper, and hot pepper flakes. Toss well and adjust seasonings as necessary. Add bread crumbs and toss again. Serve warm or at room temperature.

CHAPTER

09

celery

(including celery root)

Perhaps worse than being hated is being ignored or taken for granted. Such is the case with celery.

Most of us don't hate celery unless we're on a diet and that's all we think we can eat. But we don't love it either, or even think about it much.

It's not as if we get cravings for celery and have to go out and buy a bunch every once in a while. Mom doesn't say, "We're having your favorite tonight, dear—celery." No, celery is just there, doing its thing in thousands of dishes that wouldn't be the same without it.

Celery is one of the "big four" vegetables for chefs the world over, along with onions, carrots, and parsley. These four are the foundation for virtually all stocks, many sauces, and a lot of other dishes. No professional kitchen would be without any of these "aromatics," as they are sometimes called.

Celery by itself might not seem terribly appetizing, but look at it this way: What would a potato, tuna, chicken, or shrimp salad be without it? Or your favorite Thanksgiving stuffing? Celery is crucial to many ethnic dishes as well. Caponata, one of Sicily's most famous dishes (page 109), just wouldn't be the same without celery. The reason is that celery contains an essential, highly aromatic oil that lends its perfume and flavor to numerous dishes. So it's not surprising that celery is the sixth best selling vegetable in supermarkets.

Celery root or celeriac (sometimes called apio) is quite literally the underground kin of celery. Wild celery produced two offspring: the more familiar aboveground celery and the more sinister-looking root. The root, more commonly called a knob, looks as if it would be the *plat du jour* of that bar in *Star Wars:* bumpy, dirty skin with dangling roots. But underneath that nubby, dirty exterior is an intense celery flavor that wins many friends.

WHERE GROWN

California produces 75 percent of the celery grown in the United States. Florida is second. Other producing states of note are Arizona, Michigan, New York, Ohio, Wisconsin, and Washington. Some celery is imported from Canada and Mexico. Most celery root comes from California.

VARIETIES

The vast majority of celery on the market today is the Pascal or green celery. There is also a bleached white celery.

Celery roots come in two varieties: a smaller knob version sold earlier in the fall and a larger knob version that comes later.

SEASONS

Celery is available year-round with no real peak season. California produces celery all year long, with the peak of the crop occurring in November and December. Florida celery is available from October through July; Michigan, July through October.

Celery root is available from November through April, though it may show up as early as September and last until June. Peak supplies and best quality are in late fall and early winter.

SELECTION, HANDLING & STORAGE

Celery stalks should have a nice, glossy finish and a medium- to light-green color. Ribs should be crisp and not too thick. Leaves should be bright green and fresh looking.

Celery roots should be firm and heavy for their size. Check for any decay under clinging dirt. If green tops are attached, they should be fresh looking. Medium-size knobs are best for overall quality and ease of preparation.

To store celery, trim the base and remove any leaves or ribs that are damaged or bruised. Rinse and place in a plastic bag in the high-humidity crisper section of the refrigerator. It will last about two weeks. As with carrots, to refresh limp stalks, trim the ends and place in ice water for a few hours. Cut celery (unwashed), stored in well-sealed plastic bags, will last about three days.

If you have a cool, moist cellar like your grandma did, celery root will last there for several weeks or months. Otherwise, it's best stored in the refrigerator, wrapped in plastic.

NUTRITION

Despite its reputation (or notoriety) as a dieter's food, celery may not really be a good idea if you're trying to lose weight. Despite its low caloric content—two medium stalks, about 110g (3.9 ounces), contain only 20 calories— celery has appetite-stimulating properties. Another seeming contradiction is that while celery is mostly water, it is also a mild diuretic, which helps you lose water.

The compounds contained in celery have been shown to help lower blood pressure. In fact, it is a traditional blood-pressure remedy among Vietnamese. Celery also contains several compounds that fight cancer, notably stomach cancer.

A serving of celery contains 5g of carbohydrates, 2g of dietary fiber, and 1g of protein. It contains 15% of the DV for vitamin C, 2% each for vitamin A and iron, and 4% for calcium. Celery is also a good source of potassium (350mg) and folic acid.

Celery root has about twice the calories of celery and is not as broadly nutritious, though it does have twice the iron, four times the phosphorous, and twice the magnesium of celery as well as similar amounts of calcium and vitamin C.

YIELD

First a note about terminology. A stalk of celery is the same as a bunch, the whole celery plant. A rib is just one arm or branch of that plant. One medium bunch or stalk of celery normally weighs about 1 1/2 pounds and yields about 4 to 5 cups of diced or sliced celery. One large rib will yield about 1/2 cup diced. One pound of celery root yields about 2 1/2 cups chopped.

Tony's Tip

If you're in a hurry, or you don't want to buy a whole bunch of celery for one dish, check out the salad bar at your supermarket for already cut celery. Yes, it's more expensive per pound, but you won't be using that much.

PREPARATION

Once trimmed of any bruised tops or bottoms and removed of any leaves, celery stalks are most commonly diced or cut into crescents. To dice, cut ribs in half or quarters, lengthwise, depending on size, then chop crosswise. For crescents, cut ribs crosswise to whatever width you desire.

Celery can be a valuable addition to stir-fries. Cut the celery in crescents 1/4 to 1/2 inch wide, depending on how crunchy you want it to be. For a fancier touch, cut the crescents on the diagonal.

Leaves are valuable additions to soups and stocks and can be treated like an herb such as parsley. Celery with the leaves attached can be used as a baster for grilled meats, poultry, and fish. For a festive presentation, use a 6-inch piece of a celery rib with the leaves attached for a swizzle stick in a spicy tomato juice cocktail.

Celery root is delicious with potatoes, mashed or in gratins. It makes a nice change to add regular celery in cold composed salads. It also adds a great deal to soups and stews.

Mom's Olive Salad

Sam's mom makes olive salad to go with sandwiches (especially on Thanksgiving night) or with homemade sausages grilled in the backyard. Sam's wife, Mary, actually loves the celery and onions more than the olives, so he's upped the quantities of both. It's essential that this salad mellow for twenty-four hours so that the flavors meld and the onions lose some of their bite.

Makes 8 servings as a condiment with cold meats or sandwiches

1 pound large green olives, preferably from a store that sells them in bulk

6 good-size ribs celery, cut in $1/4$- to $1/2$-inch-wide crescents on the diagonal, about 3 cups

2 small to medium red onions, cut into rings as thin as possible, about 3 cups

$1/4$ cup capers, drained

5 tablespoons olive oil

6 tablespoons cider or wine vinegar

$1^1/2$ teaspoons dried oregano (preferably Greek)

Kosher salt and freshly ground black pepper to taste

1. Rinse olives and pat dry. Crack each just so the pit is exposed—do not "smash." Put in a mixing bowl with celery, onions, and capers.

2. Mix remaining ingredients in a cup or small bowl. Pour over olive mixture and toss well. Cover and refrigerate 24 hours. Bring to room temperature, taste, and adjust seasonings as needed.

Celery Root Rémoulade with Fresh Dill

This is a low-fat version of a classic French salad.

Makes 4 servings

5 tablespoons low-fat mayonnaise or equal amounts of mayonnaise and low-fat sour cream

2 tablespoons coarse-grained mustard

2 tablespoons fresh dill, chopped

1 teaspoon fresh lemon juice

Kosher salt and freshly ground black pepper to taste

1 knob celery root, about $1^1/4$ pounds

1. Combine mayonnaise (with sour cream if desired), mustard, dill, lemon juice, salt, and pepper.

2. Peel and shred celery root in a food processor or by hand. Put in a mixing bowl. Pour dressing over and toss well. Refrigerate at least a few hours. Bring to room temperature. Adjust seasonings if necessary.

Turkey Stuffing

The key to the Thanksgiving stuffing Sam's mom made every year is celery. The recipe can easily be doubled.

Makes 5 or 6 servings

1-pound loaf of sliced white bread
3 tablespoons butter or margarine
2¹/₂ ribs celery, cut into crescents
(about 1¹/₄ cups)
2 medium onions, chopped
(about 2 cups)

1¹/₂ tablespoons fresh sage, finely
chopped, or 1 tablespoon dried
Kosher salt and freshly ground black
pepper to taste

1. Dip bread, two slices at a time, lightly in warm water and squeeze out excess moisture. Crumble bread coarsely into a large bowl.

2. In a large, nonstick skillet over medium heat, melt 1 tablespoon of the butter. Add celery, cover, and cook, stirring occasionally, just until it softens, about 5 minutes. Add to bread. Add onions to skillet, cook, covered, until softened, 5 to 7 minutes. Add to bread.

3. Add seasonings to bread mixture and mix well. Put remaining butter in the skillet over medium-high heat. When sizzling stops, add stuffing. Cook, turning periodically to prevent burning, until stuffing is evenly browned all over, about 10 minutes. Cool and stuff turkey or reheat separately. If you're not stuffing a turkey, moisten the stuffing with about ¹/₃ cup Chicken Stock (page 9) and put in a greased casserole dish. Bake at 350°F for about 40 minutes or until heated through.

Sam's Cooking Tip

Don't used powdered sage. It doesn't have the nice perfume that fresh or dried leaf sage does. If using dried leaf sage, first crumble it, then measure.

Stir-Fried Chicken with Celery

This dish can easily be made an all-vegetarian affair by increasing the celery and onion to 2 cups and 1 cup, respectively, and doubling the amount of mushrooms.

Makes 4 servings

1 tablespoon peanut oil

1 pound boneless chicken breasts, cut into ³/₄-inch cubes

2 ribs celery cut on the diagonal, about 1¹/₂ inches long tip to tip (about 1¹/₄ cups)

1 small onion, thinly sliced, about ³/₄ cup

1 cup sliced shiitake mushrooms

³/₄ cup Chicken Stock (page 9) or Vegetable Stock (page 64) mixed with 2 teaspoons cornstarch

³/₄ to 1 teaspoon dried thyme

Kosher salt and freshly ground black pepper to taste

1. Put oil in a wok over medium-high heat. When it begins to smoke, add chicken and stir-fry about 2 to 3 minutes.

2. Add celery, onion, and mushrooms. Cook 2 to 3 minutes. Add chicken stock mixture, thyme, salt, and pepper and cook until mixture thickens. Serve over rice.

Bean and Celery Salad

This is a substantial salad that goes well on a buffet or as the quick part of a cold dinner with perhaps some good bread and cold sliced chicken or ribs.

Makes 6 servings

One 15-ounce can small white beans, rinsed and drained

One 15-ounce can pink beans, rinsed and drained

One 15-ounce can black beans, rinsed and drained

2 large ribs celery, chopped (about 1¹/₂ cups)

1 to 2 jalapeño peppers, seeded and minced

2 to 3 tablespoons chopped cilantro

3 tablespoons olive oil

3 tablespoons cider vinegar

Kosher salt and freshly ground black pepper to taste

1. Put beans, celery, jalapeño peppers, and cilantro in a mixing bowl.

2. Combine other ingredients in a cup and pour over bean mixture. Toss and let sit 30 minutes before serving. Check seasonings and adjust as needed.

chicory

(including endive, radicchio and escarole)

Americans like things sweet. We

consume oceans of sugary soda pop and moun-

tains of candy and desserts. But foods that are

bitter haven't quite caught our fancy the way they

have in Europe.

In Italy, bitter liqueurs such as Campari are an institution. So are various forms of chicory such as radicchio. Belgium, home of the famous Belgian endive, those ivory white bitter cylinders, has the highest per capita consumption of chicory in the world. France grows half of the world's chicory, most of it in the cooler north.

We probably get our lack of appreciation for chicory from our British ancestors. They think of it as, well, bitter. But in recent years the French have tried to change things there with aggressive marketing programs that show how to use chicory beyond the salad bowl.

Maybe the French—or the Belgians or the Italians—should help us out over here too. Americans are missing the boat when it comes to chicory in their diets. Yes, Belgian endive and radicchio can be delicious in salads. But what about escarole soup, braised endive, and grilled radicchio?

Chefs have already recognized these greens and are using them in numerous dishes, particularly the more trendy radicchio. We hope this chapter helps Jane and John Q. Public know that these lettuces aren't bitter pills to swallow.

WHERE GROWN

Florida is the number-one endive- and escarole-producing state, followed by New Jersey and California. Other states that produce endive and escarole are Arizona, Illinois, Michigan, New York, Colorado, Ohio, and Texas.

Radicchio is grown in California and New Jersey and is imported from Italy and Mexico.

Belgium is the largest producer of Belgian endive, and while it consumes most of what it grows, increasing amounts of that country's production are exported. America is the fastest-growing market.

VARIETIES

As difficult as it is to get the American palate to appreciate chicory, endive, and escarole, it may be more difficult to describe them. Here's what Joe Carcione said in his book *The Green Grocer* (Chronicle Books, 1972), "There's hopeless confusion between the botanical and common names of these three salad greens. If you can keep them straight, you're doing a better job than many professional produce men I know."

Well, let's give it a try. Endive, chicory, and escarole are all members of the *Compositae* family (sometimes called the sunflower family) and are contained in the subcategory or chicory "tribe" called *Cichorieae*. Endive and escarole are variants of *Cichorium endivia*, chicory of *Cichorium intybus*.

Cichorium endiva includes endive and curly endive (which some people mistakenly call chicory). It has narrow, ragged, green outer leaves that resemble the leaves of dandelion. The outer leaves are bitter; the inside leaves are smaller, more tender, and yellow to creamy white.

There are several varieties of **curly endive** that are grown during different times of the year. They vary in the size of the heart, or center, with peak winter varieties such as the Ruffec having the biggest. Some varieties are longer than others.

Escarole is a broader leaf version of endive and is not as bitter. Both endive and escarole are native to the Mediterranean or perhaps the Near East. Some say they originated in Sicily. The major variety of escarole on the market is Full Heart Batavian. It is about 12 to 15 inches across with deep green, closely bunched foliage that produces a heart that is well blanched.

Frisée (confusingly called French endive by some) is almost a miniature version of curly endive or perhaps is more like the inner portion or heart of that plant. The outer leaves of frisée are light green to yellow, and the yellowing continues inside and becomes white at the center with a lacelike pattern. The taste is milder than curly endive. Frisée is limited to specialty markets and supermarkets with extensive produce sections.

Cichorium intybus. **Chicory** was cultivated long after endive and escarole, perhaps not until the early seventeenth century. **Belgian endive** is a variation of a chicory plant created by accident in September 1830 in the early days of Belgian independence (which is why we know the date rather precisely). A farmer by the name of Jan Lammers had covered some chicory plants with earth before fleeing the hostilities of war. When he returned, he found white shoots growing up through the ground. They had a pleasantly bitter taste that soon caught on.

In 1872, Witloof (meaning "white leaf") chicory, as it was called in Belgium, was exported to France. The French liked the vegetable but apparently not the name. They called it endive and thereafter Belgian endive stuck, though it is also called French endive. (Incidentally, the French pronunciation of endive is *ahn-DEEV* as opposed to the English *EN-dive*). The creamy white cylinders, sometimes compared to fat cigars, with pale yellow tips derive their color (or lack of it) from being deprived of sunlight. Because they require hand labor and two plantings—one to obtain a root and one to produce the actual plant—the cost is fairly high.

Radicchio is an Italian red chicory (sometimes called Italian red lettuce) that looks somewhat like a miniature red cabbage but with distinct white veins running through more velvety leaves. Radicchio comes in two main varieties. Radicchio di Verona, also known as rosso di Verona or red Verona

chicory, is the cabbage-style radicchio with a deep red, almost purple color. It is by far the more widely available of the two varieties. Radicchio di Treviso or red Treviso chicory has elongated leaves and a color ranging from pink to deep red. It may range in size from as small as a Belgian endive to as large as a head of romaine lettuce.

SEASONS

All of the chicory family is available year-round. Endive and escarole have peak supplies from December through April and less availability in summer months. Belgian endive begins peaking in November and starts to trail off in late spring.

SELECTION, HANDLING & STORAGE

Endive, escarole, and p should be bright and fresh looking without bruises. Leaves should have no withering or discoloration. Heads should be crisp and firm. Some careless produce managers allow endive to dry out and wither. All should be kept cold and moist.

At home, remove any damaged leaves, wash in cool water, and drain. Then wrap loosely in paper towels and store in plastic bags in the crisper section of the refrigerator for no more than three days.

Belgian endive, which is often displayed in its wooden shipping crates, should have smooth, white leaves with yellow tips that are closed. Heads should be about 6 inches long, firm, and with no discoloring (such as rust-colored spots or edges). Heads should be kept dry in a cool, dark place. Wrap them in paper towels and store in plastic in the refrigerator. Use within a day or two.

Radicchio should have a firm core. Leaves should have a deep, rich red color with no blemishes or discoloration. Put heads in a plastic bag and store in the crisper section of the refrigerator for a week or more, but try to use within five to seven days.

NUTRITION

Endive isn't particularly nutritious, but then it doesn't have many calories to waste—10 for ³/₄ cup of chopped greens (75g, about 2.6 ounces). Endive is a very good source of folid acid, however, and a fair source of potassium. A serving also contains 2g of carbohydrates, 1g each of protein and dietary fiber, and 2% of the DV for both iron and calcium.

The nutrition numbers for Belgian endive aren't much different except that it has no folic acid or iron and has 2% of the DV for vitamin C. Radicchio has less going for it than either endive or Belgian endive, though some nutrition charts give it decent amounts of vitamins A and C. (The FDA has no official nutritional information on radicchio.)

YIELD

The government-recommended ³/₄-cup serving size of endive is, as usual, a bit light. A large head of a pound or more will yield about four servings. For Belgian endive, figure one head per person.

PREPARATION

Once trimmed and washed, endive and escarole can be broken up by hand into salads, preferably mixed with other greens to soften their bitterness somewhat, and dressed with an assertive vinaigrette.

Both can also be gently braised as a vegetable in stock with perhaps a bit of smoked pork. If you've got a strongly flavored sandwich, try

them instead of the usual iceberg or romaine lettuce.

To prepare Belgian endive, cut off about ¹/₈ inch from the stem end, then cut a ¹/₂-inch-deep cone into the stem end. The leaves can then be easily separated for use in a salad as is or cut into strips, lengthwise. Favorite accompaniments are blue cheese and walnuts. Try some apples too.

Belgian endive leaves make a particularly attractive presentation as part of an hors d'oeuvre platter. They are perfect scoops for dips. And they can be filled with everything from caviar and sour cream to grain salads like tabbouleh.

Tony's Tip

The root of the chicory plant is dried, roasted, and ground, and used to make a coffeelike drink that is popular in Louisiana.

Braised endive is more popular in Europe than here, but it is easily done. (See Braised Belgian Endive, page 86). This side dish is particularly good with a roast of pork or veal.

Radicchio is good in all the above presentations. Because it can be frightfully expensive, radicchio is best used judiciously. A small head goes a long way and don't toss those outer leaves. One nifty idea is to peel off the leaves and use them as cups for chicken, shrimp, or other kinds of salad that might make a light lunch dish.

Radicchio is also an increasing favorite on the grill. First halve or quarter (depending on size), then brush with olive oil and put over medium heat about 5 minutes, until soft but not mushy.

Radicchio and Chickpea Salad

*This salad improves with age, especially for those who like the bitter edge
from the radicchio somewhat mellowed.*

Makes 6 servings

1 small head radicchio

Two 15-ounce cans chickpeas, rinsed and
  drained

1 bunch scallions, trimmed, white and
  1 inch of green cut into thin slices

1 medium carrot, shredded (about
  3/4 cup)

3 tablespoons fresh parsley

3 tablespoons extra-virgin olive oil

3 tablespoons fresh lemon juice

2 teaspoons toasted, ground cumin

Kosher salt and freshly ground black
  pepper to taste

1. Separate leaves of radicchio. Lay one on top of the other and cut into thin strips.
Wash and drain in a colander or salad spinner. Put into a large bowl. Add chickpeas,
scallions, carrot, and parsley.

2. Mix remaining ingredients in a small bowl. Pour over vegetables and toss well. Let sit
at least 1 hour at room temperature before serving.

Braised Belgian Endive

The sweet saltiness of prosciutto marries well here with the bittersweetness of the endive.

Makes 4 servings

4 heads Belgian endive, about 6 ounces each

4 very thin slices prosciutto, about 2 ounces total

1 tablespoon butter

Kosher salt and freshly ground black pepper to taste

$^1/_4$ cup minced shallots

1 tablespoon flour

$^1/_4$ cup dry white wine

$1^1/_4$ cups Chicken Stock (page 9)

$^1/_4$ cup flavored bread crumbs

Butter-flavored cooking spray

1 tablespoon chopped fresh parsley

1. Cut off about $^1/_8$ inch from the stem end of each endive, then cut a $^1/_2$-inch-deep cone into the stem ends. Set aside. Preheat oven to 400°F.

2. Wrap a slice of prosciutto around each of the Belgian endive. Put butter into a non-stick skillet over medium to medium-low heat. Brown endive all over, about 10 minutes, then remove to a gratin dish just large enough to hold all in one layer. Season with salt and pepper.

3. Add shallots to skillet over medium heat and cook until soft, a minute or two. Add flour and stir another minute. Add wine, then stock, and bring to a simmer, stirring until it just thickens to the consistency of a thin gravy.

4. Pour sauce over endive. Bake, covered, 25 minutes or until endive is just tender. Raise oven heat to 500°F, sprinkle endive with bread crumbs, and spray with butter-flavored cooking spray. Bake about 8 to 10 minutes or until top is nicely browned.

5. Remove endive to a platter. Whisk sauce and pour around endive. Sprinkle parsley on top of endive.

Escarole Soup with Spicy Meatballs

This is a traditional Italian soup lightened with chicken instead of beef or pork meatballs. The key, however, is the quality of the stock.

Makes 6 servings

Kosher salt

1 head escarole, about 1 pound

$^1/_2$ cup bread crumbs from day-old Italian bread

4 ounces ground chicken breast meat

1 egg white

$^1/_3$ cup Parmesan cheese

2 tablespoons chopped fresh parsley

$^1/_4$ teaspoon cayenne pepper

Freshly ground black pepper to taste

3 quarts defatted Chicken Stock (page 9), preferably homemade, cooked over medium-high until reduced to 2 quarts

$^1/_3$ cup *acini di pepe* or other tiny pasta for soups

1. Bring 3 quarts of water and 1 teaspoon salt to a boil. Have a large bowl of ice water ready. Remove bottoms from escarole. Stack and roll leaves. Cut crosswise into $^1/_2$-inch strips. Wash, drain, and put into boiling water. Stir and cook 3 minutes. Drain and put into ice water. When cool, drain.

2. In a mixing bowl, moisten bread crumbs with a few tablespoons of water. Add chicken, egg white, 2 tablespoons of the Parmesan, parsley, cayenne pepper, and salt and black pepper to taste. Mix well and form into very small meatballs, slightly larger than a marble. You should have about 30.

3. Bring stock to a boil and add pasta. Cook 5 minutes, stirring. Add meatballs and cook 2 minutes. Add escarole and salt and pepper to taste. Cook 5 minutes. Serve, sprinkling each serving with remaining cheese.

Sam's Cooking Tip

To facilitate making meatballs, periodically dip the fingertips of the hand that does the rolling in a dish of water.

Curly Endive with Bacon and Blue Cheese

This is a lower-fat version of one of Sam's wife's all-time favorite salads, which she first had in Paris.

Makes 4 servings

1 head curly endive, about 1 pound
1 ounce lean bacon, finely chopped
3 tablespoons balsamic vinegar
1 teaspoon sugar

Kosher salt and freshly ground black
  pepper to taste
2 ounces blue cheese, crumbled

1. Wash, dry, and break endive into bite-size pieces. Set aside.

2. Put bacon in a wok or large skillet over medium-low heat and cook until crisp, about 5 minutes.

3. Add vinegar, sugar, and one tablespoon of water to bacon fat, bring to a boil, then reduce heat to low. Add curly endive and toss. Season with salt and pepper and continue tossing until coated with dressing and barely wilted but still quite crisp.

4. Remove to a serving bowl. Add blue cheese, toss, and serve.

corn

If bread is the staff of life, then corn

is life's scepter, certainly for the Western World.

Corn isn't just something we eat on the cob with

melted butter in summer when it's "as high as an

elephant's eye." The fact is, of all the corn grown,

we consume less than 1 percent as fresh, frozen, or

canned corn, even cornmeal. The rest goes into a $20 billion a year business that creates fuel for automobiles, oil for cooking, syrup for soft drinks, and talcum powder for babies' bottoms. It's even used in embalming fluid, a final salute to this amazing vegetable.

But if corn is important today, it was even more important to the Indians who inhabited the Americas before Columbus. The cuisine that was built around corn was a rich and complex one in the Mayan, Aztec, and Inca cultures. (The Incas alone developed some forty-eight varieties of corn.)

But corn was more than just food. Corn was sacred. The maize god was at the center of the pantheon of Mayan deities. The god-man Quetzalcoatl gave maize to the Aztecs. And the Inca calendar was based on the life cycle of the corn crop.

Today, corn is grown around the world from Beijing to Brazil, Indonesia to India. And while corn is generally considered the fodder of the poor, we can recall the endless fields of corn in the Dordogne region of France. That corn was destined to fatten the local geese whose livers produced the luxurious and very expensive foie gras.

WHERE GROWN

What state do you think of when you think of corn? Iowa, right? Maybe Nebraska. Sorry, but the number-one corn-producing state is the land of grapefruit and orange juice, Florida. California is second. Other significant producing states are Georgia, New York, and Illinois. Some corn is imported from Mexico.

VARIETIES

The five ancient types of corn still exist, but not all are used for fresh consumption by the general public. Dent corn is used for grits and hominy. Flour corn is preferred for grinding into tortillas. Flint corn is often the choice in colder regions because of its hardiness. And popcorn is used for guess what?

That pretty much leaves sweet corn, which is divided into yellow, white, and bicolored corn. Within each are numerous varieties or hybrids, more than two hundred in all. Some of the best-known names are Silver Queen, Golden Cross Bantam, Kandy Korn, and Honey and Cream.

In recent years, growers have developed sweeter and sweeter varieties to the point that you almost feel as if you're eating that orange and yellow candy corn that comes out on Halloween. Nearly 100 percent of the corn in Florida is some type of yellow supersweet variety. White corn isn't as widely planted and is usually higher in price. Bicolored corn isn't an equal mix of yellow and white but about 80 percent yellow and 20 percent white.

At the retail market it's unlikely you'll know what kind of corn you're getting. However, almost every region has its local crop. So quiz your local farmer about the varieties he plants.

Huitlacoche (pronounced *wheat-la-COE-chay*), a corn fungus, sometimes referred to as corn smut, is an ancient Mexican delicacy that is becoming popular in trendy Mexican and Southwestern restaurants in the United States. The kernels affected by the fungus are swollen and black. The flavor is somewhat reminiscent of wild mushrooms or truffles. In fact, huitlachoche is sometimes marketed as corn mushroom or Mexican truffle. It is very scarce but can be ordered by mail—fresh from March through December and frozen in January and February—from Burns Farms in Montverde, Florida, (407) 469-4490.

SEASONS

Despite the fact that we think of it mostly in summer and early fall, corn is a year-round crop. Florida's crop runs from October through June, peaking from April to June. In California, the season starts in May, ends in October, and peaks in June and July. New York runs from July to September, peaking in August and September.

SELECTION, HANDLING & STORAGE

The standard way for most people to check on the freshness of corn—and to see if any kernels are missing from the cob—is to rip open the husk and examine it. And this is fine as long as you don't beat up the corn for the next guy. The exposed kernels should be firm and plump with no indentations. You can, however, find out if the kernels are all there and also plump by just feeling the top of the closed husk. The husk, incidentally, should be evenly green with no darkness on the bottom.

Most experts tell you to pass by any evidence of worm damage. But Betty Fussell, author of *Crazy for Corn* (HarperPerennial, 1995), has a different philosophy: "it will not only do you no harm, granted that you remove it when you take the silks from the cobs, but today it may testify that the corn has been grown without the pervasive chemicals that do us all harm."

Getting to know the local farmer who sells at a roadside stand or the weekly farmer's market is one way to ensure fresh, quality corn. Go back to him or her again and again until you've had your fill for the season. Ideally, the corn you buy should have been picked that morning (while it's still cool). Don't buy any fresh corn that's more than a few days old at the most.

Once you get corn home, refrigerate it in the high-humidity storage bins in the natural casings that Mother Nature has provided. You can put it in a plastic bag but don't be tempted to hold it for more than a day, especially if it's to be consumed right off the cob, because the longer corn sits, the more its sugar turns to starch.

NUTRITION

One medium ear of corn (90g, 3.2 ounces) contains 80 calories, 1g of fat, 18g of carbohydrates, and 3g each of protein and dietary fiber. A serving also contains 2% of the DV for vitamin A and iron and 10% for vitamin C. Corn is also a decent source of potassium (240mg).

Corn has some antiviral and anticancer properties. In small amounts, it may help to neutralize stomach acid. Corn and corn products are among the most common foods that can cause allergic reactions in people. They are also implicated in some forms of chronic fatigue.

YIELD

One small to medium ear of corn yields about $^1/_2$ cup of kernels.

Tony's Tip

If you're able to get very fresh, tender corn from a farmer's market or roadside stand (or if you grow your own), try eating an ear raw, right there.

PREPARATION

Obviously, if corn can be eaten raw, the less it gets cooked the better. The simplest method is to put ears in a kettle of water (with no salt) at a rolling boil for a minute or two but no more. Fussell suggests cooking the corn in its husk (but removing an outer layer) for more intense flavor. But this causes the corn to remain in the boiling water longer to get it to the appropriate temperature.

Steaming is preferred by some because flavor isn't lost in cooking water, but it takes longer,

5 minutes or more depending on how many ears you have. Microwaving is fine if you only have a few ears. A full-power oven will cook two ears in about 5 minutes, a few minutes longer in a lower-wattage oven.

Grilling is a fabulous way to cook corn. Some prefer to soak the husks in water before grilling to prevent burning. But this gives more of a steamed-grilled flavor than a pure grilled flavor. (The same is true when corn is husked and wrapped in foil.)

Instead, cook ears directly on the grill with or without the husks. Husked corn will take about 3 minutes, unhusked about 6 to 8 minutes. The flame should be of about medium intensity. You can brush the corn with some melted butter for either method. Pulling the husk down to the stem instead of removing it entirely gives a decorative touch for presentation.

For apartment dwellers without access to grills, follow the grill method in a 500°F oven.

To remove kernels on cooked or raw corn, hold the ear upright with one hand firmly holding the top. Then, starting halfway up the ear, slice down all around. Turn the ear upside down and repeat the process. For added flavor in soups and other prepared dishes, scrape the cob with the dull side of a knife to remove the flavorful "milk" from the cob. Cobs can also be boiled for a stock for corn chowder or soup.

Perhaps because they are also native to the Americas, we like chile peppers with corn. Spicy chile-flavored butter is a piquant change of pace and a good alternative for those watching salt intake. We also like corn with onions, especially scallions and red onions, with beans, particularly black beans, and with toasted and ground cumin seeds, cilantro, basil, and tomatoes.

Corn off the Cob with Chili Butter

Makes 4 servings

4 large ears fresh corn, shucked
2 tablespoons butter
1 teaspoon chili powder

1. Slice kernels off each ear of corn. Put corn in a skillet with $1/3$ cup water and cook, stirring a few times, over medium heat until water evaporates, about 3 minutes.

2. Add butter and chili powder. Lower heat slightly and cook about 3 minutes, stirring a few times.

Sam's Cooking Tip

Chili powder is actually a spice mix like curry. You could make your own chili powder using ground chiles (New Mexico, Ancho), salt, and pepper.

Corn and Black Bean Salad

This is a colorful salad that could be served any time of the year, but would look especially nice with grilled or barbecued chicken.

Makes 4 servings

2 cups cooked corn kernels, about
 4 ears (page 91)
One 15-ounce can black beans, rinsed
 and drained
1 cup chopped tomatoes
$1/2$ cup chopped mild onions
2 tablespoons chopped cilantro

1 tablespoon lime juice
1 tablespoon rice vinegar or other mild
 vinegar
2 tablespoons olive oil
Kosher salt and freshly ground black
 pepper to taste

1. Combine corn, beans, tomatoes, onions, and cilantro in a bowl.

2. Mix remaining ingredients in a cup. Pour over corn mixture and toss well. Let sit at least 30 minutes at room temperature. Check for seasonings.

Corn Sauté with Herbs and Peppers

Fresh summer herbs are a natural with corn, as are sweet and hot peppers.

Makes 4 servings

2 tablespoons butter

1 red bell pepper, chopped, about $1/2$ cup

1 or 2 jalapeño peppers, depending on taste, finely chopped

1 small onion, chopped, about $1/2$ cup

1 rib celery, chopped

3 cups corn kernels, about 6 ears

1 teaspoon fresh sage, chopped, or $1/2$ teaspoon dried

1 teaspoon fresh summer savory or thyme, or $1/2$ teaspoon dried

2 tablespoons chopped chives

Kosher salt and freshly ground black pepper to taste

1. Put butter in a large skillet over medium heat. Add the peppers, onion, and celery. Cook about 5 minutes until onion softens.

2. Add corn and remaining ingredients and cook, stirring, about 5 minutes. Check for seasonings.

Sam's Cooking Tip

In addition to the total number of peppers, you can adjust the heat from hot peppers by using or discarding all or part of the seeds and membranes where most of the heat from hot peppers resides.

Corn Chowder with Lobster

You don't have to go to Maine to enjoy this dish, which makes for a hearty first course or a light lunch with crusty bread and a green salad.

Makes 6 servings

Two $1^1/_4$-pound lobsters

3 cups corn kernels (6 ears), cobs saved

$^1/_2$ pound red-skinned potatoes, unpeeled

2 tablespoons butter

$^1/_3$ cup chopped shallots

1 rib celery, cut in half lengthwise and thinly sliced

2 tablespoons flour

1 cup warm milk

Kosher salt and freshly ground black pepper to taste

Large pinch cayenne pepper

3 tablespoons chopped chives

1. Put lobsters in a large pot with a steamer basket and 1 inch of boiling water. Cover and steam 10 minutes. Cool, remove meat, and retain shells and cooking water. Cut meat into $^1/_2$-inch pieces. (A lot of suburban supermarkets will steam lobsters for you if you feel squeamish about cooking them yourself.)

2. Add enough water to the lobster pot to make 2 quarts. Break the corn cobs in half and add along with the lobster shells. Bring to a boil, skimming any scum that forms on the surface. Reduce heat and simmer 45 minutes. Strain, pressing the solids with the back of a spoon to extract any remaining liquid. You should have about 1 quart.

3. Meanwhile, steam potatoes (see Mussel and Potato Salad, page 218), cool, and cut into $^1/_2$-inch cubes. Set aside.

4. Melt butter in a small kettle or large saucepan over medium heat. Cook shallots and celery, stirring, until shallots soften, about 3 to 4 minutes. Add flour and stir a few minutes. Add lobster-corn stock and bring to a boil, stirring. Lower heat and simmer 10 minutes.

5. Add corn kernels, potatoes, milk, salt, pepper, and cayenne pepper. Cook 5 minutes. Add reserved lobster and chives. Heat a few minutes. Check for seasonings.

Corn Bread

Try this with the Collards on page 144. Add another jalapeño pepper if you like your cornbread really spicy.

Makes 9 squares, about 6 to 8 servings

Butter-flavored cooking spray
1 cup yellow cornmeal
3/4 cup all-purpose flour
1 teaspoon Kosher salt
1 tablespoon baking powder
2 tablespoons sugar
1 cup buttermilk

2 eggs, well beaten
1 tablespoon canola oil
1/3 cup nonfat sour cream
1 cup fresh corn kernels
1 large jalapeño pepper, roasted, peeled, seeded, and chopped (page 205)
1/4 cup chopped cilantro

1. Spray an 8-inch-square baking pan with butter-flavored cooking spray. Preheat oven to 400°F.

2. Combine cornmeal, flour, salt, baking powder, and sugar in a bowl.

3. Whisk buttermilk, eggs, oil, sour cream, corn, jalapeño pepper, and cilantro together in a small bowl. Add to the dry mixture. Mix until just barely combined.

4. Pour into the baking pan and bake about 25 minutes or until a toothpick tester comes out clean and edges just begin to come away from the side of the pan.

Cucumbers

There are a lot of expressions about life and descriptions of people that involve fruits and vegetables. A person or a thing that's well liked is called a "peach." An attractive young woman is called a "tomato." One of our favorites is "cool as a cucumber."

Maybe we like that one because, unlike the others, which convey rather vague and subjective descriptions that can sometimes be downright erroneous (some pretty ugly tomatoes are delicious), cucumbers really are cool. The inside of a cucumber can be as much as 20°F cooler than the outside air. If you don't believe us, put some cucumber slices on your forehead on a hot day.

But cucumbers can also be cool and soothing when we use them in a more traditional manner, like eating. Cucumber salads or cucumbers in salads, cold cucumber soups, and cucumber with yogurt as a condiment are perfect light-eating fare on sweltering summer days. In addition to being cool, cucumbers are more than 95 percent water. That helps keep our internal radiators filled and keeps us cool too.

Maybe that's why cucumbers were favored by desert tribes. If they don't know how to keep cool, nobody does.

If you have a garden or can visit a place where cucumbers grow you'll notice a curious similarity between how cucumbers and squashes and melons grow. That's because cucumbers, squashes, and melons are all members of the *Cucurbitaceae* family.

WHERE GROWN

Florida is the biggest producer of cucumbers in the United States. Other significant producing states are California, New York, North Carolina, South Carolina, Texas, and Virginia. A fair amount of cucumbers is imported from Mexico.

VARIETIES

There are many varieties of cucumbers that most of us aren't aware of unless we're home gardeners. But there are three main types.

The slicing cucumber is the most familiar. It has dark green skin that is often heavily waxed

and thus can be chewy and indigestible. Popular commercial slicing varieties include the Ashley, Marketer, Palomar, Long Market, Marketmore, Poinsett, Straight Eight, Cherokee 7, Gemini, Hybrid Ashley, and High Mark II.

The pickling cucumber, sometimes called the Kirby or West Indian Gherkin, is short and very crisp with a bumpy skin. It is most often used for pickles but makes an excellent cucumber salad or part of a relish tray.

The English cucumber is dark green, long (up to 18 inches), rather narrow, and seedless or mostly seedless. Since the seeds promote gas, this variety is called "burpless." It is also called a European or Hot House cucumber. This cucumber does not have some of the bitterness that can be associated with the slicing cucumber.

Less widely available varieties include the Lemon, a mild, burpless variety that looks more like a green tomato and doesn't have a lemony flavor. The pale and undulating Armenian (also called Syrian and Turkish) ranges in length from 10 to 18 inches and in diameter from about 1 to 2 inches. It has a mellow flavor that can be enjoyed when eaten fresh or cooked. The dark and slim Japanese is part of the Armenian branch of the cucumber family. It is similar in shape to European cucumbers though shorter and with a slightly prickly skin.

SEASONS

Cucumbers are available year-round. Florida's crop wanes in July but others, particularly local varieties, pick up nicely. In fact, summer is the best time for price and availability (not to mention appropriateness) of cucumbers. The English cucumber peaks from March to November.

Pickling cucumbers are at their most abundant in late summer when thoughts turn to, you guessed it, pickling. California supplies of pickling and Armenian cucumbers come in

July and August. Lemon cucumbers from California come in from late May through mid-July. The year-round Japanese cucumber peaks from June through September.

SELECTION, HANDLING & STORAGE

Choose cucumbers that are firm with a good green color. They should be well shaped but not too large. (Smaller cucumbers are less likely to be bitter.) Small bumps and occasional whitish or light green spots are not an indication of poor quality. Avoid cucumbers that have withered or shriveled ends (indicating toughness and bitterness), a dull or yellowed color, puffiness, soft spots, or pitting.

Most commercial slicing cucumbers are waxed to extend shelf life. For similar reasons, the European cucumber is wrapped in cellophane.

Cucumbers should be refrigerated but not in the coldest part of the refrigerator, as they are more sensitive to cold than other vegetables. At between 45°F and 50°F, stored in plastic bags, cucumbers will last a week. Don't wash cucumbers until you're ready to use them.

NUTRITION

Cucumbers are a low-calorie wonder with only 15 calories in a 99g serving, $1/3$ of a medium cucumber (about 3.5 ounces). A serving also contains 3g of carbohydrates, 1g each of protein and dietary fiber, 4% of the DV for vitamin A, 10% for vitamin C, and 2% each for iron and calcium.

YIELD

To get about 2 cups of sliced cucumbers, you'll need about $1^1/2$ pickling cucumbers (each about 3 to 4 inches long), one slicing cucumber, or about $2/3$ of an English cucumber. A normal serving is about $1/2$ of a slicing cucumber per person.

Tony's Tip

Garnish a Bloody Mary with an unpeeled cucumber spear instead of a rib of celery.

PREPARATION

Slicing cucumbers bought at retail markets should be peeled to remove the tough wax covering. But locally grown cucumbers need only to be scrubbed before slicing unless you want to remove the peel for aesthetic reasons or because it is particularly indigestible. The peel can be bitter so it's best to taste a small piece before leaving the skin on.

If all systems are go and you're leaving on the skins but want a decorative look, try one of two methods. The simplest one is to scrape the tines of a fork down the outside of the cucumber, lengthwise, before slicing. A zester makes deeper ridges. You can also slice off strips of skin, such that you create a squarish or six-sided look for slices.

Seeds can also be bitter. The best way to remove them is to halve the cucumber lengthwise first. You'll notice that one end seems to be more open than the other; scoop the seeds in that direction (a melon baller is the best tool).

Don't overlook cucumbers as a vegetable, sautéed in butter and oil with fresh dill. Dill along with mint are the best matching herbs for cucumbers.

Greek Salad

Any Greek worth his taramasalata knows that a Greek salad can't possibly contain lettuce and tomatoes because local salad greens are gone by the end of June and local tomatoes don't ripen until mid-July. That's why true Greek salads have cucumbers instead of salad greens.

Makes 6 servings

1 medium red onion

$^2/_3$ cup plus 2 tablespoons good red wine vinegar (the Greek Glykadi if you can get it)

3 to 4 large Kirby cucumbers or 2 medium waxy cucumbers

1 large, ripe tomato

2 tablespoons extra-virgin olive oil

1 teaspoon crushed oregano (preferably the Greek variety)

Kosher salt and freshly ground black pepper to taste

3 ounces feta cheese, crumbled or cut into small cubes

8 kalamata olives, pitted and quartered, lengthwise

1. Cut the onion into very thin rings. Put it in a shallow bowl with $^2/_3$ cup vinegar and marinate 30 minutes, tossing a few times.

2. Meanwhile, trim cucumbers, halve lengthwise, and cut into half-moon shapes, about $^3/_8$ inch thick. Put into a mixing bowl. Core tomato, halve, then cut into wedges. Halve wedges and add to the cucumber. Drain the onion and add to the cucumbers and tomato.

3. Put olive oil, oregano, salt, pepper, and remaining 2 tablespoons vinegar in a small mixing bowl or large cup. Mix and add to vegetables. Toss well and let sit, covered 30 minutes to 1 hour at room temperature. Add feta and olives. Toss. Check for seasonings.

Sam's Cooking Tip

Though they're thought of more for pickles, I like to use Kirby cucumbers fresh because they have a less watery flavor than most waxy cucumbers.

Quick Cucumber Soup

In the dog days of summer, when we have plenty of cucumbers to go along with tomatoes and zucchini, we don't want to spend a lot of time cooking.

Makes 4 servings

4 scallions, trimmed

2 medium cucumbers, peeled, seeded, and coarsely chopped

2 cups low-fat buttermilk

3 tablespoons fresh dill, minced

Salt and white pepper to taste

3 tablespoons toasted chopped walnuts

1. Detach the green parts of the scallions and mince about 3 tablespoons. Set aside.

2. Put the white parts of the scallions and cucumbers in a food processor or blender and puree. Add buttermilk, dill, salt and pepper and blend until smooth. Refrigerate at least an hour, preferably several. Check seasonings and adjust if necessary. Stir in walnuts and sprinkle with the green parts of the scallions.

Sam's Cooking Tip

Though you can often substitute dried herbs (especially thyme and sage) for fresh, don't try it with dill. I find dried dill to be bitter and flavorless. Thankfully, fresh dill is available year-round.

Tabbouleh

The classic tabbouleh is a somewhat wet Middle Eastern salad of parsley and bulgur with emphasis on the parsley. This version is fluffier and nuttier with less parsley and the addition of cucumbers.

Makes 8 to 10 servings

2 cups bulgur wheat

1 to 1$\frac{1}{2}$ cups boiling water

1 cup thinly sliced scallions (white parts and 1 to 2 inches of the green parts)

1$\frac{1}{2}$ cups seeded, peeled, and diced cucumbers (3 Kirbys)

1$\frac{1}{2}$ cups diced tomato

$\frac{1}{2}$ cup chopped fresh mint

$\frac{1}{2}$ cup chopped fresh parsley

$\frac{1}{4}$ cup fresh lemon juice

3 tablespoons olive oil

Kosher salt and freshly ground black pepper to taste

Large pinch cayenne pepper

1. Put bulgur in a large mixing bowl, pour 1 cup boiling water over, and fluff with a large fork. Wait about 10 minutes and taste. If too firm, add more boiling water, $\frac{1}{4}$ cup at a time.

2. Meanwhile, prepare vegetables and herbs. Mix lemon juice, oil, salt, pepper, and cayenne pepper in a cup.

3. When bulgur is at the proper consistency, add all other ingredients and mix well. Chill a few hours before serving.

Sam's Cooking Tip

In Middle Eastern grocery stores, bulgur is often sold in two or three different grinds. The finest grind is normally used for tabbouleh, but I prefer a grind slightly more coarse. Experiment for yourself. Or try making tabbouleh with other grains such as barley, rice, and couscous.

Tzatziki

Serve this as an appetizer with toasted pita triangles, as part of a Middle Eastern meze (appetizer) with stuffed grape leaves and hummus, or as an accompaniment to roasted leg of lamb or lamb kebabs.

Makes 4 to 6 servings

$3^1/_2$ cups nonfat yogurt

1 English cucumber, peeled and grated

Kosher salt

1 large clove garlic, minced

1 tablespoon chopped fresh dill

1 tablespoon chopped mint

1 tablespoon extra-virgin olive oil

2 tablespoons Glykadi or other quality red wine vinegar

Freshly ground black pepper to taste

1. Line a strainer with a double thickness of cheesecloth and put strainer over a bowl. Put yogurt into cheesecloth and refrigerate for at least 8 hours. Put the strained yogurt (you should have about 2 cups) into a mixing bowl. Discard the water.

2. Meanwhile, put cucumber in a colander and sprinkle with a tablespoon of salt. Toss well and leave at least an hour. Squeeze out as much moisture as you can and pat with paper towels. Add to yogurt.

3. Add remaining ingredients and taste for salt.

eggplant

There are two issues involving egg-

plant. One is the name; the other is salt. (Actually

there are three, but the third one, oil, is dealt

with in Preparation, page 108.) Issue number one

is how the eggplant got its name. That's easy. Early

versions of the eggplant were white and about

the size of an egg.

The issue of salt is more complicated. It involves bitterness, which may involve seeds, but probably not sex. Huh? Many recipes call for routinely salting eggplant slices or cubes to leach out bitterness. But some believe that knowing the sex of the eggplant helps to avoid bitterness in the first place.

According to this theory, it's the female's fault. She's got the abundance of seeds. The gender of the eggplant can be determined by the blossom end, the one opposite the stem. The distaff side has an oval scar or indentation at that end. The male a round scar. Another theory says that the female eggplant has a sheen on the outside and the male has a dull appearance.

At a Turkish cuisine conference a few years ago (the Turks love eggplant), Paula Wolfert, the author of many cookbooks and an expert on Mediterranean cuisine said, in effect, "Baloney." Others we've consulted or read about seem to concur. In Craig Claiborne's *The New York Times Food Encyclopedia* (Times Books, 1985), the author says he consulted a botanist who pooh-poohed the sex theory, saying, among other things, that an eggplant has both female and male parts.

However, not all eggplant is bitter. Younger eggplant is usually not bitter.

But Wolfert says you never really know how old an eggplant is even if it has all the positive characteristics. So Wolfert says to choose eggplant that is lighter in weight, and will thus have fewer seeds that cause bitterness, even though the conventional wisdom says to choose eggplant that is heavy. The *Produce Availability and Merchandising Guide,* the bible of the produce industry, would seem to concur with Wolfert when it advises in its 1995 edition, "Product should be firm and light in relation to size."

In an article in *Cook's* magazine some years ago, Alice Waters, owner of the famed Berkeley, California, restaurant Chez Panisse, said the key to nonbitter eggplant is freshness. That means eggplant that is not too large and is shiny on the outside with taut, deep-colored skin. The flesh should spring back when pressed. Dull skin and rust-colored spots are a sign of age. The inside of the eggplant should be white with few seeds and no green. Green indicates an immature eggplant. Also, eggplant that is not used right away will have a tendency to become bitter.

Claiborne thinks all the fuss about salt and bitterness is just hooey anyway. He says, "I never thought that salt improved either the flavor or texture."

WHERE GROWN

Florida provides most of the U.S. crop. New Jersey is second and California third. A substantial amount of eggplant comes from Mexico.

VARIETIES

The egg-shaped globe or American eggplant (which to us often looks like a giant purple roma tomato) has many commercial varieties, the main ones being Black Beauty, Florida Market, Myers Market, Florida High Bush, New York Purple, and New Hampshire. Most are deep purple, almost black in color with a green stem and green calyx or leaf protrusion that shoots out from the base of the stem and wraps the top of the eggplant like the cap of an elf. Some of the smaller varieties of the globe-shaped eggplant are called Italian eggplants, which should not be confused with the Rosa Bianco, a more obscure purple and white eggplant with a pronounced calyx.

Also purple and white (but more purple than white) and with a distinct calyx is the Puerto

Rican Rayada eggplant, though its shape is more cylindrical than the Rosa Bianco.

The smaller, thinner Japanese eggplant has a purple skin with a calyx that may also be purple instead of green. It is sweeter than larger globe varieties with less tendency toward bitterness. The primary variety is Millionaire. There is a miniature version of the Millionaire that has violet and purple streaks and is straighter than the full-size Japanese eggplant.

The French Bonde de Valence is a deep purple, medium-size eggplant whose calyx and stem are somewhere between the Japanese and globe in color.

White eggplants are generally somewhat larger than their egg-size ancestor. Ghost Buster is the main white variety, about 6 to 8 inches long. But you may also see other white varieties in specialty and ethnic markets. There is the softball-size Easter egg and the smaller White egg. The Casper is another white eggplant, about the shape of a large zucchini. The Chinese white eggplant is similar in size to the Japanese eggplant.

In recent years, with the increased popularity of Asian cuisines, Thai eggplants are becoming more evident, though they are still a specialty item. They are small and round and may be green-streaked, purple, or white. One variety, the green bunch, comes in clusters like grapes.

SEASONS

The globe or American eggplant is a year-round commodity, though supplies may dwindle somewhat in late spring. Florida produces from October through July, New Jersey from July through October, and California from May through December. Mexico provides a substantial supply from January through March. Local crops of eggplants are at their peak in mid-to-late summer and early fall.

Japanese eggplants come from Mexico and California in February, March, and April, with baby versions coming from May through October.

SELECTION, HANDLING & STORAGE

All eggplants should be shiny and firm (but not rock hard) with taut skin that is free of blemishes (such as worm holes or dark brown spots) or bruises. Heavy scarring is an indication of poor handling, but small scarring may just signal wind damage. The color should reflect the specific variety. Even with the larger globe variety, avoid eggplants that are too large. (Lois Burpee's *Gardener's Companion and Cookbook*, Harper and Row, 1968, suggests eggplants that are less than 3 inches in diameter.) The stem, which should always be on the eggplant, should be bright green when it is appropriate to the variety.

Eggplant does not like severe cold; 46°F to 54°F is the ideal temperature range for storage. Because eggplant is ethylene sensitive, store it away from ethylene-producing items such as apples. Kept in a plastic bag (to retain moisture), eggplant will last up to five days.

NUTRITION

Eggplants are like potatoes in one respect. As long as you keep the fat off them, they're a low-calorie food. An 84g serving (barely 3 ounces) has only 25 calories as well as 2g dietary fiber, 5g carbohydrates, and 1g protein. A serving also contains 2% of the DV for vitamin C and iron.

Eggplant may have some beneficial effects on stomach cancer. It may help to lower blood cholesterol and counter the negative effects that fatty foods produce in the blood. Eggplant also acts as a diuretic.

YIELD

Depending on the type of preparation, one large eggplant (about 1½ pounds) will serve four people. It will yield about 4 cups of chopped or cubed eggplant, peeled and trimmed.

Tony's Tip

Because eggplant is susceptible to bruising, don't stack other food on top of it. And be wary of retailers who do.

PREPARATION

The first decision you need to make is to peel or not to peel. With most preparations, such as eggplant Parmesan, grilled eggplant, and caponata, we like to keep the skin on. If you do need to salt the eggplant, or you just want to salt it as a precaution against bitterness, cut the eggplant into slices, the thickness of which accommodates your recipe. Sprinkle both sides with salt and line the slices inside a large colander for at least 30 minutes. Then rinse, pat dry with paper towels, and prepare as directed.

As we alluded, oil is a problem because eggplant soaks it up like a sponge. For this reason, we like to broil or grill eggplant instead of frying it. Before doing either, slices (prepared as above) are sprayed with olive oil cooking spray, one of the great low-fat inventions of the twentieth century as far as we're concerned. You can also panfry slices after spraying, but only in a nonstick skillet.

If the recipe calls for cubed eggplant, follow all the directions for salting and cooking slices. Once the slices are cooked, cut them into cubes.

Eggplant lends itself to a multitude of ethnic preparations from Indian to Moroccan, with Mediterranean and Middle Eastern dishes in between. Garlic, onion, tomatoes, peppers, olive oil, and sesame oils are merely a few of the many seasonings and vegetables that go with eggplant.

Caponata

This is one of the signature dishes of Sicily. It is most often served as an appetizer, sometimes topped with albacore tuna. However, we think this fresher and more intensely flavored version is best used as a condiment with roasted meats (hot or cold), or as an hors d'oeuvre spread on rustic bread—plain, toasted, or grilled.

Makes 6 servings

2 medium eggplants (unpeeled), cut into $\frac{1}{2}$-inch slices
Kosher salt
1 medium onion
3 inner ribs celery
6 fresh plum tomatoes or 8 canned
1 tablespoon olive oil
1 anchovy fillet, rinsed and minced
3 tablespoons capers (one 3-ounce jar), rinsed

$\frac{1}{2}$ cup pitted green olives, whole if small, halved or quartered if large
$\frac{2}{3}$ cup quality red wine vinegar or balsamic vinegar
1 tablespoon sugar
Olive oil cooking spray
$\frac{1}{4}$ cup toasted pine nuts garnish (see page 28)

1. In a large bowl, sprinkle eggplant with 1 tablespoon of salt, then line the slices in a colander. Set aside for 30 minutes for moisture to be drawn out. Line a sheet pan with paper towels, line eggplant on sheet pan, cover with more paper towels, then press down with a cutting board to squeeze out any more moisture, and pat slices dry. Preheat oven to 500°F.

2. Meanwhile, chop onion, cut celery into very thin crescents, and trim and dice tomatoes. Put oil in a large skillet over medium heat. Add onion and celery and cook just until onion softens, 3 or 4 minutes. Add tomatoes and cook about 10 minutes. Add anchovy, capers, olives, vinegar, and sugar. Simmer 10 minutes.

3. Spray a baking sheet with olive oil cooking spray and layer eggplant slices on the sheet. Spray with olive oil cooking spray and bake 20 minutes (turning slices over once) or until soft and browned but not falling apart. Remove, cut into $\frac{1}{2}$-inch dice, and add to onion/celery/tomato mixture.

4. Simmer 15 minutes, stirring occasionally and adding a little water if necessary. Adjust seasonings—it should be pleasantly sweet and sour and quite thick. Cool and serve at room temperature topped with pine nuts. It's just as good or better the next day.

Sam's Cooking Tip

If you don't use anchovies often, try buying anchovy paste in a tube. Just squeeze out what you need, reseal, and refrigerate. One anchovy fillet equals $\frac{1}{2}$ teaspoon of paste. An opened can of fillets will last at least two months under refrigeration when tightly covered.

Eggplant Caviar

This dish is so-called because poor folks can mound it on pita bread (or crackers or bread) the way rich folks mound real caviar on toast points. Variations on this theme run the length of the Mediterranean.

Makes about 3 cups, 8 to 10 servings

2 small to medium eggplants, 1½ to 2 pounds

1 small onion

1 clove garlic

1 small tomato, seeded, juiced, and diced

1 tablespoon sesame oil

1 tablespoon fresh lemon juice

3 tablespoons flat Italian parsley, minced

Kosher salt and freshly ground black pepper to taste

1. Make a few slits in the eggplants and bake in a 450°F oven about 30 minutes or until they collapse and become soft. (This can also be done on a charcoal or gas grill.) Cool.

2. Mince onion and garlic by hand or puree in a food processor. Scrape out flesh from eggplants into a mixing bowl with onion and garlic, discarding skins. Mash with a fork or puree in a food processor along with remaining ingredients.

3. Use as is for a dip. For use as a sandwich spread (delicious on a baguette, sprinkled with creamy feta cheese), drain in a sieve for 15 minutes to remove excess moisture.

Sam's Cooking Tip

Unlike most versions of eggplant caviar or baba ganooj (as it's called in the Middle East) that use a fair amount of olive oil or tahini (sesame paste), this version uses sesame oil, which is so intensely flavored you can use a small amount.

Eggplant Parmesan

This interpretation of a most clichéd dish, inspired by Palermo restaurant in San Jose, California, is light and fresh, unlike the heavy and fat-laden versions in most mom-and-pop Italian restaurants. Serve it at room temperature as part of an antipasto table (the way it's served at Palermo). You can also serve it by itself as a first course for dinner, or as a light entrée for lunch.

Makes 6 to 8 servings as a first course

1 tablespoon extra-virgin olive oil

1 medium onion, minced

1 clove garlic, minced

One 28-ounce can tomatoes, seeded and chopped with their juice

1 1/2 tablespoons tomato paste

1/8 teaspoon hot pepper flakes

Kosher salt and freshly ground black pepper to taste

3 tablespoons fresh basil, chopped

2 medium eggplants, about 2 pounds

Olive oil cooking spray

1/4 to 1/3 cup grated Parmesan cheese

2 to 4 basil sprigs

1. Heat oil in a saucepan over moderate heat. Add onion and cook a few minutes. Add garlic and cook until onion is soft but not browned. Add tomatoes, tomato paste, hot pepper flakes, salt, and pepper. Stir, bring to a boil, and simmer 20 to 25 minutes. Remove from heat, add basil and let cool at room temperature. Check for seasonings.

2. Meanwhile, trim (but don't peel) eggplants. Cut into 1/4-inch-thick slices. Spray a nonstick skillet with olive oil cooking spray and cook slices over medium-high heat in batches until nicely browned, 3 to 4 minutes on each side. (Add more spray to skillet—off the heat—or eggplant slices, as needed.) As eggplant slices are done, put them on a serving platter, slightly overlapping each other. Season slices with salt and pepper.

3. Pour tomato sauce over eggplant, sprinkle with cheese, and garnish with basil sprigs.

Sam's Cooking Tip

As the Italians have long since found out with their sumptuous antipasto tables, many room-temperature foods taste as good or better than foods that are hot or cold. That's because the flavors aren't masked by extreme temperatures at either end of the spectrum.

Eggplant Pizza

Making regular pizza from scratch isn't hard, it's just time consuming because you have to knead the dough and wait for it to rise. But with rapid-rising yeast you can make the dough and let it rise while you prepare the toppings.

Makes 2 to 4 servings

$2^1/_4$ cups unbleached all-purpose flour

1 package quick-rising yeast such as Rapid-Rise from Fleischmann's

1 teaspoon sugar

1 tablespoon kosher salt

1 teaspoon extra-virgin olive oil

1 cup barely hot water at 125°F to 130°F

Olive oil cooking spray

1 medium eggplant, about 1 pound

$^1/_2$ teaspoon freshly ground pepper

2 medium tomatoes or 3 plum tomatoes, thinly sliced

$^1/_4$ cup chopped fresh basil

$^1/_2$ cup grated Parmesan cheese

1. Turn on broiler. Put 2 cups of flour, yeast, sugar, and half the salt in the bowl of a food processor. With the motor running, add olive oil and $^3/_4$ cup of the water. Add more water, 1 tablespoon at a time, until the dough forms a ball. Then continue processing another 30 seconds to knead. Spray a bowl with olive oil cooking spray and put dough in it. Spray again and cover with plastic wrap and a towel. Set bowl in a warm, draft-free place. (If mixing by hand, knead dough about 10 minutes before setting aside.)

2. While dough rises, trim (but don't peel) eggplant. Cut into $^1/_4$-inch-thick slices. Spray a baking sheet that will fit inside the broiler with olive oil cooking spray. Put eggplant slices on the tray and spray the tops. Put in the broiler and brown, about 5 minutes. Turn and brown other side. Remove from the oven and reduce heat to 500°F. Sprinkle eggplant with half the remaining salt and half the pepper.

3. After the dough has doubled in size (20 minutes or more), punch down and roll out the dough on a work surface dusted with remaining flour. Dough should be 14 inches in diameter for a thin-crust pizza, about 12 inches for a thicker pizza. Place on a pizza stone, pizza pan, or on the back of a baking sheet. Top with eggplant, then tomato slices. Sprinkle tomato with basil, remaining salt, and pepper. Spray edges with olive oil cooking spray.

4. Bake 12 to 15 minutes for thin-crust pizza, adding cheese halfway through. Add 3 to 5 minutes for thicker pizzas. Pizza should be crisp and nicely browned underneath.

Quick Ratatouille with Poultry Sausage

Ratatouille is normally stewed for 45 minutes or longer. This version is quick, light, and fresh and becomes a vegetarian entrée when the sausage is omitted.

Makes 4 servings

1 tablespoon olive oil

1 medium red bell pepper, diced

1 small medium-hot pepper

1 medium onion, diced

3 cloves garlic, chopped

1 medium zucchini or yellow squash, diced

1 small to medium eggplant, diced

1 medium tomato, chopped

8 to 10 ounces cooked poultry sausage, cut into ½-inch slices

2 tablespoons fresh basil, chopped

2 tablespoons parsley, chopped

Salt and freshly ground black pepper to taste

3 cups cooked rice (according to package directions)

1. Put oil in a wok over high heat. Add peppers, onion, garlic, zucchini, and eggplant. Cook 5 minutes, stirring frequently. Add tomato and cook about 3 minutes.

2. Add sausage, herbs, and salt and pepper to taste. Cook 3 minutes. Serve over rice.

Sam's Cooking Tip

Most supermarkets and butcher shops now carry poultry sausages of some kind. Check the labels, however, and don't assume it's low fat just because it's poultry. The sausage I used in this recipe totaled 9 grams of fat for three links, about 9 ounces.

fennel

Sometimes we forget that not everybody has been eating fennel as long as we have—essentially since we were both old enough to eat solid food. Periodically, when either of us picks out a bulb of fennel at the supermarket, someone watching us will say, "What is that?" We can't blame them. Fennel does look a little weird with its pale green stalks shooting up as if they were some kind of oxygen tubes and its darker green fronds looking like the last bit of hair on a balding Martian. If fennel doesn't look like a vegetable from another planet, at the very least it resembles a mutant celery stalk.

The Italian community knows fennel as *finocchio.* This celerylike vegetable has a wonderful crisp texture and a pleasant licorice flavor.

Until the past decade or so, fennel was available only in Italian markets and specialty stores. Now you can find it in mainstream supermarkets where it is frequently, and incorrectly, called sweet anise. (It is also called Florence fennel, but you'll rarely see that name.)

Think of fennel as celery on steroids and you'll be just fine. As a matter of fact, fennel is a good alternative to celery if you're trying to lose weight. Try it as a snack, by itself, or as a celery substitute in such dishes as tuna salad. Then you'll agree with us that fennel is out of this world.

WHERE GROWN

Fennel is grown primarily in Italy, France, Greece, and the United States. In the United States, fennel is grown almost exclusively in California, particularly Northern California where you can see it wild almost everywhere, even coming up through cracks of the sidewalks in cities like Berkeley.

VARIETIES

For all practical purposes there is only one variety of fennel, the Florence fennel. This squat bulb has a subtle licorice flavor that diminishes with cooking. Taller, more spindly wild or herb fennel has a much more pronounced fennel flavor and produces seeds used for seasoning.

SEASONS

Fennel season starts in September and continues into May. Peak periods with lowest prices occur in November and December.

SELECTION, HANDLING & STORAGE

Fennel can weigh from 8 ounces to over 2 pounds. Generally the smaller the fennel bulb, the more tender. Larger ones can be fibrous. Fennel normally has three distinct elements: the round white bottom, the stalks, and the leaves or fronds. The stalks and fronds should be a bright, light green. The bulb, which has virtually all of the usable meat, should be creamy white with no cracks and no withering. Any browning or yellowing means that the fennel is old.

Fennel that is not consumed within a few days will lose as much as 50 percent of its distinctive licorice flavor. Store fennel in a plastic bag in the high-humidity crisper section of the refrigerator for no more than a few days.

NUTRITION

A cup of sliced fennel (about 87g) has only 27 calories. So it's great for dieters and a welcome change from celery. A serving also has about 1g of protein, 6g of carbohydrates, a trace of fat, and a small amount (less than a gram) of fiber. Fennel is a good source of potassium, and depending on which nutrition guide you believe—there are no FDA numbers for fennel—a fair source of vitamins A and C.

Tony's Tip
Put fennel on your crudité platter instead of celery or serve it with Sicilian oil-cured olives in a relish dish.

PREPARATION

Most fennel dishes require that the pale green stalks and darker green fronds be removed, leaving a white bulb that looks a little like a softball with the top and bottom sliced off. Whether the outermost layer of the bulb is used depends on the size of the bulb (large ones can be tough) and its condition (bruises, splits, etc.).

Very often you'll want to slice the trimmed bulb in half lengthwise, then cut the halves into wedges for braising, or thin crescents for salads. Or the halves can be diced as you would an onion or celery stalk.

Don't discard the fronds and stalks when you trim a fennel bulb. The stalks can go into fish stock, especially one that's destined for bouillabaisse. Use the fronds as you would parsley or dill. The fronds are particularly good with fish baked in parchment. You can also wet the fronds and stalks and throw them on the grill in lieu of wood chips. In addition to fish, they'll provide excellent flavor to poultry, pork, and lamb.

To perk up the flavor of fennel dishes you can add a splash of Pernod or Ricard, French anise liqueurs.

Fennel and Parmesan Salad

This dish perfectly exemplifies the precepts of Italian cooking: quality ingredients used simply. Don't try it unless you're willing to splurge on real Parmesan cheese.

Makes 3 servings

1 fennel bulb
1 tablespoon extra-virgin olive oil
1 clove garlic, smashed but left whole
2 teaspoons fresh lemon juice

Salt and freshly ground black pepper
  to taste
Parmesan cheese (preferably Parmigiano-
  Reggiano)

1. Trim stalks and fronds from bulb and slice off the woody ¼ inch from the bottom. Wash and dry fronds and chop. Halve bulb vertically and remove layers as you would an onion. Slice each layer into strips about ¼ inch wide and put into a mixing bowl with all but 1 teaspoon of the fronds.

2. In a small bowl, mix olive oil with garlic and set aside for a few minutes. Whisk in lemon juice, salt, and pepper. Pour over fennel and remove garlic. Toss and put on a serving platter.

3. Using a vegetable peeler, shave about 3 tablespoons of Parmesan evenly over the fennel. Garnish with additional black pepper and remaining fronds.

Braised Fennel with Tomatoes

Makes 4 servings as a side vegetable

2 fennel bulbs, about 1½ pounds
1 tablespoon olive oil or butter
1 clove garlic, chopped
Kosher salt and freshly ground black
  pepper to taste

½ cup chopped tomatoes
1 cup Chicken Stock (page 9)
1 tablespoon Pernod or other anise-
  flavored liqueur, or 1 teaspoon ground
  fennel seeds

1. Trim fennel. Cut each bulb, lengthwise, into eight wedges. Chop fronds and set aside.

2. In a cast-iron or similar skillet, heat oil or butter over medium heat. Add fennel and gently cook a few minutes, stirring once. Add garlic, salt, and pepper and cook a few minutes more, stirring. Add remaining ingredients, cover, and simmer about 15 minutes or until fennel is just tender but not mushy.

3. With a slotted spoon, transfer fennel to a serving platter and keep warm. Turn heat under skillet to high and reduce juices until they become slightly syrupy. Pour over fennel. Sprinkle with 1 tablespoon of reserved fronds and serve.

Blood Orange and Fennel Salad

This crisp and refreshing salad would go particularly well with roasted chicken or veal.

Makes 4 servings

2 fennel bulbs

2 blood or navel oranges

1 small red onion

$1/2$ cup orange juice

$1/4$ cup sherry vinegar or 1 tablespoon dry
  sherry and 3 tablespoons good-quality
  red wine vinegar

2 tablespoons extra-virgin olive oil

Kosher salt and freshly ground black
  pepper to taste

6 basil leaves

1. Trim the fennel, removing stalks, fronds, and woody $1/4$ inch off the bottom. Cut fennel into vertical slices as thin as possible. Peel oranges, removing all the white pith. Segment or slice thinly. Alternate slices of fennel and orange on platter in concentric circles.

2. Cut onion into very thin rings. (You should be able to see the blade of the knife as it cuts through each slice.) Spread rings over fennel and oranges. Mix orange juice, vinegar, olive oil, salt, and pepper together and pour over fennel, oranges, and onion. Stack basil leaves on top of each other and roll tightly as if making a cigar. Cut across roll making thin shreds. (This is called a chiffonade.) Sprinkle over salad. Let salad sit at room temperature 1 hour before serving.

Fennel à la Grecque
with Portobello Mushrooms

Fennel seeds have always been a primary seasoning for à la Grecque presentations— essentially vegetables poached in aromatic broth. So it made sense to cook the fennel vegetable itself à la Grecque.

Makes 4 servings

2 fennel bulbs	1 dried chile pepper
2 tablespoons olive oil	1 teaspoon kosher salt
$1/2$ teaspoon fennel seeds	1 lemon, juice and all
$1/2$ teaspoon coriander seeds	$1/2$ cup dry white wine
$1/2$ teaspoon thyme	1 large portobello mushroom,
$1/2$ teaspoon marjoram	about 4 ounces
$1/4$ teaspoon whole black peppercorns	Kosher salt and freshly ground black
2 bay leaves	pepper to taste

1. Remove stalks from fennel. Put stalks, with fronds attached, half the olive oil, and the remaining ingredients along with 1 quart of water in a 4-quart pot. Bring to a boil, reduce heat, and simmer 5 minutes. Add whole fennel bulbs, cover, and simmer gently about 15 minutes or until bulb is easily pierced with the tip of a knife. Turn off heat and let fennel cool in broth about 30 minutes.

2. Strain broth into a saucepan and cook over medium-high heat until reduced to $1/3$ cup. Meanwhile, remove stem from mushroom, brush the cap with the remaining oil, season with salt and pepper, and grill under a broiler 3 to 5 minutes on each side, or until softened and lightly charred. Chop coarsely.

3. Remove very bottom $1/8$ inch of fennel, cut into $1/2$-inch slices, and arrange on a platter. Sprinkle mushroom over and pour reduced fennel liquid over. Serve at room temperature.

CHAPTER 15

green beans

We rarely give botanists the credit they are due. Once in a while someone like Norman Borlaug, considered the founder of the green revolution in farming, is recognized at the highest levels—in this case with the 1970 Nobel Peace Prize for making a major dent in world hunger with the development of high-yield crops.

But most of the time botanists just go about their business improving our lives in little bits and pieces with better tasting tomatoes or easier peeling oranges. That's what happened with the string bean. Years ago the string bean really did have a string. It ran down the seam of the pod and had to be removed before cooking because it was tough and indigestible. All those Norman Rockwell pictures of Grandma preparing string beans on the porch on a lazy summer afternoon made her look as if she was having a gay old time. But removing the string was tedious.

Then a botanist came along and developed a hybrid string bean that had no string. Grandma had more time to spend with her grandchildren or to play bingo. But did people whoop and holler? Did they thank botanists they met on the street or take them out to lunch? No.

As a matter of fact, they acted as if nothing had changed. They kept calling the string bean a string bean, even though there was no string. Today we still say string bean instead of snap bean or green bean, the more proper names.

And we take our snap beans for granted until, by some quirk of nature, a string pops up in one of our beans. But rather than saying, "Oh well, one out of every 100,000 isn't so bad," we say, "Darned botanists, can't they do anything right?"

WHERE GROWN

Florida is the leading producer of green beans. California and Georgia are second and third, respectively. New York, New Jersey, North Carolina, and Virginia produce significant amounts as well. Green beans are also imported from Mexico.

VARIETIES

Snap beans can be divided into green and yellow types. Leading varieties in the green category are Triumph, Opus, Podsquad, Strike, and Sprite. Yellow wax beans, which look like snap beans except for a pale yellow, almost translucent color, are mostly of the Golden Rod and Gold Rush varieties.

Occasionally you'll see purple snap beans, which are the same as green snap beans except for the color, which is lost in the cooking process.

Blue Lake snap beans are the classic shaped, rounded beans familiar to many. Romano beans (sometimes called Italian string beans) are flat, wide snap beans with a meaty texture that Italian Americans favor. Kentucky Wonder (also called KY) beans are somewhere in shape between the rounded snap bean and the flat Romano. Varieties include the Magnum and Green.

Haricots verts, also called baby French green beans, are tiny, tender green beans, no more than about 3 inches long. Because they are expensive, they are normally relegated to specialty markets and upscale grocers.

Chinese long beans (or yard-long beans) are not in the snap bean family, but rather related to black-eyed peas. They measure between 18 and 36 inches in length, and the color ranges between light and dark green. The texture is crunchier than snap beans.

SEASONS

Snap beans are a year-round commodity except for yellow wax beans, which run from October to June. The peak season for snap beans is April through June. *Haricots verts,* which come from Southern California, are available from February through November. Peak supplies for

Chinese long beans (coming from Mexico and California) occur in late summer and early fall.

SELECTION, HANDLING & STORAGE

Green beans, whether rounded snap or flattened pole, should be fresh looking with a bright color that will range from light to dark green. They should be plump and firm with a velvety feel and no signs of decay such as blemishes or wilting. Smaller beans will be more tender.

Beans should be kept cool, ideally between 40°F and 45°F. To retain their moisture, they should be kept in plastic bags. Properly stored, snap beans will last several days but should be consumed within two or three.

NUTRITION

A ³/₄-cup serving of green beans (about 83g, 3 ounces) contains 25 calories, 5g of carbohydrates, 3g of dietary fiber, and 1g of protein. A serving also has 4% of the DV for vitamin A and calcium, 2% for iron, and 10% for vitamin C. Green beans are also a decent source of potassium (200mg). Yellow wax greens have twice the vitamin C of green beans, half the vitamin A and iron, and less potassium. They also contain a fair amount of folic acid (6% of the DV).

YIELD

One pound of green beans will yield about 3¹/₂ cups of whole beans or 2³/₄ cups cut beans. A pound will serve four.

Tony's Tip

Don't think of green beans as just a side vegetable. Put them in salads or on relish or vegetable trays after they have been blanched and chilled.

PREPARATION

The standard way to trim green beans is to snap or cut off both ends before cooking. Increasingly, restaurants only remove the stem end. Grandma probably wouldn't have approved, but it does give the bean a more interesting look.

To speed up the process of preparing green beans, grab a bunch (six or so), line them up quickly, then slice off the ends with a chef's knife—they don't have to be exactly even. If you're removing both ends, turn the beans around and do the same to the other end. After a while, you'll be moving at lightning speed, able to do a few pounds of beans in a matter of minutes. (Your job will be made easier if you have beans of uniform size. Uniform beans will also cook more evenly.)

Larger beans, especially some of the pole varieties, may need to be halved before cooking. You can also cut the beans in slivers, called French style, with a gizmo that can be purchased in many cookware shops.

In general, we think beans should be firm but well cooked, absent of that raw taste.

As with most green vegetables, the choice is usually steaming, boiling, or microwaving. A pound of trimmed, boiled green beans will be ready in 5 to 7 minutes. If you choose the boiling method, you don't need a large pot of water, unless you're cooking large quantities (more than 1¹/₂ pounds). An inch or two of water in a skillet will do. Bring the water to a boil with a teaspoon of salt, then add the beans and cook. Green beans should be tender but quite firm.

Blanching is also a good way to get ahead for a dinner party. Boiled or steamed beans are plunged into ice water to stop the cooking and retain color. Once chilled and drained, the beans can be put into salads or on vegetable trays. When it's time to finish the green beans for a hot presentation, sauté them in butter or oil with any number of accompaniments. We especially like bread crumbs, garlic, sliced mushrooms, sliced almonds, minced shallots, and fresh herbs, especially dill and chives. Blanched green beans can also be frozen.

Steaming the beans will take about 8 to 10 minutes for a pound of regular green beans (large pole beans will take longer, smaller *haricots verts* or cut beans considerably less). Microwaving at full power is somewhere in between boiling and steaming, about 6 to 8 minutes. For stir-frying, cut the beans in 1- to 2-inch pieces and cook them from the raw state in a small amount of oil for a few minutes. Then add a little liquid, such as Chicken Stock, and cook 3 or 4 minutes more.

Sautéed Green Beans with Bread Crumbs

This was a frequent side vegetable in Vincenzo's, Sam's first restaurant in Philadelphia.

Makes 4 servings

1 pound green beans, trimmed
1 tablespoon butter
1 tablespoon extra-virgin olive oil
2 tablespoons minced shallots

Kosher salt and freshly ground black
  pepper to taste
3 tablespoons seasoned bread crumbs
1 tablespoon chopped fresh parsley

1. Boil or steam beans, then chill in ice water as described in Preparation (page 123). When the beans are completely cooled, about 10 minutes, drain them well.

2. To finish off the beans, heat butter and oil in a large skillet or wok over medium-high heat. Add shallots and cook about 30 seconds. Then add beans, salt, and pepper. Cook 2 minutes, stirring frequently. Add bread crumbs and parsley. Cook, stirring frequently, until the bread crumbs are crisp and nicely browned and the beans are hot, about 2 minutes.

Stewed Romano Green Beans with Tomatoes and Olives

These meaty green beans go well with roasted meats such as leg of lamb, roast pork, or roast chicken.

Makes 4 servings

1 pound Romano (Italian) green beans, each 7 to 8 inches long

1 tablespoon extra-virgin olive oil

1 medium onion, halved and thinly sliced

2 cloves garlic, minced

1 cup fresh chopped tomato, preferably plum

12 oil-cured black olives, pitted and cut in halves or thirds

1 to 2 tablespoons chopped fresh basil

Kosher salt and freshly ground black pepper to taste

1. Trim and halve beans crosswise. Set aside.

2. Put oil in a large skillet or wok over medium-low heat. Add onion and cook, stirring, just until soft, about 3 minutes. Add beans and garlic and cook a minute or two, stirring a few times. Add tomato and olives and cook, covered, until beans are barely tender, about 20 minutes. Check a few times and add 1/4 cup or so of water if needed.

3. Add 1 tablespoon of basil, and salt and pepper to taste and cook a few minutes more. Taste and add remaining basil, if desired, and any additional salt and pepper.

Warm Bean and Potato Salad

Beans and potatoes go well together, especially if you can get local varieties of both in early summer.

Makes 6 servings

1 small sweet red onion
3/4 pound small red potatoes (unpeeled),
  cut into 1/4-inch slices
1 pound green beans, each about
  4 to 5 inches long, trimmed
1/2 cup chopped red bell pepper

1 tablespoon chopped fresh basil
1 tablespoon chopped fresh parsley
2 tablespoons extra-virgin olive oil
1 tablespoon balsamic vinegar
Kosher salt and freshly ground black
  pepper to taste

1. Halve the onion and cut it into very thin crescents. Put it into a bowl of ice water for 20 minutes. Drain.

2. Put potatoes in the bottom of a steamer basket inside a large saucepan with 1/2 inch of water. Cover pan and turn heat to medium high for 5 minutes. Reduce heat to medium low, put beans on top of the potatoes. Steam 15 more minutes or until beans and potatoes are tender.

3. Combine bell pepper, basil, and parsley in a mixing bowl with drained onion. Mix oil, vinegar, salt, and pepper in a cup.

4. When potatoes and beans are done, add them to the onion mixture and toss. Pour oil mixture over and toss again. Let sit 10 minutes and toss again.

Green Beans with Lemon and Anchovy

This is a green bean dish even anchovy haters will like.

Makes 4 servings

1 pound green beans, trimmed
2 tablespoons extra-virgin olive oil
1 teaspoon minced anchovy fillet
1 teaspoon grated lemon rind
Kosher salt and freshly ground black pepper to taste

1. Blanch beans and chill as described in Preparation (page 123).

2. Put oil in a nonstick skillet over very low heat. Stir in anchovy until completely incorporated, 1 to 2 minutes. Add beans and increase heat to medium. Cook a minute, tossing a few times. Add lemon rind, salt and pepper. Toss and continue cooking until beans are heated through, 3 to 4 minutes.

greens, salad

We've divided greens into three chapters, since it's such a diverse subject. If you've been reading alphabetically, you've already seen the chapter on chicory, the bitter salad greens that can also be used in cooking. After this chapter comes cooking greens, hardy greens such as kale and broccoli raab. This chapter is devoted to more traditional salad greens.

Craig Claiborne, the former food editor of *The New York Times,* once wrote that America is doubtless the most dedicated salad-eating nation in the world. We agree, especially after having visited many other countries where salads as we know them are not nearly as common. We can recall coming back from vacations in France when we ate fabulous food, but somehow at the end of it all, we were dying for a good, crispy salad.

Most of us grew up eating salads that were composed primarily of iceberg lettuce. Even today, one is hard-pressed to find a salad bar, diner, or other mainstream American restaurant that doesn't have iceberg in some form. And who could forget all those banquets where the salad was hearts of lettuce: a huge wedge of iceberg, usually slathered with far too much Russian dressing?

But even though iceberg is still popular, Americans have a great variety of salad greens from which to choose these days: butter, limestone, Bibb, Boston, romaine, watercress, arugula, oak leaf, mache, those attractive (and pricey) mesclun mixes, and a host of local greens when in season. These greens, along with supermarket aisles of dressings and other salad accoutrements, have helped Americans to create, as Claiborne put it, the greatest number and some of the most imaginative salads on earth.

But America hasn't always been a great salad-making country. In an interview with Sam a few years ago, Julia Child said that before Caesar salad became the rage during Prohibition, Americans didn't eat salad, particularly in the East. "Salads were considered foreign and sissy food," she said.

Child said that the addition of eggs and garlic (not to mention croutons, Parmesan, and anchovies) probably helped to elevate this salad beyond sissy status. Since Caesar Cardini created the Caesar salad, Americans have matched his inventiveness with salads almost daily. We just wish they'd ease up on the Russian dressing.

WHERE GROWN

Salinas, Kansas, may be in the middle of America's bread basket, but Salinas, California, is at the epicenter of America's salad bowl. The warm days and cool nights of this region along the central coast of California are ideal for lettuce. After California, Arizona is the second largest producer of lettuce in the country. Florida is third.

Some of the more obscure specialty lettuces are only available locally because there isn't a big enough market for them. Some are imported. Mache, for example, is brought in from Holland.

VARIETIES

There are four main types of lettuce and many varieties within each type.

Crisphead lettuce or roundhead lettuce is best characterized by iceberg lettuce. Iceberg got its name from the way it was stacked with lots of ice to keep it fresh during transport. This tightly packed, pale green head is usually wrapped in cellophane for sale. Crisp and juicy, it is still the most popular lettuce despite being maligned by food critics. (Claiborne says he never puts iceberg in his salads.)

Butterhead lettuce (sometimes referred to as cabbage lettuce because of its shape) is sold under that name but also as Boston and Bibb lettuce. The leaves are thin and soft, almost buttery, with less prominent veins than iceberg. Varieties include Big Boston, White Boston, May King, and Limestone. Limestone is a type of Bibb that gets its name and distinctive lime-stone flavor from the limestone fields of Kentucky where it originated.

Loose-leaf or bunching lettuce does not form a head like crisphead or butterhead lettuces. Instead it grows in loose bunches on a stalk. The leaves can be smooth or curly and are softer than crisphead but not as soft as butter-head leaves. Red leaf and green leaf lettuces, which both have curly leaves, are the two most common types of loose-leaf lettuce. Major varieties include Black-seeded Simpson, Prize Head, Grand Rapids, and Salad Bowl.

Oak leaf lettuces are a type of loose-leafed lettuce with oak-shaped leaves that are thin and tender. Colors can range from red to green to bronze. When fully mature, the reddish version is called Red Oak Leaf. As baby lettuce it's called Royal Red Oak Leaf.

Lollo Rossa is a loose-leaf lettuce characterized by a red or reddish bronze fringe at the end of its leaves.

Romaine or cos lettuce has a loaf-shaped appearance with long, upright outer leaves that are dark green and have a white central spine. As you reach the center, the leaves become smaller and more yellow. The outer leaves can be quite sturdy while the inner leaves (which were the only ones originally used in Caesar salad) are more tender.

Red romaine and ruby red romaine are more obscure variations of standard romaine with colors that range from red to reddish bronze.

Watercress is the best known of the cress family of water- and land-grown plants. While it isn't thought of as fitting into the formal lettuce family, it is an important salad component as well as a commonly used ingredient in sandwiches. It adds a refreshing peppery bite to dishes. The round, nickel-sized leaves are attached to stems that can be as long as 10 inches, making watercress a versatile garnish as well.

Other salad greens that may be available at specialty retailers or at selected supermarkets include:

Arugula, also called rocket or roquette, has notched leaves that look somewhat like dandelion. It may be nutty and peppery in cooler weather and become more pungent and "hotter" in warm weather.

Mache is also known as lamb's lettuce, field, and corn salad. More of a green like mustard greens than a true lettuce green, mache has small, spoon- or tongue-shaped leaves that are delicate with a nutty, peppery taste.

Mustard greens are thought of more as cooking greens, but when small and young they can be used in salads (and are often part of a mesclun mix). Baby red mustard leaves add a nice bite, as does mizuna, which looks like a kind of dandelion.

A growing segment of the salad industry is salad mixes, already trimmed and washed. The most common example is what is generally called gourmet salad mix or mesclun, which is derived from the French Niçoise dialect word for *mélange.* These mixes can have as many as fifteen different lettuces from red oak leaf to radicchio. Mesclun is expensive if you look at the price per pound. But there is no waste and salad greens don't weigh very much. Other salad mixes include Caesar salad with its own croutons and dressing. We don't recommend that one unless you're in a real hurry.

(Note: Dandelion greens and spinach are dealt with in other chapters, pages 139 and 245, respectively.)

SEASONS

The major types of lettuce are available year-round from California and fall through spring from Arizona. Cooler states such as New York and New Jersey have supplies as the weather warms.

SELECTION, HANDLING & STORAGE

In general, lettuce should be crisp and bright with good color and no yellowing, bruises, blemishes, withering, or rust spots. Iceberg should have round and well-formed heads that are not too hard (they should give somewhat under pressure) or pale. The stem or butt end should be creamy in color and smell sweet. Smell is especially important on lettuce if the butt has been trimmed to deflect the appearance of age.

For leaf lettuce, make sure the leaves are firm with good color and no slime. Romaine should have dark outer leaves that are tightly closed. Though soft in texture, the leaves on butterhead lettuce should be firm.

Watercress should be displayed in water or well iced and have no signs of yellowing.

Lettuce likes moisture and cool temperatures, as low as 32°F. It will hold up longer if washed before storing (see Preparation, this page). Wrapped in paper towels and stored in plastic bags (preferably perforated), lettuce will last several days in the crisper section of the refrigerator. Since lettuce is ethylene-sensitive, don't store it near ethylene-producing food such as apples or pears, or it will develop rust spots.

NUTRITION

The four major lettuce types are relatively close in nutritional content. For example, a serving of leaf (85g, 3 ounces or 1½ cups shredded) and iceberg (89g, 3.2 ounces or ⅙ of a medium head) lettuces each contains 15 calories, 1g of protein and 6% of the DV for vitamin C.

Iceberg has 1g of dietary fiber, 3g of carbohydrates, 2% of the DV for both calcium and iron, and 4% for vitamin A.

Leaf lettuce contains 4g of carbohydrates, 2g of dietary fiber, 40% of the DV for vitamin A, 4% for calcium, no iron, and about twice the potassium of iceberg (230mg versus 120mg). Leaf lettuce is also a good source of folic acid. Romaine lettuce is somewhere in between leaf and iceberg.

Lettuce, particularly dark green lettuce, has been shown to be helpful in fighting cancer, especially stomach and lung cancers.

YIELD

A pound of salad greens will yield about 6 cups chopped.

Tony's Tip

> When preparing salads, make sure the salad greens (and everything else, for that matter) are absolutely dry. Otherwise the dressing won't cling to the leaves.

PREPARATION

The best investment you can make for preparing greens is a salad spinner. It removes moisture better than any other method we know. For lettuce other than iceberg, put the leaves in lots of cool water in the sink. (Particularly sandy lettuce such as arugula may need two baths.) Then break up or cut the leaves and fill the salad spinner. But don't overfill or it won't work as well as it should. (For large heads, you'll need to do more than one batch.)

Water whips out through the side slats of the spinner and falls to the bottom. Empty it and repeat the spinning a few times to remove all the moisture. Store lettuce in the spinner or in plastic bags.

For iceberg lettuce, remove the core by smashing it on the counter to loosen first, then pulling it out. Rinse the cavity with cool running water, then break apart and spin dry in the salad spinner. Try this method with other lettuce such as romaine by first cutting a V shape from the stem end. Then run cool water through the bottom area while firmly holding the head in the middle.

Some people think it's a no-no to cut lettuce with a knife because the lettuce will rust where it is cut. But that rule only applies to the older, pure carbon-steel knives, the kind that rust if not wiped right after washing. Stainless steel knives will not rust lettuce. However, they should be sharp or they may bruise the lettuce.

Enlightened Caesar Salad

We try to minimize the use of products like egg substitute but in this dish it works perfectly well, helping to keep fat and calories down.

Makes 4 to 6 servings

Olive oil cooking spray

2 cups French bread, cut into 3/4-inch cubes

2 cloves garlic

3 anchovy fillets

2 tablespoons egg substitute

2 tablespoons extra-virgin olive oil

2 tablespoons fresh lemon juice

1/2 tablespoon Worcestershire sauce

A few drops of Tabasco

1 teaspoon Dijon mustard

Kosher salt and freshly ground black pepper to taste

1/3 cup grated Parmesan cheese

1 large head romaine lettuce, cleaned and torn into bite-size pieces

1. Spray a baking sheet with olive oil cooking spray. Spread French bread cubes evenly on the sheet. Spray tops of the croutons and put in a preheated 350°F oven. Cook 10 minutes, tossing once. Then turn off the oven and leave the croutons inside for 15 minutes. Allow to cool.

2. With the motor of a food processor running, put garlic down the feed tube. Scrape down the sides and add anchovy fillets. Scrape down again and add remaining ingredients except cheese and lettuce. Put into a small bowl and fold in cheese.

3. Put lettuce in a wide salad bowl with croutons. Add dressing and toss. Taste and adjust seasonings. Toss again.

Arugula Pasta Salad with Wild Mushrooms

This is a warm salad in which the arugula barely gets wilted from the heat of the pasta. It includes low-fat goat cheese that may not be available in your area. But since the amount is so small, regular goat cheese won't add that much more fat.

Makes 4 servings

1 ounce dried porcini mushrooms

Kosher salt

1 pound orecchiette (ear-shaped) pasta or other short pasta

2 bunches arugula

1½ tablespoons extra-virgin olive oil

2 tablespoons dry white wine

1 tablespoon balsamic vinegar

2 tablespoons minced shallots

Freshly ground black pepper to taste

2 ounces prosciutto

2 ounces low-fat goat cheese, crumbled

1. Put mushrooms in a small bowl with 1 cup hot water for 30 minutes. Drain through a cheesecloth, reserving liquid. Chop coarsely or cut into thin strips.

2. Meanwhile, bring 4 quarts of water and 1 teaspoon salt to boil on the stove for pasta. Cook orecchiette until just tender, about 10 minutes. Drain.

3. While pasta cooks, trim roots from arugula, wash in lots of cool water, and drain. Cut crosswise into ½-inch-wide strips. Put arugula in a large mixing bowl. In a small bowl, combine oil, wine, vinegar, shallots, salt, pepper, and ¼ cup of reserved mushroom liquid (save the leftover liquid for soups or stocks).

4. Stack slices of prosciutto and cut crosswise into thin strips. Add cooked pasta to arugula along with prosciutto, cheese, and reserved porcini. Add dressing and toss.

Sam's Cooking Tip

Normally prosciutto is sliced very thin at the deli or butcher shop. For this recipe and others like it, ask for thicker slices, about six per four ounces. This makes the prosciutto easier to cut into strips.

Taco Salad

Normally taco salads are dreadful concoctions of "plastic" cheese, cold hamburger meat, and deep-fried tortilla shells. This one, however, is light and fresh. It's probably the only time we use iceberg lettuce.

Makes 4 servings

1 pound tomatoes, coarsely chopped
Kosher salt
3 cups shredded iceberg lettuce
1 cup shredded red cabbage
1 medium to large sweet onion such as
  Vidalia, thinly sliced (about 1½ cups)
2 jalapeño peppers
⅓ cup cilantro, chopped
2 tablespoons extra-virgin olive oil
1 tablespoon each cider vinegar and lime
  juice

2 teaspoons toasted cumin, ground
  (page 300)
Freshly ground black pepper
2 ounces shredded reduced-fat Cheddar
  cheese
About 40 low-fat baked tortilla chips
  such as Guiltless Gourmet (1g fat/
  20 chips), lightly crushed

1. Toss tomatoes with 1 teaspoon of salt in a small bowl and set aside for 30 minutes.

2. Meanwhile, shred lettuce and cabbage, slice onion, and seed and chop jalapeño peppers. Put all in a mixing bowl. Add ¼ cup of the cilantro.

3. Drain tomatoes, saving juice, and add tomatoes to lettuce mixture. Combine 2 tablespoons of the tomato juice with the olive oil, vinegar, lime juice, cumin, and salt and pepper to taste. Add about ¾ of the dressing to the salad and toss well. Taste and add more dressing if desired.

4. Put salad on 4 plates. Top with cheese, then tortilla chips. Sprinkle on remaining cilantro.

Salad with Goat Cheese Dressing and Garlic Croutons

This simple salad is made even easier with a ready mix of salad greens or mesclun that many markets now carry.

Makes 4 servings

12 cherry tomatoes
Kosher salt
8 slices French bread
Olive oil cooking spray
2 cloves garlic, peeled and smashed
  but not chopped
1½ tablespoons extra-virgin olive oil

1½ tablespoons balsamic vinegar
1 teaspoon chopped fresh thyme
Freshly ground black pepper to taste
2 ounces low-fat goat cheese
5 cups mixed salad greens such as
  butterhead, Bibb, red leaf lettuce, or a
  prepared salad mix, cleaned and dried

1. Halve the cherry tomatoes. Toss with a teaspoon of salt and set aside for 30 minutes at room temperature. Drain, saving tomato liquid.

2. Meanwhile, preheat oven to 400°F and spray a cookie sheet and both sides of the bread slices with olive oil cooking spray. Rub both sides of slices with garlic cloves and bake until crisp and light brown, about 15 minutes.

3. Mix oil, vinegar, and thyme with 1 tablespoon of the reserved tomato liquid and salt and pepper to taste. Add half the cheese and mix thoroughly.

4. Toss greens and tomatoes with dressing. Put on 4 salad plates and crumble an equal amount of the remaining goat cheese over each. Garnish each plate with 2 slices of garlic croutons.

Sam's Cooking Tip

Because this dressing is rather thick when the cheese is added, it is best mixed by hand. If that sounds a little yucky, be advised that most restaurants mix their salads this way. Just make sure your hands are clean first.

greens, cooked

With some notable ethnic exceptions such as Asians, non-Italians are real Johnny-come-latelies when it comes to appreciating hearty greens like broccoli raab and dandelion. But we've enjoyed these greens since we were kids.

Tony can remember driving with his family through the Santa Clara Valley of California in the winter and spring when all of a sudden his father, Giovanni, would stop the car and order his sons to pick broccoli raab growing wild on the side of the road or on nearby hillsides. "We felt silly," Tony says, "but Dad acted as if he struck gold." After they couldn't fit any more broccoli raab into the trunk, they returned home where Tony's mother cleaned and prepared this slightly bitter green in many ways, including as an accompaniment to pasta.

Check out a lot of the trendy restaurants from New York to San Francisco today. Many of them have broccoli raab on the menu, often with some sort of pasta. Combining it with sausage and orecchiette (ear-shaped pasta) seems to be a favorite.

As soon as the snow cleared in Buffalo, New York—which sometimes wasn't until just before Easter—Sam's mother, Anna Gugino, was on her hands and knees, digging up dandelion on the front and back lawns. She used an old rusty knife with a broken wooden handle. It wasn't exactly a weed cutter but looked more like a relic from an exhibit at the historical society featuring primitive tools from the Bronze Age. (Legendary green grocer Joe Carcione says old women [we assume Italian] could be seen gathering dandelion along the fairways of golf courses.)

The dandelion was trimmed on newspapers spread out on the kitchen table and washed in several changes of water. Then it was boiled and dressed with oil and garlic, or put in omelets, a very popular meat substitute during Lent. And like Southerners with their "pot lickker," Anna Gugino encouraged her kids to drink the liquid in which the dandelion was cooked.

WHERE GROWN

For dandelions, just look out your window in the spring. Mainstream commercial varieties come from Texas and Florida. Long Island, Virginia, and New Jersey are the main producers of kale. Southern states such as Florida, South Carolina, Alabama, Georgia, and Virginia are the leading producers of collards and mustard greens. Mustard greens are also grown in California, Michigan, Ohio, Indiana, New Jersey, and Arizona.

VARIETIES

Broccoli Raab (also called broccoli rabe, broccoli di rape, and rapini): Sold in tight bunches looking like a cousin of more traditional broccoli but with smaller stalks and florets. Pleasantly bitter, peppery flavor.

Chard or Swiss Chard: Has a tart quality that sets it apart from other greens. Comes in red and green varieties. The green has white veins running through the leaves and a white or creamy white stem. Red chard has a red stalk that is often thinner than the stalk on green chard and red veins that may run through green or red leaves. Red chard is sometimes called rhubarb chard, which is one of the several varieties of chard along with Burpee's Rhubarb Chard, Lucullus, Giant Lucullus, Fordhook Giant, and Dark Green White Ribbed.

Collard Greens: White-veined, wide green leaves whose leathery texture (and often size) can be reminiscent of elephant ears. Large bunches require long cooking, so look for ones with leaves as small as possible and stems that are not too thick. More of a cabbagelike flavor than other greens. Main varieties include Georgia, Vates, Morris Heading, and Louisiana Sweet.

Dandelion Greens: The local wild and field-grown versions of this pleasantly biting green have smaller, more severely saw-toothed leaves than the mass-produced, nationally distributed varieties. Larger dandelion greens can be tough and quite bitter, needing more cooking (up to 10 minutes) than the young varieties, which should be cooked quickly (as little as 3 minutes). Commercial varieties include Thick Leaf, Improved Thick Leaf, and Arlington Thick Leaf.

Kale: This sturdy green loves the cold and is often displayed outdoors because of its tolerance to cold weather. There are two commercial types. Scotch kale has curly edged leaves with color that can range from spruce green to bluish or grayish green, depending on the variety. Smooth-leafed kale has leaves with very little curl. Small and tender kale can be used in salad mixes.

Mustard Greens: The most common variety is light, almost lime green with softer and more delicately ruffled leaves than kale. Some varieties have deep red or maroon leaves with green highlights. As the name implies, it has a tangy, mustardlike flavor. Smaller leaf varieties such as baby red mustard greens are often found in salad mixes now common in supermarkets and specialty stores.

Turnip Greens: While most turnip greens are attached to their bulbs as an afterthought, some varieties of turnips are grown especially for their thin, dark greens. As with mustard greens, their sharp flavor (as well as their coarse texture) mellows with cooking. Turnip greens can be cooked like mustard greens or collards or added in strips to stir-fries and soups.

SEASONS

Thanks to companies like D'Arrigo Brothers, broccoli raab, which was previously available from August through March, has become a year-round vegetable. Chard is available April through November, with most supplies coming June through October. Collards are available all year with peaks December through April and shorter supplies from June through August.

Dandelion greens are available virtually year-round (much of the crop is grown in hothouses), though supplies dwindle from December through February. The best are local wild and field-grown varieties that peak in April and May. Kale is available year-round, but supplies are best from December through February. Mustard greens are most abundant from December though April and less available in July and August. Turnip greens are generally available October through March.

SELECTION, HANDLING & STORAGE

With all greens, choose those that have good, green color with leaves that show no or little yellowing, withering, or blemishes and with stems that look freshly cut and are not thick, dried out, browned, or split. Often greens are bunched so that the inner parts of the bunch are subject to decay and slime.

For broccoli raab, look for bunches with few flowers on top and even, deep green color. Turnip greens should have very firm leaves that have been kept moist. Kale leaves should be frilly and bright (though a gray-green cast is fine). Collards are often sold too large and tough. Seek out bunches with smaller leaves and thinner stems. Leaves should be free of insect holes.

Locally grown dandelion is light and delicate with thin stems and pronounced saw-toothed leaves. It is often sold with roots attached. Other varieties can be tough so be careful to select more tender bunches. Mustard greens should be bright, though color may range from lighter to darker green. Leaves are delicate and frilly. Be wary of evidence of slime. Swiss chard should be firm with good color. Avoid bunches with leaves and stalks that are too large and with leaves that are decaying.

Once home, discard any bruised or yellow leaves and remove any bands or ties that hold bunches together. Wash greens in plenty of cool water, drain, and store loosely in plastic bags (preferably perforated) and gently wrapped in paper towels. Keep moist (but not wet or they will rot) and cool (as low as 32°F) in the lower part of the refrigerator in the high-humidity bin. Local dandelions, beet, and turnip greens should be used within two days. Other greens will last up to four days.

NUTRITION

Most greens are very high in vitamin A with dandelion greens leading the pack at a whopping 14,000 IU for 3½ raw ounces, almost three times the DV for vitamin A. Kale is next, with about twice the DV for vitamin A, followed closely by mustard greens, collards, chard, and turnip greens.

Greens have fair amounts of vitamin C. Kale is way ahead of the pack with 120mg, twice the DV. Turnip and mustard greens have 100% of the DV, dandelion and chard about 50%, and collards about 30%. In terms of fiber, kale leads again with 6.6g dietary fiber, followed by turnip greens and dandelion. Dandelion and turnip greens each have just under 20% of the DV for calcium, and kale 13%. In iron, dandelion leads with 3.1mg, about 17% of the DV. Kale is the best source of potassium followed by dandelion. Broccoli raab is a good source of vitamins A, C, and potassium. Mustard greens are high in folic acid.

All this for between 20 calories (turnip greens) and 53 calories (kale) in a 3½-ounce serving. As if this weren't enough, dark, leafy greens, particularly those in the cruciferous or cabbage family (kale, collards, turnip greens, broccoli raab), have been shown to have enormous cancer-fighting potential. Kale (and to a lesser extent collards) is particularly high in lutein, an antioxidant that can help lower blood cholesterol and blood pressure, reduce the inflammation of arthritis, increase fertility, and minimize the formation of cataracts.

YIELD

Yield will vary depending on the green. However, it's best to remember that all will shrink when cooked, sometimes to ⅛ of their original volume. As a rule of thumb, figure about ½ pound of raw, untrimmed greens per person if the greens are to be used as a side vegetable. That amount can be reduced if the greens are a component in a soup, stew, or pasta.

Tony's Tip

Gather your own dandelion greens just like Sam's mom. Just make sure the area hasn't been sprayed with pesticides and the dandelions haven't yet flowered.

PREPARATION

Clean greens in lots of cool water. Local dandelions with roots attached are particularly gritty and will need to be washed in two changes of water. Greens can be drained in a colander, spun dry in a salad spinner, or cooked with their clinging water as you would spinach. Often we like to roll stacked, uncleaned leaves and cut them crosswise before cleaning.

These strips can then be cooked quite easily by boiling, steaming, or braising. We usually cook the stems unless they are very thick. Just cut them in small pieces. Steaming and quick boiling help to minimize nutrient loss. But nutrients can also be retained by saving the cooking liquid for soups, broths, or as part of the dish, soaked up by crusty bread.

All of theses greens stand up to assertive seasonings. Broccoli raab goes well in Italian preparations such as pastas, and in polenta, bean, and potato dishes. Flavorings include garlic, olive oil, olives, balsamic vinegar, anchovies, and pork meats such as sausage and pancetta.

Collards are among the sturdiest of greens. Their common companions are smoked or salted pork. To lower fat and sodium, use smoked pork to flavor cooking broth (smoked turkey can also be used) and then discard or use the meat minimally. Or braise the collards in homemade, defatted Chicken Stock with garlic and/or chiles.

Kale is also very hearty but more versatile than collards. Stir-fry or braise in a wok with garlic and oil or a smidgen of cured pork. It's excellent as a steamed green vegetable and great with pasta on its own or as a substitute for broccoli raab. When small and tender, it can be used in salads as an accent to other greens. Kale also makes a superb garnish or liner for salad bowls or trays because it won't wilt like other greens. (Good salad bars have known this for some time.)

The strong mustard bite in mustard greens will dissipate somewhat with longer cooking. So too will the sharp flavor (as well as the coarse texture) of turnip greens. Mustard greens go nicely with lentils in soups, stews, or salads.

Chard can be cooked quickly when young or gently braised if older and larger. Stems, which can be fibrous and trimmed like celery, are often cooked separately from leaves. Stems and leaves are often recombined (very popular with the French) in gratins. Leaves can be stuffed like cabbage leaves and stems added to soups or stews.

Though dandelion has a strong flavor, it has a rather delicate texture and tends to be over cooked. Boiling 5 minutes or less is usually enough. It goes marvelously with garlic, olive oil, and freshly ground black pepper. Also, it's very good tossed with bacon fat (pancetta if you prefer) and a little red wine vinegar.

Collards with Smoked Pork

This is normally a high-fat dish made even worse by cooking the greens to death. Here, however, the stock is flavored judiciously with pork and the broth consumed along with the greens.

Makes 4 servings

2 smoked ham hocks, about 1¹/₄ to 1¹/₂ pounds

1 quart defatted Chicken Stock (page 9)

1 quart water

2 small bunches collard greens, about 1¹/₂ pounds total

3 cloves garlic, chopped

1 medium onion, chopped

2 teaspoons corn or peanut oil

¹/₂ teaspoon kosher salt

¹/₄ teaspoon freshly ground black pepper

Hot pepper flakes or sauce to taste

1. Put hocks, stock, and water in a large saucepan or pot, bring to a boil, cover and gently simmer 1 hour. Remove hocks and set aside. Chill or freeze liquid until any fat rises to the top and can be skimmed off.

2. Trim about ¹/₂ inch from the bottoms of the collards. Cut crosswise into strips, about ³/₈ inch wide at the bottom of the leaf and up to 1 inch wide toward the top. Wash thoroughly in a large tub of cool water. Drain.

3. In a large saucepan or small stockpot, cook garlic and onion in oil over medium-high heat until soft, 3 to 5 minutes. Add collards and stock and bring to a boil. Lower heat and simmer, uncovered, about 25 minutes or until thickest stem pieces are tender. Season with salt and pepper and hot pepper to taste.

4. Meanwhile, remove all the fat and skin from the hocks and dice about ¹/₂ cup of the lean meat. Remove collards with a skimmer to 4 shallow bowls or soup plates. Add ¹/₂ cup of broth to each plate and sprinkle on diced pork. Make sure good country bread is on hand for dunking.

Sam's Cooking Tip

This is not a Mediterranean dish as are most of the recipes in the book. But you can make it somewhat Mediterranean by using the ends of a prosciutto instead of ham hocks. Delis will sometimes sell these ends at a lower price than the center portion of the prosciutto.

Potato and Kale Soup

This is a lower fat version of a well-known Portuguese dish.

Makes 4 to 6 servings

4 ounces turkey kielbasa or similar spicy
 poultry sausage
1 tablespoon extra-virgin olive oil
1 small onion, chopped
1 clove garlic, minced
1 pound small red potatoes, quartered

6 cups defatted Chicken Stock (page 9)
1/2 bunch kale, about 1/2 pound
Kosher salt and freshly ground black
 pepper to taste
Hot pepper sauce to taste

1. Slice sausage thinly, then halve each slice. Put oil in a Dutch oven or similar pot over medium heat. Add sausage. When the meat is nicely browned and slightly crisped, remove with slotted spoon to dish lined with paper towels.

2. Add the onion and garlic to the pot. Cook until onion wilts, about 5 minutes. Add potatoes and cook a few minutes, stirring. Add stock and bring to a boil. Lower heat and simmer, covered, 20 minutes or until potatoes are soft. Mash coarsely in the pot with a potato masher or large fork.

3. Meanwhile, roll kale and cut crosswise into thin strips. Put in a colander and rinse thoroughly. Add to pot and stir well. Add salt and pepper. Cook 15 minutes or more, depending on how tough the kale is.

4. When kale is just tender, add sausage and hot pepper sauce to taste and cook 5 minutes more. Taste and adjust seasonings.

Dandelions with Garlic and Olive Oil

The best dandelion greens are local varieties. They don't last long so don't dally before you enjoy them.

Makes 3 to 4 servings

1 pound dandelion greens
2 tablespoons extra-virgin olive oil
2 large cloves garlic, chopped
Kosher salt and freshly ground black pepper to taste

1. Trim off the roots and the very bottoms of any tough stems. Remove any leaves that are bruised or yellowed. Plunge leaves into a sink of cool water. Swish around and drain in a colander. Repeat process.

2. Bring a 4-quart pot of water and a tablespoon of salt to a boil. Add the dandelions and cook 5 minutes. Remove with a skimmer (if you want to save the cooking liquid) or drain in a colander. Gently squeeze out any excess moisture.

3. In the same pot, heat oil and add garlic over medium heat. When the garlic is just turning golden, add the dandelion. Toss well, coating with oil and garlic. Add salt and pepper and toss again.

Mustard Greens with Lentils

A welcome addition to any buffet table as well as a terrific vegetarian entrée.

Makes 8 servings

1 bunch mustard greens, about 1 pound
Kosher salt
1 bay leaf
3 cloves garlic, peeled and lightly
  crushed
2 cups lentils

3 tablespoons extra-virgin olive oil
2 tablespoons balsamic vinegar
2 tablespoons minced shallots
$^1/_4$ teaspoon freshly ground black pepper
3 ounces crumbled low-fat goat cheese

1. Cut off the bottom $^1/_2$ inch of the mustard greens. Then, with the bunch on its side, cut crosswise into strips, no more than $^1/_2$ inch wide at the bottom of the leaf and about 1 inch wide at the leafy top. Wash in a tub of cool water. Drain.

2. In a 4-quart pot, bring 2 quarts of water and 2 teaspoons of salt to a boil. Add mustard greens, cover and allow to return to a boil as quickly as possible. Cook 7 minutes total, stirring once or twice to cook evenly. With a skimmer, remove greens to a colander to drain, saving the cooking water. Run cool water over greens to retain color.

3. Add bay leaf, garlic, 1 teaspoon salt, and lentils to mustard green broth. Bring to a boil and lower heat to simmer. Cook 20 to 25 minutes or until just tender. Drain, removing garlic and bay leaf.

4. Meanwhile, gently squeeze out some of the moisture from the mustard greens. Put in a mixing bowl. In a small bowl, mix olive oil, vinegar, shallots, 1 teaspoon salt, and the black pepper.

5. Add cooked lentils to the mustard greens. Pour dressing over and toss. Sprinkle with goat cheese. Serve warm.

Sam's Cooking Tip

Coach Farms in upstate New York makes a marvelous low-fat goat cheese that has only 2.5g of fat per ounce. If you can't find such a cheese where you live, try a farmer's cheese or regular goat cheese that is as low in fat as possible.

Swiss Chard and White Bean Salad

Makes 6 servings

2 bunches Swiss chard, about 1½ pounds
Two 15-ounce cans cannellini or great
  northern beans, rinsed and drained
3 tablespoons lemon juice
3 tablespoons extra-virgin olive oil

1 clove garlic, finely minced
Kosher salt and freshly ground black
  pepper to taste
1 teaspoon *herbes de Provence*

1. Separate chard stems from leaves. Stack and roll leaves, cigar-style, and cut into ½-inch strips. Cut stems crosswise into ³/₈-inch-wide crescents. Wash in lots of cool water. Drain.

2. Put stems in a steamer basket over ½ inch of boiling water in a large saucepan. Cover and cook 5 minutes. Add leaves and cook 5 minutes more. Drain and gently squeeze out any excess moisture from the leaves.

3. Put chard in a bowl with beans. Combine remaining ingredients in a small bowl and pour over chard and beans. Toss and cover with plastic wrap 1 hour before serving.

Swiss Chard and Grilled Polenta

This makes a satisfying lunch dish or a hearty first course for dinner.

Makes 6 servings

1¼ cups cornmeal

3 teaspoons kosher salt

½ teaspoon freshly ground black pepper

1 quart skim milk

Butter-flavored cooking spray

1 bunch Swiss chard, about 1 pound

1 tablespoon olive oil

1 small onion, chopped

6 ounces wild or domestic mushrooms, sliced

3 cloves garlic, minced

¾ cup dry red wine

One 28-ounce can plum tomatoes, drained and chopped

2 teaspoons tomato paste

¼ cup chopped fresh parsley

1½ tablespoons fresh sage or 2 teaspoons dried

¾ cup grated Parmesan cheese

1. Prepare polenta by combining cornmeal, 2 teaspoons salt, ¼ teaspoon pepper, and milk in a microwaveable, 2-quart casserole. Cook at full power in a microwave oven, uncovered for 12 minutes, stirring once. Let stand 3 minutes. Spray an 8×8-inch baking pan with butter-flavored cooking spray and pour polenta into it, spreading out evenly. Put in the refrigerator to cool. When completely cooled, cut into 6 equal pieces.

2. Meanwhile, separate chard stems from leaves. Stack and roll leaves, cigar-style, and cut into ½-inch strips. Cut stems crosswise into ⅜-inch-wide crescents. Wash in lots of cool water. Drain.

3. Put oil in a large skillet or wok over medium-high heat. Add onion and mushrooms and cook, stirring, until onion and mushrooms begin to soften. Add garlic, cook a few minutes more, then add wine, tomatoes, and paste. Bring to a boil, add chard, and season well with remaining salt and pepper. Reduce heat and simmer 25 minutes. Add parsley and sage during the last 5 minutes. Preheat broiler.

4. Spray a small baking sheet with butter-flavored cooking spray. Distribute polenta pieces evenly and spray the tops. Broil about 5 minutes on each side or until nicely browned. To serve, put a piece of polenta on each of 6 plates (preferably soup plates), top with chard, and sprinkle with 2 tablespoons of Parmesan.

Sam's Cooking Tip

Polenta, soft or firm, is so much easier to make when microwaved, but if you're one of the few who doesn't have a microwave oven, you can make polenta on top of the stove by adding the cornmeal to a saucepan of boiling salted water or milk in a stream. Stir with a wooden spoon until it comes away from the sides of the pan, about 20 minutes.

Broccoli Raab with Roasted Garlic and Fusilli

Almost all cooking greens go well with pasta, but none better than broccoli raab.

Makes 4 servings as a main course, 6 as an appetizer

1 head garlic
Kosher salt
1 bunch broccoli raab, about 1 pound
1 pound fusilli or other short pasta

3 tablespoons extra-virgin olive oil
Freshly ground black pepper to taste
Dash hot pepper flakes (optional)
Grated Parmesan cheese

1. Slice $1/4$ inch off the top of the garlic head, wrap in aluminum foil, and bake in a 375°F oven about 30 minutes. Remove cloves from skin and slice. Set aside.

2. Put a pot with 4 quarts of water and a teaspoon of salt on the stove over high heat.

3. Cut off the bottom $1/2$ inch from the stems of the broccoli raab. Then lay the bunch on its side on a cutting board and cut crosswise. The stem portions should be no more than $3/8$ inch wide; the leafy tops can be cut somewhat wider, as much as $3/4$ inch.

4. Rinse the broccoli raab in a colander and put into the pot when the water comes to a boil. Cook 7 minutes or until just tender. Scoop out with a skimmer into the colander and return the pot to a boil. When it reaches the boil again, add the pasta and cook until just tender.

5. Put the broccoli raab in a large skillet—a wok is ideal for this—and turn the heat on low. Drain the pasta in the colander and add to the broccoli raab with the garlic, half the olive oil, salt and black pepper to taste, and pepper flakes (if desired). Toss and cook a few minutes, just until flavors meld. Add remaining olive oil and serve with Parmesan.

CHAPTER

18

Jerusalem artichokes

When we asked the clerk in the produce section of a local supermarket where the Jerusalem artichokes were, he said, "The artichokes are over there, but I have no idea where they came from."

Such is the problem with the misnamed Jerusalem artichoke. Producers of this tuber have tried to overcome the confusion by advertising the product as the sunchoke. On one-pound trays from Frieda's, the Los Angeles specialty produce company, the word sunchokes stands out in bold letters on a green banner. But underneath that word in less prominent type are the sunchoke aliases: Jerusalem artichokes and topinambours.

And it doesn't stop there. The Jerusalem artichoke is also called *girasole* and *Racine de Tournesol.* But not until very recently was it called sun roots, which was the name originally given to the tuber by North American Indians, according to Elizabeth Schneider's superb *Uncommon Fruits and Vegetables: A Commonsense Guide* (Perennial Library, 1989).

The prevailing opinion has been that the term *Jerusalem artichoke* is a corruption of *girasole articiocco,* meaning "sunflower artichoke," a name that was given to the vegetable by the Italians. However, according to *The Curious Cook* by Harold McGee (North Point Press, 1990), there is evidence that it is instead an English corruption of the Dutch word *Terneuzen,* the name of a city in the Netherlands where the tuber was grown. It has nothing to do with Jerusalem, although apparently some do grow there.

As to topinambours, that name came about because a group of Brazilian Indians from the Topinamboux tribe happened to be in Paris about the same time Jerusalem artichokes (or whatever) were arriving. Somehow, street vendors who sold the chokes thought the name *Topinamboux* was catchy and stuck it on the tubers, which is a little like giving Florida grapefruit that is sold in Moscow the name

Miami Dolphins. It's not clear why the "x" at the end of the name became an "r."

If only we'd stuck with the original Indian name we would have saved a lot of confusion. And we'd be correct. The botanical name of the Jerusalem artichoke is *Helianthus tuberosus,* meaning that it is from the sunflower family (which it is) and that it's a root (two for two).

WHERE GROWN

Jerusalem artichokes like cool growing climates. The primary growing areas are central California, Washington, and Minnesota.

VARIETIES

There are two varieties. The western Jerusalem artichoke is beige and mostly round. The midwestern or northeastern type is longer and knobbier with a reddish exterior. Both varieties are the same inside.

The Jerusalem artichoke looks like a nubby new potato or a knob of fresh ginger. Inside the dusty brown skin is a creamy white, crisp, and sweet interior with a taste that is very much like a water chestnut or perhaps a jicama. (Others liken it to artichoke hearts and salsify.)

Sometimes Jerusalem artichokes are confused with tiny Chinese artichokes, which are imported from France. But they are not the same vegetable.

SEASONS

Jerusalem artichokes are technically available all year, but late spring and summer availability can be spotty. The best time for them is fall and winter. According to *The Essential Root Vegetable Cookbook* by Sally and Martin Stone (Clarkson Potter, 1991), in areas of the northeast and midwest, some of the tubers are left in the ground over the winter to be harvested in early spring.

The later ones are sweeter, say the Stones. Others disagree, claiming the fall and winter-picked Jerusalem artichokes are best.

SELECTION, HANDLING & STORAGE

When selecting, choose Jerusalem artichokes that are evenly sized for easier handling (though that may be difficult because Jerusalem artichokes are often packaged, and just as often with sizes ranging from that of a golf ball to a knob of ginger). They should be firm with no wrinkles, green spots, blotches, or sprouting. However, protrusions and unevenness on the skin are perfectly fine.

Stored in plastic bags, they will keep a week or more in the refrigerator in the low-humidity bin.

NUTRITION

The Jerusalem artichoke is not exactly a nutritional powerhouse, but it does have two important features. One is that it is low in calories, with only 35 per 100g (about 3.5 ounces). That, and its sweet crunchiness, make the Jerusalem artichoke a good, low-fat snack for kids and adults alike.

For vegetarians the good news is that Jerusalem artichokes are a good source of iron, with 3.4mg per serving. That's more than lean ground beef and about 19% of the DV for iron. A serving also contains 2.3g of protein, .1g of fat, 16.7g of carbohydrates, .8g of dietary fiber, and 6% of the DV for vitamin C.

YIELD

Figure on three or four servings per pound, depending on how much peeling or cleaning is needed and the nature of the dish. One pound yields about 2 cups sliced or chopped.

PREPARATION

The major decision to be made when preparing Jerusalem artichokes is which weapon to choose, the scrub brush or the peeler. Scrubbing removes dirt and grit but not all the skin. And it requires some elbow grease. Peeling does remove what some consider the less-than-aesthetic skin, but small pieces are a chore and scrapes are not uncommon. Pick your poison.

Jerusalem artichokes are extremely versatile because they can be used raw or cooked, whole, diced, sliced, or julienned. Try adding them to a roast as you would potatoes or carrots. Or just roast them as you would potatoes for a side dish.

Jerusalem artichokes can be cooked in soups, stews, gratins, or purees with other root vegetables such as potatoes or with fennel. They are excellent in stir-fries as a substitute for water chestnuts (especially the canned ones) or as just part of the mélange to add sweetness and crunch.

When raw, they are a refreshing addition to salads, folded into tuna or chicken salads, or sprinkled onto tossed salads. (They won't turn color if cut with a stainless steel knife.) Jerusalem artichokes are perfect candidates for pickling.

Tony's Tip

One of the problems of Jerusalem artichokes is that they produce a lot of gas, even more than dried beans. Some of this can be reduced by prolonged cold storage (a month or more), according to Harold McGee in The Curious Cook. McGee also suggests boiling sliced chokes in lots of water for 15 minutes. Neither is an ideal solution, so keep portions of Jerusalem artichokes modest.

Jerusalem Artichoke Gratin

*This hearty side dish, a good accompaniment to roasts and other meats,
looks a lot richer than it really is.*

Makes 6 to 8 servings

1 tablespoon butter

1 shallot, minced

2 tablespoons all-purpose flour

2 cups skim milk, warmed

$^1/_2$ teaspoon grated nutmeg

$^1/_2$ teaspoon ground ginger

Kosher salt and freshly ground black
   pepper to taste

Butter-flavored cooking spray

1 pound Jerusalem artichokes, scrubbed
   or peeled and cut into very thin slices

1 pound sweet potatoes, cut into $^1/_4$-inch-
   thick slices

$^1/_2$ cup shredded low-fat Jarlsberg cheese

$^1/_3$ cup bread crumbs

2 tablespoons chopped fresh parsley

1. Put butter in a large saucepan over medium heat. Add shallot and cook until soft, a few minutes. Add flour and stir until well incorporated. Add milk and whisk until mixture thickens and is smooth with no flour taste, about 5 minutes. Season with nutmeg, ginger, salt, and pepper.

2. Preheat oven to 350°F. Spray a 2-quart gratin dish with butter-flavored cooking spray. Alternately layer Jerusalem artichokes and sweet potatoes, seasoning each lightly with salt and pepper.

3. Pour cream sauce over, cover with foil, and bake about 55 minutes until vegetables are tender. Raise heat to 500°F. Mix cheese with bread crumbs and parsley. Remove foil, sprinkle gratin with cheese mixture, and spray with butter-flavored cooking spray. Return to the oven and bake until top is nicely browned and crusty, 5 to 10 minutes.

Sam's Cooking Tip

Jarlsberg Lite is one of the better low-fat cheeses, a good Swiss-style cheese substitute.

Chicken Salad with Jerusalem Artichokes

This is a good dish for using those leftovers from the holiday turkey.

Makes 6 servings

$^1/_4$ cup low-fat mayonnaise

$^1/_3$ cup nonfat sour cream or yogurt

1 tablespoon Dijon mustard

Juice of 1 lime

$^1/_4$ cup chopped cilantro

Kosher salt and freshly ground black pepper to taste

1 pound Jerusalem artichokes, scrubbed or peeled

1 pound cooked boneless, skinless chicken or turkey breast, cut into $^1/_2$-inch cubes

1 red bell pepper, chopped

1 teaspoon minced jalapeño or other hot pepper

1 bunch scallions, trimmed and cut into thin slices (white and 1 inch of green)

1. Mix first seven ingredients in a small bowl. Set aside.

2. Cut Jerusalem artichokes into a combination of very thin slices and 1$^1/_2$-inch match-sticks. Combine Jerusalem artichokes, chicken, pepper, and scallions in a bowl. Season with salt and pepper.

3. Add dressing and mix well. Refrigerate at least 1 hour before serving. Bring to room temperature for serving.

Roasted Jerusalem Artichokes

Cooked this way, Jerusalem artichokes taste like a cross between turnips and potatoes.

Makes 4 servings

4 cloves garlic, smashed, then chopped
2½ tablespoons extra-virgin olive oil
1½ pounds Jerusalem artichokes
Kosher salt and freshly ground black pepper to taste
1 tablespoon chopped fresh parsley

1. Preheat oven to 500°F. Put garlic and oil in a microwaveable dish. Cover with a paper towel and cook in microwave oven at half power for 2 minutes (3 if a low-wattage oven). Set aside.

2. Peel Jerusalem artichokes and cut into pieces the size of golf balls. Put in a shallow roasting pan large enough to hold all in one layer comfortably. Strain garlic from oil and pour oil over the chokes. Add salt and pepper and toss.

3. Cook about 20 minutes (tossing once or twice) or until tender. Sprinkle on the parsley and serve.

Jerusalem Artichoke and Carrot Salad

This dish emphasizes the crunchy sweetness of Jerusalem artichokes.

Makes 6 to 8 servings

1 pound Jerusalem artichokes, peeled or well scrubbed

1 pound carrots, peeled or well scrubbed and trimmed

$1/4$ cup chopped chives

2 tablespoons chopped dill

2 tablespoons extra-virgin olive oil

3 tablespoons freshly squeezed lemon juice

Kosher salt and freshly ground black pepper to taste

2 tablespoons capers, rinsed

1. Use the slicing attachment of a food processor to thinly slice the chokes. Then stack the halves and julienne. Put the shredding attachment on the food processor and grate the carrots. (An alternative is to slice the chokes by hand and use a hand grater for the carrots.) Put vegetables into a mixing bowl with chives and dill.

2. Mix remaining ingredients in a cup. Add to vegetables and toss. Let sit 30 minutes before serving.

mushrooms

Some Sunday afternoon in the fall, instead of watching a football game on television, go on a mushroom hunt. It's so fascinating you may wind up forgetting what a nickel defense is.

Years ago we went on just such a hunt with Jack Czarnecki, a man who knows more about mushrooms than anyone we can think of. Czarnecki is the chef and owner of Joe's Bistro 614 in West Reading, Pennsylvania, and the former chef and owner of the now-closed Joe's, an award-winning restaurant in Reading, Pennsylvania, that specialized in mushroom dishes, even to the point of putting pickled mushrooms in martinis instead of olives.

Czarnecki's mushroom knowledge was largely handed down from his father, Joe. Joe's father, Joe Sr., started Joe's as a workers' bar in 1916. The rest of what Czarnecki learned was on his own. He's a trained bacteriologist and an insatiable mycophile (a person who loves mushrooms). His knowledge is so astonishing, he's regularly called upon by local health officials investigating cases of mushroom poisoning.

One of the reasons mushrooms are so interesting is that there are some thirty-eight thousand species known to exist. The Latin names for these fungi are somewhat daunting, but the nicknames are charming: hen-of-the-woods, Black Trumpet, and Woolly Bear just to name a few.

Mushrooms add a wonderful earthy quality to dishes, even plain, white domestic mushrooms, which Czarnecki says can be just as flavorful as some wild ones.

Sometimes these wild mushrooms can be frightfully expensive, upwards of fifteen dollars a pound or more. But mushrooms don't weigh very much and a little goes a long way. Besides, the price goes down considerably when you pick them yourself.

If you do decide to change your couch potato ways and go mushroom hunting, Jack Czarnecki has a few suggestions.

- Do some reading. There is an extensive bibliography in Czarnecki's most recent book, *A Cook's Book of Mushrooms* (Artisan, 1995).
- Contact your local mycology society about field trips.
- Know what you don't know. They say a little knowledge is a dangerous thing, but with wild mushrooms it can be fatal.

We'd add one more simple note of caution: Don't eat any mushrooms that came from a source in which you're not absolutely confident, whether it's a friend or a friendly forager.

WHERE GROWN

As Gilroy, California, is to garlic, Kennett Square, Pennsylvania, is to mushrooms, at least as far as the familiar button or domestic mushroom is concerned. So it's not surprising that Pennsylvania is the leading mushroom-producing state. Since Kennett Square is so near the Delaware border, that state is also a major supplier, as are California, Michigan, and Illinois. Many of the specialty mushrooms come from Northern California, Oregon, and Washington.

VARIETIES

The *Agaricus bisporus* or just Agaricus is the mainstay of the fresh mushroom market. Also called a **white or button mushroom,** its color ranges from white to beige. It is very mild when eaten raw but the flavor increases when cooked. Generally it is available in three sizes. The smallest is about the size of a button and is used whole in stews (see Coq Au Vin recipe, page 189). The medium size is generally sliced or chopped and the larger size can be stuffed, chopped, grilled, or roasted. Flavor does not change with size.

Crimini mushrooms (also spelled cremini) are also called golden Italian and Italian brown mushrooms. They are a variation of button mushrooms with a deeper color that can go as dark as a rich brown. Though their color gives the impression of wild mushrooms, their taste is fairly close to the button. In fact, it's questionable whether they're worth two or three times the price of button mushrooms.

Portobello mushrooms seem to have come out of nowhere to become a staple in markets and restaurants. In fact, in *The Edible Mushroom* by Margaret Liebenstein (Fawcett Columbine, 1986) and *Joe's Book of Mushroom Cookery* by Jack Czarnecki (Atheneum, 1986), the portobello is not even mentioned. Essentially a giant crimini, the portobello is the Arnold Schwarzenegger of mushrooms with a wide, flat cap that can be 8 inches across and a stem the thickness of a broccoli stalk. Occasionally roots are left on the stem. Its meaty flavor and firm texture make it ideal for grilling and roasting and a good meat substitute. The portobello is sometimes called portabella, a name the mushroom industry prefers.

Enoki are pure white mushrooms with tiny caps and spaghettilike stems that are often attached to a base like a book of matches. Czarnecki compares enokies in appearance and taste to Q-Tips and we agree. But they do make nice garnishes.

Oyster mushrooms (also called Pleurotus or Pleurotte) get their name because their convex cap, off-white or silver-gray color, and fluted shell shape reminds some of oyster shells. We think they look more like those fans used to keep potentates cool. The texture is thick and soft, almost flabby. The flavor is rather mild. Angel trumpets are a white hybrid of oyster mushrooms.

Shiitake mushrooms, also known as golden oak, black forest, black, oakwood, oak tree, and Chinese mushrooms, have really taken off in the past decade. In the wild and under cultivation, they are grown on oak logs. In Japan, where shiitakes have been grown for more than a thousand years, it's common for households to have their own supply of shiitakes growing outside. The umbrellalike cap has the color of brown suede and the underbelly and stem are off-white with flecks of brown. The long thin stem is inedible unless the mushroom is very young. But the cap is full of woodsy flavor, which intensifies when cooked. Domestic shiitakes are the same as those grown in Japan and China, including the dried mushrooms that are often found in Chinese markets.

The following mushrooms are more likely to be available through specialty stores and upscale markets.

- **Chanterelle mushrooms** have many other names such as Girolle, which is what the French call them. They look somewhat like horns—some have suggested umbrellas turned inside out—with colors that can range from pale yellow to reddish orange, the color (and the shape) varying with the species. Chanterelles are among the most flavorful of all wild mushrooms with hints of apricot, pepper, and nuts. They are also more widely available than many of the exotic and expensive mushrooms.

- **Horn of Plenty**'s shape is similar to the chanterelle's, but it is a different, though related species. It is more delicate than the chanterelle and can be larger, up to 3 inches long, and the entire mushroom can be used. The flavor is equally delicate when fresh, though more intense and buttery when dried and reconstituted. The color ranges from dark brown to black. When black it may be called a Black Chanterelle or Trumpet of Death.

- **Hen-of-the-woods**, like many wild mushrooms does not have the traditional cap and stem. It has folded fronds that are reminiscent of the feathers of a sitting hen. The related chicken-of-the-woods derives its name from the fact that when cooked, it has a chickenlike flavor and texture; it is also called a sulfur mushroom because the underside of its red-orange cap is bright yellow. Both mushrooms grow on hardwood stumps and can be huge, some reaching 50 pounds. The hen's flavor is much more delicate than that of the chicken and needs less cooking time. Sometimes chicken-of-the-woods requires extensive boiling to soften before it can be sliced and sautéed.

- **Hedgehog** (also called a Sweet Tooth among others) has a yellow-orange cap with a thick white stem that is somewhat off center. Instead of gills underneath, it has teethlike protrusions. The flavor is mild.

- **Lobster**, as expected, has a red-orange color on its irregular shape. You be the judge if it has fishlike flavors.

- **Porcini** (the singular is porcino) are also known as *cèpes* (in France), *Steinpilz* (in Germany), and *borowick* or *borovicki* (in Poland; the Poles are big wild mushroom eaters). All are members of the large *Boletus* family of mushrooms distinguished by spores under their caps instead of the gills found on domestic (white) mushrooms. Size will vary depending on where it comes from. (It can go as high as 5 pounds.) Flavor may also vary. Porcini from Italy are somewhat less intense than their cousins from Poland, Germany, and France. Most often we see them sold dried (which intensifies the flavor), but twice a year they are available fresh. The stems are thick, tapering to the cap. (In fact, the French term is taken from the word for

"trunk" in the Gascon dialect. The Italian word means "piglets.") The caps are thick and rusty brown. The texture is meaty and the flavor buttery and nutty. Good for all kinds of cooking but especially grilling and stuffing.

- **Morels** are related more to truffles than true mushrooms, but that's a botanical game of inside baseball we don't have to play except to realize that morels are probably second only to truffles in desirability. Their deep, earthy flavor adds a special dimension to many foods. Morels can be distinguished by their honeycombed or spongelike brown cone-shaped caps. Both the stems and caps are hollow. The caps are traditionally used for more delicate dishes since the stems are tougher. Imported morels, usually from France, are smaller and darker with a smokier flavor than domestic morels. Like porcini, morels are most often purchased dried.

SEASONS

Because they are raised in hothouse environments, most of the more common mushrooms are available year-round. That includes the common button, crimini, enoki, oyster, shiitake, and portobello.

The more exotic mushrooms are seasonal. Chanterelles are available from September through April, black chanterelles from January through March. Hen-of-the-woods are in the market in late summer and early fall. Hedgehogs can be seen from December through March. Lobster mushrooms are available in mid- and late summer. Morels are available from late March through early May. Porcini have two seasons, spring (May and June) and fall (October).

SELECTION, HANDLING & STORAGE

The standard mushroom axiom used to be to choose mushrooms with tight caps and no gills (the brown ridges underneath the cap) showing, and to pass up mushrooms whose gills were exposed. However, with the popularity of portobello mushrooms, which are almost always sold with gills exposed, has come a recognition that open gills are not a sign of poor quality, just age. In fact, mushrooms with open or exposed gills are further along in their development and thus have a more intense mushroom flavor. However, they should be used right away. For aesthetic reasons, tightly closed caps may still be necessary in certain dishes.

Fresh mushrooms should be firm with no soft spots. Button mushrooms should have a dry, but not wrinkled, look. Wild mushrooms can look a bit moist, but a moistness that conveys brightness and freshness, not mushiness. Button mushrooms will have a faint earthy or musky smell, wild mushrooms more so. A neutral smell on wild mushrooms means some of the flavor has probably been lost, but the mushrooms are still good, just not as flavorful as they might be. An obvious off-putting odor indicates poor quality.

With wild mushrooms check for any holes that indicate insect damage. A few are okay, but more than that indicates excessive infestation. (Look on the underside of the stem primarily but also under the cap.)

Shiitake mushrooms should have caps that curl under. The size of the cap, which can be as wide as 8 inches, is not a determinant of quality. Mushrooms should not normally be purchased if broken, though the hedgehog is so brittle it is often in pieces when sold. However, the flavor should not be affected if all the other signs are right.

Paper bags are commonly recommended for storing mushrooms. But the bag absorbs moisture from the mushrooms. Instead, put the paper bag in a larger plastic bag, perforated if possible. This creates a kind of air lock that allows mushrooms to breathe but not go dry. Store mushrooms in the cool, high-humidity part of the refrigerator; they can stand temperatures as low as 36°F. But keep them away from other foods with strong odors since mushrooms act as a sponge for odors. Properly stored mushrooms should last several days. Don't clean or chop mushrooms until you're ready to use them.

Mushrooms should not be frozen unless first blanched, then covered in the blanching water before being put into the freezer. They are good candidates for drying, canning, and pickling.

NUTRITION

Five medium mushrooms (about 84g, 3 ounces) contain only 20 calories as well as 3g of carbohydrates, 1g of dietary fiber, and 3g of protein. Unfortunately, they don't contain much else in the way of vitamins, only 2% of the DV for both vitamin C and iron, though they do contain a good amount of potassium (300mg) and 20% of the DV for riboflavin. And while no other health effects have been uncovered for the everyday button mushroom, a number of therapeutic benefits have been attributed to Asian mushrooms like the shiitake. These mushrooms are thought to lower blood cholesterol, reduce the likelihood of certain forms of cancer (especially breast cancer and leukemia), and act as treatment for viruses such as influenza and possibly even AIDS.

YIELD

A pound of raw whole mushrooms yields about 5 cups sliced, 6 cups chopped. Once cooked, a pound of sliced mushrooms will reduce to about 2 cups.

Tony's Tip

If you want to keep white mushrooms nice and bright, wipe them with a paper towel that has been dipped in lemon juice.

PREPARATION

To wash or not to wash, that is the question when it comes to mushrooms. We say yes, and no. We routinely rinse button mushrooms in a colander, then dry them quickly in paper towels. With more delicate wild mushrooms, we generally brush off dirt and debris with a regular old paint brush—one that has not been used for painting, obviously. More stubborn dirt can be removed with a damp cloth or paper towel.

After cleaning, a thin slice is removed from the stem. In the case of shiitake mushrooms, the fibrous stems are removed and discarded (though they can be thrown into a stock if you like). For other mushrooms such as morels and porcini, the stems and caps frequently are used for different purposes.

To remove the stems, hold the cap firmly in one hand, then push the stem firmly in one direction or twist it until it snaps off.

Caps have more uses than stems. They can be stuffed with everything from crab to spicy sausage. But don't overdo it or the stuffing will obliterate the mushroom flavor. Our favorite stuffing includes simply the chopped caps and scallions sautéed in butter, then combined with parsley, thyme, and flavored bread crumbs.

Mushroom stems are ideal for duxelles, one of the great flavor enhancers in any kitchen. (See Artichokes Stuffed with Duxelles, page 10.) They're also great for stuffings.

Mushrooms carry many flavors well. Among the best are garlic, onions (especially scallions and shallots), butter, olive oil, thyme, and parsley. But they also give an added flavor to so many dishes from sautéed green beans and asparagus to risottos and pastas.

The best way to bring out the flavor of mushrooms is to sauté them, preferably in butter, but olive oil works well too. It's almost always preferable to cook mushrooms this way (or in a similar fashion) before adding them to a dish. For example, mushrooms sprinkled on a pizza are much more flavorful if sautéed first rather than merely used raw. When sautéed, mushrooms go through three stages: They shrink, then they exude a tremendous amount of water, then the water evaporates and the flavor concentrates.

Oven roasting is also excellent for mushrooms, especially meaty ones. One of the best mushroom dishes we've ever eaten was roasted shiitakes the size of hubcaps, slathered with olive oil and grilled with thyme branches that were large enough to fell power lines.

With rare exceptions we don't particularly care for raw mushrooms, any more than we do raw cauliflower or broccoli. According to nutrition writer Jean Carper, there are some who believe raw button mushrooms are toxic.

Portobello Mushroom Sandwich

Mushrooms are often described as "meaty," but none is meatier than the portobello. In fact, we've heard some vegetarians won't eat it because it looks too much like meat.

Makes 2 servings

2 portobello mushrooms, about 5 to 6 ounces each

2 tablespoons porcini mushroom oil or extra-virgin olive oil

2 tablespoons balsamic vinegar

1 teaspoon fresh thyme, chopped

Kosher salt and freshly ground black pepper to taste

2 round toasted sesame rolls, halved horizontally

1 large roasted red pepper, peeled, seeded, and halved lengthwise (see Preparation, page 205)

Watercress

Thinly sliced red onion rings (optional)

1. Heat broiler or grill. Remove stems from mushrooms and set them aside for another use. Clean mushroom caps.

2. Mix oil, vinegar, thyme, salt, and pepper in a glass. Season mushrooms with additional salt and pepper and brush one side with slightly less than half the oil and vinegar mixture. Put caps under a broiler or on the grill for about 4 minutes. Turn over, brush with all but 1 tablespoon of remaining oil and vinegar mixture. Broil 4 minutes more or until nicely browned and tender.

3. Brush the inside of each bun with remaining oil and vinegar mixture. Top with mushroom cap, then roasted pepper half, then watercress. Add onion rings if desired.

Sam's Cooking Tip

Flavored oils, especially those by Consorzio, have become very popular in the past few years. They can give new flavors to a dish or intensify existing flavors. Consorzio makes a porcini mushroom oil that is perfect for adding more depth of flavor to wild mushroom dishes.

Wild Mushroom Crostini

This is a terrific hors d'oeuvre that can be made ahead if needed.
Serve warm or at room temperature.

Makes 6 to 8 servings as an hors d'oeuvre

1 tablespoon extra-virgin olive oil

1 pound mushrooms, any mixture of wild and cultivated, thinly sliced

1 small onion, minced

1 clove garlic, minced

$1/4$ cup dry white wine, Chicken Stock (page 9), or mushroom liquid from soaking dried mushrooms

2 tablespoons chopped fresh parsley

1 teaspoon kosher salt

$1/4$ teaspoon freshly ground black pepper

1 French baguette, cut into $1/4$-inch slices and toasted

1. Heat the oil in a large skillet (a wok is ideal for this) over medium-high heat. Just before it smokes, add mushrooms, onion, and garlic. Cook, stirring, until mushrooms wilt and begin to turn brown, about 5 minutes.

2. Add wine, parsley, salt, and pepper and cook until the liquid evaporates. Remove to a cutting board and chop finely. Spread on toasted bread.

Turkey Cutlets with Mushrooms and Dry Vermouth

This is the kind of restaurant dish most people wouldn't cook at home, but it's quick and easy. Just don't try it for more than four people.

Makes 4 servings

4 turkey cutlets, cut from the breast, each about 5 ounces

3 tablespoons all-purpose flour

1¹/₂ teaspoons chopped fresh thyme, or ³/₄ teaspoon dried

Kosher salt and freshly ground black pepper to taste

1¹/₂ tablespoons clarified butter (see page 284), or regular butter

2 tablespoons minced shallots

4 ounces thinly sliced wild or domestic mushrooms, or a combination of the two

²/₃ cup dry vermouth or dry white wine

1 tablespoon chopped chives

1. If the butcher hasn't done it already, pound cutlets between two sheets of butcher paper or aluminum foil until ¹/₄ inch thick or less. Combine flour, thyme, salt, and pepper. Dredge cutlets in flour mixture and shake off any excess.

2. In a skillet large enough to hold all cutlets comfortably in a single layer, heat clarified butter over medium heat. When fat is hot, add cutlets and cook about 3 or 4 minutes on one side, then 2 or 3 minutes on the other side.

3. Remove cutlets to a warm platter or individual plates. Add shallots and mushrooms and more salt and pepper to the skillet. Stir a few minutes until mushrooms and shallots soften. Add vermouth and raise heat to medium high. Scrape up particles from the bottom of the pan with a wooden spoon.

4. As soon as sauce thickens, about 2 minutes, pour over cutlets. Sprinkle with chives.

Sam's Cooking Tip

I always keep a dry vermouth in my refrigerator so I don't have to open a bottle of white wine when a small amount is needed for a recipe. Because vermouth is fortified, it will last a lot longer than table wine.

Mushrooms à la Grecque

This is a good substitute for fatty cheese and nacho chips as an hors d'oeuvre before dinner. Get small mushrooms so guests can pop them into their mouths.

Makes 6 to 8 servings

2 teaspoons kosher salt

$3/4$ teaspoon black peppercorns

$3/4$ teaspoon coriander seeds

$3/4$ teaspoon fennel seeds

2 bay leaves

A few branches of fresh thyme
   or $1/2$ teaspoon dried

1 whole chile pepper or a pinch of hot
   pepper flakes

3 cloves garlic, crushed

6 fresh parsley stems

1 lemon, juiced

2 tablespoons extra-virgin olive oil

1 pound small mushrooms

1 tablespoon minced fresh parsley

1. Combine all ingredients, except mushrooms and minced parsley, with 1 quart of water in a large saucepan. Bring to a boil and simmer at least 10 minutes, stirring a few times.

2. Add mushrooms to the saucepan, stir, and bring to a boil. Simmer 5 minutes. Turn off heat and let cool to room temperature.

3. Refrigerate several hours or overnight. Bring to room temperature, then drain just before serving. Serve as part of an antipasto spread sprinkled with parsley or as an hors d'oeuvre with toothpicks.

Sam's Cooking Tip

The seasonings that go into any vegetable prepared à la Grecque vary widely. The core usually consists of peppercorns, bay leaves, thyme, fennel seeds, olive oil, and lemon juice. Other herbs can include basil, rosemary, sage, parsley (stems, not leaves), or oregano (especially the Greek variety). Spices may include coriander, cumin, and mustard seeds. In addition, or in lieu of garlic, you can use onion. Celery tops are another option. You can also add dry vermouth or dry white wine.

Loin of Venison with Wild Mushrooms

Game and wild mushrooms go perfectly together. Accompany this with a sturdy red wine from the Rhone or an Italian Barolo.

Makes 6 servings

$^1\!/_2$ pound wild mushrooms such as shiitakes, oysters, and chanterelles

1 tablespoon butter

$^1\!/_4$ cup minced shallots

1 teaspoon kosher salt

$^1\!/_4$ teaspoon freshly ground black pepper

$^1\!/_2$ cup port wine

1 cup beef stock mixed with 2 teaspoons arrowroot

2-pound boneless loin "New York Strip" of venison

1 teaspoon canola oil

1 tablespoon chopped chives

1. Brush off dirt from mushrooms or rinse lightly, then pat dry. Halve, quarter, or slice mushrooms depending on size.

2. Put butter in a skillet over medium heat. Add shallots and cook about 2 minutes. Raise heat to medium high, add mushrooms, half the salt and pepper, and cook another 2 minutes, stirring. Add port and cook 2 minutes. Add stock with arrowroot and cook just until the sauce begins to thicken, about 3 minutes. Set aside until the venison is cooked. (This step can be done up to 2 hours ahead of time.)

3. Preheat oven to 500°F. If refrigerated, remove the venison from the refrigerator at least 30 minutes before cooking. Season the outside of the meat with the remaining salt and pepper and rub with canola oil. Put on a rack in a shallow roasting pan large enough to easily accommodate the entire loin. Cook 17 to 20 minutes. It should be rare to medium rare. Remove from the oven and cover with foil for 8 minutes.

4. While the venison rests, reheat the sauce, adding a tablespoon or more of port if needed. Check for and adjust seasonings as desired. Slice venison into 12 even pieces, 2 per person. Top each with an equal amount of mushroom sauce. Sprinkle with chives.

Sam's Cooking Tip

Canned beef broth can be quite salty, so adjust the addition of salt accordingly.

Okra is the kind of vegetable only a

mother could love—or a staunch Southerner, even

if he or she is living in Chicago or New York. But

outside this loyal circle okra gets a puzzled look, a

scrunched up nose, or a firm "No, thank you."

Why? It's the slime, or to put it more delicately,

that slightly sweet, viscous liquid that exudes

from okra. This slippery quality, sometimes called "roping," turns a lot of people off.

But okra aficionados love their vegetable in spite of this gooey substance, and maybe a little because of it. Okra, mainly fried, was a mainstay of the resurgence of soul food some years ago. And in dishes such as gumbos it was part of the equally resurgent creole cooking.

However, changes are afoot with okra. Other cuisines such as that of India and the countries of Northern Africa and the Eastern Mediterranean are using okra in many unusual ways. So too are young American cooks who revel in indigenous ingredients, though generally not the cooking methods that accompany them. Not long ago we had dinner at the prestigious Beard House (the former home of food legend James Beard), where pickled okra the size of railroad spikes was sitting on every table, spread out like the spokes of a wagon wheel. Delicious, and a minimum of slime to boot.

WHERE GROWN

Florida, California, and Georgia are the leading okra-producing states. Quite a bit of okra is imported from Mexico.

VARIETIES

For the most part okra is a medium-green pod shaped like a thin spinning top, about 1½ to 3 inches long on average with ridged sides, a tapered point at one end, and a cap at the other. It can grow considerably longer, which is probably how okra got one of its nicknames, ladies' fingers. The dark-green Chinese okra, for example, a variety grown in California, can reach a length of 10 to 13 inches.

The most common okra varieties are the Perkins, Spineless, Dwarf Long Pod, and Clemson Spineless. Less common is purple okra, which you may see at peak times. And even more rare is a version grown in New Guinea, which is grown for its leaves that resemble sorrel.

SEASONS

Okra is a year-round vegetable with supplies at their peak in June, July, and August.

SELECTION, HANDLING & STORAGE

Indian cook par excellence Madhur Jaffrey suggests that one should select okra as one would green beans. "Pick a pod up and snap it, and if it is young and crisp, you buy it. Otherwise, walk on."

She might also have mentioned that the okra should have a good green color with no dullness or blemishes. Pods shouldn't look shriveled but neither should they show signs of obvious moisture. The caps should be light in color, darkness being a sign of age. The smaller the pods—less than 3 inches, preferably closer to 2 inches—the better. It is normal for okra to have a slightly scratchy surface.

Keep okra cool but not cold, about 43°F to 45°F. In a plastic bag, unwashed, it should last in the refrigerator for three days in the high-humidity bin. Okra is ethylene sensitive and should be stored away from ethylene-producing foods such as apples and pears.

NUTRITION

A 3-ounce serving of okra (83g, about six pods) contains about 30 calories, 6g of carbohydrates, 1g dietary fiber, 2g of protein, 20% of the DV for vitamin C, 10% for vitamin A, 6% for calcium, and 4% for iron.

Okra is also a decent source of potassium and a good source of folic acid.

YIELD

A pound of okra will yield about 2¼ cups, chopped, and will serve about four people.

Tony's Tip

> When trimming the tops of okra, be careful not to cut off too much or you'll expose the insides.

PREPARATION

The slime factor can be minimized in two ways. First, leave the okra whole. In gumbos okra is traditionally sliced. In most preparations the very tops of the okra are trimmed.

The second way to minimize, but not entirely eliminate, the slime factor is to not overcook okra. Exactly how long is a matter of personal taste. A pound that is boiled should be ready in 5 to 10 minutes, about twice as long when steamed.

Stir-frying is a good idea too, but only if the okra are very small. Avoid cooking okra in cast iron, aluminum, copper, or brass because this turns okra black, though it does not affect flavor.

Larousse Gastronomique suggests that regardless of the preparation, okra should be blanched first in salted water. This is probably one of several antislime attempts, along with soaking in vinegar, that aren't necessary and don't really work, according to produce maven Elizabeth Schneider.

As far as natural companions to okra, tomatoes come immediately to mind. Moroccans do a wonderful cold salad of okra and tomatoes. Corn and onions are also good with okra as are hot and sweet peppers and eggplant. If these sound as if okra might be a candidate for a Southern-style ratatouille, please be our guest.

Corn Pudding with Okra

Though corn and okra peak in late summer, both are available virtually year-round. And this would make a nice side dish for a Southern-style Thanksgiving.

Makes 6 servings

$^1/_2$ pound okra

Kosher salt and freshly ground black
  pepper to taste

2 tablespoons butter

1 small onion, chopped

2 tablespoons all-purpose flour

2 cups milk, warmed

3 cups corn kernels

1 egg

Healthy pinch cayenne pepper

Butter-flavored cooking spray

$^1/_2$ teaspoon sweet paprika

1. Trim stems from the okra and steam about 5 to 7 minutes (depending on size) until barely tender but still quite firm. Cut into $^1/_2$-inch slices, season with salt and pepper, and set aside. Preheat oven to 350°F.

2. Put the butter in a large saucepan over medium heat. Add onion and cook about 5 minutes until onion softens. Add flour, stir, and cook a few minutes. Add milk and bring to a boil. Simmer 5 minutes, stirring a few times.

3. Remove from heat and add okra, corn, egg, salt and pepper, and cayenne pepper.

4. Spray a 2-quart casserole or soufflé dish with butter-flavored cooking spray. Pour in corn and okra mixture and dust with paprika. Bake about 40 minutes or until pudding just begins to pull away from the sides of the pan.

Moroccan Okra Salad

*This is typical of the numerous salads Moroccans eat at the beginning of a meal.
Traditionally, the salads are scooped up with pieces of bread. No forks.*

Makes 4 to 6 servings a first course or as part of an antipasto table

1 teaspoon cumin seeds

1 teaspoon coriander seeds

$1/2$ teaspoon sweet paprika

Pinch hot pepper flakes

2 tablespoons extra-virgin olive oil

1 pound okra, trimmed and cut into 1-inch pieces

2 cloves garlic, minced

1 pound tomatoes, cored and chopped

Kosher salt and freshly ground black pepper to taste

1 tablespoon fresh lemon juice

2 tablespoons chopped cilantro

1. Toast cumin and coriander seeds in a cast-iron or other skillet over low heat until fragrant, about 10 minutes. Put in a spice mill with paprika and pepper flakes. Grind until fine. Set aside.

2. Put oil in a wok or other large skillet over medium-high heat. Add okra and stir-fry a few minutes. Add garlic and reserved spices, toss a minute, then add tomatoes and salt and pepper to taste. Bring to a boil, lower heat, and cook, covered, about 10 minutes. Remove cover and cook another 5 to 10 minutes or until okra is just tender and most of the juices have evaporated.

3. Remove from heat, add lemon juice, and stir in cilantro. Cool to room temperature, check and adjust seasonings, and serve.

Pickled Okra

Try these pickled okra with almost any kind of pork or beef barbecue. Put them on small plates in a pinwheel fashion with tips pointing to the center.

Makes 4 half pints

1 pound okra, each about 3 inches long
1 cup distilled white vinegar
1 cup water
2 tablespoons Kosher salt
2 tablespoons sugar

4 cloves garlic
2 teaspoons pickling spice
4 sterilized $1/2$-pint canning jars with lids
  and screw tops

1. Rinse okra and dry with paper towels. Trim stems but do not pierce pods.

2. Bring vinegar, water, salt, and sugar to a boil in a saucepan. Divide garlic and pickling spice evenly among the jars. Pack okra vertically into the jars, alternating stems up and down. Pack tightly but do not jam them in. You should get 8 to 10 okra in each jar.

3. Pour vinegar solution over okra, leaving a gap of about $1/2$ inch to the top of each jar. (The okra may float to the top initially, but it will drop down. Okra should be completely covered—by about $1/2$ inch—with the brine.)

4. Seal jars and put into a pot with enough hot water to cover the jars by at least 2 inches. Cover, bring to a boil, and boil 10 minutes. Remove carefully and put on several layers of newspaper. Store at least a few weeks before using.

Sam's Cooking Tip

To sterilize jars, cover by 2 inches of hot water in a pot and boil, covered, 10 to 15 minutes. Put in jar lids for the last few minutes. Leave jars in hot sterilizing water until they are ready to be filled. Handle hot jars carefully. (You may want to use special canning tongs that securely grip the jars for easy removal from the water. They can be purchased wherever canning supplies are found, in good cookware and hardware stores.)

Okra and Corn Salad

Okra and corn are commonly found in the same dishes because both were used so frequently in the Deep South.

Makes 4 to 6 servings

¹/₂ pound okra

2 cups fresh corn kernels (about 3 ears)

1 cup chopped tomatoes

¹/₂ cup chopped scallions (white and 1 inch of the green)

¹/₂ cup finely chopped red bell pepper

1 small jalapeño pepper, seeded and minced

¹/₄ cup chopped fresh parsley

3 tablespoons extra-virgin olive oil

1 tablespoon cider vinegar

1 teaspoon toasted, ground cumin (see page 310)

Kosher salt and freshly ground black pepper to taste

1. Steam okra until just tender, about 10 minutes. Cool under running water. Cut into ¹/₂-inch slices and put into a mixing bowl.

2. If corn is very fresh, tender, and sweet, use as is. Otherwise, cook a few minutes in a few cups of salted water. Cool and add to okra.

3. Add tomatoes, scallions, bell pepper, jalapeño, and parsley to okra and corn.

4. Mix remaining ingredients in a cup, pour over okra mixture, and mix well.

Paella with Okra

Okra normally goes into gumbo, a famous American rice dish. So we thought, why not put it into paella, an equally famous Spanish rice dish, instead of green beans or peas? It works!

Makes 6 servings

1 tablespoon extra-virgin olive oil

6 skinless chicken drumsticks

Kosher salt and freshly ground black pepper to taste

6 ounces spicy turkey sausage such as kielbasa, cut into $1/4$-inch slices

1 cup chopped onion

1 large red bell pepper, cut into strips $1/4$ inch wide by 2 inches long

1 tablespoon chopped garlic

6 cups Chicken Stock (page 9) or water

$3/4$ teaspoon crushed saffron threads mixed with one 12-ounce bottle of clam juice

$1^1/2$ cups seeded and chopped tomatoes (fresh or canned, cored if fresh)

3 cups short-grain rice

24 small clams, well scrubbed

$3/4$ pound small whole okra, about 2 inches long

24 mussels, well scrubbed with beards removed

2 tablespoons chopped fresh parsley for garnish

1. Put oil in a paella pan, casserole, or wok over medium heat. Cook drumsticks until well browned, about 8 to 10 minutes. Remove to a plate and season with salt and pepper. Add sausage, onion, bell pepper, and garlic to pan and cook until onion and pepper begin to soften. Preheat oven to 375°F.

2. Bring stock and clam juice with saffron to a boil in a saucepan. Add tomatoes, salt, and pepper to wok. Cook 10 minutes on top of the stove. Add rice and clams to wok along with boiling stock.

3. Bring to a gentle boil on top of the stove. Add okra, mussels, and drumsticks. Cover and put in the oven 10 minutes. Uncover and cook 10 minutes more. Remove from heat, cover, and let rest 10 minutes. Do not stir. Adjust seasonings if needed. Sprinkle with parsley.

Sam's Cooking Tip

Paella normally calls for short-grain rice, which isn't always easy to get; try the Hispanic section of your supermarket. But I've substituted long-grain rice successfully and have even seen paella recipes that use basmati rice.

onions

The Crying Game was a popular movie several years ago, but it could be the label attached to the ritual we go through when we chop onions. Those unstable sulfur compounds in onions have caused many teary eyes over the years, and almost as many remedies.

Our friend Jesse Cool, who writes a weekly produce column for the *San Jose Mercury News,* had these suggestions in an April 23, 1993, column:

- Hang a piece of bread from your mouth, as long as it doesn't block the view of the knife, the onion, and most importantly, your fingers.
- Hold the onion under running water while you peel it.
- Hold your breath, or at least don't open your mouth while chopping.
- Wear swimming goggles.
- Wrap your head with plastic wrap, leaving breathing holes, and open the refrigerator. Then cut the onion on the top shelf.

All these sound pretty weird to us, especially the ones that call for holding your breath and using plastic wrap.

In *The Food Lover's Tiptionary* (William Morrow, 1994), author Sharon Tyler Herbst, who has become a kind of Hints from Heloise for foodies with this and her excellent book *Food Lover's Companion* (Barron's, 1990), agrees with the goggles suggestion that Jesse Cool gives. However, she recommends safety goggles instead of swimming goggles. She also has these suggestions:

- Freeze onions for 20 minutes before chopping.
- Hold a wooden kitchen spoon between your teeth.
- Bite down on two kitchen matches, sulfur tips pointing out so they're positioned under your nose. (Honest folks, we're not making these up.)
- Turn on the stovetop exhaust fan and chop on top of the stove.

We're not sure if any of these work except the first method Herbst suggests. That's because it's a lot like what we do all the time, and we've never had to resort to sticking matches in our mouth or mummifying our head with plastic wrap.

Our method is simple: Store the onions in the refrigerator. Normally, people will tell you not to store onions in the refrigerator because it's too cold and moisture can build up, spoiling the onions. But we've never seen any ill effects and we use onions so frequently they don't have a chance to spoil.

However, if you have a problem with storing onions in the refrigerator, we suggest two other pieces of advice. One, (which Herbst also suggests), is to make sure that the knife you use is sharp so that it will chop quickly, minimizing tears. (That applies to almost anything you cut in the kitchen, tears or no tears.) One final possibility is a food processor (see Preparation, page 185). It's not as good as chopping, but better than crying your eyes out.

WHERE GROWN

Onions are grown all over the United States. The largest producers are California, Texas, New York, Oregon, Colorado, Idaho, Michigan, New Mexico, Georgia, and Washington. Mexico is responsible for more than 70 percent of imports. Other significant importing countries are Canada, Chile, and New Zealand.

When most people think of sweet onions, they think of Vidalia, a place in Georgia famous for sweet onions. Despite that, more sweet onions are grown in California's Imperial Valley and in Texas. Sweet onions are also grown in New Mexico, Washington, and Arizona.

The largest suppliers of scallions are California and Mexico. Other producers include Arizona, Texas, New Jersey, Ohio, Colorado, Illinois, and Washington. California, New Jersey, Michigan, and Virginia are the main growing areas for leeks. New York and New Jersey are the primary domestic suppliers of shallots, while France is the main importer.

About 90 percent of the domestically consumed garlic is produced in California. Gilroy is the self-proclaimed garlic capital of the world, but this title is less a reflection of growing and more of processing (more than a million pounds a day during the peak of the season). Garlic is imported from Mexico, Argentina, Chile, and China.

VARIETIES

Onions can be divided into types: sweet onions and hot or storage onions. Storage onions are the kind with which we are most familiar. They sting when you bite into them and make you cry because of strong sulfur compounds. Sweet onions have much less of a bite and don't make you cry.

Sweet or mild onions are planted in late fall or very early spring for harvest in early spring to summer. That's why they come from warm areas. The Maui Sweet, for example, comes from Hawaii; the Sweet Imperial from California's Imperial Valley; the Texas 1015 Supersweet from Texas; the Vidalia from Georgia; the Italian Red from California; and the Walla Walla from Washington. In recent years another sweet variety called OSO Sweet has been coming in from Chile.

Most of these onions are good sized, averaging about $1/2$ to $3/4$ pound each, though the Vidalia can come in smaller sizes. (Smaller sweets can be hotter.) The shape varies from round to globe shaped to tops that are somewhat flattened. Their skin is thin, like a new potato. It's also delicate, bruises easily, and doesn't store for extended periods of time. Sweet onions are very crisp with a high water and sugar content. Some are sweet enough to eat like an apple. Since these onions are mild, they are most often used raw, in salads, and on hamburgers.

Storage or hot onions are the more traditional onions that form the backbone of cooking all over the world. Though generally round, shapes vary from large and round to small and round, flattened at one or both ends, or shaped like a torpedo. Colors can be yellow (which includes deeper shades like golden to almost copper colored), white, or red.

However, size, shape, and color do not alter the onion's heat with two minor exceptions. Spanish onions, the large yellow onions, tend to be a bit milder because of their higher water content. Red onions are also a little milder. All storage varieties can be stowed for longer periods of time than sweet onions, though the white onion is somewhat more perishable.

Generally, storage onions are not marketed by name. Spanish and Bermuda onions are merely two types of yellow storage onions that are grown neither in Spain nor in Bermuda. Incidentally, Bermuda onions no longer exist, so if your retailer is advertising Bermuda onions, they are most likely Spanish. Despite the fact that they are called storage onions, there is a steady supply of these onions throughout the year from various areas in and outside the country.

Pearl onions are small onions the size of marbles and come in red, yellow (or gold), and white, which is the most widely available. They are mild with a crunchy texture and add a nice accent to vegetable dishes such as fresh peas. Pearl onions are sometimes called pickling onions because they pickle well. Creamed pearl onions are a favorite Thanksgiving side dish. Pearl onions are usually sold in pint containers.

Boiler or boiling onions are similar to pearl onions in shape although they are larger and somewhat hotter. They are typically used in stews and casseroles although they can be creamed like pearl onions.

Shallots look like small onions. They are cased in a papery skin that is usually rust colored (the American variety) but sometimes a bluish gray (the French variety). Shallots sometimes come in clusters with two or three bulbs or cloves attached. (If a recipe calls for one shallot, it usually means just one of these cloves.) Many recipes suggest that when shallots can't be found, scallions can be substituted. (In some places such as Louisiana, scallions are sometimes called shallots.) But shallots have a more assertive flavor than scallions, which is probably why they are so favored by restaurant chefs and why they are rarely used raw.

Green onions or scallions are mild-tasting, fresh or immature onions with long thin bulbs to which the root ends are attached. Both the bulb and bright green tops are edible. Recipes will typically call for using only the white part or both the white and green part of the scallion. Generally, the white part is cooked, and the green part is used as a garnish or in cold preparations. In a pinch you can substitute the green part for chives. White Lisbon is the most widely grown variety. Others include Crystal Wax, Eclipse, Spanish, White Sweet Spanish, Southport, White Globe, and White Portugal. Scallions are sold in bunches.

When the scallion is allowed to grow a little longer and form a more substantial white bulb, it is called a creaming onion as well as a green onion (which can be confusing). Because they have matured longer, these onions are somewhat hotter than scallions. Like scallions, they are sold in bunches.

Leeks look like overgrown scallions, but a single leek can be as thick as a bunch of scallions, though there are times when a leek can be almost as thin as a scallion. Leeks have a heartier flavor than scallions and are used mostly in cooking, particularly in soups and stews. They can also be served as a vegetable, very often braised or served à la Grecque. The main varieties of leeks grown in the United States are American Flag (also called London Flag), Blue Leaf, Carentan (also called Winter), and Musselburg. They are sold in bunches of two, three, or four, depending on their size.

Garlic, "The Stinking Rose" as it is sometimes called, is the bulb of a delicate plant with snowy white flowers. In season, the flowers are sold in local farmer's markets and add a nice zing to salads. The bulb is composed of eight to twelve sections called cloves, each of which is individually wrapped in a parchmentlike covering and tightly bound together, attached at the base.

There are some three hundred varieties of garlic grown the world over. But in California the two main types of garlic are California Early and California Late. California Early has a white or off-white skin and is harvested in June. The bulb is somewhat rounder and flatter with larger cloves than the Late. California Late is a smaller variety with skins that have a purple or pink hue, which is why it is sometimes called pink garlic. It is harvested in July and August. Late garlic is preferred commercially because of its longer storage capabilities.

In local farmer's markets during July and August you may see a purplish bulb called Rocambole. This is a mild garlic with thick-skinned cloves. Yellowish Elephant garlic has cloves that are two or three times the size of normal garlic cloves. But the flavor is milder. Other varieties of garlic include Argentina White, Mexican Purple, and Mexican White. Colors range from snowy white to light purple.

In the past several years, prepared garlic has become a big business. In many markets you can now buy whole, peeled cloves, which are sold refrigerated. Chopped garlic in oil comes in small jars and is found on store shelves with condiments and oils. Braided garlic is more for ornamentation than cooking, particularly at the prices charged.

Among the specialty items in the onion family are the following:

- **Cipolline** onions are small, flat, sweet onions imported from Italy. They are delicious when featured by themselves on an antipasto table for example. The classic way to prepare them is in a sweet-and-sour sauce.
- **Ramps** are wild mountain leeks. They look like scallions, though their stems taper to a slightly larger bulb and their leaves are wider. Ramps are gleaned by foragers from forests in the eastern United States and have a very short season much like local dandelions. Look for them from the end of March to early May.

SEASONS

Texas 1015 Supersweets are the first to arrive in March. Then come the Vidalia, Sweet Imperial, and Italian Reds. All are gone by the end of June except the Italian Reds, which last into August. Walla Walla onions are available in June and July. OSO Sweets begin arriving in late December or early January and last until the end of March. Maui Sweet onions are generally available year-round.

Hot or storage onions are a year-round crop though certain types will only be available at certain times of the year. Peak supplies are from August to March. White pearl onions arrive in July followed by red and gold. The pearl onion season runs through March.

Scallions are available year-round, peaking in May, June, and July and dipping somewhat in January and February. Leeks are available year-round with peaks in September, November, and in the spring. Shallots are a year-round crop.

Because there are so many growing areas, garlic is in steady supply year-round. However, July and August are the peak times for garlic, when California production is in full swing. From January to March garlic arrives from Argentina, from April to July from Mexico. Elephant garlic comes from Chile from February to June and the rest of the year from California and Oregon.

SELECTION, HANDLING & STORAGE

Sweet onions should be firm and free of bruises or soft spots. They should have thin, papery skins. Sweet onions like cool but not cold temperatures, about 50°F to 55°F with relatively low humidity as far as produce is concerned, about 65 to 70 percent. For this reason refrigeration is not normally recommended—hanging them in knotted pantyhose in a well-ventilated area is a favorite technique. However, the Vidalia Onion Committee says onions wrapped individually in foil will last as long as a year in the refrigerator.

Storage onions should have a firm, tight skin with no soft spots, blemishes, or sprouting. The skin will often have a brittle, papery feel. Store in cool, dry places, though as we said, the refrigerator is fine with us. Choose and store pearl and boiler onions in a similar fashion. Avoid onions with any sign of sprouting. They're old. If the onions at home show signs of sprouting, cut away the sprouts and use them immediately.

Both leeks and scallions should have bright green tops and firm white bottoms. Scallions can occasionally show evidence of slime, while the green tops on leeks may look withered from age or mangled from poor handling. Never buy leeks that have had their green parts trimmed. It's a good indication that the leeks are older than the retailer wants to let on.

Scallions like cool, moist conditions, as low as 32°F with high humidity. Store scallions away from odor-sensitive foods such as corn and mushrooms, which will absorb the odor of the onions. Store leeks in a similar manner. Remove any rubber bands and any damaged leaves and store in plastic bags in the crisper section of the refrigerator. They'll both last up to five days.

While we store scallions, leeks, and onions in the refrigerator, shallots are always kept at room temperature, preferably away from the stove or heater. Shallots will last several weeks this way. Even under these conditions, shallots don't have the effect on the eyes that onions do.

Garlic should have firm, tight bulbs that are plump with no signs of sprouting, shriveling, soft spots, or broken skin. Color is not an indicator of quality. Stored in a dark, cool, dry place with plenty of ventilation, garlic will last several weeks. The Fresh Garlic Association says that under optimum conditions, fresh garlic can be kept for a year. That's sort of like saying that technically you can travel at the speed of light. Try to use fresh garlic within a few weeks. If you can't, then you're not using enough garlic. Do not refrigerate unless the garlic has been peeled or chopped.

NUTRITION

One medium onion (about 148g, 5.3 ounces) contains 60 calories, 14g of carbohydrates, 3g of dietary fiber, 2g of protein, 20% of the DV for vitamin C, 4% for calcium, and 2% for iron. Onions are also a decent source of potassium (240mg).

The serving size for the DV of green onions is about one-sixth that of regular onions (25g, .9 ounces). However, if you compare the same amount of green onions and regular onions, green onions have more impressive nutritional statistics. In 1½ cups of chopped green onions (150g) you'd get 48% of the DV for vitamin C, 12% for vitamin A, twice the dietary fiber (6g) of regular onions and almost twice the potassium (420mg). This amount also contains 12g of carbohydrates and the same number of calories as regular onions.

Onions have been considered a tonic for many maladies going back thousands of years. We now have scientific confirmation that those ancient health claims associated with onions are true, and then some.

Onions, including chives, leeks, scallions, and shallots, are powerful antioxidants which combat a variety of diseases, including several forms of cancer. Shallots and yellow and red onions in particular are the best source of quercetin, one of the most potent antioxidants. It works through the immune system as an anti-inflammatory, antibacterial, antiviral, and antifungal agent. It also helps to keep arteries unclogged and lower overall blood cholesterol but raise "good" (HDL) cholesterol. It is effective against asthma, hay fever, chronic bronchitis, and diabetes. Quercetin also works as a sedative.

Garlic has had more myth and lore written about its salutary benefits than almost any food. And while it may not be the antidote for unrequited love, vampires, or baldness, it is, according to Jean Carper, author of *Food: Your Miracle Medicine* (HarperCollins, 1993), an all-around wonder drug. Garlic works as an antibiotic against various bacteria, intestinal parasites, and viruses. It lowers blood pressure and blood cholesterol. It contains numerous anticancer compounds. It strengthens the immune system, which helps to fight colds among other things. It helps relieve gas (in small doses; in larger doses it may promote gas in some people). It works as a diuretic, helps quell diarrhea, and acts as a decongestant, expectorant, and as an anti-inflammatory agent.

Since the effects of garlic vary depending on whether it is consumed cooked or raw, a combination of both forms is a good idea to get the maximum benefit.

YIELD

One medium onion will yield about 3 cups of onion rings, 2 cups coarsely chopped, and 1 1/2 cups finely chopped. One pound of leeks yields about 2 cups chopped. Nine small to medium scallions with green tops included will yield about 1 cup sliced. Two cloves of garlic yield 1 teaspoon chopped.

Tony's Tip

Restaurants usually buy large onions because they use a lot of them. If you use a lot of onions, buy larger sizes so you'll have less waste and less work. On the other hand, if you're always using a half or a third of an onion, maybe you're buying onions that are too large.

PREPARATION

We prefer to peel onions after they have been halved lengthwise, and the ends trimmed. It's much easier. Also, there are times when you've discovered after chopping half the onion that it's enough. The other half will stay fresher when stored with the skin on.

To chop an onion efficiently, place one of the halves, cut side down, on a cutting surface. Make two or three (depending on the size of the onion) horizontal cuts to the root end but not quite cutting all the way through the root. This will give you two or three stacked slices. Then, make even lengthwise vertical cuts down through the slices toward the root but again, not cutting through the root. Finally, cut crosswise down through the onion. The width between cuts is partially determined by how big a dice you want. When you get to the root end, you'll have a very small piece that can be dispatched with several quick cuts. Repeat with the other half.

(There is a theory that most of the tear-causing compounds are stored in the root end of the onion, which may explain why chopping that part last helps to minimize watery eyes.)

The food processor is not a bad choice, especially if you're chopping lots of onions. But it requires a little practice. You can't just turn on the machine and walk away. It only takes a few seconds to go from chopped onions to a soggy puree. Peel and quarter onions and place them in the bowl of the processor fitted with a metal blade. Then pulse (turn on and off) three times with each pulse lasting no more than one second. That will give you coarsely chopped onions. Scrape down the work bowl and repeat once or twice for more finely chopped onions. Even under the best of circumstances, onions chopped in a food processor will be "wetter" than those chopped by hand. But with some care, you can still achieve a desirable result.

To slice onions, put the peeled onion half cut side down. Cut crosswise into half moons as thin as you like. This shape is good for caramelizing as in onion soup.

For rings, you should peel the onion without halving it. Just be careful to get the onion as stable as you can on a cutting surface—and keep those fingers tucked in!

For pearl onions and shallots, soaking in warm water helps to remove the peel.

Leeks are notoriously sandy and must be washed thoroughly. First trim off the root and green tops. Then slit the leeks lengthwise. Rinse off the dirt between the layers under a running tap or swish the leek in a tub of water while holding it firmly so it doesn't fall apart. We like to separate the leaves in a flapping motion to make sure all the grit is removed.

Most of the time, leeks are cut crosswise into crescents before they are sautéed in butter or oil for a dish. If they are to be roasted or braised, the two halves can be left intact.

Scallions are prepared like leeks except dirt and grit are not an issue. Trim the roots and the green tops; we like to leave about an inch of green where it's fairly light green. Then cut crosswise into thin slices or halve lengthwise, then chop crosswise for smaller pieces.

Shallots can be chopped like an onion, in theory. But since they are so small, a chef's knife can be a bit cumbersome. Instead, try using a razor-sharp paring knife. Just follow the same procedure for dicing onions.

The standard method for peeling garlic first involves separating the cloves from the bulb. A good smash on the counter with the heel of your hand will do. Then put the side of a chef's knife (or the back of a wooden spoon) over a clove (or two) and pound with your fist. This will loosen the peel and begin to release some of the garlic's flavor. If you're doing a lot of cloves, or you want to keep the cloves whole without a lot of laborious hand work (obviously the smash routine won't do here), we recommend the Garlic Peeler by Élan, a wonderful gizmo that rubs off the peel using a rubber tube.

Older cloves will have sprouts that look like tiny scallions in the center. If they're obvious we pluck them out with the tip of a paring knife.

Don Christopher, the owner of Christopher Ranch, a major garlic processor in Gilroy, California, once told us, "The more you do to garlic, the more flavor is released." In other words, leaving cloves whole gives less garlic flavor than slicing, slicing less than chopping, and so on. Smashing and finely chopping cloves or putting them through a garlic press releases the maximum flavor. And if you're the old-fashioned type, try pounding garlic in a mortar and pestle to release a torrent of garlic flavor.

Conversely, to add just a whisper of flavor, gently crush a clove and put it in a vinaigrette, for example. Mix and let sit an hour. Then taste. Remove if there is just enough garlic flavor or let remain for a little longer. (Poaching garlic in water also tames its power.) Incidentally, we rarely use a garlic press because it takes too much time and is a pain to clean. But it does have the advantage of not having to peel the garlic first.

Need we tell you that garlic's pungency turns into mellow, sweet nuttiness when cooked? But be careful not to overcook. Garlic can easily burn and turn bitter. For this reason, in recipes that call for sautéing garlic with other ingredients such as onions, we usually cook the onions first, then add the garlic. To bake a whole head of garlic, cut off the top $1/4$ inch from the head as if you're giving the bulb a crew cut. Remove the papery outer layers, making sure you don't separate the cloves. Rub the whole head with olive oil, wrap in foil, and bake in a 350°F oven for about an hour.

Braised Ramps and Sausage

Normally we'd serve this dish over pasta. But ramps (wild mountain leeks) are such an American rural dish that rice seemed more appropriate. And we like Konriko Original Brown Rice of Louisiana to add to the country feel. It's a wonderfully fragrant and nutty rice that holds up well to the assertive ramps. Substitute some other pork product with the ramps, as long as you don't go too far. Ramp purists would probably use bacon.

Makes 3 servings

2 bunches ramps
1 link Italian sweet sausage, about 4 ounces
$^1/_2$ cup defatted Chicken Stock (page 9)
Kosher salt and freshly ground black pepper to taste
$2^1/_2$ cups cooked rice, approximately

1. Remove roots from ramps and separate bulbs from leaves. Chop bulbs coarsely. Stack the leaves and cut crosswise into $^1/_2$-inch-wide strips. Wash both thoroughly.

2. Remove sausage from casing and cook in a large skillet until browned. Put ramp bulbs into skillet and cook over medium-low heat until soft. Add leaves, stock, salt, and pepper and cook, covered, about 10 minutes, stirring a few times. Serve over rice.

Greek-Style Pizza with Red Onions

Raw red onions are ubiquitous in so-called Greek salads that one finds in gyros and souvlaki parlors. But cooked lightly they lend a nice flavor to this pizza.

Makes 2 to 4 servings

2¼ cups unbleached all-purpose flour
1 package quick-rising yeast such as
  Fleischmann's Rapid-Rise yeast
1 teaspoon kosher salt
1 teaspoon sugar
1 teaspoon extra-virgin olive oil
1 cup barely hot water at 125°F to 130°F
Olive oil cooking spray

1 medium red onion
One 14-ounce can artichoke hearts
15 kalamata olives or other Greek black
  olives
4 ounces feta cheese, crumbled
2 teaspoons crushed oregano, preferably
  Greek oregano

1. Put 2 cups of the flour, yeast, salt, and sugar in the bowl of a food processor. With the motor running, add olive oil and ¾ of the water. Add more water, 1 tablespoon at a time, until the dough forms a ball. Then process 30 seconds to knead. Spray a bowl with olive oil cooking spray, put the dough in the bowl, spray the top of the dough, and cover with plastic wrap and a towel. Set aside in a warm, draft-free area. (If mixing by hand, knead dough about 10 minutes before setting aside.)

2. While dough rises, preheat oven to 500°F. Peel and thinly slice onion. Cut artichoke hearts in sixths or eighths if large. Pit and cut olives in half or quarters if large. Chop or crumble feta.

3. After dough has doubled in size (about 20 minutes), punch down and roll out to a diameter of 14 inches for thin-crust pizza, 12 inches for thicker-crust pizza. Place on a pizza stone, pizza pan, or back of a baking sheet. Spread onion slices on the pizza, leaving a border of ½ inch all around. Top with artichoke hearts and olives. Sprinkle with cheese, then oregano. Spray edges with olive oil cooking spray.

4. Bake 12 to 15 minutes for thin crust, 3 to 5 minutes longer for thicker crust or until edges are crisp and bottom nicely browned.

Sam's Cooking Tip

Unlike the sharp, often unpleasant oregano available in most supermarket spice sections, Greek oregano has a wonderful floral aroma and sweet flavor. It is sold in Middle Eastern stores in dried bunches. When you need to use some, just take a sprig out of the bunch and crush the dried leaves between your fingers.

Coq au Vin

This is a slimmed down version of the French classic. Serve it over noodles or rice.

Makes 4 servings

16 small pearl onions

2 ounces prosciutto, chopped

2 teaspoons olive oil

3 tablespoons all-purpose flour

Kosher salt and freshly ground black
  pepper to taste

4 chicken breast halves (8 ounces each),
  skinned but still on the bone

2 shallots or 1 small onion, chopped

3 cloves garlic, chopped

$^1/_4$ cup brandy, or more red wine

1 cup dry red wine

$1^1/_2$ cups defatted Chicken Stock
  (page 9)

2 teaspoons tomato paste

1 tablespoon fresh thyme or 1 teaspoon
  dried

2 bay leaves

16 small, whole crimini or other small
  mushrooms

1 tablespoon arrowroot

2 tablespoons chopped fresh parsley

1. Put onions in a bowl with warm water for 20 minutes. Peel and set aside.

2. Meanwhile, cook prosciutto in a large, nonstick skillet over low heat until it becomes crisp. Remove to a Dutch oven or casserole with a cover.

3. Put oil in the same skillet over medium heat. Put flour in a pie plate with 1 teaspoon salt and $^1/_2$ teaspoon pepper. Coat breasts with flour mixture and shake off excess. Add chicken to skillet and brown well, about 5 minutes on each side. Do not crowd pan.

4. Add shallots and garlic to chicken and cook, stirring until both begin to brown, about 3 minutes. Add brandy and carefully ignite with a match. When flames die down, pour the contents of the skillet into the casserole with the prosciutto. Add red wine, stock, and paste to the skillet. Bring to a boil and stir with a wooden spoon, scraping up any bits on the bottom of the pan.

5. Add wine mixture to chicken along with thyme, bay leaves, mushrooms, and pearl onions. Season with salt and pepper to taste and cover. Simmer 30 minutes or until chicken and onions are tender.

6. Remove chicken to a platter. Mix arrowroot with 1 cup of the liquid in the pot and return it to the pot. Stir well and reduce liquid to thicken. Taste for seasonings and remove bay leaves. Pour sauce over chicken and noodles or rice. Sprinkle with parsley.

Sam's Cooking Tip

Flaming dishes isn't as dangerous as it may seem, but you need to take some precautions. Don't wear loose clothing. Keep your hair pulled back. Pour the brandy from a cup or ladle and not from the bottle. Use long-stemmed matches if you have them. Have a cover close by to dampen flames if they get out of hand.

Mashed Potatoes with Garlic and Anchovies

This dish is flavorful enough so you won't miss the normal addition of cream and butter.

Makes 4 to 6 servings

2 pounds russet or red-skinned potatoes
1$\frac{1}{2}$ teaspoons kosher salt
12 cloves garlic, peeled
1 cup skim milk

$\frac{1}{2}$ teaspoon finely minced anchovy fillets
   or anchovy paste
$\frac{1}{4}$ teaspoon freshly ground black pepper
1 tablespoon snipped chives

1. Peel potatoes if using russets and cut into 1$\frac{1}{2}$-inch chunks. Put potatoes in a pan with half the salt and the garlic. Add just enough cold water to cover. Bring to a boil and cook at a moderate boil about 20 minutes or until potatoes are easily pierced by a fork but not falling apart.

2. Drain potatoes and garlic. Return them to the pan over very low heat for a minute or two. Warm the milk with the anchovies in a small saucepan.

3. Put potatoes in the bowl of an electric mixer with a paddle attachment and mix on low speed, gradually adding milk, $\frac{1}{4}$ cup at a time. (You can also mash by hand or use a hand-held mixer or food mill. Do not use a food processor.)

4. After $\frac{3}{4}$ cup of milk has been added, check to see if it is the texture you desire. Add more milk if you want it looser and "creamier." Season with remaining salt and pepper. Put in a warmed serving bowl and sprinkle with chives.

Shrimp, Vidalia Onion, and Couscous Salad

This is a delicious hot-weather dish. Have it as a main course or part of a Mediterranean buffet with Greek Salad (page 100) and room-temperature Eggplant Parmesan (page 111).

Makes 4 servings as a main course, up to 8 as part of a buffet

1 pound medium shrimp (31 to 35 count)

$1/4$ teaspoon saffron mixed with $1/3$ cup white wine, Chicken Stock (page 9), or clam juice

One 10-ounce package of couscous (about $1^2/3$ cups)

1 medium Vidalia or other sweet onion, chopped, about 1 cup

One 15-ounce can chickpeas, rinsed and drained

1 jalapeño or other fresh chile pepper, seeded and minced

1 medium to large tomato, diced

$1/2$ cup fresh mint, chopped

$1/4$ cup extra-virgin olive oil

2 tablespoons lemon juice

Kosher salt and freshly ground black pepper to taste

Romaine or other lettuce for garnish

1. Bring 1 quart water to a boil. Add shrimp and cook 5 minutes. Skim off any scum, remove shrimp with a slotted spoon, and cool. Save 2 cups of the shrimp cooking water.

2. While shrimp are cooling add wine/saffron mixture to the 2 cups reserved shrimp water. Use this liquid to cook the couscous. (If package calls for more or less liquid, adjust accordingly.) Cool couscous, fluffing occasionally with a large fork.

3. Peel shrimp (devein, if you like) and put in a large bowl with onion, chickpeas, jalapeño, tomato, and mint. Add couscous and mix well.

4. Combine olive oil, lemon juice, salt, and pepper and pour over couscous mixture. Toss well and adjust seasonings as needed. Chill until ready to serve. To serve, line plates with lettuce and spoon out salad.

Clarence Birdseye, you spoiled us.

Thanks to your pioneering in frozen vegetables in

the 1920s you created a frozen pea that nine times

out of ten beats the pants off of fresh peas.

Don't get us wrong. There is still nothing like an

absolutely fresh pea stripped from its pod, then

boiled quickly and tossed with some sweet butter and salt. Nothing else is really needed.

But how often do we get that perfect pea? Most of the time the pods we buy are too old and that sweet pea has become starchy and dull. The old saw about putting a pot of water on to boil before you went out and picked your corn goes double for peas.

However, frozen peas don't have that problem. They are picked at the peak of ripeness and frozen immediately. Thus, they retain that wonderful pea sweetness and tenderness as well as a bright, verdant color that we never seem to achieve with the fresh peas we cook ourselves.

Peas take so well to freezing that by the mid-1950s less than 10 percent of the pea crop—at the time the second-largest vegetable crop in the country—was sold fresh. That ended what was called pea-time, the period from June to September when fresh peas were sold in local markets.

With a greater emphasis on farmer's markets we're getting more local and fresher peas than we did twenty years ago. But we'll probably never return to pea-time.

Clarence Birdseye, you rascal, you.

WHERE GROWN

With year-round supplies, California is the leading producer of peas. New York, South Carolina, Oregon, Idaho, Texas, New Mexico, Florida, Washington, New Jersey, and Virginia are also pea-producing states. Guatemala is the largest importer to the United States. Peas are also imported from Mexico, China, Honduras, and the Dominican Republic.

VARIETIES

Like beans, peas are divided into two categories: those with edible pods and those without them. The pea we know as the green pea,

English pea, and garden pea, falls into the latter category. As to specific varieties, most commercial peas are either called garden or English peas and that's that. Petit pois are not a variety of pea but merely green peas that have been picked before full maturity. Thus, they are smaller than normal green peas.

Snap peas look like miniature versions of the pods of green peas. The difference is that these pods are edible. Sugar snap and Sugar Daddy are the two varieties of snap peas, the latter being a cross between the green pea and the snow pea. In addition, the Sugar Daddy is a stringless sugar snap pea. However, even sugar snaps with strings don't necessarily need to be stringed before cooking. (See Preparation, page 195.)

Snow peas used to be seen only in Chinese restaurants. Now they're available everywhere. The pale green, edible pods are flat and wide with little bulges—the immature peas inside—rippling throughout the pod. There are often strings, but again, they need not be removed. Snow peas are also called sugar peas, China peas, and in French *mangetout,* meaning "eat all."

SEASONS

For green peas the peak period is January through June but supplies from local farmers may be available through the summer. Sugar snap peas peak from February through September, though they are available all year. Snow peas are available year-round with the peak period from November to March.

SELECTION, HANDLING & STORAGE

For green peas, your first assignment is to find a retailer who gets them in soon after they are picked. Better yet, seek out a farmer's market or roadside stand and ask when the peas were picked. The closer you are to the time of picking, the better.

That's at least half the work. The rest involves checking the pod, which should be firm, crisp, and bright green with a fresh appearance and a velvety touch. Tough, thick-skinned pods are an indication of overly mature peas. Also avoid pods that have poor color (such as gray specks or yellowing) or show any sign of decay or wilting. Don't buy peas that are already shelled because you never know when they were shelled; earlier than you'd like is a good guess. Don't even ask how long they'll last in storage.

Snow peas and snap peas should also have good color (light for snow, darker for sugar) and a firm crispness. The ideal size for snow peas is about 3 to 3½ inches long and about ¾ inch wide. For snap peas, the most desirable size is 2½ to 3 inches long.

Snap and sugar peas have a somewhat longer shelf life than green peas, up to three days, unwashed, in plastic bags under refrigeration as low as 33°F. But they should be used within a day or two. Snow peas like less humidity than sugar snap peas so take that into account in deciding where in the refrigerator to store them, or perforate the plastic bag you put them in.

NUTRITION

A 100g or 3.5-ounce serving of cooked green peas has 70 calories, 12g of carbohydrates, less than .5g of fat, 2g of dietary fiber, about 30% of the DV for vitamin C, about 10% for vitamin A, 10% for iron, and 2% for calcium. Peas are an excellent source of protein, with more than 5g protein per serving, a good source of folic acid, and a decent source of potassium (though the FDA does not have an official nutritional label for green peas).

Sugar and snow peas have a similar nutritional profile with some exceptions. On the plus side, they are somewhat higher in calcium and vitamin A as well as being lower (43 calories for 100g) in calories. On the minus side they have less copper, zinc, iron, potassium, and vitamin C.

YIELD

One pound of green peas in the pod yields about a cup when shelled. A pound of sugar snap or snow peas will feed four.

Tony's Tip

When selecting green peas, run your finger to the top of the pod to make sure the peas are not too large but fill up the whole pod. If the pod is not completely filled, the peas won't be as sweet as those in a full pod.

PREPARATION

Shelling green peas is somewhat time-consuming but not difficult. Do it in front of the television. As to cooking them, there are two, possibly three methods. One is steaming, one is boiling. And the boiling is divided into whether one salts the water or not. *Larousse Gastronomique* says to salt and James Beard, dean of American cookery, says not to salt. Steaming, of course eliminates the salting controversy.

In any event, the fresher the peas (and we know how difficult that is) the shorter the cooking time, about 5 to 10 minutes. After butter and salt, chives and mint are our favorite pea flavorings.

Sugar snap peas have strings, but whether or not they are removed is personal choice or habit, not an obligation. When we talked to Johna Dystra of Go West Distributing, a

California grower and shipper of sugar snap peas, she said she never strings them. The only thing that you may want to remove (and some growers already do this) is the calyx or cap at one end.

We agree with our friend Janet Fletcher, author of *More Vegetables, Please* (Harlow and Ratner, 1992), who, in addition to bemoaning the poor quality of fresh green peas, suggests boiling snap peas for about 3 minutes and refreshing them in ice water to set their bright color. Then they can be stir-fried with other vegetables, heated through on their own with butter and herbs or put into cold preparations such as pasta salads.

As with sugar snaps, snow peas have strings but they needn't be removed. Some have a calyx and that should be removed for aesthetic as well as practical reasons. A quick snap of the wrist, with or without a paring knife, will do it.

Snow peas are ideal for stir-fries or as a vegetable by themselves with perhaps some minced ginger, garlic, or hot pepper—or all three. Or they can be part of a stir-fry mélange with shrimp or strips of chicken or pork.

If you have some patience, or extra hands in the kitchen, try opening the pods of snow peas and piping in a cream cheese spread (with salmon perhaps) for an attractive hors d'oeuvre.

Bow-Tie Pasta with Peas and Prosciutto

Peas and prosciutto are a favorite combo with Italians. Yes, prosciutto is expensive, but you only need to use a little.

Makes 4 servings

1 tablespoon butter	1 cup shelled peas
$1/4$ cup chopped shallots	$1/2$ teaspoon nutmeg
2 ounces prosciutto, chopped	Kosher salt and freshly ground black
$1/2$ cup defatted Chicken Stock (page 9)	pepper to taste
12 ounces bow-tie (farfalle) pasta	$1/2$ cup grated Parmesan cheese

1. Bring a pot with 4 quarts of salted water to boil on the stove.

2. Put butter in a large skillet, preferably a wok, over medium heat. Cook shallots and prosciutto until shallots soften. Add Chicken Stock and continue to cook until liquid is reduced by half, about 5 minutes.

3. When pasta water boils, add pasta and cook until just beyond half done, about 7 minutes. Add peas and cook until peas and pasta are done, about 5 minutes more. Drain both in a colander.

4. Reheat shallot mixture and add pasta and peas. Season with nutmeg, salt, and pepper and toss. Turn off heat and add cheese. Toss again.

Sam's Cooking Tip

There are many types of prosciutto, but as with Chablis, the name alone doesn't guarantee success. Look for Prosciutto di Parma for quality. Domestic prosciutto is often salty with a less silky texture.

Sugar Snap Peas with New Potatoes

This is a delight when the first new potatoes come in.

Makes 4 servings

10 ounces sugar snap peas
Kosher salt
1 pound very small new potatoes
2 tablespoons butter

1 tablespoon chopped chives
2 tablespoons chopped fresh mint
Freshly ground black pepper to taste

1. Remove strings from peas. Put peas in boiling water with 1 teaspoon salt for 3 minutes. Drain and plunge into ice water until cold. Drain well.

2. Wash potatoes well and do not peel. If potatoes are not very small (no larger than golfball size), quarter or halve as necessary. Place in a steamer basket in a large pot and steam 15 to 20 minutes or until just tender.

3. In a large skillet or wok, melt butter over low heat until it begins to look nutty brown and smells like nuts. Add peas and potatoes, raise heat to medium, and toss well. Add chives, mint, and salt and pepper to taste. Toss again until well coated.

Risi e Bisi

Risi e bisi is a classic Venetian dish of rice and peas, a kind of soupy risotto that's a good first course or luncheon main dish.

Makes 4 servings

2 tablespoons butter
4 scallions, white and green parts, sliced
1 cup arborio rice
5 cups Chicken Stock (page 9)
1 cup shelled peas (about 1 pound unshelled)

2 tablespoons chopped fresh mint
Kosher salt and freshly ground black pepper to taste
¹/₃ cup grated Parmesan cheese

1. Heat butter in a large, heavy-bottomed saucepan. When hot, cook scallions until soft over medium heat. Add rice and stir.

2. Add half of the stock mixture, cover and cook 5 minutes over medium-low heat. Stir, add remaining liquid, and cook 5 minutes more. Add peas, stir, and cook until rice is tender, about 5 to 7 minutes more.

3. Add mint, salt, and pepper to taste. The dish should be soupy, though still quite thick. Pour into 4 soup plates. Sprinkle with cheese.

Snow Peas with Three Peppers

Freshly ground black pepper is the third pepper, in case you were wondering.

Makes 4 servings

1 tablespoon peanut oil
1 dried chile pepper
2 teaspoons cumin seeds
1 pound snow peas, trimmed

1 small red bell pepper, cut into thin
   strips
Kosher salt and freshly ground black
   pepper to taste

1. Put oil in a wok or large skillet over medium-high heat. Add chile pepper and cook a few minutes until color starts to darken.

2. Remove chile pepper and add cumin seeds. Stir a minute, raise heat to high, and add snow peas and bell pepper. Turn frequently and season with salt and black pepper. Cook until bell pepper and peas begin to soften, about 3 or 4 minutes.

When Columbus landed in the New World,

not only did he and his immediate followers misname

the natives they met, they stuck an erroneous and

confusing moniker on one of the vegetables.

Columbus was looking for a shorter route to the

countries of Asia that produced valuable spices

like black pepper, *Piper nigrum* botanically. But Columbus bumped into North and South America along the way. So, like a good politician, he declared victory. He called the natives Indians, even though he was farther away from India than he had been before he left Spain. And he named the local hot chiles "peppers" because they spiced up the bland food he and his sailors had been eating just the way black pepper did.

It took about two centuries for botanists to figure out that chiles and sweet peppers belong to a totally different botanical family than black pepper. That genus is called *Capsicum*. (To clear up one other confusion you'll note that chile is spelled with an *e* at the end, not an *i*. The latter is the name of a stew with meat, and sometimes beans, and is only related to the former by the fact that some of the versions contain copious amounts of hot peppers.)

But the confusion that Columbus created hasn't stopped people from using chile peppers all over the world. According to *Blue Corn and Chocolate* by Elisabeth Rozin (Knopf, 1992), "Chiles, in the few centuries since their discovery, have become the single most widely used spice in the world, eaten on a daily basis, it is reported, by at least one quarter of the world's adult population."

Columbus may have been politically incorrect, but who's going to argue when you're enjoying your favorite spicy Thai or Indian dish?

WHERE GROWN

California and Florida are the two largest bell pepper–producing states. Others include New Jersey, North Carolina, and Texas. Peppers are imported from Mexico and Holland. Mexico and California are the two largest hot pepper–growing areas.

VARIETIES

The familiar green bell pepper we know is really an immature pepper. Depending on the variety, that green pepper, if left on the vine, will eventually turn red, orange, purple, or even brown. However, the most common mature pepper is the red bell pepper. (Yellow peppers can be found in immature and mature varieties.) When bell peppers mature, their sugar content increases, so they're sweeter. They also develop more nutrients, primarily vitamins A and C.

California Wonder is the most popular type of bell pepper. It has four lobes or rounded sections and is about 4 inches high. Early Cal-Wonder, a hybrid and successor to California Wonder, is the second most widely planted variety. Other varieties include the Burlington, Yolo Wonder, Neopolitan, Chinese Giant, and Harris Early Giant. The Le Rouge Royale is a large red bell pepper developed by Sun World in Southern California. It can grow up to 10 inches long and weigh up to 2 pounds.

The **Italian sweet or frying pepper** is not a bell pepper or chile pepper. It is normally pale green but can also be orange to red. It is used almost exclusively in cooking, frequently fried or roasted, rather than in raw presentations. Sweet Italian peppers are also known as banana peppers and Cubanelles.

The variety in chile peppers today is remarkable. Though they vary in size, color, and flavor, one way to categorize chiles is by their level of heat as measured in Scoville heat units; the higher the number of Scoville heat units, the hotter the pepper. Here are the major varieties with the number of Scoville heat units in parentheses where appropriate. Note that depending on the grower, retailer, and part of the country, chiles may be called different names.

- **Anaheim** (1,000 to 1,500). Long (6 to 8 inches) and narrow, this light to medium green pepper roasts wonderfully and is the kind that often comes roasted and peeled in cans in the Mexican food section of supermarkets. It can be stuffed and used where mild chile flavor is called for. When mature it turns bright red. Also called a long green, long red, Texas, or New Mexico chile. When dried it is called a California or New Mexico chile.
- **Poblano** (2,500 to 3,000). The pepper of choice for stuffing as in *chiles rellenos,* this dark green chile has broad shoulders that taper to a point at the end. Also used for sauces. When dried it is called a mulato.
- **Pasilla** (3,000). Often confused with the poblano, the true pasilla is a long, dark green chile that tapers to a blunt end. It is interchangeable with the poblano in many instances. Mild to medium hot, it is used in tamales and quesadillas. Also called a *chilaca* chile, and when dried, a *negro* chile.
- **Jalapeño** (3,500 to 4,500). Perhaps the most widely used chile pepper, it's hot if you aren't used to chiles but medium if you're more experienced. The color is a medium to deep green with a bullet shape and meaty skin. Sometimes a jalapeño will have stripes called striations running lengthwise. These are generally older varieties but the quality is not affected. You'll also occasionally see red jalapeños, which, like red bell peppers, are merely mature versions of the pepper. A dried and smoked jalapeño is called a *chipotle.*
- **Serrano** (7,000 to 25,000). Similar in color to the jalapeño but about half to one-third the size and not as shiny. However, it is hotter. Rick Bayless, one of

the best proponents of Mexican cuisine in the country, says he uses serrano peppers over jalapeños because he believes jalapeños have been bred to be too mild and flavorless.
- **Cayenne** (35,000 to 40,000). More common dried and ground, this thin, tubular red pepper is occasionally available fresh. Curved, slightly wrinkled, and up to 4 inches in length, the cayenne may go under several other names such as a Thai, arbol, or bird.
- **Thai pepper** (70,000 to 80,000). Long and thin, this pepper is usually green but may be available red when fully mature. Also known as a bird chile.
- **Arbol** (15,000 to 30,000). More common when dried, it is bright green when immature, turning bright red at maturity. This sharp and hot pepper is slender and tubular, about 2 to 3 inches long. It is also known as a type of cayenne and in some places, a Thai or bird chile.
- **Habanero.** There are two types of this supremely hot pepper. The most common is the Scotch Bonnet (200,000 to 300,000). It is yellow orange to bright orange with a vary distinctive flavor if you use it judiciously and don't let the heat overpower you. The trademarked Red Savina habanero is even hotter (300,000 to 400,000), perhaps the hottest pepper available commercially.
- **Yellow Chile or Yellow Wax peppers** are conical with a pale yellow color and waxy look. They are sometimes called Yellow hot, Caribe, or Caloro. Heat varies.
- **Fresno.** Usually harvested when immature or pale green. But it also may appear when mature and bright red. Tapered like a yellow chile. Heat will vary.

SEASONS

Supplies of bell peppers from California, Florida, and Mexico overlap, ensuring a year-round supply and different peak periods. Florida peppers are available from November through July with peaks in November, December, April, and May. The California season runs from May through December with the peak occurring from June through October. Mexico's year-round production peaks from January through May.

The main types of chile peppers are generally available year-round. Some are more limited such as the Red Savina habanero, which is only available from August through November.

SELECTION, HANDLING & STORAGE

Bell peppers should have smooth, firm, glossy skin with no soft spots or shriveling. Generally the same is true for chile peppers.

Bell peppers like cool but not cold temperatures, ideally about 45°F to 50°F with good humidity. Since they are ethylene sensitive, they should not be stored near ethylene-producing food such as pears or apples. Chile peppers can tolerate more cold than bell peppers, as low as 38°F, with humidity somewhat less than for bell peppers.

Put peppers in plastic bags and they will keep up to five days in the refrigerator.

NUTRITION

One medium green bell pepper (148g, 5.3 ounces) contains 30 calories, 7g of carbohydrates, 2g of dietary fiber, 1g of protein, 8% of the DV for vitamin A, 190% for vitamin C, and 2% for iron and calcium. For a comparable serving of red bell peppers, vitamin A increases by a factor of 5 and vitamin C increases about 15%. Green and red bell peppers are fair sources of potassium while red bells alone are moderately high in folic acid.

Because of their high vitamin C content, bell peppers are high in antioxidants, which are beneficial to fighting everything from the common cold to heart and circulatory disease to cancer.

Pound for pound, or more likely ounce for ounce, chile peppers are higher in vitamins A and C than green bell peppers, and in some cases more than red bell peppers. But since you're less likely to eat the same volume of, say habaneros, as green bell peppers, that nutritional fact has to be put into perspective. One chile pepper, 45g or about one-third the serving size of a green bell pepper, contains 80% of the DV for vitamin A and 170% for vitamin C.

In addition to the antioxidant benefits of sweet peppers, chile peppers have other benefits courtesy of capsaicin, the compound that gives chiles their heat. Capsaicin acts as a painkiller and headache remedy. It speeds up metabolism, which helps to lose or maintain weight. It acts as a decongestant and expectorant. And capsaicin opens up sinus and air passages, something anyone who has eaten chiles can attest to.

YIELD

One medium bell pepper will yield 1 cup chopped. Depending on size, about three bell peppers will equal 1 pound. Because chile peppers vary significantly in size and heat, yields and amounts used will vary. But, for example, a jalapeño pepper will yield 4 minced teaspoons.

Tony's Tip

> *How do you put out the fire in hot chiles? Water only spreads the fire because capsaicin isn't soluble in water. The best two remedies are starch, like bread, potatoes, and rice, and dairy products such as yogurt, sour cream, and milk.*

PREPARATION

When preparing raw sweet peppers, remove the stem, seeds, and webbing or membrane before cutting into strips (and then diced, if desired) or rings.

Roasting peppers intensifies the flavor and eliminates the skin, which some find indigestible. There are several methods. One of the most frequently suggested is holding peppers over a gas flame until the pepper blisters and blackens all over. This is tedious and time consuming, especially if you want to do several peppers.

We suggest oven roasting, grilling, or broiling. Put peppers on a sheet pan lined with foil and roast in a hot (500°F) oven, under the broiler, or on the grate of a barbecue grill. The more intense the heat, the more often you need to turn the peppers. They should be blackened and blistered rather evenly when done. This can take anywhere from 15 to 30 minutes depending on which method you use. But you won't have to stand over a flame with a pepper at the end of a fork like a kid at a marshmallow roast.

When done, put peppers in a plastic bag or in a bowl covered with plastic wrap. When peppers are cool, remove stems, slip off the skins, and scrape off the seeds. Don't do this under running water. Water washes away flavorful oils and juices. Instead, let the water run and periodically rinse your hands as you work.

The roasted peppers can be used immediately, or put in olive oil, with garlic or other seasonings, or refrigerated for use in a number of dishes from pastas to frittatas. They also make a fine addition to any antipasto table.

Chile peppers can be roasted like sweet peppers, though they are a bit more difficult to handle because of their size. In raw preparations, the stems and seeds are usually removed. Since much of the heat is contained in the seeds and membranes, you can adjust the level of heat in a dish by removing all or part of them.

Unless you are scrupulous about cleaning work surfaces and hands with warm soapy water the second you have finished, you should wear gloves when you prepare hot peppers. These peppers can cause painful burns or nasty irritations when hands and fingers that have come in contact with them touch eyes and other sensitive parts of the body. Because they are thinner and adhere to hands more tightly, gloves that physicians use are more practical than kitchen gloves.

Treat hot peppers like salt. When too much is put in a dish, it's very hard to remove. By all means experiment with substituting one kind of chile for another, as long as you understand heat differences.

Both sweet and hot peppers can be frozen once they have been roasted, skinned, and seeded. They can also be frozen without any preparation, save seeding and slicing, but the texture will be a bit wimpy.

Scallops on a Ragout of Sweet Peppers

This makes a nice, light, summer entrée with crusty French bread.
If you want to bulk things up a bit, put it over rice or pasta.

Makes 4 servings

1^1/$_2$ tablespoons extra-virgin olive oil

1 each red, yellow, and green bell
pepper, cored, seeded, and cut into
^{1}/$_4$-inch-wide strips

1 small to medium onion, thinly sliced

2 cloves garlic, minced

2 bay leaves

Kosher salt and freshly ground black
pepper to taste

1 pound sea scallops

^{1}/$_2$ cup white wine or clam juice

2 tablespoons chopped fresh parsley

1. Heat 1 tablespoon of oil in a large skillet or wok. Add peppers, onion, garlic, and bay leaves and cook, covered, over medium-low heat 15 to 20 minutes until peppers are very soft. Season with salt and pepper and keep warm.

2. Meanwhile, remove the white strip of muscle or "hinge" from the side of each scallop and cut scallops as necessary to ensure uniform size.

3. In another skillet, heat remaining oil until very hot. Add scallops and cook, stirring, until they begin to firm up and are just browned, about 2 minutes. Remove to a warm plate with a slotted spoon and add wine to the skillet. Raise heat and cook until reduced by half. Add scallops to warm and season with salt and pepper. (If using clam juice instead of wine, reduce the amount of salt somewhat.)

4. Remove bay leaves and put ^{1}/$_4$ of the pepper mixture on each of 4 plates, then top with scallops. Sprinkle with parsley.

Sam's Cooking Tip

Sea scallops are larger and less expensive than bay scallops. However, I still prefer sea scallops because they have fuller flavor and hold up better in cooking. Unfortunately, unlike the smaller bay scallops, they aren't uniform in size and require cutting so that all the pieces cook evenly.

Hot and Sweet Pepper Sauce

This is a spicy hot dish but not overpowering. However, if you're sensitive to hot peppers, you may want to cut down to just one. Serve over pasta or grilled meats.

Makes about 2 cups, enough for about 4 servings of pasta

2 medium-large red bell peppers
1 medium-large green bell pepper
2 jalapeño peppers or a combination of jalapeño and other fresh hot chile such as serrano
1 tablespoon extra-virgin olive oil
1 medium onion, chopped
2 cloves garlic, chopped
$^3/_4$ cup defatted Chicken Stock (page 9), approximately

1 tablespoon chopped fresh basil or 1 teaspoon dried
Kosher salt and freshly ground black pepper to taste
8 kalamata, gaeta, or other black olives, pitted and quartered lengthwise
1 tablespoon chopped fresh parsley (only if dried basil used)

1. Roast, peel, and seed peppers as in Preparation, page 205. Cut into thin strips.

2. Meanwhile, heat oil in a saucepan or deep skillet and sauté onion over medium heat until soft, 4 or 5 minutes. Add garlic and peppers and cook 5 minutes. Add $^1/_4$ cup stock and cook another 5 minutes.

3. Put mixture in a food processor with $^1/_4$ cup of the remaining stock. Pulse until you get a mildly chunky texture. Pour back into the saucepan. Rinse out the bowl of the processor with the last $^1/_4$ cup of stock. Add the remaining stock, the basil, salt, black pepper, olives, and, if needed, parsley.

4. Cook gently about 10 minutes. Adjust seasonings as necessary.

Pan Bagna

Pan bagna—literally "bathed bread"—is one of the world's great sandwiches and a favorite of ours for picnics because the longer it sits, the better it gets (within reason, of course). Feel free to alter the stuffing with things such as artichoke hearts, cucumbers, hard-boiled eggs, or leftover grilled fish such as tuna or swordfish instead of the canned. Anchovies, preferably the whole, salt-packed variety, are also a common ingredient.

Makes 4 servings

4 large cloves garlic, pressed or chopped

$1/4$ cup extra-virgin olive oil

1 French baguette or similar Italian loaf, about 16 inches long and 3 inches wide

1 or 2 tablespoons chopped basil or parsley

One $6^{1}/_{2}$-ounce can water-packed albacore tuna

12 black olives, preferably oil cured, pitted and halved

2 tablespoons large capers, drained

1 large red bell pepper, roasted, seeded, and cut into thin strips (see Preparation, page 205)

1 small red onion, cut into very thin rings, soaked in ice water 30 minutes, and drained

2 ripe medium tomatoes, thinly sliced

Kosher salt and freshly ground black pepper to taste

$1/2$ teaspoon *herbes de Provence* (see tip below)

1. In a small bowl, mix the garlic and oil and set aside 30 minutes or more while you prepare the remaining ingredients (or steep 10 minutes over very low heat). Halve the bread lengthwise and scoop out some of the fluffy insides.

2. Strain garlic oil through a fine sieve or strainer, pressing the garlic with the back of a spoon to squeeze out all juices. Then brush each side of the bread with the garlic oil. Sprinkle the top half with the basil or parsley.

3. Mix the tuna, olives, and capers in another bowl and spread evenly on the bottom of the bread. Then top with bell pepper, onion, and tomatoes. Season with salt and pepper, then sprinkle with *herbes de Provence*, crushing the herbs between your fingers as you do.

4. Wrap well with aluminum foil. Put on an oval dish and weight down with cutting board topped with cans or some other handy weights. Refrigerate overnight. (The easiest way to serve is to cut portions right through the foil, then unwrap.)

Sam's Cooking Tip

Herbes de Provence *is a common herb mixture used in France. If you can't find it in specialty markets (it's often sold in a small beige crock), you can reasonably approximate it with two parts each thyme and marjoram, and one part each oregano and summer savory.*

Cold Sweet Pepper Soup with Sage

The hue of this remarkably simple dish will vary depending on the variety of sweet peppers used. We like a combination of red, yellow, and orange.

Makes 4 servings

1 tablespoon butter
1 medium onion, chopped
2 pounds red, or a combination of
   red, yellow, and orange bell peppers,
   roasted, peeled, and seeded (as in
   Preparation, page 205)

1 quart defatted Chicken Stock (page 9)
Kosher salt and freshly ground black
   pepper to taste
2 to 3 teaspoons fresh sage, finely
   chopped
1 cup evaporated skim milk

1. Put butter in a large saucepan or small Dutch oven, preferably with a heavy bottom, and melt butter over medium heat. Add onion and cook until softened, about 3 or 4 minutes.

2. Dice peppers and add to the pan. Cook a few minutes, stirring—do not let onion or peppers brown—and then add the Chicken Stock.

3. Bring to a boil and simmer gently 30 minutes. Puree in a food processor or food mill. Add salt, pepper, 2 teaspoons of the sage, and the milk and return to the pan. Cook 10 minutes more without boiling. Adjust seasonings and chill.

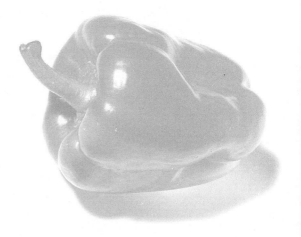

potatoes

When is a potato not a potato? When it's

a sweet potato.

Potatoes, *solanum tuberosum,* are members of

a totally different family from sweet potatoes,

which are in the morning glory family. The sweet

potato probably got linked up as a potato with the

corruption of the word *batata,* the Indian word for sweet potato.

And while we're on the subject of confusion, when is it a yam and when is it a sweet potato? Yams are in the lily family, a totally different botanical family from sweet potatoes. In addition, sweet potatoes are not even from the same part of the plant. Sweet potatoes are the roots of the plant, whereas yams are rhizomes, creeping stems that grow horizontally at or under the surface of the soil. (Potatoes are tubers.)

There are more differences. Yams are moister and much sweeter than sweet potatoes. Yams are larger, too, with some surpassing 30 pounds.

How did all this get started? According to the U.S. Sweet Potato Council, it began with African slaves calling sweet potatoes *nyami,* their word for a starchy, edible root. Perhaps they were recalling the yams of their continent, which had been grown in Africa for thousands of years and had some physical resemblance to sweet potatoes.

Elizabeth Schneider, author of *Uncommon Fruits and Vegetables* (HarperCollins, 1990), also points to the 1930 introduction of a very sweet, orange-fleshed sweet potato. Growers decided to call it a Louisiana yam to distinguish it from the more common white sweet potato. The ploy worked and retailers obliged by mislabeling these as yams ever since.

What makes the confusion even worse is that this orange sweet potato isn't even a real sweet potato but a boniato. But for our purposes, we'll consider that familiar orange, er, thing, a sweet potato or we'll all go crazy.

WHERE GROWN

When you think of potatoes, you think Idaho. And the reason, in addition to very good marketing, is the fact that Idaho ships more potatoes, by a factor of three, than the next leading state, California. Washington is a solid number three. Other large potato-producing states, in descending order, are Colorado, Oregon, Wisconsin, Maine, and North Dakota. Most potato imports come from Canada.

North Carolina is the largest producer of sweet potatoes followed by Louisiana and California.

VARIETIES

In 1994, per capita consumption of potatoes was 138.3 pounds, which works out to about a potato a day according to the National Potato Board. One in four restaurant meals that Americans eat includes potatoes. At home, Americans prefer baked potatoes 34% of the time to 28% for mashed and 15% for french fries.

According to the Snack Food Association, during the summer of 1994 Americans consumed more than 605 million pounds of potato chips. In the west central region of the United States, potato chips were most popular, followed by the Southeast. New England consumed the smallest amount of potato chips.

The **Russet Burbank** is the workhorse of potatoes. Oblong and russet brown in color with a netted or somewhat rough skin, it is primarily used for baking and french fries because its high starch content makes it turn fluffy when cooked. Other varieties of the Russet that give the name more versatility in boiling, mashing, and roasting include the Russet Norkotah, Centennial Russet, and new Russets such as the HiLite Russet, Frontier Russet, and Ranger Russet.

The general category of **round red potatoes** is distinguished by a rosy red skin and white flesh. The main red potatoes are the red Norlands (there are a few varieties), Pontiac, Red Lasoda, Sangre, and Larouge. Less common are the Chiefton, Viking, and Red Ruby. These can be used for any cooking purpose, but their waxy texture makes them preferred for boiling. However, try them unpeeled, mashed, and in potato salads for a different look.

Another group is called **round whites,** the Superior being a good example. Light to medium brown in color, this potato is an all-purpose potato used mostly for boiling and baking. Long whites such as the White Rose are grown mostly in California in spring and summer. They have an oval shape with a thin, light tan, almost translucent skin and are good for boiling and roasting as well as in potato salads.

One of the significant potato developments in the past decade has been the popularity of **yellow-fleshed potatoes.** Whether illusion or fact, their yellow flesh does seem richer and less in need of butter. Yukon Gold is the best-known name of yellow-flesh potatoes. Also look for Yellow Finn or Finnish. Steam, roast, or mash them.

Blue potatoes are still somewhat of a novelty, though they've been around for thousands of years. The outside is deep blue or purple and the flesh ranges from dark blue to white. To preserve their color, try microwaving them.

There are so many other potato varieties, an entire book is needed to do them justice. One of our favorites is the Fingerling, which is about the length of your pinkie and wonderful for roasting. Another is the pinkish Desiree, good for roasting and steaming.

Among sweet potatoes, the top varieties are Beauregard, Jewel, Hernandez, and Garnet. The uniformly shaped Beauregard, which accounts for half the U.S. sweet potato production, has firm stringless flesh. (Some sweet potatoes left in storage until March or April will tend to become stringy. The Beauregard is less likely to do so.)

The Hernandez is a fairly new variety developed in North Carolina for its uniform size and good storage capabilities. It has soft, deep orange flesh and russet skin. The purple-skinned, twisting Garnet also has a soft flesh inside and a very sweet taste. The Yellow Jersey has a tan skin and pale yellow flesh.

Retailers will often refer to two types of sweet potatoes as dry and moist, though those terms do not accurately reflect moisture content. Moist varieties, such as the Jewel, tend to have a deep orange flesh and darker, reddish brown skins. These are the ones most often mislabeled as yams. They have a higher starch content and are thus sweeter when cooked. The dry, such as the Yellow Jersey, have less sweet flavor and may also be more fibrous.

Both types of sweet potatoes are cured—that is, they are put into warm, moist rooms—for a few days. This gives them a darker color on the outside and helps to convert their starch to sugar, making them sweeter when cooked as well as giving them a smoother texture. Generally, only sweet potatoes harvested after October are cured.

SEASONS

Supplies from Idaho and Washington are consistently available throughout the year. They are also available year-round from California, though peak production from that state occurs in June and July. Maine potatoes are available from September to June, Colorado's October through April, and Wisconsin's August through May. The season for Minnesota's Red River Valley, a large producing area, runs from

September to June. Yukon Gold potatoes from Michigan are available from August to early March.

Despite their association with Thanksgiving and Christmas, sweet potatoes are available year-round, though there are usually peak supplies from September through January and lulls in June and July.

SELECTION, HANDLING & STORAGE

Potatoes, regardless of their variety, should be firm and relatively smooth with good color. They should have few eyes, no cuts, dark, or soft spots, and no wrinkles or wilted skin. Potatoes that have a green tint have been exposed to light. If you happen to notice some green at home, cut it away when preparing the potatoes.

Russet Burbanks in particular should have a good oval shape, nice russet brown color, and net-textured skin.

There is a tendency to think that all red or all small potatoes are new. New potatoes are potatoes that have just been dug up, regardless of size, though they are often small. The best way to know if you have a new potato is to examine the skin. It should be papery and thin enough to easily rub off with a decent scrubbing.

Seek out these potatoes from late spring through summer at local markets. Don't be put off by their often prosaic appearance. Simply steamed and tossed with butter, salt, and maybe some fresh chives, they're heaven.

Potatoes like cool (45°F to 50°F), humid (but not wet) surroundings. But refrigeration can turn the starch in potatoes to sugar and may tend to darken the potatoes when cooked. So they are best kept in the coolest, nonrefrigerated part of the house, away from light and well ventilated. Under ideal conditions they can last up to three months this way. But more realistically, figure three to five weeks.

When buying sweet potatoes, select those that are firm and free of blemishes or decay. Choose uniform sizes that are thick in the middle and taper at both ends for easier handling and to minimize waste. Since sweet potatoes bruise easily, they should be handled with care. Store sweet potatoes as you would regular potatoes, though at slightly warmer temperatures, between 55°F and 65°F. They'll last four to six weeks.

NUTRITION

One medium potato (148g, 5.3 ounces) has 100 calories and contains 26g of carbohydrates, 3g of dietary fiber, 4g of protein, 45% of the DV for vitamin C, 2% for calcium, and 6% for iron.

Potatoes are the best source of potassium among the major vegetables, a single serving supplying 720mg. Potatoes contain glutathione (white potatoes only) and protease, both significant cancer fighters. They may relieve constipation and, conversely, diarrhea as well. (However, in some people potatoes can contribute to irritable bowel syndrome.)

Sweet potatoes are even more nutritious than potatoes. In fact, they are one of nature's most nutritious vegetables. Nutrition writer Jean Carper calls them, "a blockbuster source of the antioxidant beta-carotene, linked to preventing heart disease, cataracts, strokes, and numerous cancers."

Sweet potato power comes from its huge amount of vitamin A, the precursor of beta-carotene. A medium sweet potato (130g, about 4.6 ounces) contains 440% of the DV for vitamin A, as well as 30% of the DV for vitamin C, and 2% each for calcium and iron. A serving also contains 130 calories, 33g of carbohydrates, 4g of dietary fiber, and 2g of protein. Though they have less than half the potassium of regular potatoes, sweet potatoes still have a good amount at 350mg.

YIELD

Three medium potatoes will equal about a pound. A pound of peeled potatoes yields 3 cups sliced, 2¼ cups diced, 2 cups mashed, and 2 cups cut for french fries. Three medium sweet potatoes are also about a pound and will yield about 2 cups when mashed.

> If you do store potatoes in the refrigerator, you can reverse the effects of the cold temperature by bringing the potatoes completely to room temperature before you prepare them.

PREPARATION

The guidelines for which potato is best for which dish are to be loosely followed at best. For example, as strange as it may seem, the Russet baking potato is considered to be the ideal potato for mashed potatoes because of its high starch content, allowing for maximum absorption of cream and butter, which, we

suspect, are the real reasons people like mashed potatoes anyway.

An increasing number of chefs have opted for red-skinned potatoes, very often mashed with skins on. We've tried several different spuds, including some organics from California, and have found that Russets and small red-skinned potatoes work equally well for mashed potatoes.

Potatoes cook well in the microwave, about 5 minutes at full power for two good-size potatoes, about 45 minutes less than baking them at 400°F. In addition to chives, parsley and dill go well with potatoes.

Because sweet potatoes are so high in nutrition and sweet enough to obviate the need for gobs of butter, we'd like to see more people bake them like Russets. (They're also more nutritious with skins on.) For this you'll need somewhat smaller sweet potatoes that are uniform in size. Dress them with just a dab or no butter and a smidgen of brown sugar or maple syrup. We think many people don't like sweet potatoes because far too many cooks have sweetened them to death.

Try them with roast pork. Sweet potatoes should also be considered for oven roasting, purees, and soups. They naturally go well with other sweet vegetables such as parsnips and carrots. But they can also handle assertive flavoring such as garlic, sage, rosemary, allspice, nutmeg, mace, and cinnamon.

Slow-Roasted Mashed Sweet Potatoes

The best sweet potatoes we've ever eaten were cooked by Scott Peacock, chef of the Horseradish Grill in Atlanta. Scott's method is absurdly simple: slow roasting to bring out maximum flavor and the barest of seasonings.

Makes 6 servings

3 pounds sweet potatoes
1 tablespoon butter, softened
$1/2$ teaspoon ground cardamom
Kosher salt and freshly ground black pepper to taste
1 to 2 tablespoons brown sugar

1. Put the potatoes on a baking sheet in a 300°F oven for 2 hours. Remove, scoop out the flesh, and mash or puree (but not in a food processor).

2. Add butter, cardamom, salt, pepper, and 1 tablespoon of the brown sugar. Mix well and taste. Add remaining sugar if desired. (Can be made ahead and reheated in a double boiler or microwave oven.)

Sam's Cooking Tip

If you're using a food mill, you don't have to peel the cooked sweet potatoes. Just cut them in chunks and put them through the mill. The skins will stay behind.

Spanish Potato Tortilla

Eggs have gotten a bad rap in recent years because of their cholesterol. But used judiciously, they can be the basis for a fine main dish, especially when they're used as a binder for vegetables as in this version of the Spanish tortilla or omelet (not to be confused with the Mexican bread).

Makes 4 servings

Olive oil cooking spray

2 medium potatoes, peeled and cut into
  $1/2$-inch dice

1 small onion, peeled and cut into
  8 wedges

Kosher salt and freshly ground black
  pepper to taste

1 teaspoon sweet paprika

6 eggs

$1/2$ cup each frozen green peas and
  lima beans, cooked

1. Preheat oven to 500°F. Spray a sheet pan with olive oil cooking spray. Add potatoes and onion, but keep separate. Season both with salt and pepper and sprinkle the potatoes with paprika. Cook about 15 minutes, until the onions begin to char and soften. Remove and coarsely chop. Cook the potatoes about 5 minutes more or until they become tender. Toss a few times to cook evenly.

2. Meanwhile, beat eggs in a mixing bowl and season with salt and pepper. Add peas and lima beans. When the potatoes and onion are done, add them to the egg mixture. Combine all ingredients well.

3. Turn oven to broil. Spray a cast-iron skillet with olive oil cooking spray. Heat skillet over medium heat. Just before it smokes, add egg mixture. With a wooden spoon gently push the eggs a few times as if making scrambled eggs. When the eggs are about half set, put the pan under the broiler. Cook about 90 seconds, turning the pan to cook evenly. When just set—be careful not to overcook—remove and let cool until warm or room temperature.

Sam's Cooking Tip

Potatoes can soak up a fair amount of oil but in this dish, instead of being fried in lots of olive oil, they're baked in a hot oven, coated only with a small amount of olive oil cooking spray.

Mussel and Potato Salad

Makes 4 servings

20 to 24 mussels

$1/3$ cup dry white wine

10 small to medium red-skinned potatoes, about $1^1/2$ pounds, scrubbed but
not peeled

1 red bell pepper, roasted, peeled, and
seeded (see page 205)

10 black, oil-cured olives, pitted and
halved

2 teaspoons chopped fresh marjoram
or 1 teaspoon dried

1 medium to large tomato, cored and cut
into 12 wedges

1 small, mild red onion, halved lengthwise and cut into thin crescents

2 tablespoons extra-virgin olive oil

2 tablespoons balsamic vinegar

Kosher salt and freshly ground black
pepper to taste

2 tablespoons chopped chives

1. Scrub the mussels well under cool running water, removing "beards" (the fibrous tuffs that protrude). Discard any that do not open.

2. Put them in a large saucepan with the wine, cover, and put over high heat. Remove them as soon as they open (8–10 minutes) and place in a bowl. Discard any that do not open. Strain remaining liquid in the pot through cheesecloth and set aside.

3. Put potatoes in a steamer basket in a large pot with 1 inch of water. Bring to a boil and steam, covered, for 20–25 minutes, or until tender, then cool and cut into $1/2$-inch cubes.

4. Cut bell pepper into $1/2$-inch squares and put in a bowl. Remove mussels from their shells and add to the bell pepper along with the potatoes, olives, marjoram, tomato, and red onion.

5. In a small bowl, combine oil, vinegar, salt, and pepper with 2 tablespoons of the reserved mussel broth. Pour over mussel-potato mixture and stir. Sprinkle with chives.

Sam's Cooking Tip

There are two kinds of mussels generally available in the United States: the Prince Edward Island variety and the green-lipped New Zealand. The former are smaller, cheaper, and more strongly flavored (fishier). The latter are larger, more expensive, and milder.

Spicy Oven-Roasted Potatoes

When this is done right, the potatoes come out crisp on the outside and fluffy on the inside. The key is to have them at just the right size, coated with just enough oil, and roasted in a hot oven.

Makes 4 servings

1 teaspoon paprika
$^{1}/_{2}$ teaspoon turmeric
1 teaspoon freshly ground cumin
1 teaspoon kosher salt
1 pound small potatoes, about the size
of golf balls

$1^{1}/_{2}$ tablespoons hot pepper oil (you can
substitute plain oil—if so, use hot
paprika instead of regular and/or add
$^{1}/_{4}$ teaspoon cayenne pepper to seasoning mix)
Olive oil cooking spray

1. Preheat oven to 500°F. Combine paprika, turmeric, cumin, and salt in a small dish. Set aside.

2. Cut the potatoes in half and put in a mixing bowl. Add oil and toss well to coat. Add seasonings and toss again.

3. Spray a shallow roasting pan or cooking sheet with olive oil cooking spray. Spread out potatoes evenly on the pan and put in the oven. Cook 15 to 18 minutes or until easily pierced with a paring knife. Shake once or twice during cooking to cook evenly.

Potatoes with Peppers and Onions

Fried potatoes sound fattening, but this dish uses only a tablespoon of oil.

Makes 4 servings

1 tablespoon olive oil

1 medium green bell pepper, seeded and
cut into thin strips

1 small to medium onion, thinly sliced

4 medium red potatoes, washed and
thinly sliced

Kosher salt and freshly ground black
pepper to taste

Pinch hot pepper flakes

2 bay leaves

1. Heat oil over medium heat in a large, heavy-bottomed skillet. Layer half the pepper, then half the onion, and half the potatoes, seasoning each layer with salt, pepper, and a pinch of hot pepper flakes. Repeat. Stick the bay leaves among the vegetables.

2. Reduce heat to medium low. Cover and cook about 25 minutes or until potatoes are soft. Stir every 5 minutes with a wide spatula.

radishes

The cruciferous family of vegetables has gotten a lot of good press over the past several years because of the numerous health benefits attributed to it. But somehow kale, cabbage, and broccoli have gotten all the glory, and one of the members, the radish, has been left in the cold.

Didn't know that radishes were a cruciferous vegetable? Neither did we until we started doing this book. The cruciferous (also called mustard) family, incidentally, is so-designated because all the members have cross-shaped flowers.

The word *radish* comes from the Latin *radix,* which became *raedic* in Old English and finally radish. The botanical name is *Raphanus sativus.* Raphanus comes from the Greek, meaning "quick appearing," though it has been loosely translated to mean "easily reared," a reference to the fact that radishes germinate quickly and grow in many climates.

WHERE GROWN

California is the major producer of bunched red radishes, those with their greens attached, secured with rubber bands or twist ties. Topped, bagged, or "cello" radishes, those whose greens have been clipped and that have been put in small plastic bags, are produced in more than thirty states. Florida is the second-largest producer overall.

VARIETIES

The major type of radish is the familiar red globe, with sizes that vary from that of a marble to larger than a golf ball. Varieties include the Cherry Belle, Red Devil, Red Prince, Scarlet Globe, Red Silk, and Fuego.

Increasing in availability because of our burgeoning Asian population and Asian-influenced cuisine is the daikon, Japanese, or Oriental radish. It is large and white, like a big, fat, white carrot. (They can be huge, as much as 50 pounds, but most commercially available ones are about $1\frac{1}{2}$ to 2 pounds.) As with the red radish, it is occasionally sold with the green tops (mostly in Asian markets). It is slightly hotter than a red radish, particularly in spring and summer. If you've ever eaten sushi or sashimi, it was likely accompanied by a shredded daikon salad.

Black radishes, sometimes called winter radishes, look more like large, dark turnips than radishes but can be used like either vegetable. The interior is white and drier than red radishes, and the flavor is pungent and sharp, almost as powerful as horseradish (which is also a member of the mustard family). There is also a baby version of the black radish.

Other varieties of radishes are considered specialty items with very limited production. The Sparkler, a favorite of home gardeners, is distinguished by a pronounced white tip. The White Icicle looks exactly the way it sounds and is about $4\frac{1}{2}$ to $5\frac{1}{2}$ inches long. The California Mammoth White is about 7 to 8 inches long, 2 to 3 inches in diameter with a mildly pungent flesh.

SEASONS

The major varieties of radishes are available year-round. Peak supplies occur from March to May. Daikon and black radishes are available year-round from California, but black radishes may be more in evidence in the winter and early spring.

SELECTION, HANDLING & STORAGE

Red globe radishes are typically sold two ways: in plastic bags with the tops removed and in bunches with their greens. We highly recommend the latter for two reasons. First, you can readily see how fresh the radishes are by the quality of the greens, which should be bright, green, and fresh looking, much like the tops of beets. Second, those greens are edible, quite tasty in fact, and nutritious.

When you buy radishes with green tops—varieties such as the Sparkler or White Icicle are usually sold this way—immediately separate the two when you get home. The radishes will last a week or more in plastic bags in the crisper section of the refrigerator, the greens only a few days. Keep both well chilled.

If you're forced to buy them in plastic bags, the red radishes themselves should be firm when given a gentle squeeze. If they yield to pressure, they're likely to be fibrous. They should be smooth and well formed with no cracks and good color.

Daikon radishes should be smooth, firm, and bright, almost gleaming. They get flabby quite easily, so they should be kept in plastic bags in the refrigerator for several days.

Unlike red radishes, black radishes should be purchased with roots and greens trimmed because they draw moisture away from the vegetable. Otherwise they should be inspected as you would red or white radishes. They'll last forever in the refrigerator as long as they are not too damp. A perforated plastic bag is a good wrapper.

NUTRITION

A single serving of seven red radishes (83g, about 3 ounces) contains 15 calories, 3g of carbohydrates, 1g of protein, 30% of the DV for vitamin C, and 2% for iron. Red radishes are also a decent source of potassium (230mg).

In many nutritional areas white or Asian radishes and the red radishes are similar. However, red radishes contain a few nutrients that white radishes do not such as magnesium, pantothenic acid, vitamin B_6, folic acid, zinc, and copper.

YIELD

A good-size bunch of red radishes will weigh about $3/4$ pound with greens and yield about $1^1/2$ to $1^2/3$ cups sliced. (A bunch normally contains a dozen radishes.)

Tony's Tip

In addition to making radishes crisper, putting radishes in ice water for a few hours removes some of their pungency.

PREPARATION

With some exceptions noted below, greens should be removed from radishes. Roots are always removed. Use the greens as you would hearty salad or cooking greens like arugula, kale, or beet greens.

Radishes are one of the better vegetable garnishes. A rose can be made by slicing a strip down four sides, not quite to the bottom of the radish. Then put it in ice water to open. Another common method is to slice a thin layer off the top, then make six or so parallel cuts down to but not through the bottom. Turn the radish 90° and make six more cuts at right angles to the first. Put in ice water to open.

Red radishes are good, carved or not, on relish trays. The white-tipped Sparkler is particularly pretty. If the greens are in good shape, leave some of them on.

Black radishes should be washed thoroughly before being cooked or put into salads, but they need not be peeled. Food authority Elizabeth Schneider points out that for radishes that are "diced or cut into julienne, the black edging, tiny and tidy, is most attractive." Schneider also suggests salting and weighing down sliced, chopped, or shredded black radish (with 1 teaspoon salt per $1^1/4$ cups vegetable) for an hour to remove some of its sharpness.

Daikon should be peeled like a carrot before being sliced or shredded. Unlike carrots, however, they cook rather quickly. They're fine in stir-fries, but we like them better raw, shredded in salads, or pickled.

Radish and Broccoli Slaw

Are you one of those people who buys the precut broccoli florets because you don't know what to do with the stems? Or worse yet, you buy whole bunches of broccoli and discard the stems? Shame on you! There's actually more flavor in those stems, once you get past the woody skin.

Makes 4 servings as a side dish

Stems from one large bunch about
 1¹/₂ pounds broccoli, peeled
4 radishes, trimmed
2 medium carrots, trimmed and peeled
2 tablespoons soy sauce
1 tablespoon sesame oil
1 tablespoon defatted Chicken Stock
 (page 9)

2 tablespoons rice wine or other mild
 vinegar
1 tablespoon grated ginger root
1 clove garlic, smashed but left whole
1 tablespoon toasted sesame seeds
 (15 minutes at 350°F)

1. Using the grating attachment of a food processor (or the large holes of a hand-held, four-sided grater), grate broccoli stems, radishes, and carrots. Put the vegetables in a mixing bowl.

2. Mix remaining ingredients in a small bowl or cup and pour over vegetables. Allow to marinate at least 30 minutes. Remove the garlic before serving.

Sautéed Radishes with Dill

This unusual side dish should be served with a fatty roast like lamb, beef, or pork so that the bite of the radishes can counter the richness of the meat.

Makes 4 to 6 servings

3 bunches red radishes
1 bunch scallions
2 tablespoons butter
4 teaspoons chopped fresh dill
Kosher salt and freshly ground black pepper to taste

1. Wash and trim radishes. Slice by hand or with the slicing attachment of a food processor to a thickness of $3/16$ inch. You should have about 3 cups. Trim scallions and thinly slice, using all the white portion and about 1 inch of the green.

2. Put butter in a large, nonstick skillet over medium heat. When butter stops sizzling, add radishes and scallions and sauté about 8 minutes or until scallions are soft but not brown and radishes start to become translucent but are still firm.

3. Add 3 teaspoons of the dill, salt, and pepper and stir well. Put into a serving dish and sprinkle with remaining dill.

Pasta with Radishes and Radish Greens

Makes 4 servings

2 bunches radishes with green tops
1½ tablespoons extra-virgin olive oil
1 medium onion, chopped
Kosher salt and freshly ground black pepper to taste

12 ounces short pasta such as penne, cooked according to package directions and drained, with ¼ cup cooking water reserved
⅓ cup freshly grated Romano cheese plus more for passing at the table

1. Separate the greens from radishes. Wash greens and spin dry in a salad spinner or drain in a colander. Wash and trim the radishes. Thinly slice radishes so you have 2 cups. Save any extra radishes for another dish.

2. Put half the oil in a wok or large skillet over medium heat. Add onion and cook just until it begins to soften. Add radishes and greens. Cover and cook 7 minutes or until greens wilt and radishes become translucent. Season with salt and pepper.

3. Add drained pasta to skillet along with remaining oil and toss. Add reserved cooking water as needed a tablespoon at a time to avoid dryness. Toss with cheese and serve. Pass additional cheese at the table.

Risotto with Radishes and Radish Greens

Makes 4 servings

2 bunches radishes with green tops
5 cups defatted Chicken Stock (page 9)
1 tablespoon butter
1 small onion, chopped
2 teaspoons finely chopped garlic

$1^1/_2$ cups arborio rice
Kosher salt and freshly ground black pepper to taste
$^1/_4$ cup freshly grated Romano cheese
$^1/_4$ cup freshly grated Parmesan cheese

1. Separate the greens from the radishes. Wash and spin dry the greens in a salad spinner. Coarsely chop. You should have about 3 cups. Wash and trim one of the bunches of radishes. (Reserve the other bunch for another use.) Chop radishes into about $^1/_4$-inch dice.

2. Heat Chicken Stock in a saucepan.

3. Put butter in a large saucepan over medium heat. Add onion, garlic, and radishes and cook just until onion begins to soften, about 3 to 4 minutes.

4. Add rice and stir to coat. Begin adding stock, a cup or so at a time, stirring occasionally while risotto is at a simmer. Continue adding stock as the rice absorbs the previous amount of liquid. Just before the last addition of stock, fold in radish greens. When risotto is tender, after 20–25 minutes, but still firm (you may not need all the stock), remove from heat. Season with salt and pepper. Stir in cheeses and serve.

rhubarb

When Sam was growing up, rhubarb was a big favorite in the Gugino household. That is, until Sam's brother Frank got hives one day from eating rhubarb pie. Ever since then, rhubarb was a forbidden fruit.

Make that a vegetable. Though we eat rhubarb as a fruit it's a vegetable, at least botanically. Legally it's a fruit. In 1947, the U.S. Customs Court in Buffalo, New York (which coincidentally is Sam's hometown), ruled that because rhubarb is used principally as a fruit at home, it's a fruit. (This enabled the imported rhubarb to pay a smaller duty than if it were a vegetable.)

Like a lot of old-fashioned vegetables (or fruits), rhubarb has been forgotten. Many young people probably never had rhubarb to begin with and just don't know what to do with it. And perhaps there are some who don't want to add all the sugar rhubarb needs to make it palatable.

Another roadblock to appreciating rhubarb is its limited versatility in people's minds. It was called the pie plant because that's pretty much what people used rhubarb for in colonial days. And as one produce retailer told us, "Who makes pies anymore?"

We do. We make a lot of other things with rhubarb too like sauces and soufflés. And we're glad that a lot of young chefs are discovering the joys of rhubarb. Gray Kunz, chef at Lespinasse, the four-star New York restaurant, has a rhubarb dessert soup on the menu. The Four Seasons restaurant, also in New York, serves rhubarb compote with roast duck. And nobody gets hives.

WHERE GROWN

Washington is the leading rhubarb producer. Oregon, Michigan, and California are also rhubarb producers of note.

VARIETIES

There are two types of rhubarb: hothouse and field rhubarb. Hothouse rhubarb is also called strawberry rhubarb because of its pinkish hue.

Grown in greenhouses, this type has smaller, less stringy stalks than field rhubarb. It is also less coarsely textured and sweeter than field rhubarb. Outdoor-grown field rhubarb has a more pronounced, tart rhubarb flavor. The stalks are darker red, and thus this type is called cherry rhubarb. (Wholesalers command the highest prices for fat, dark rhubarb.)

SEASONS

Hothouse rhubarb is normally available from January through April, usually with a two-week peak in mid-February. Field rhubarb overlaps, beginning in March and going through August and into the early fall. The peak period is April and May.

SELECTION, HANDLING & STORAGE

Choose rhubarb that is firm with good color for its type and no blemishes or flabbiness. The leaves, if attached, should look fresh and green, not yellow. The leaves, incidentally, are quite toxic and must be removed before cooking. Rhubarb will last up to two weeks when put in a plastic bag in the coldest part of the refrigerator.

NUTRITION

A 61g serving of rhubarb (about 2.2 ounces, $1/2$ cup diced) has 1g protein and 2g carbohydrates as well as a gram of dietary fiber and only 15 calories. But it shoots up to 141 calories when sugar is added for cooking. Nonetheless, rhubarb contains almost 4% of the DV for calcium and 8% for vitamin C. Rhubarb is also a fair source of potassium.

One health warning: Because it is high in oxalates, rhubarb may contribute to the formation of kidney stones. So you may want to avoid large quantities, especially if you are prone to kidney stones.

YIELD

One pound of rhubarb yields 3 cups sliced.

Tony's Tip

> If you've got more rhubarb than you can handle when it's at the peak of the season, freeze it. Cut stalks into 1-inch pieces and put them on a baking sheet in the freezer. When frozen, put the pieces in a freezer bag for up to nine months.

PREPARATION

After the leaves are removed and the stalks washed, rhubarb is cut very much like celery, crosswise into crescents. But since rhubarb breaks down much more quickly than celery, those crescents should normally be fairly wide, an inch or so.

The basic way to cook rhubarb is to stew it very much like cooking cranberries. Add about $1/4$ cup water and sugar to taste ($1/2$ to 1 cup) to a pound of cut-up rhubarb. Cover and cook gently about 5 to 10 minutes. Be careful not to let the rhubarb disintegrate.

And as with cranberries, you can add all manner of seasonings to stewed rhubarb. Orange juice or orange liqueurs go nicely with rhubarb. So do lemon and ginger. Spoon the rhubarb over ice cream, waffles, and pancakes.

Compotes are just a step up from stewed rhubarb and make good low-fat desserts or breakfast dishes. Just add some dried fruits such as prunes, raisins, and apricots; or perhaps some other fresh fruit like strawberries. Strawberries are the most favored companions to rhubarb, which is why you see so many strawberry-rhubarb pies, crisps, and compotes. Kirsch marries nicely with both.

Rhubarb Soup

This is a dessert soup that's particularly refreshing after a heavy meat-and-potatoes meal. You could also serve it as a first course on a hot day.

Makes 5 servings

2¹/₂ pounds rhubarb, trimmed of leaves and cut into ¹/₂-inch pieces

1¹/₂ cups sugar

1 cinnamon stick

¹/₂ cup dry white wine

2 tablespoons lemon juice

2 large mangoes

3 kiwi

2 navel oranges

5 fresh mint sprigs

1. Put rhubarb in a large saucepan with sugar, cinnamon stick, and wine. Add 6 cups of water and simmer, uncovered, 45 minutes.

2. Strain liquid through a sieve and add lemon juice. Cool. You should have about 6 to 7 cups.

3. Cut mangoes into ¹/₂-inch cubes. Peel kiwi, halve lengthwise, and cut into ¹/₄-inch-thick crescents. Peel oranges and section, removing all membrane and pith.

4. Pour soup slowly into a soup bowl or shallow soup plate, stopping before you get to the cloudy and unattractive dregs. You will have about 5 cups. Put one cup into each of 5 soup plates. Divide fruit equally among the plates so that it looks attractive. Put a mint sprig in the middle.

Pork Tenderloin with Rhubarb Sauce

Because of its natural sweetness, pork and fruit (or vegetables that act like fruit such as rhubarb) naturally go together.

Makes 4 servings

1¹/₂ teaspoons kosher salt

¹/₂ teaspoon freshly ground black pepper

¹/₂ teaspoon ground coriander

¹/₂ teaspoon ground ginger

1 tablespoon canola or vegetable oil

2 pork tenderloins, about 11 to 12 ounces each

¹/₂ pound rhubarb

¹/₄ cup sugar

¹/₂ teaspoon grated orange rind

2 tablespoons water

2 ounces raspberry vinegar, raspberry liqueur, or raspberry brandy

¹/₂ cup defatted Chicken Stock (page 9)

1. Preheat oven to 500°F. Mix salt, pepper, coriander, and ginger in a teacup. Rub oil over the tenderloins. Then rub on spices.

2. Put tenderloins in a cast-iron or other ovenproof skillet and put in the oven. Cook about 20 to 25 minutes or until the internal temperature of the thickest part reaches 155°F to 160°F.

3. Meanwhile, wash rhubarb and peel if tough, as you would celery. Cut into 1-inch pieces (smaller if the pieces are very wide) and combine in a heavy-bottomed saucepan with sugar, orange rind, and water. Cover and cook over medium-low heat 5 to 7 minutes or until rhubarb is very soft. Set aside.

4. When tenderloins are done, remove to a warm platter. Put skillet on the stove over medium heat. Add raspberry vinegar or liqueur or brandy and scrape any particles on the bottom of the skillet with a wooden spoon. Add stock and reduce volume by half. Add rhubarb and reduce slightly until sauce thickens. Taste for seasonings. Then strain through a sieve (use the back of a ladle to press) into a saucepan.

5. Cut pork into approximately ³/₈-inch-thick slices, reserving the juices from slicing. Add juices to the rhubarb sauce and heat to thicken if necessary. (The sauce should not be thick but gently coat the meat.) Put pork on a platter or individual plates and pour sauce over.

Sam's Cooking Tip

Pork tenderloins—the tubes of meat that run down the back of the hog—are delicious and remarkably lean cuts of meat with half the fat of skinless dark meat chicken. Because they don't have a lot of fat, it's important not to overcook them, as people so often do with pork. Since the trichina worm is killed at 137°F, I give a little cushion and suggest that meat be cooked to 155°F or so, recognizing that some thermometers are off.

Rhubarb-Strawberry Crisp with Kirsch

Strawberries and rhubarb go together like bacon and eggs. Depending on the sweetness of the strawberries and your preference for tartness, you may want to increase the sugar somewhat in this recipe. We like this dish a little on the tart side.

Makes 6 to 8 servings

$3/4$ cup Grape Nuts cereal or similar nugget cereal

$1/3$ cup brown sugar

2 tablespoons granulated sugar

$1/4$ teaspoon cinnamon

3 tablespoons butter, softened

$1^1/2$ pounds rhubarb

1 pint strawberries

$2/3$ cup sugar, or more to taste

$1/4$ teaspoon ground nutmeg

1 tablespoon kirsch or framboise (raspberry liqueur)

3 tablespoons flour

Butter-flavored cooking spray

1. Mix cereal, sugars, and cinnamon. Work in butter with a pastry knife or large fork until you have an even, crumbly meal. Set aside. Preheat oven to 350°F.

2. Wash rhubarb and peel if tough, as you would celery. Cut into $3/4$-inch pieces (shorter if stalks are wide) and put into a bowl. Wash, hull, and halve strawberries and add to rhubarb. Add sugar, nutmeg, and kirsch to fruit and toss well. Add flour and toss well again.

3. Spray a 9×14-inch gratin dish with butter-flavored cooking spray. Spread the fruit mixture in the dish evenly and top with cereal mixture. Bake 40 to 45 minutes or until juice bubbles up through the crust and crust is nicely browned. Serve warm or at room temperature.

Sam's Cooking Tip

Kirsch, the clear cherry brandy, adds a delicious flavor accent for both strawberries and rhubarb. We like the kirsch made by St. George Cellars in Northern California. It's smooth and fruity (though strong, to be sure) but without the throat-scorching harshness of most kirsch. You can substitute framboise (raspberry liqueur) or an orange liqueur such as Triple Sec.

Rhubarb Compote with Prunes and Apricots

This is a sweet and spicy way to eat rhubarb, as a low-fat dessert or for breakfast the next morning. It's best at room temperature, so be sure to take it out of the refrigerator at least 30 minutes before serving.

Makes 4 to 6 servings

2 pounds rhubarb

1 cup pitted, dried apricots

1 cup pitted prunes

1 cup dessert wine such as a late harvest
  Riesling

$^2/_3$ cup sugar

1 tablespoon grated fresh ginger

$^1/_4$ teaspoon grated nutmeg

1. Trim rhubarb and cut into 1-inch pieces, smaller if stalks are more than 1 inch wide. Halve apricots and prunes if large.

2. Combine all ingredients, except rhubarb, in a covered, heavy-bottomed saucepan. Bring to a simmer. Add rhubarb and simmer 5 to 7 minutes, stirring gently a few times, until rhubarb just softens but does not get too mushy.

3. Cool and serve at room temperature over pound cake or with frozen yogurt or low-fat ice cream.

Sam's Cooking Tip

If you like your compote on the spicy side, increase the amount of ginger by another teaspoon or two. And if you like your compote a bit sweeter, increase the sugar to $^3/_4$ cup.

Rhubarb Soufflé with Rhubarb-Strawberry Coulis

Emile Mooser has been known to make more than two hundred soufflés in an evening at Emile's, his restaurant in San Jose, California. This adaptation of one of Emile's soufflé recipes eliminates the normal cream-laden mousseline sauce but keeps the fat-free fruit coulis. Instead of making this in a 2-quart soufflé dish, you can also use two 1-quart soufflé dishes or four half-quart dishes. If you use smaller soufflé dishes, start checking for doneness after 30 minutes.

Makes 6 to 8 servings

3 tablespoons butter
3 tablespoons flour
³/₄ cup whole milk, warmed
Kosher salt
2 egg yolks
¹/₂ cup Sugar Syrup (page 382)
1 cup diced rhubarb

³/₄ cup sugar
1 teaspoon cornstarch
12 egg whites
1 ounce framboise (raspberry liqueur), brandy, or Triple Sec
Rhubarb-Strawberry Coulis (recipe follows)

1. Preheat oven to 350°F. Melt butter in a saucepan and whisk in flour, stirring for a few minutes. Add milk and a pinch of salt and mix thoroughly with a whisk over low heat until it thickens and comes clean from the bottom of the pan. Remove from heat and cool slightly (a few minutes) and whisk in egg yolks, one at a time, mixing thoroughly. Put into a large mixing bowl and set aside to cool.

2. Bring Sugar Syrup and rhubarb to boil in a small saucepan. Cook gently about 3 or 4 minutes. Drain and set aside.

3. Mix sugar and cornstarch together. Set aside. Beat egg whites until soft peaks form. Add cornstarch mixture and beat a few seconds to mix.

4. Add framboise to egg yolk mixture and mix until smooth. Mix a small amount of the egg whites into egg yolk mixture. Fold in cooked rhubarb, then remaining egg whites. Pour mixture into a buttered 2-quart soufflé dish to about ¹/₂ inch below the rim. Do not overfill.

5. Put soufflé dish in the oven. Bake 40 minutes or until a tester comes out clean. Serve with Rhubarb-Strawberry Coulis.

Rhubarb-Strawberry Coulis
Makes about 2$\frac{1}{2}$ cups

$\frac{1}{2}$ pound (one thick, long stalk) peeled
  rhubarb, cut into $\frac{3}{8}$-inch dice
$\frac{1}{2}$ pound (6 to 8 large) strawberries,
  coarsely chopped

1 cup sugar
$\frac{1}{3}$ cup white wine, preferably an
  off-dry wine such as chenin blanc or
  Riesling

Put all ingredients in a medium saucepan. Cook over medium heat until rhubarb is tender but not mushy, about 10 to 12 minutes. Cool to room temperature.

Sam's Cooking Tip

Most people think soufflés are difficult desserts that require lots of last-minute work. Not so. The white sauce (made in the direction above) and coulis are a snap and both can be done a day or two ahead. To prevent skin from forming on the white sauce, put plastic wrap directly on the surface.

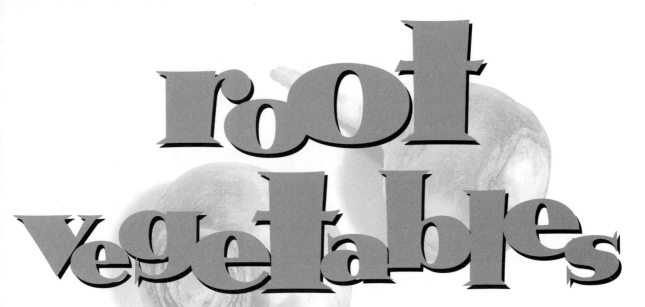

root
vegetables

There was a time when asparagus wasn't

available in December, lettuce in January, and zuc-

chini in February. It was a time—and this is most

of recorded history in temperate climates—when

people had to stock up on the earth-toned vegeta-

bles of fall to last them through the winter.

No greens, few reds, but a lot of whites, browns, yellows, and oranges.

These are root vegetables for which a special place was made: the root cellar. We've talked elsewhere about other root vegetables—potatoes, onions, and the like—but this space is reserved for those hard-core root vegetables that aren't quite as glamorous: turnips, rutabagas, and parsnips.

Root vegetables are often referred to as lowly, more of an indication of their status than of their location. When someone questions your intelligence, the appropriate response might be, "Hey man, I didn't just fall off a turnip truck." And then there are the stories of families so destitute they are reduced to eating turnips.

James Beard said that parsnips were one of our most neglected vegetables, though he personally loved them and preferred them to sweet potatoes for Thanksgiving.

But root vegetables are experiencing a kind of renaissance. Not long ago, we heard Joel Patraker, the special projects manager of the Greenmarket Farmers Market in New York City, waxing poetically on the radio about rutabagas. And one of the signature dishes at the Union Square Cafe, one of New York City's best restaurants, is creamy mashed turnips (they actually use rutabagas) with crispy shallots. Chef Michael Romano says he also likes to make parsnip pancakes as a side vegetable with roast venison.

So it looks like those subterranean Rodney Dangerfields are finally getting some respect. As the authors of the fine book *The Essential Root Vegetable Cookbook,* Sally and Martin Stone, put it "we forget that the most expensive, glamorous, exotic, rare and idealized foodstuff of all, the truffle, is truly a buried treasure." Treasure, indeed. We hope this chapter is the shovel to help you dig up your own.

WHERE GROWN

The major turnip- and rutabaga-producing states are California, Colorado, Indiana, New Jersey, Ohio, Oregon, Texas, and Washington. A significant amount of both are imported from Canada. Parsnips are also grown in Canada as well as in Arizona, California, Colorado, Florida, Massachusetts, Michigan, Minnesota, New York, Oregon, Pennsylvania, Texas, and Wisconsin.

VARIETIES

Both rutabagas and turnips are members of the mustard family. All **turnips** have a snowy white flesh. The differences in varieties mostly involve outside coloring and size. Some have reddish rings around the crown of the vegetable, others purple. Flavors are essentially the same although larger turnips (3 or more inches in diameter), which appear later in the winter, tend to be more pungent than the smaller (1½ to 2 inches) turnips that appear earlier in the season. Major turnip varieties include Purple Top, White Globe, White Egg, Golden Ball, Amber, and Yellow Amberdeen.

Instead of white flesh, **rutabagas** have a yellow-orange flesh that, like yellow-flesh potatoes, gives an impression of richness or butteriness. They're also sweeter and denser than turnips, with less moisture. On the outside rutabagas are half yellow-orange, half burgundy or purple. To add to their shelf life most rutabagas are waxed. Commercially available rutabagas tend to be larger than turnips. The three main rutabaga varieties are American Purple Top, Laurentian, and the Thomson strain of the Laurentian.

It's no coincidence that the **parsnip** resembles a carrot that has seen a ghost. The pale yellow parsnip and the carrot are in the same family. Parsnips, however, are more irregular in shape, though they generally follow the same carrot tapered look with lengths varying from 5 to 10 inches. Some have likened them to sweet potatoes, but we think parsnips have a taste all their own, somewhat starchy like a potato, sweet like a carrot, and a little nutty as well.

SEASONS

Turnips and rutabagas are available year-round, with peak supplies available from October through March. Parsnips generally run from fall (usually after the first frost) into spring.

SELECTION, HANDLING & STORAGE

Select small to medium turnips that are heavy for their size (indicating good moisture content), with good color and firmness and no bruises, soft spots, or shriveling. The stem end may be somewhat flattened. Winter turnips may be larger with tougher skin, so choose carefully during that time of the year. If greens are attached, they should be bright and fresh looking. As we mentioned in the Cooking Greens chapter (page 139), turnip greens are nutritious and delicious. Remove them immediately if they come attached to the turnips and store them separately in plastic bags. The greens will last three or four days.

Rutabagas should be medium-size, about 4 to 5 inches across, because exceptionally large ones can be a bit much to handle. And they should be heavy for their size. Lighter ones may be woody. The wax on the surface of some is merely applied to prolong shelf life.

Turnips and rutabagas like cold (as low as 32°F) and moist surroundings. In plastic bags in the refrigerator in the high-humidity bin, turnips will last as long as two weeks. If waxed, rutabagas need not be in plastic. They'll last even longer, up to two months under proper conditions.

Choose parsnips that are firm with a good creamy color and no spots, blemishes, cuts, or cracks. They should have a good, uniform shape (about 4 to 5 inches long) and should not be limp or shriveled. Avoid those that are particularly large since they may be woody, and those that are particularly small since they are not as economical and require more preparation time. Parsnips like cool temperatures. Store them in plastic bags in the refrigerator and they'll last up to two weeks.

NUTRITION

A 3.5-ounce serving (100g) of turnips has 30 calories, 6g of carbohydrates, 1g each of protein and dietary fiber, 60% of the DV for vitamin C, 2% for iron, and 3% for calcium. Turnips are also a fair source of potassium and folic acid.

A 100g serving of rutabagas contains 36 calories, 7g of carbohydrates, 1g each of dietary fiber and protein, 11% of the DV for vitamin A and 43% for vitamin C. Rutabagas are also a decent source of potassium and folic acid.

The good news is that because turnips and rutabagas are in the same family as cabbage and other cruciferous vegetables, they have many of the same health benefits, particularly as cancer fighters. The bad news is that like other cruciferous vegetables, they too produce a fair amount of gas.

A serving of parsnips (100g, 3.5 ounces) contains 76 calories, 17g carbohydrates, .5g fat, 1g protein, 2g dietary fiber, 26% of the DV for vitamin C, and 5% each for calcium and iron. Parsnips are a good source of potassium.

YIELD

A pound of parsnips (about four medium) will yield about 2 cups peeled and chopped. A pound of turnips will yield about 2½ cups chopped. Rutabaga yields will be a little less because of the waste from waxing (you have to cut off the waxed outside and discard it).

Tony's Tip

Parsnips love cool weather. Frost, or even frozen ground, does not harm them. In fact, their flavor actually improves with cool temperatures. At low temperatures, their starch converts to sugar, giving them a delicately sweet, nutty taste.

PREPARATION

Turnips are normally peeled before being used, but if the turnips are small and young and their skins thin, treat them like potatoes and roast them unpeeled after a good scrub.

And in other ways you can treat turnips like potatoes, quartering them and roasting them, steaming them, or boiling and mashing them. Rutabagas can be treated likewise, except that we think they are superior to mashed turnips.

But you'll need a sturdy vegetable peeler (like the ones with fat handles) to get through the wax and skin of rutabagas.

Seasonings for turnips include garlic, parsley, and dill. For rutabagas, seasonings lean more toward those used for sweet potatoes: nutmeg, cinnamon, allspice, and mace.

Parsnips are usually peeled, unless you get your hands on a particularly pristine organic bunch. James Beard said he rarely peeled parsnips, preferring just to scrub them before cooking. Parsnips roast well accompanied by carrots and perhaps turnips and rutabagas. They puree marvelously with potatoes or other root vegetables. Steaming and microwaving are also good ideas. And don't overlook the possibility of small chunks, slices, or julienne strips of parsnips quickly sautéed.

Carrot seasonings are appropriate for parsnips. That means nutmeg, parsley, dill, and orange flavoring. Roasted garlic turned nutty and sweet is also a good seasoning.

Mashed Parsnips with Roasted Leeks and Nutmeg

Root vegetables mash nicely by themselves or in combination with other root vegetables. Try them instead of the usual mashed potatoes.

Makes 4 to 6 servings

1$^{1}/_{2}$ pounds parsnips, peeled and cut into
  1-inch chunks
$^{1}/_{2}$ pound potatoes, peeled and cut into
  1-inch chunks
Olive oil cooking spray
1 large or 2 small leeks, white part only,
  halved lengthwise and washed
  thoroughly (see "Preparation" in the
  Onion chapter, page 185)

$^{1}/_{2}$ to $^{2}/_{3}$ cup skim milk, warmed
1 tablespoon butter, softened
$^{1}/_{4}$ teaspoon ground nutmeg
Kosher salt and freshly ground black
  pepper to taste

1. Preheat oven to 500°F. Put parsnips and potatoes in large saucepan and cover with water. Bring to a boil and boil gently, about 12 minutes, or until very tender.

2. Meanwhile, spray a cast-iron frying pan with olive oil cooking spray. Halve leeks again, crosswise if using only one large one. Add to pan and put in the oven. Cook about 15 minutes until browned all over. Turn a few times to cook evenly. Remove, chop, and set aside.

3. When parsnips and potatoes are cooked, drain well and return to the pan over low heat. Mash, adding milk and butter as you do. Add just enough milk to get the texture you prefer, and leave a few lumps if you like. Fold in leeks and season with nutmeg, salt, and pepper.

Roasted Winter Vegetables with Basil Oil

This dish is so substantial it could be the main part of the meal.
Feel free to substitute other winter vegetables.

Makes 4 servings

3 medium red-skinned potatoes, washed but unpeeled

3 small turnips, peeled

3 medium parsnips, peeled

1¹/₂ pounds butternut or other winter squash, peeled and seeded

3 medium carrots, peeled

¹/₄ cup Chicken Stock (page 9) or Vegetable Stock (page 64)

2 tablespoons basil oil or extra-virgin olive oil

2 teaspoons kosher salt

¹/₂ teaspoon freshly ground black pepper

8 to 10 small onions, peeled

Olive oil cooking spray

1 tablespoon chopped fresh basil or 1 teaspoon dried (omit if using basil oil)

1. Preheat oven to 400°F. Cut potatoes, turnips, parsnips, and squash into 1¹/₄- to 1¹/₂-inch-square chunks. Cut carrots into 1¹/₂-inch lengths. Mix stock with 1 tablespoon of the oil and half the salt and pepper. In a large mixing bowl, pour mixture over vegetables and toss.

2. Put potatoes, turnips, parsnips, carrots, and onions in a large roasting pan greased with olive oil cooking spray. Roast 15 minutes. Add squash and cook 30 to 35 minutes longer, stirring a few times, until nicely browned and easily pierced with a fork. Toss with remaining oil, salt and pepper, and basil.

Sam's Cooking Tip

One of the great ways to get intense basil flavor when fresh basil isn't in season is to use basil oil. (Yes, fresh basil is often available year-round these days. But winter basil doesn't have the intensity of flavor that summer basil has.) I like the basil oil by Consorzio best, but Loriva also makes a credible one. If you use either, eliminate the dried or fresh basil.

Turnip, Potato, and Parsnip Gratin

Gratins, like mashed potatoes, can be vehicles for lots of fat. But this one uses defatted Chicken Stock, skim milk, and a minimum of butter.

Makes 8 servings

Butter-flavored cooking spray
1 tablespoon butter
2 tablespoons flour
$^1/_2$ cup defatted Chicken Stock (page 9)
$1^1/_2$ cups skim milk
Kosher salt and freshly ground black
  pepper to taste
$^1/_4$ teaspoon grated nutmeg
1 pound turnips, peeled and thinly sliced

2 medium leeks, white only, halved
  lengthwise and thinly sliced
$^1/_2$ pound parsnips, peeled and thinly
  sliced
$^1/_2$ pound potatoes, peeled and thinly
  sliced
$^1/_2$ cup grated Parmesan cheese
$^1/_2$ cup bread crumbs
2 tablespoons chopped fresh parsley

1. Preheat oven to 350°F. Spray gratin dish with butter-flavored cooking spray and set aside.

2. Heat butter in a saucepan until the foam subsides. Add flour and whisk a few minutes. Add stock and stir vigorously until well incorporated. Add milk and whisk until mixture returns to a boil. Simmer a few minutes. It should have the consistency of a thin white sauce. Season with salt, pepper, and nutmeg.

3. Arrange half the turnips on the bottom of the gratin dish. Sprinkle with $^1/_3$ of the leeks. Add parsnip slices. Then $^1/_3$ more leeks. Then potatoes, remaining leeks, and remaining turnips. Season each layer with salt and pepper.

4. Pour sauce over, cover, and bake 30 minutes. Mix cheese, bread crumbs, and parsley. Sprinkle on top and bake 30 minutes more uncovered.

Clay Pot Curried Winter Vegetable Stew

Curry is a blend of spices, which was made into a convenient single yellow powder by the British during their occupation of India. Most Indians would make their own blend, as you can too for this dish, if you have the time and inclination.

Makes 4 servings as a main course, 8 as a side dish

1 tablespoon extra-virgin olive oil

4 cloves garlic, chopped

1 tablespoon curry powder

1 teaspoon ground, toasted cumin

$1/4$ teaspoon cayenne pepper

One 16-ounce can tomatoes, seeded and chopped, with juice

2 cups Chicken Stock (page 9) or Vegetable Stock (page 64)

Kosher salt and freshly ground black pepper to taste

1 large onion, peeled and thinly sliced

3 medium parsnips, peeled and cut into 1-inch chunks

3 medium to large carrots, peeled and cut into 1-inch chunks

1 medium rutabaga, peeled and cut into 1-inch chunks

3 medium turnips, peeled and cut into 1-inch chunks

1 pound wedge winter squash, peeled and cut into 1-inch chunks

1 fennel bulb, trimmed, and cut into sixths, lengthwise

One 15-ounce can chickpeas, rinsed and drained

2 tablespoons chopped fresh mint or parsley for garnish

1 tablespoon toasted sesame seeds, for garnish (page 28)

1. Soak a clay pot in cold water for 15 minutes. Meanwhile, in a large saucepan, heat the olive oil and cook, stirring, until it just starts to turn color. Add garlic, curry, cumin, and cayenne pepper and cook a few minutes, stirring, so that garlic does not burn. Add tomatoes, stock, and salt and pepper to taste. Bring to a boil and simmer 10 minutes.

2. While stock mixture cooks, toss onion, parsnips, carrots, rutabaga, turnips, squash, and fennel in a large bowl with salt and pepper. Fold in chickpeas and put in the clay pot. Pour stock mixture over. Put in a cold oven and turn the heat to 450°F.

3. Bake, covered, 1 hour or until all vegetables are tender. Garnish with parsley and sesame seeds and serve in soup plates with good country bread or over couscous or basmati rice.

Sam's Cooking Tip

The clay pot is a great way to seal in juices for roasts, stews, and any number of braised meats or vegetables; you can even make an apple pie in it. The three most important things to remember when using a clay pot are: (1) soak it before you use it, (2) put it in a cold oven, and (3) make sure the cover is always secure.

CHAPTER

28

spinach

If you thumb through enough cookbooks, you'll see that just about everything labeled "Florentine" has spinach in it. In fact, just the other day we looked at *Cook's Ingredients* (The Reader's Digest Association, 1990). In this otherwise fine book, this phrase appears in the spinach section: "The word *Florentine* denotes its use in recipes."

On the surface it appears to be true. There is flounder Florentine (stuffed with spinach), eggs Florentine (on a bed of spinach), even Florentine dressing with chopped spinach in it. Thus, the following conclusions might be reached: Either spinach was invented in Tuscany, the Italian province in which the city of Florence is located, or the Florentines perfected all aspects of cooking that involve spinach.

Think of it, the entire culinary repertoire of one of the most cultured cities in the world revolving around spinach. Piazzas with statues to Popeye and the Jolly Green Giant. Michelangelo's *David* with a spinach leaf instead of a fig leaf.

There is a logical reason as revealed in *The Great Food Almanac: A Feast of Facts from A to Z* (Collins, 1994). Author Irena Chalmers says that Catherine de Médici, who left Florence to marry the king of France, was so fond of spinach she wanted it at every meal. So the royal cooks found all sorts of ways to weave spinach into dishes, and the Florentine moniker for things with spinach stuck. Though why those dishes weren't *alla de Médici* we're not sure.

WHERE GROWN

Spinach likes three conditions for growing: sandy soil, cool temperature, and relative dryness. So it thrives during the winter months in California, far and away the leading producer, and Texas, which is number two.

VARIETIES

There are three main types of spinach: savoy, semisavoy, and flat-leafed. The savoy has crinkled leaves and is the primary commercial variety. The semisavoy has partially crinkled leaves and is used for processing as well as in the fresh market. Flat-leafed spinach is used mainly for processing. Varieties include Bloomsdale, Old Dominion, and Virginia Savoy, all grown in the eastern United States; Dixie Market, Melody, and 621 from Texas; and Polka and New Zealand from California.

Botanically New Zealand spinach is not a true spinach, but it looks and tastes very much like spinach. It has dark green leaves and a tang when used raw. That tang mellows when cooked.

SEASONS

Consistently available year-round, spinach peaks from December to May.

SELECTION, HANDLING & STORAGE

Spinach should look fresh and crisp with good green color and no wilting or yellowing. Leaves should be well developed with minimal bruises or blemishes. Generally, the smooth leaf spinach has smaller stems than the curly leaf spinach and is therefore a better buy. But we rarely have a choice of one or the other.

A good deal of spinach comes in plastic or "cello" bags weighing 10 ounces. This spinach is already washed and picked through with long stems removed. Obviously, bagged spinach is more expensive but it saves time. However, it's important to inspect the package to make sure there are no obvious signs of decay or age such as slime and wilting.

When you get bunched spinach home, untie the bunches. Then remove any blemished leaves and stems and wash thoroughly in lots of cool water. Repeat to make sure all the grit is gone. Spin dry in a salad spinner or drain well, then put into clean plastic bags very loosely wrapped with paper towels. It will last up to three days this way. Packaged spinach can be left in its bag but we prefer to remove it, check for any slime or damaged leaves, then repackage it in clean bags. Cold, moist surroundings are best for spinach storage, as low as 32°F and about 95-percent humidity.

NUTRITION

An 85g (3 ounces) serving of shredded spinach (1½ cups) contains 40 calories, 10g carbohydrates, 5g dietary fiber, 2g protein, 70% of the DV for vitamin A, 25% for vitamin C, 6% for calcium, 20% for iron, and 20% for folic acid.

Mom was right: Spinach is good for us. But not for hydrant-size forearms like Popeye has. Spinach is an excellent source of antioxidants that are major cancer fighters. Spinach has four times the beta-carotene of broccoli, which is no slouch. It is also very high in lutein, another significant antioxidant. The nutrients in spinach also help lower blood cholesterol. For maximum benefit of all these goodies, spinach should be eaten raw or lightly cooked. One negative note is that spinach is high in oxalate, which may promote kidney stones.

YIELD

Anyone who has cooked fresh spinach knows that the yield is like getting gold nuggets out of a mountain (a small return, but every bit valuable). Figure on a pound for two people. The yield will be greater with bagged spinach, where a 10-ounce bag will serve two, and less if the spinach has especially large stems. A pound of raw spinach will yield about 4 cups when cleaned, 1 cup when cooked.

Tony's Tip

Spinach reacts adversely to a lot of metals. Don't chop it with a pure carbon-steel blade, cook it in aluminum, or serve it on silver.

PREPARATION

We generally like to remove the stems of spinach by hand before cooking, a bit tedious but worth it in the end. The work that is needed in cleaning and preparing spinach is rewarded by the quickness with which spinach is cooked.

Ideally, the freshly washed and stemmed spinach is put with its clinging water into a large pot—a wok is perfect—then covered and cooked, shaking and stirring a few times, for 3 to 5 minutes (the water on the leaves is enough to steam cook the spinach). Once done, you can dress the spinach any way you like. Garlic, freshly cracked black pepper, and olive oil are favorites. Butter is fine, too, as is a small grating of nutmeg.

If the spinach is to be used later in a more complex dish, you may want to blanch it in a large amount of water just until it wilts, then plunge it into ice water to preserve its color.

Cooked, chopped spinach makes a great filling for pastas, either in lasagna or tube pasta like cannelloni. You can also use it to stuff a butterflied leg of lamb or breast of veal.

Spinach soufflé makes a light and impressive side dish. And who could resist creamed spinach? (But make a béchamel with skim milk instead of a cream sauce to keep the fat in check—see step 3, page 38.)

In salads, serve spinach with sliced mushrooms and a light bacon dressing mixed with a good red wine vinegar.

Baked Oysters on Spinach

This dish is an adaptation of a recipe that appeared in The Cooking of Italy by Waverley Root (Time-Life Books, 1968). It was a favorite at Vincenzo's, Sam's first restaurant in Philadelphia.

Makes 4 servings

2 tablespoons butter

1 tablespoon finely chopped garlic

1 cup Italian-style bread crumbs

1 pound spinach

Kosher salt and freshly ground black
  pepper to taste

$1/4$ teaspoon freshly ground nutmeg

Rock salt (optional)

16 freshly shucked oysters with 16 half
  shells, both at room temperature

Butter-flavored cooking spray

1. Put butter in a heavy-bottomed skillet over medium-low heat. When butter stops sizzling, add garlic, cook a minute, then add bread crumbs. Stir until bread crumbs are nicely browned and toasty, 5 to 7 minutes. Set aside. Preheat oven to 400°F.

2. Trim spinach and wash in lots of cool water to remove grit. Drain briefly, then, with clinging water, put spinach into a large pot over medium heat. Stir and cook just until spinach wilts. Squeeze out excess moisture, chop coarsely, and season with salt, pepper, and nutmeg.

3. If using, put about $1/2$ inch of rock salt in an ovenproof dish. Put 16 oyster shells on top of rock salt, rough side down. Place about 1 tablespoon of spinach in each shell cavity. Top with an oyster and spoon about 1 tablespoon of bread crumbs over each oyster. Spray with butter-flavored cooking spray.

4. Bake oysters about 15 minutes, slightly longer if oysters are especially large.

Sam's Cooking Tip

Call your fishmonger ahead of time to make sure he or she sets aside the shells for you.

Creamed Spinach with Mushrooms

For some reason, creamed spinach is de rigueur as a side vegetable at all the great steak houses. This version doesn't require steak, nor does it have any cream.

Makes 4 to 6 servings

3 bunches spinach, each about 3/4 pound
Kosher salt and freshly ground black
  pepper to taste
2 tablespoons butter
2 ounces shiitake mushrooms, stemmed
  and chopped

2 tablespoons minced shallots
3 tablespoons all-purpose flour
1 1/2 cups skim milk, warmed
Pinch cayenne pepper

1. Wash spinach thoroughly and remove any thick stems or blemished leaves. Put with clinging water into a large pot or wok. Over medium heat, cook, stirring, until just wilted, about 5 minutes. Drain and gently squeeze out excess moisture. Chop, season with salt and pepper, and set aside. You should have about 3 cups.

2. Put butter in a large, heavy-bottomed saucepan over medium heat. When foaming stops add mushrooms and shallots. Cook, covered, until both wilt, about 3 or 4 minutes.

3. Add flour and stir a few minutes, making sure flour is fully incorporated. Add milk and bring to a simmer, stirring with a whisk. Season with salt, pepper, and cayenne pepper and cook until thickened, about 5 minutes. Add spinach and cook, stirring gently until heated through.

Spinach Salad with Lemon and Prosciutto

We prefer spinach slightly wilted rather than uncooked or well cooked. It still has texture but doesn't taste raw or soggy.

Makes 4 servings

3 bunches spinach, each about $3/4$ pound
$1^1/2$ tablespoons extra-virgin olive oil
$1^1/2$ tablespoons fresh lemon juice
Kosher salt and freshly ground black
  pepper to taste

Hot pepper flakes to taste
2 ounces prosciutto, chopped
$1/4$ cup shaved Parmesan cheese

1. Clean spinach in two changes of water. Remove stems and any blemished leaves. Dry thoroughly in a salad spinner.

2. Mix oil, lemon juice, and salt and pepper to taste in a cup, adding hot pepper flakes to taste. Set aside.

3. Put prosciutto in a large skillet or wok over low heat. Cook, covered, until crisp. Remove with a slotted spoon to paper towels.

4. Add spinach to wok and toss until barely wilted, about 5 minutes. Drain off any excess liquid from skillet and add olive oil mixture. Toss well. Add prosciutto and toss again.

5. Put on each of 4 plates. With a vegetable peeler, shave a few strips of Parmesan on top of each plate.

Pasta with Spinach and Red Potatoes

Our friend Andy Schloss, one of the country's most inventive cooks, points out that potatoes with pasta isn't as weird as you might think. When thoroughly cooked, potatoes provide creaminess without the fat.

Makes 4 servings

10 ounces small, red-skinned potatoes, washed but unpeeled

1¹/₂ tablespoons extra-virgin olive oil

5 cloves garlic, chopped

1¹/₂ pounds spinach, cleaned and cut into strips about ¹/₂ inch wide or less

Kosher salt to taste

¹/₈–¹/₄ teaspoon freshly ground black pepper

2 teaspoons fresh thyme, chopped, or a heaping ¹/₂ teaspoon dried

14 ounces short pasta such as penne or ziti, cooked according to package directions and drained with about ¹/₃ cup of cooking water reserved

6 tablespoons grated Parmesan cheese plus additional for the table

1. Cut potatoes into very thin slices. Put into a saucepan fitted with a steamer basket and about ³/₄ inch of water. Cover and steam over medium heat until very tender, about 20 minutes.

2. Put ¹/₂ tablespoon of the oil in a wok or large skillet over medium-low heat. Add garlic and cook 1¹/₂ to 2 minutes, just until it begins to turn a very light golden color. Add spinach and cook, tossing a few times until just wilted, about 5 minutes.

3. Add potatoes, salt, pepper, and thyme to skillet and toss again.

4. Add pasta, remaining oil, and just enough cooking water until mixture has a light coating but isn't soupy. Add Parmesan, toss, and serve with additional grated Parmesan at the table.

Sam's Cooking Tip

Potatoes, pasta, and spinach all require a good deal of seasoning, so don't think the amounts of garlic and black pepper are a misprint. Match the pepperiness with a spicy zinfandel.

CHAPTER

29

Most people have grown up with a

pretty one-dimensional view of squash. Make that

two dimensional: summer and winter.

In the summer, we groan about the surplus of

zucchini from our garden, or we try to find ways

to politely decline the "gifts" from our neighbor's

garden. In August and early September the newspaper food sections are flooded with zucchini recipes to help rid us of this squash scourge.

In the fall and winter, it's jack-o'-lanterns for Halloween and pumpkin pie for Thanksgiving. Oh, we might have an acorn squash here and there. But that is about it.

How limiting our squash repertoire is! In between the acorns and the zucchini you've got buttercup, butternut, calabaza, delicata, hubbard, kabocha, pattypan, scallopini, spaghetti, sunburst, sweet dumpling, turban, and yellow crookneck squashes. And how about those delicate and delicious squash blossoms?

Part of our lack of squash appreciation stems from not knowing how to cook them, which usually means overcooking them. Here is a cooking instruction for summer squash from an early nineteenth-century cookbook written by Eliza Leslie: "Wash them, cut them into pieces and take out the seeds. Boil them about three quarters of an hour or until quite tender. When done, drain them and squeeze them well till you have pressed out all the water. Mash them with a little butter, pepper and salt. Then put the squash, thus prepared, into a stew pan, set it on hot coals, and stir it very frequently til it becomes dry."

No wonder we cringe when the zucchini appear on our doorstep.

WHERE GROWN

Florida is the largest producer of squash, followed closely by California. Georgia and New Jersey are also large squash-producing states. Other states include Texas, Massachusetts, New York, Michigan, Oregon, and South Carolina. A large amount of squash, mostly summer squash in the late fall and winter, is imported from Mexico.

VARIETIES

Squash is normally divided into winter and summer varieties. But since both types are available almost year-round, it makes more sense to divide them into soft- and hard-shelled varieties.

Soft-shelled squash are harvested before they become fully mature and before their seeds and skins become hard. Thus, the whole squash except for the stem end can be eaten. The most common is **zucchini** or Italian squash (courgette in French). It is generally cucumber-sized but can range from a few inches to over a foot. The flesh of zucchini is white or pale green, the skin green subtly streaked with white, and the stem end somewhat squarish. Golden zucchini is exactly the same except the skin is yellow (though the stem remains green). English zucchini is somewhat more bulbous with a skin that is almost evenly streaked with white and green. The cocozelle or Italian marrow squash is very much like a zucchini but with more pronounced dark green and white stripes and a thicker, more tubular shape.

The **yellow crookneck squash** has a medium to bright yellow exterior accented by a slightly bumpy texture. It has a bottle shape with a narrow, gently curved neck. The yellow straightneck is similar except that its neck does not curve. The flesh of both is similar to that of a zucchini but with more obvious seeds.

Scallopini squash looks like a zucchini that has been compressed into the shape of a top, or perhaps a small turban with a scalloped edge. Its flesh is similar to a zucchini. Also similar in texture and shape are the pattypan and sunburst. The **pattypan** is somewhat flatter and pale green or white. The **sunburst** is a bright yellow pattypan with a green stem.

In some markets that cater to Italian clientele you may see *cucuzza* (sometimes called long squash or Siciliano squash), a pale green, long, smooth squash, which food writer Mary Taylor Simeti says, "is proverbial for its lack of character yet much loved by Sicilians." In the peak of its season cucuzza may also be sold with its tendrils, which old-timers chop and cook with the squash, some tomatoes, and garlic, then toss with pasta.

Hard-shelled squash has grown to maturity with thicker, harder skins and firm, fully developed seeds. This category contains more variety in color, size, shape, and flavor than the soft-shelled varieties. They range in size from a small acorn squash, which can weigh not much more than a Rome apple, to the banana squash that can weigh 70 pounds.

Acorn squash (also called table queen, Des Moines, and Danish) has an acorn shape with distinct furrows. It is mostly dark green, though there is a golden acorn that can range from yellow to orange in color. (Some green acorn squash will have yellow or orange blotches and, in fact, this is desirable as long as it does not cover more than half the surface.) The flesh of both is yellow-orange and the flavor is mild and sweet. More flavorful is the light tan, bell-shaped butternut squash (also called an African bell) with a deeper orange flesh.

The behemoths of the hard-shelled squashes are the banana and Hubbard. The **banana** is tan and tubular with tapered ends. The flesh is bright yellow, hearty, and moist. The **Hubbard** has a bumpy, thick skin with golden, bluish-gray or green color. The flesh is rich and slightly sweeter than the banana.

Somewhat newer squash include the **Delicata**, also called a sweet potato or bohemian squash. It is somewhat cylindrical, though the base may flare out a bit. The yellow shell has furrows with green stripes and reddish-brown mottling. The flesh is pale yellow-orange, the aroma and

mild flavor reminiscent of fresh corn. The **sweet dumpling** looks like a squatter cousin to the Delicata with a pale yellow, green-streaked outside coloring, though the flesh is a deeper, richer orange. The flavor is exceptionally sweet.

The **Japanese or Kabocha squash** is round with a flattened top and a dark green color punctuated by white streaks. The deep orange flesh is flavorful but less moist than most other squash, akin to the fluffiness of a Russet potato. Though *calabaza* is the generic Spanish term for squash (usually from Mexico or the Caribbean), what is available commercially under that name is usually round and tan with a mild yellow-orange flesh.

Spaghetti squash is noted for its cooked flesh that turns into spaghettilike strands when scooped out. It is large, yellow, and oval, looking more like a melon than a squash. The Mediterranean squash looks like a large butternut on the outside with a similar flesh; it weighs 8 to 10 pounds.

One of the more dramatic-looking winter squashes is the **turban squash,** which looks as if it is wrapped in layers. It is mostly red-orange with green and white accents. Though most turban squash, particularly the larger varieties, are better to look at than to eat, the smaller, dark green buttercup has a nutty, sweet, deep orange flesh with a mealy texture that is good for pies.

Pumpkins that make great jack-o'-lanterns don't make great eating. They're stringy and tasteless. Look for smaller varieties. Pumpkin varieties good for pies and the like include Sugar Pie or Sweetie Pie, Small Sugar or New England Pie, Sugar Baby, Lumina (white skin but yellow flesh), Autumn Gold, Prize Winner (very large), Spirit, Spookie, and Triple Treat (for carving and pies). The Golden Nugget is also a pumpkinlike squash with a round, orange ridged shell and slightly sweet flesh. Minipumpkins that can fit into your hand are great for stuffing.

SEASONS

Though summer squash is available year-round in some form, the peak for price, variety, and availability is late spring and early summer. Some winter squash is available year-round, but the season runs from August through March with the peak period from October to December.

SELECTION, HANDLING & STORAGE

Summer squash should have bright, smooth skin. Dull skin is a sign of old age, and pitting is caused by cold. Varieties that are supposed to have dark green skin should have no sign of yellowing. Also avoid any with soft spots and those that are especially large (particularly zucchini), which can be tough and bland. Unless they're going to be stuffed, choose the smallest summer squash you can find.

Winter squash is more difficult to select because defects are not as apparent. However, choosing a squash that is heavy for its size is a good indicator of quality. That means greater moisture and less of a tendency to be dry and stringy. Shells should be hard with no cracks or soft spots, but the skin should not be shiny. Winter squash should also be true to its color. Butternut squash that is deep orange instead of light tan on the outside, for example, should be avoided.

Summer squash should be kept cool but not cold, about 41°F to 50°F with good humidity. Put it in plastic bags and it will last several days in the refrigerator. Winter squash should not be refrigerated unless cut. The best temperature range is 50°F to 55°F with relatively low humidity. It should be stored away from light and with good ventilation. Kept this way, winter squash will last one to two months.

NUTRITION

Though there is some minor variation from variety to variety, a serving of summer squash ($1/2$ medium squash, 98g, about 3.5 ounces) contains 20 calories, 4g of carbohydrates, 1g of protein, 2g of dietary fiber, 6% of the DV for vitamin A, 30% for vitamin C, and 2% each for iron and calcium. Summer squash is also a pretty good source of potassium (260mg) and a fair source of folic acid.

Like summer squash, there is some variation with winter squash. In general, a 100g (3.5 ounce) baked serving contains 63 calories, 15g of carbohydrates, 2g each of protein and dietary fiber, 82% of the DV for vitamin A, 21% for vitamin C, 4% for iron, and about 3% for calcium. Winter squash is a fairly good source of potassium, but its limited supply of folic acid is lost in cooking.

YIELD

Two pounds of winter squash, when peeled and trimmed, will yield about 4 cups chopped or four servings. A pound of summer squash will yield about 3 cups chopped or sliced, about three or four servings.

Tony's Tip

Large pumpkins, hollowed out, are great containers for a winter stew.

PREPARATION

Summer squash needs a good washing to remove grit. Then, once the ends are trimmed, it can be diced, sliced, or shredded. Stir-frying or sautéing is the best method for cooking. Steaming just emphasizes the wateriness of the vegetable as does microwaving.

Shredding and salting before stir-frying or sautéing helps to remove a lot of that undesired moisture. To shred zucchini or summer squash, use the second-largest holes of a four-sided grater or the shredding attachment of a food processor. Then put the squash in a colander, toss with salt, and let drain for 30 minutes. Put it in a clean dish towel and squeeze out as much moisture as possible.

Generally, we're not fond of summer squash raw. However, try a salad of small and sweet sliced zucchini with roasted red bell pepper strips, olive oil, vinegar, and herbs. Summer squash marries well with garlic and fresh herbs, especially basil, oregano, thyme, and mint.

Winter squash is not usually peeled before cooking though there is no reason why it can't be. The best way to accomplish this is to take a butternut squash, for example, halve it lengthwise, then put it cut side down on a work surface. Peel the skin with a sturdy vegetable peeler. For rounder squash, leaving them whole makes more sense before peeling. Just make sure the squash is stable on the work surface. If not, cut a slice off the bottom to keep it from rolling.

Once peeled, halve the squash and remove the seeds and any stringy fiber. Then halve again and cut into cubes or other desired shapes for steaming, boiling, or baking. Though it's not as commonly done with winter squash as with summer squash, there's no reason why winter squash can't be cut into small pieces (or shredded) and sautéed until tender. A splash of stock or water may be needed if the pan dries before the squash is completely cooked.

More commonly, the squash is steamed or baked, unpeeled. For an acorn squash, for example, halve lengthwise, remove the seeds, and put it cut side down in a shallow baking pan with half an inch of water. It will be cooked in a 375°F oven in about 45 to 55 minutes, depending on size. Steaming takes about the same amount of time. Microwaving (uncovered at full power) takes about 10 minutes.

After cooking squash this way, particularly acorn and butternut varieties, the flesh can be scooped out for purees or the skin can be peeled (a lot easier than when raw). But we have seen cooks puree a butternut squash with its skin when cooked very soft.

The cavities of some squash are perfect for stuffing. Acorn offers the most variety in size and you can probably get ones small enough to allow two servings when the halves are stuffed. Delicata also has a good cavity for stuffing.

Seasonings for winter squash are similar to what goes well with sweet potatoes: brown sugar, vanilla, cinnamon, nutmeg, allspice, cloves, and ginger (fresh, powdered, or candied). Cooked garlic adds a nutty mellowness and Chinese five-spice powder adds an exotic note. The exception is spaghetti squash, which in many ways can be treated like a pasta with the same kinds of sauces, especially tomato sauce.

To toast the seeds of winter squash, rinse them well in a colander and let them dry. Spread them on an oiled before stir-frying or sautéing sheet pan and bake at 250°F for 1 hour, raising the temperature to 400°F during the last 5 minutes to brown lightly. Salt if desired and store in an airtight container.

Curried Zucchini and Corn Soup

A great hot-weather soup that uses low-fat buttermilk instead of cream.
If you don't like buttermilk, use whole, regular milk.

Makes 6 servings

1 large onion, minced

1 tablespoon canola oil

2 teaspoons curry powder

6 medium zucchini, trimmed and cut into
 $^3/_4$-inch chunks

$3^1/_2$ cups Chicken Stock (page 9)

2 large ears corn, kernels removed

Kosher salt and freshly ground black
 pepper to taste

1 cup low-fat buttermilk

1. In a large, covered, heavy-bottomed saucepan, cook onion in the oil over low heat until soft but not browned, about 10 minutes. Add curry and cook a few minutes more, stirring. Turn up heat to medium and add zucchini. Stir a few minutes, add stock, and bring to a boil. Simmer 20 minutes or until zucchini are tender. Add corn and cook 5 minutes more. Season with salt and pepper and let cool slightly.

2. Puree in a food processor or blender. Refrigerate until cold. Add buttermilk and mix well. Check for seasonings. Serve lightly chilled.

Sautéed Zucchini with Corn and Avocado

This dish features a triumvirate of classic summer vegetables. (A quartet if you include the bell pepper.)

Makes 6 servings

3 medium zucchini, trimmed

2 teaspoons avocado oil or olive oil

1 red bell pepper, diced (about 3/4 cup)

6 trimmed scallions with 1 inch of green,
  thinly sliced

2 cloves garlic, minced

2 cups corn kernels, preferably fresh

1 avocado, peeled and coarsely chopped

1 teaspoon toasted cumin, ground
  (page 300)

1 teaspoon kosher salt

1/4 teaspoon freshly ground black pepper

1. Grate zucchini using a hand grater or the grater attachment of a food processor. Set aside.

2. Heat oil in a large skillet or wok and add pepper, scallions, and garlic. Cook 2 minutes over medium heat. Add zucchini and corn. Cook 5 minutes. Add remaining ingredients and cook just until avocado softens, but vegetables are still firm.

Roasted Summer Squash with Fresh Herbs

Use any combination of summer squash you like in this recipe, remembering to choose smaller sizes whenever possible.

Makes 8 servings as a side dish

Olive oil cooking spray

3 pounds summer squash to include zucchini, crookneck squash, scallopini, pattypan, and sunburst squash, all cut in ³/₄-inch cubes

2 medium red bell peppers, cut into 1-inch squares

3 small red onions, peeled and halved, each half cut into ¹/₂-inch-wide wedges (or 16 small boiler-type onions left whole)

Kosher salt and freshly ground black pepper to taste

1 tablespoon chopped fresh thyme or summer savory

2 tablespoons chopped fresh basil

2 tablespoons chopped chives

2 tablespoons extra-virgin olive oil

1. Preheat oven to 500°F. Spray a large, shallow roasting pan with olive oil cooking spray.

2. Add all vegetables, spray well with olive oil cooking spray, and toss. Add salt and pepper and toss again.

3. Put in the oven and cook 8 to 10 minutes. Toss and cook 8 to 10 minutes more. Add herbs, toss, and cook 5 minutes or until vegetables are cooked but still maintain their shape. Add olive oil and toss.

Sam's Cooking Tip

The larger and more shallow the roasting pan, the more the squash will brown and the faster they will cook.

Zucchini Pancakes

Here's a way to use up the pulp leftover from the Summer Squash Skins recipe (page 262). It makes a nice side dish with roasted chicken or as part of a Sunday brunch.

Makes 10 pancakes, enough for 5 or more servings

1½ pounds zucchini, shredded, salted, and squeezed (see Preparation, page 256)

2 teaspoons kosher salt

¼ cup minced onion

⅓ cup grated Parmesan cheese

2 teaspoons fresh thyme or 1 teaspoon dried

Freshly ground black pepper to taste

⅓ cup all-purpose flour

2 eggs, beaten

2 tablespoons canola oil

Nonfat sour cream (optional)

1. Put shredded zucchini in a mixing bowl with remaining ingredients except oil and sour cream.

2. Put oil in a nonstick skillet over medium heat. Add ¼ cup of zucchini mixture and form a pancake. Continue adding more pancakes but don't crowd the pan. Cook about 4 minutes on each side. Keep pancakes warm in a low oven until all are done.

3. Serve topped with nonfat sour cream, if desired.

Summer Squash Skins with Garlic Bread Crumbs

Somewhere, we're not exactly sure where, we read about a restaurant using the skins of summer squash rather than the whole squash. We tried it. It works!

Makes 4 servings

Olive oil cooking spray
4 cloves garlic, chopped
$1/4$ cup fresh bread crumbs
$3^1/2$ pounds zucchini or combination of
 zucchini and yellow crookneck squash,
 each no longer than 6 inches

1 tablespoon butter
1 tablespoon extra-virgin olive oil
Kosher salt and freshly ground black
 pepper to taste
3 tablespoons chopped fresh parsley

1. Preheat oven to 400°F. Spray a small baking sheet with olive oil cooking spray. Combine garlic and bread crumbs and spread evenly on the baking sheet. Spray again with olive oil cooking spray and bake 10 to 15 minutes or until nicely browned. Stir a few times to toast evenly.

2. Meanwhile, trim ends of the squash. Holding each squash upright (vertically), slice off the skins into long, narrow slices all around. (You should have about $1^1/4$ pounds.) Cut slices into long strips, about $1/4$ inch wide. Use the inside pulp for Zucchini Pancakes (page 261).

3. Put butter and oil in a large skillet or wok over medium-high heat. Add squash strips, raise heat to high, and toss. Cook, tossing occasionally, until squash strips are just beginning to soften but are still slightly crunchy, about 5 minutes.

4. Add garlic bread crumbs and parsley, toss, and serve.

Stuffed Winter Squash

This is a delicious main course for vegetarians at holiday time. But don't let them have all the fun. Meat eaters will love it too.

Makes 4 servings

2 large acorn or small butternut squash

Kosher salt and freshly ground black
  pepper to taste

One 6-ounce package wild rice

4 cups Vegetable Stock (page 64) or
  water

1 tablespoon butter or oil

8 ounces mushrooms, any combination of
  domestic and wild, sliced

1 cup chopped onions

1 rib celery, finely chopped

1/2 cup toasted nuts, any combination
  of pine nuts, hazelnuts, walnuts, and
  pecans, coarsely chopped (page 28)

2 tablespoons chopped fresh parsley

2 tablespoons fresh herbs such as thyme,
  chives, or marjoram, chopped

1 whole egg and 1 egg white

1. Preheat oven to 400°F. Cut squash in half lengthwise, scoop out the seeds, and put in a roasting pan, cut side down, with 1/2 inch of water. Bake about 40 minutes or until just tender. Remove, season with salt and pepper, and lower oven to 350°F.

2. Meanwhile, rinse wild rice and cook in stock or water about 45 minutes or until tender. Drain and put in a mixing bowl. Heat butter or oil in a large skillet over medium heat. Add mushrooms, onions, and celery. Cook until mushrooms wilt and onions soften, about 5 minutes. Add to wild rice along with nuts, parsley, herbs, salt, and pepper. Add egg and egg white and mix well.

3. Put stuffing into squash cavities, mounding slightly. Cover with foil and bake in a lightly greased baking dish 25 minutes or until heated through.

Squash Ravioli with Parmesan-Sage Cream

*A ravioli crimper, which looks like a ridged pizza cutter,
makes the job of making ravioli a lot easier.*

Makes 4 servings

1 to 1¹/₂ pounds pumpkin or other winter
  squash
¹/₂ teaspoon grated nutmeg
Kosher salt and freshly ground black
  pepper to taste
1 tablespoon butter
2 tablespoons all-purpose flour
2 cups skim milk, warmed

1 tablespoon fresh sage, finely chopped,
  or 2 teaspoons dried
6 tablespoons grated Parmesan cheese
  plus additional cheese for passing
12 sheets fresh lasagna noodles, each
  5×7 inches, enough for 36 ravioli
Cornmeal

1. Cut pumpkin in half, remove seeds, and place, cut side down, in a baking pan with ¹/₂ inch water. Bake in a preheated 350°F oven about 40 minutes or until very tender. (Microwaving takes less than half the time.) Scoop out flesh and puree with nutmeg, salt, and pepper. You should have about 1¹/₄ cups.

2. Meanwhile, put butter in a heavy-bottomed saucepan over medium heat. Add flour and stir a few minutes. Add milk slowly and bring to a bare simmer, whisking constantly. Cook until thickened and you can no longer taste any flour, about 10 minutes. Add sage, cheese, and salt and pepper to taste. Remove from heat and put plastic wrap on the surface to prevent skin from forming.

3. Spoon out pumpkin puree in 2 rows across and 3 rows down on one lasagna sheet using 1 teaspoon per ravioli. Brush another sheet with water. Gently put the second sheet on the first, wet side down. Run a ravioli cutter down the middle between the two rows and then across, sealing each ravioli with a ³/₈-inch border of dough all around. Without a ravioli cutter, press down with the side of your hand along the rows between the fillings, removing any air pockets. Seal with your fingers and cut ravioli free with a knife. Then crimp with the tines of a fork. Repeat with remaining pasta and filling until you have 36 ravioli. (To prevent sticking, put ravioli, as you make them, on a baking sheet sprinkled with cornmeal.)

4. Bring a pot with 4 quarts of water and 1 teaspoon salt to a boil over high heat. While water heats, gently reheat cream sauce. Add ravioli to cooking water, stir and cook, covered, about 3 or 4 minutes. All ravioli should rise to the surface. Drain.

5. Put half the cream sauce into the pasta pot over medium-low heat and add the ravioli. Add remaining sauce and gently stir, coating all the ravioli. Serve at once with more cheese passed at the table.

Baked Acorn Squash Rings

We wouldn't be at all surprised if the kids suddenly started eating squash after they try this recipe.

Makes 4 servings

1 medium acorn squash, about 1½ pounds
⅓ cup maple syrup mixed with 2 tablespoons
  bourbon or rum
Kosher salt to taste

1. Preheat oven to 400°F. Trim ends of squash and cut crosswise into 4 rings of equal thickness (about ¾ inch thick). Remove seeds and stringy material.

2. Put rings on a shallow baking pan. Add enough water to come halfway up the sides of the rings. Bake about 30 minutes, turning once, or until rings are just tender. Pour off any remaining water.

3. Brush one side of each ring with maple syrup mixture and season with salt. Bake 5 minutes. Repeat on the other side.

Sam's Cooking Tip

My wife likes to eat the skin and all with this dish. You may want to cook it a little longer if you plan on doing that yourself. Also, wash the skin well before cutting the rings.

Pumpkin Risotto

Pumpkin may seem like an all-American vegetable, but the Italians do wondrous things with it as well as with other winter squash, all of which they call zucca.

Makes 4 servings as a main course, 6 as an appetizer

7 to 8 cups Chicken Stock (page 9)
1 tablespoon butter
1 small onion, finely chopped
2 cups arborio rice
1 1/2 cups cooked butternut, acorn, or other winter squash, cut in 3/8-inch cubes

6 sage leaves, minced
Kosher salt and freshly ground white pepper to taste
1/2 cup grated Parmesan cheese
4 sage leaves for garnish

1. Heat stock to a bare simmer in a saucepan. Heat butter in a large, heavy-bottomed saucepan next to it on the stove. Add onion to the butter and cook over medium heat, stirring, until onion turns translucent. Add rice, stir, and add 1 1/2 cups of stock.

2. When the rice has absorbed most of the liquid, add another 1 1/2 cups of stock. Add another 1 1/2 cups in the same fashion along with the squash and minced sage. Repeat with another 1 1/2 cups stock and salt and pepper to taste.

3. After most of the stock has been absorbed, after 25–30 minutes, taste rice. It should be firm but tender. If too firm, add some or all of the remaining stock, again tasting to discover when it is just right. Leave the risotto a little runny before adding the cheese so it will have a nice creamy texture.

4. Dish into soup plates and stick a sage leaf in the middle of each plate. Serve immediately.

In _Can You Trust a Tomato_ *in January?*

(Simon and Schuster, 1993) author Vince Staten

writes, "There's a price to pay for year-round pro-

duce. Taste. The apples and tomatoes of today

aren't as tasty as they were thirty or forty years

ago. They've been bred for looks and long hauls in

trucks and boats. And for mass-market tastes, which means a blander tasting product."

Forty years ago, nobody expected tomatoes in January. They waited until summer and got their fill, along with corn and other foods that say summer, but not winter.

And for those who wanted the taste of delicious summer tomatoes in winter, there was canning. Sam's mother used to can more than two hundred quarts of tomatoes every summer, just for his family of six (seven when Grandpa stayed with them).

Granted, few have the time to can today. But does that mean the only alternative is a tomato that looks like a pink tennis ball— and tastes like one? We don't think so. If you've got to have tomatoes in a cooking recipe, buy canned tomatoes that are full of flavor because they were picked and packed when ripe. And if you're making a salad in January and want something to go with all that green, instead of adding tomatoes, try sliced radishes, grated red cabbage, thinly sliced red onions, shredded carrots, radicchio leaves, pomegranate seeds, sliced Fuyu persimmons, and red bell pepper rings.

WHERE GROWN

It's hard to imagine a state where tomatoes aren't grown, but the major commercial states are Florida and California. Florida is responsible for 50 percent of the domestic crop, about $1.5 billion in annual sales. A huge number of tomatoes are imported from Mexico.

VARIETIES

The major commercial varieties in Florida are Sunny, Solar Set, Bonita, Agriset, and BHN-26. The top California varieties are the Shady Lady, Merced, Olympic, Sunbolt, and Sunbrite. But, as the 1995 *Produce Availability and Merchandising Guide* notes, tomatoes are sold by types rather than by varieties. Whether field, stake, or pole grown, these types are described as mature green, vine pink or vine ripe, plum or roma, cherry, greenhouse, and hydroponic.

The workhorse of the mainstream tomato market is the **slicing or beefsteak tomato.** It is made to be sliced for sandwiches or cut into wedges for salads.

The major commercial tomatoes in this group are either picked mature green, meaning fully green, or they are picked somewhere during the next three stages of development up until they reach 30 percent, but no more than 60 percent, red or pink (called vine pink). Mature green tomatoes are "gassed" with ethylene gas to ripen them, whereas the vine pink are already sufficiently ripened.

Roma or plum tomatoes are considered sauce tomatoes because their thick skin, meaty pulp, and lack of juice is more conducive to making sauce. They can come in yellow or red varieties, but red is by far the most common. Despite their use in sauces they can still be used fresh and are often seen sliced with fresh mozzarella cheese and basil leaves.

Cherry tomatoes are about the size of a large cherry and can be red or yellow, though again, red is the main color. Mostly for salads, they can also be hollowed and stuffed or sliced and sautéed. Sweet 100s are a particular type of cherry tomato that has exceptional flavor and sweetness.

Pear-shaped tomatoes look like teardrops and come in yellow and red, though more yellow than red. Use them like cherry tomatoes, though in general they tend to be sweeter.

There are enough specialty varieties of tomatoes to warrant books on their own. The best way to find them is to frequent local farmer's markets where farmers are more likely to experiment with obscure tomatoes like green striped, yellow, and orange tomatoes.

SEASONS

As noted, tomatoes are regrettably a year-round vegetable. Florida's crop runs from October through June, while California's runs from May through December. Domestic peak supplies occur from May to July. The Mexican production is concentrated from January through April.

SELECTION, HANDLING & STORAGE

We think our friend Janet Fletcher has the right piece of advice for selecting good tomatoes: "Tomatoes should smell like tomatoes. If they have no aroma, put them back." Some of the best tomatoes we've ever eaten were butt ugly, yet they had a fabulous tomato aroma. On the other hand, some real beauties smelled as if they had just been removed from a hermetically sealed room.

Because good tomatoes are fragile and seasonal, frequent local farmer's markets for the best ones. Buy them at different stages of development so they don't all ripen at once. For example, buy a few dead ripe ones you'll use that night, a few others that will be ready in a day or two, and maybe a few more that will be ready in three or four days.

Avoid tomatoes with leathery dark patches. This is blossom end rot caused by drought following a period of rainy weather.

Unless you've just arrived from one of Jupiter's moons, you should know by now that tomatoes should never be refrigerated until or unless they (1) have been cooked, (2) have been cut or put into a raw dish like a salsa, or (3) are fully ripe and would spoil if left further at room temperature. But make sure you bring the uncooked tomatoes to room temperature before consuming them to get as much flavor out of them as possible.

The ideal temperature for holding and ripening tomatoes is between 62°F and 68°F with relatively high humidity. That means kitchen countertops and places where you keep other nonrefrigerated fresh food; place tomatoes stem end up. Don't put them on a sunny window sill to hasten ripening. Instead, put tomatoes in a sealed paper bag with or without ethylene-producing fruit such as bananas. Depending on how unripe they were to begin with, the tomatoes may take up to five days to ripen. Ripe tomatoes will hold at room temperature for two or three days.

NUTRITION

One medium tomato (148g, 5.3 ounces) contains 35 calories, 7g of carbohydrates, 1g each of protein and dietary fiber, .5g of fat, 20% of the DV for vitamin A, 40% for vitamin C, and 2% each for calcium and iron. Tomatoes are also a good source of potassium (360mg).

According to Jean Carper's *Food: Your Miracle Medicine,* tomatoes are a "major source of lycopene, an awesome antioxidant and anti-cancer agent that intervenes in devastating chain reactions of oxygen-free radical molecules." In addition, tomatoes have been shown to be helpful in reducing the incidence of pancreatic and cervical cancers.

Some people believe that tomatoes, as well as other members of the nightshade family, contribute to arthritis, but this is not a proven theory.

YIELD

A pound of tomatoes (about three medium, eight plum, twenty-five to thirty cherry) will yield about 2 cups chopped.

Tony's Tip

"Greasy" tomatoes have been sprayed with paraffin to make them shiny. Avoid these tomatoes unless that's all that is available. Then make sure you wash them thoroughly before using them.

PREPARATION

To core a tomato, use the tip of a sharp paring knife to make a shallow cut all around the stem end, then pop out the core. Slicing should be done with a serrated knife or a very sharp non-serrated knife. Or, failing both, prick the skin with the tip of the knife to get a slice going. Then follow through with the blade. Cut lengthwise (from stem to blossom end) rather than widthwise to retain more juice.

To dice a tomato, first slice the tomato. Take half of the slices and, with a flat slice on the cutting surface, cut them into strips. Then cut crosswise into dice. Repeat with the other half of the slices.

To peel a tomato, drop into boiling water about 15 to 20 seconds (longer if you're doing several tomatoes at one time or the tomatoes are very firm). Then run under cold water or plunge into a bowl of ice water until cool, about 5 minutes. The skin will slip away easily. (Some people make a small **x** opposite the stem end before putting into hot water to facilitate removing the peel.)

Seeding tomatoes is usually done more for aesthetic reasons than flavor. In fact, some nutrition is lost when seeds are removed. Nonetheless, to seed, halve the tomato horizontally. Then hold each half over a strainer sitting on a bowl. Squeeze and the seeds will be trapped in the strainer.

When cooking with tomatoes avoid aluminum pots because they give tomatoes a bitter flavor. If the tomatoes you're cooking with aren't especially sweet, add a healthy pinch of sugar. And don't hold back on the salt. Tomatoes need a healthy dose of it to bring out flavor. When using tomatoes in a salad, add them at the end so their juices won't make the salad soggy.

For stuffed tomatoes, try to find single-serving sizes. Then cut a slice off the top at the stem end and scoop out seeds and pulp with a grapefruit spoon. Invert on paper towels to let excess moisture drain out. If the tomatoes are large, halve them horizontally and follow the same process.

Broiling, grilling, and oven roasting can add more flavor to out-of-season or otherwise insipid tomatoes. Cook, turning until nicely blistered and charred.

Seasonings that go especially well with tomatoes are garlic, olive oil, basil, dill, oregano, and parsley. For a low-calorie tomato salad, try splashing sliced tomatoes with a good-quality balsamic vinegar instead of olive oil.

Salsa Cruda—Italian Style

There is nothing that brings out the flavor of ripe, locally grown tomatoes more than an uncooked pasta sauce. Some versions call for peeling the tomatoes, but we prefer to simply core them and squeeze out some of the seeds. To our way of thinking, this sauce needs no cheese. But you may want to have some Parmesan around for guests to gently add.

Makes 6 servings as a first course, 4 as an entrée

2 pounds ripe, locally grown tomatoes
2 tablespoons chopped fresh basil
2 large cloves garlic, smashed but left
  whole

2 tablespoons extra-virgin olive oil
Kosher salt and freshly ground black
  pepper to taste
1 pound pasta of your choice

1. Core the tomatoes and squeeze out some of the seeds and juice. (You'll still have some seeds left but that's okay.) Slice, then chop the tomatoes into medium dice. Put in a small mixing bowl.

2. Add the remaining ingredients except for the pasta. Stir, cover, and let sit at room temperature 1 hour. Taste for basil, salt, pepper, and garlic. The garlic flavor should be noticeable but subtle. Remove the garlic and discard. (The sauce can sit for a few more hours at room temperature if need be, but do not refrigerate.)

3. Boil a large pot of water for pasta. Cook pasta until al dente and drain well. Put tomato sauce in a serving bowl and toss with pasta.

Bread and Tomato Salad

Italians may be known for pasta, but they live on bread, especially Tuscans. Leftover bread gets transformed into wonderful dishes like this one.

Makes 4 servings

1¼ pounds ripe tomatoes
Kosher salt
2½ tablespoons each balsamic vinegar and olive oil
3 tablespoons defatted Chicken Stock (page 9)
Freshly ground black pepper to taste
1 clove garlic, smashed but left whole

1 loaf country Italian or French bread with firm texture, about ¾ pound
⅓ cup coarsely chopped celery leaves
1 cup sweet red onions, thinly sliced
½ cup fresh basil leaves, cut into thin strips
2 tablespoons capers, well drained

1. Core tomatoes, halve lengthwise, and cut into wedges no more than ⅜ inch wide. Toss with a teaspoon of salt in a large bowl. Set aside at room temperature 30 to 60 minutes. Drain tomatoes and reserve juice.

2. In a small bowl combine vinegar, olive oil, Chicken Stock, the reserved tomato juice, pepper, and garlic. Stir and set aside.

3. Cut bread into bite-size cubes or break apart with your hands for a more rustic look. Add bread to tomatoes and toss well. Add celery leaves, onions, and basil to bread/tomato mixture. Remove garlic from dressing, stir well, and pour over salad. Toss well. Let stand 30 to 60 minutes at room temperature.

4. Check salad and adjust seasonings as needed. Sprinkle with capers and serve.

Sam's Cooking Tip

Salting the tomatoes ahead of time draws out the moisture and helps to create a more flavorful dressing without a lot of oil.

Gazpacho

No dish brings together the summer bounty better than gazpacho.
This version has corn, which adds a special texture that we love.

Makes 4 servings

2 ears corn on the cob

2 pounds ripe tomatoes

3 Kirby cucumbers

1 medium sweet red or Vidalia onion,
  coarsely chopped

$1^2/_3$ cups or more spicy V-8 juice (or other
  tomato juice that is seasoned liberally
  with hot sauce)

$1^1/_4$ teaspoons ground, toasted cumin
  seeds (see page 300)

$^1/_4$ cup fresh basil leaves

Kosher salt and freshly ground black
  pepper to taste

1. Put on a few quarts of water to boil. Drop the corn on the cob in boiling water and cook about 3 or 4 minutes. (If the corn is very fresh and the kernels small, you can eliminate this step.) Cool and slice off kernels. Set aside. Keep water at a boil.

2. Drop tomatoes into the boiling water for 15 seconds and drain. Refresh tomatoes under cool water, peel, core, and chop coarsely. Set aside.

3. Peel and coarsely chop two of the cucumbers. Put them into a food processor. Trim the third cucumber and cut into small dice, unpeeled. Set it aside.

4. Put onion in the food processor and pulse with cucumber. When coarsely pureed, add tomatoes and pulse until desired consistency. Put in a bowl and add $1^2/_3$ cups V-8 juice. Add more if you want a thinner soup.

5. Add ground cumin seeds to soup. Stack basil leaves, roll cigar-style, and cut crosswise into strips. Add to soup.

6. Add diced cucumbers and corn to soup along with salt and pepper to taste. Refrigerate 1 hour or more. Adjust seasonings as desired.

Roasted Tomato Salsa

Freshly made salsa beats the stuff in cans and jars every time, not only for flavor but for price as well. Despite the number of jalapeño peppers, this salsa isn't particularly hot. In fact, you may want to roast a fourth pepper and add it at the end if you want the salsa even spicier.

Makes about 4 cups

4 large, ripe but still firm tomatoes
3 jalapeño peppers
3 cloves garlic, unpeeled
1 medium red onion, quartered

2 tablespoons chopped cilantro, or more to taste
Kosher salt and freshly ground black pepper to taste

1. Put vegetables on a sheet pan in a 500°F oven or on a charcoal or gas grill over medium heat. Cook until nicely charred and blistered. (They will char more on the grill. They will take about 30 minutes in the oven, less on the grill.)

2. Core, but don't peel the tomatoes. Peel, stem, and seed the peppers. Peel the garlic and remove the skin from the onion.

3. With the motor of a food processor running, drop the garlic down the feed tube. When pureed, scrape down the sides of the bowl. Add the onion and pulse a few times. Add tomatoes and peppers and pulse until you achieve the texture you desire.

4. Pour into a bowl and add cilantro and salt and pepper. Let sit an hour for flavors to meld and temperature to cool.

Sam's Cooking Tip

Grilling and roasting add a pleasing flavor to tomatoes and other in-season vegetables. But these cooking methods also give a flavor boost to tomatoes when they're not in season.

Pasta with Cherry Tomatoes and Pesto

Pasta with pesto made with local basil and tomatoes is one of summer's ultimate treats. Try to get Sweet 100s or a similar flavorful and sweet cherry tomato. But take care not to oversauce the pasta, which Americans have a tendency to do. You want a nice balance of pesto, pasta, and tomatoes.

Makes 4 servings as a main course, 6 as an appetizer

1 large clove garlic
1 tablespoon toasted pine nuts
  (page 28)
3 cups fresh basil leaves
Kosher salt to taste
3 tablespoons olive oil
3 tablespoons grated Parmesan and
Pecorino Romano cheeses, mixed

1 pound short pasta, such as penne
1 cup halved, small cherry tomatoes such
  as Sweet 100s
Additional grated cheese for passing
  (optional)

1. Put on a pot with 4 quarts of water and 2 teaspoons salt to boil.

2. Meanwhile, with the motor of a food processor running, drop garlic and pine nuts down the feed tube. When pureed, push down the sides and add basil, salt, and oil. Puree. Add cheese and pulse just until mixed. (This may also be done in a blender or with a mortar and pestle.) Put pesto in a small bowl. You should have about $^3/_4$ cup pesto.

3. Cook pasta according to package directions in the pot of boiling water until firm but tender, about 10 minutes. Drain pasta, reserving $^1/_2$ cup of the cooking water.

4. Put pasta in a large mixing bowl. Add between half and two-thirds of the pesto and toss, adding just enough of the cooking water to make an even sauce. Add tomatoes, toss again, and serve. Pass around additional grated cheese if desired.

Sam's Cooking Tip

Fresh basil is now available in most areas year-round. But February basil pales in comparison to August basil. Seek out locally grown basil for more intense flavor. And make sure it's dry before you chop it or it will blacken.

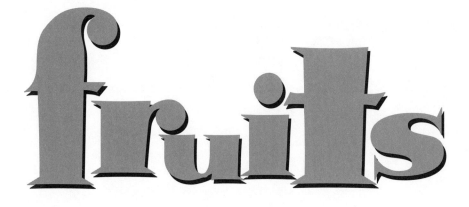

apples

Apples, the number-two consumed fruit

in the United States after bananas, seem like a

staid and steady fruit, as traditional and depend-

able as Grandma's apple pie. But changes are

afoot in the apple business. Not too long ago, the

only apples people bought were Washington

State Delicious because of their cosmetic appeal.

But new varieties are making major inroads in the apple market. For example, Fuji and Gala apples, which were not even ranked in popularity in 1992, are now two of the top-selling apples in the United States, ranked fifth and seventh respectively in 1996. Both have an unbeatable combination of sweetness and crisp flavor. As a matter of fact, we think the Fuji apple will be the number-one seller in the United States by the end of the decade. And just as well. We think Red Delicious apples are kind of boring.

WHERE GROWN

Apples, members of the rose family, are grown throughout the world in temperate climates because the trees require a change of climate, including cold weather, to trigger flowering and production cycles. Commercial crops in the United States are concentrated in the northern states of Washington (far and away the nation's biggest producer), Michigan, and New York. California and Pennsylvania round out the top five.

VARIETIES

Fifteen varieties accounted for over 90% of the 1996 domestic production. According to the U.S. Apple Association, these varieties are, in descending order of popularity, Red Delicious, Golden Delicious, Granny Smith, Rome, Fuji, McIntosh, Gala, Jonathan, Empire, York, Idared, Newton Pippin, Cortland, Rhode Island Greening, and Northern Spy.

The **Fuji,** the most extensively planted apple variety worldwide, was developed in the early 1960s by crossing the Japanese Mutsu with a California Winesap in California's San Joaquin Valley. The result is a yellow-green to blush skin apple with a perfect sweet-tart balance, outstanding juiciness, and crisp texture. The Gala has a similar shape to the Fuji but has a more polished look. The skin may be a bit thicker and more leathery than the Fuji, but the flesh is just as inviting.

The **Red Delicious** was developed in Iowa in 1881 and is currently grown in all areas of the United States except the South. Its strong points are uniformity and an attractive dark red color. But it can be a bit too sweet and can get mealy (in part because consumers and stores like to display it out of refrigeration). The Red Delicious doesn't cook well because it falls apart under sustained heat. Yellow to yellow-green and lightly freckled, Golden Delicious was developed in West Virginia in 1890. It isn't quite as sweet as the Red Delicious but it cooks much better. The distinctively striped Gravenstein is a German import (circa 1824) and is now grown mostly in California. It's more suited to cooking (especially for applesauce) than to eating out of hand.

The bright red **Jonathan,** a New York variety developed in 1880, doubles nicely as an eating and cooking apple because of its crispness and pleasantly tart flavor. The McIntosh, which originated in Ontario, Canada, in 1870 and is still grown there as well as in British Columbia, is a more tender and slightly less tart apple. For these reasons, cooking with this red and green variety is limited, but it remains a fine apple for eating fresh. Bright green Granny Smith is called "tart-sweet-tart" meaning it is mostly tart but with a hint of sweetness. Its firm texture and good size as well as flavor makes it ideal for baking.

The large, shiny red **Rome** is strictly a cooking apple, almost never eaten out of hand or in any raw preparation. Try it for whole baked apples, but not for apple pies (see Preparation, page 282). Tart Staymans have deep, purplish red skins. They're firm, tart, and juicy—ideal for baking and eating fresh. Winesaps are close enough to Staymans to be kissin' cousins.

The **Newton Pippin,** also called the Yellow Newton, was developed in New York in the early eighteenth century and should not be confused with the European Pippin. Now grown primarily in the Northwest, California, and Virginia, this medium-size apple has green to yellow coloring and a winelike flavor. The shiny red York Imperial (also known simply as the York) won't get any prizes for uniformity, but its firm texture and winey flavor make it a good candidate for baking. The firm-textured and slightly tart Empire is a fine all-purpose apple and much underrated.

Among the lesser-known varieties, the **Baldwin** apple**,** introduced in Massachusetts around 1740, is now grown in New York and Michigan as well as New England. It's slightly tart and a good apple for cooking. The mildly acidic, small- to medium-size **Northern Spy** (sometimes just called Spy) has red streaks and can be used for snacking and cooking. The **Spygold** is a mixture of Spy and Golden Delicious apples. But it is not as widely available as the **Jonagold,** a combination of Jonathan and Golden Delicious apples.

Red and green-gold **Braeburn,** a New Zealand import, is sweet, aromatic, and juicy. Tart and juicy **Idared** is a popular eating apple. And the tart **Rhode Island Greening,** sometimes just called Greening, is (as you might suspect) a Northeastern apple and just dandy for apple pies.

SEASONS

The seasons vary from variety to variety. Gravensteins and Galas start appearing in August. Cortlands, Empires, Idareds, Jonathans, McIntoshes, Newton Pippins, Staymans, and Winesaps follow in September. Most of these varieties continue well into spring or early summer, though the Jonagold has a relatively short life span from September through October. In October you'll also see Braeburns, Fujis, and Romes. Red Delicious, Golden Delicious, and Granny Smith apples are available year-round.

Through the miracle of controlled atmosphere storage, apples picked in the fall can be available well into the following spring. Since apples take in oxygen and give off carbon dioxide as they deteriorate, scientists discovered that by keeping apples in airtight rooms (which can contain as many as 100,000 boxes of apples) with reduced levels of oxygen (from around 21 percent in the air we breathe to less than 2 percent), low temperatures (30°F to 36°F), and high humidity (around 95 percent), apples can be stored up to twelve months.

SELECTION, HANDLING & STORAGE

Since so many of us buy produce from appearance, it's not surprising that the shiny Red Delicious is a best-seller. But if you look for taste, rather than cosmetic beauty, you'll often be pleasantly surprised.

The first consideration when shopping for apples is to decide how you plan to use them: in the lunch bag, baked by themselves or in pies and cakes, for salads, or in applesauce. Apples have their own characteristics and some go well with one kind of preparation but not with another. For example, Cortland apples are a good choice for salads because they tend not to turn brown once cut as other apples do. Generally though, it's a good idea to experiment and mix apples for most kinds of apple dishes to get the flavor or combination of flavors that appeals to you.

An apple's color should be vibrant with no browning near the core. The size generally is a good indicator of maturity: The larger the apple, the riper you will find it. Apples should be firm to hard and not easily bruised. There should be no broken skins or blemishes, though a few freckles are okay in some varieties.

Apples should be kept cool. If not, they become overripe quickly, which affects texture and flavor. When left out at room temperature apples become mealy and mushy. Since most apples are picked at their peak ripeness, any additional ripening actually means an acceleration in the decaying process. To stem this decay, apples should be refrigerated as soon as they are brought home from the market, no matter how nice they look in that bowl on the dining-room table.

If purchased in good condition, apples should last up to six weeks in the refrigerator. But check them often and remove any decayed apples, because one rotten apple really *can* spoil the whole bunch.

NUTRITION

One medium apple (154g, about 5.4 ounces) contains 80 calories, 22g of carbohydrates, 5g of dietary fiber, and no protein. A serving also contains 8% of the DV for vitamin C and 2% each for vitamin A and iron.

Apples are high in dietary fiber, which helps maintain regularity and avoid constipation. The soluble fiber in apples, in the form of pectin, helps to lower cholesterol levels. Pectin also aids in preventing colon cancer. Apples are rich in boron, which helps to stem the onset of osteoporosis. And apples can help boost estrogen levels in women.

YIELD

Figuring how many apples are in a pound is as easy as one, two, three, four. One pound of apples is made up of two large, three medium, or four small apples. A pound also yields about 2 to 2½ cups of chopped or sliced apples. For a 9-inch pie, you'll need between six and eight medium to large apples.

Tony's Tip

Store apples as cold as possible in the refrigerator. They won't freeze until the temperature dips to 28.5°F.

PREPARATION

Apples have a multitude of uses when raw (fruit salads, Waldorf salad) or cooked (applesauce, baked whole apples). They have a particular affinity for pork and cinnamon. But above all, apples go into the quintessential American dessert, apple pie. So we thought you'd like to know which apples make a great apple pie.

When Sam did some research for a magazine story on apple pies a few years ago, he surveyed a number of America's top dessert makers. All rejected the Rome, which, though considered a "cooking apple," is not renowned for apple pies. Nor is the Red Delicious, which can be mushy and overly sweet. Nor the McIntosh, a favorite of New England and New York as an eating apple but not quite sturdy enough for pies. Nor the soft and sweet Gravenstein, which makes far better applesauce than apple pie.

All said a good apple pie demands a hearty, tart, and aromatic apple along the lines of the Newton Pippin or a Granny Smith, the favorites of Marion Cunningham, author of *The Fanny Farmer Cookbook* (Knopf, 1990); Susan Purdy, author of *As Easy as Pie* (Collier Books, 1984); Flo Braker, author of *The Simple*

Art of Perfect Baking (Chapters, 1992); and Maida Heatter, known affectionately as America's Dessert Queen. The Rhode Island Greening also fits into that category.

Jim Dodge, former longtime pastry chef at the Stanford Court Hotel in San Francisco, likes Gala apples for their firmness, Baldwin apples (especially when still a little green), and Cortland apples for those who prefer sweetness over tartness. Sam's mother-in-law, Madge Keane, who makes a terrific apple pie, has always touted the tangy Northern Spy. Other apples to consider are the Stayman, Winesap, Jonathan, and Golden Delicious, which Braker says tastes better cooked than raw.

The time of year can also determine whether an apple is right for apple pie. People don't think of apple pies in the fall for nothing. Unripe apples in August can be watery and slightly sour. After months of storage, late winter and early spring apples can be a little mealy.

Totally confused about which apple to use? Braker has this nifty little test. Cut a slice of the apple in question and put it in a small bowl with a bit of sugar and water. Zap it for a few minutes in the microwave oven and taste it. Is it too mushy? Overly astringent? Or just right? If you're lucky enough to have more than one apple from which to choose, consider using a combination of apples for a more complex flavor.

Pork Medallions with Apples and Cider

Pork and apples always seem to go together.

Makes 2 servings

1 small pork tenderloin, about 8 ounces
2 tablespoons flour
$3/4$ teaspoon ground ginger
$1/2$ teaspoon grated nutmeg
Kosher salt and freshly ground black
  pepper to taste

$1/2$ tablespoon clarified butter (see tip)
  or whole butter
1 firm tart apple such as Granny Smith,
  peeled, cored, and thinly sliced
$1/2$ cup hard apple cider (or nonalcoholic
  sparkling cider)

1. Cut tenderloin into 1-inch-thick slices. Put slices between butcher paper or aluminum foil and pound until about $1/4$ inch thick. You should have about 6 slices.

2. Combine flour with ginger, nutmeg, and salt and pepper to taste. Dredge pork medallions in seasoned flour and shake off excess.

3. In a nonstick skillet large enough to hold all the medallions comfortably in one layer, heat clarified butter over medium heat. When butter is hot, add pork and cook about 3 to 4 minutes on each side.

4. Remove cutlets to a warm platter or serving plates. Add apple to the skillet. Cook a few minutes, turning to brown evenly. Add cider and raise heat to medium high. As soon as the sauce thickens, pour over pork.

Sam's Cooking Tip

To clarify butter, put a pound of butter in a saucepan over medium-low heat. Gently simmer 5 minutes, remove from the heat and cool 5 minutes. Skim off the top layer of foam. Pour the clarified butter gently into a bowl. Stop when you reach the milky white solids on the bottom of the pan. Don't throw out the milky solids. They're delicious on cooked vegetables. Clarified butter keeps several weeks in the refrigerator.

Sixes Wild Baked Apples

There are few desserts that are more comforting and easier to make than baked apples. At Vincenzo's, Sam's first restaurant in Philadelphia, baked apples were stuffed with raisins and pine nuts and served with crème anglaise. This recipe is a little lighter but just as satisfying. In place of dried cranberries, you can use any dried fruit such as dried cherries. Also, you can switch from sherry to Marsala, Madeira, or a fruit-flavored brandy.

Makes 6 servings

6 tablespoons dried cranberries

6 tablespoons cream sherry

6 tart apples such as Granny Smith, Winesap, or Stayman

6 teaspoons fresh lemon juice

Butter-flavored cooking spray

6 tablespoons brown sugar

6 teaspoons butter

Faux crème anglaise (see tip), about 1¹/₂ cups

1. Soak cranberries in cream sherry about 30 minutes.

2. Meanwhile, core the apples and peel the top third. Sprinkle with lemon juice.

3. Drain cranberries, reserving sherry. Spray the bottom of a baking (or microwave-safe) dish just large enough to hold all the apples with butter-flavored cooking spray. Place apples upright in the dish. Stuff the cavities of the apples with the cranberries; sprinkle cavities and tops of apples with brown sugar, then sprinkle with sherry. Dot with butter. Bake, covered in a conventional oven at 375°F for about 40 minutes. Or, in a microwave oven about 15 minutes, turning halfway through the cooking.

4. When done, apples should be soft but still maintain their shape. Serve with faux crème anglaise.

Sam's Cooking Tip

To keep this a low-fat dessert, try this recipe for faux crème anglaise, which I learned from the suzerain of slim, Jeanne Jones. Melt low or nonfat vanilla frozen yogurt or ice cream to room temperature. Add some liqueur of your choice (Grand Marnier or Amaretto), then pour a thin pool of it on a plate and top with the apple.

Madge's Apple Pie

Pies are very difficult to bring in under 10 grams of fat or 30 percent of calories per serving, because it's almost impossible to make a decent crust without a certain amount of fat. But this pie, from Sam's mother-in-law, Madge Keane, is so good we just had to share it with you. Use the same crust for the Blueberry Pie on page 319.

Makes 8 servings

Crust

2 cups all-purpose flour
¼ teaspoon kosher salt
½ cup canola oil

⅓ cup plus a few tablespoons well-chilled milk

Filling

6 cups (about 4 to 5 large) tart apples such as Northern Spy or a mixture of apples of your choice (see Preparation, page 282), peeled, cored, and thinly sliced

¾ cup plus 1 tablespoon granulated sugar
½ cup brown sugar
3 tablespoons flour
1 teaspoon cinnamon
½ teaspoon nutmeg

1. For crust, combine flour and salt in a bowl. Combine oil and milk in a covered jar and shake vigorously to mix. Make a well in the center of the flour mixture and pour in oil and milk mixture. Form two balls, one slightly larger than the other. Roll out the larger one between 2 sheets of plastic wrap so it is just large enough to cover the bottom and sides of a 9-inch pie pan. Place in pie pan.

2. Preheat oven to 450°F. Put apples in a large bowl. Combine ¾ cup granulated sugar, brown sugar, 3 tablespoons flour, and seasonings in a small bowl. Pour over apples and toss. Put apples in pie plate and spread evenly.

3. Roll out remaining ball of dough. Place over filling, pinch edges all around to secure, and make a few slits on top with a sharp knife. Brush with remaining milk and sprinkle with remaining tablespoon of sugar. Bake on a sheet pan 15 minutes. Reduce heat to 350°F and bake 45 to 60 minutes more or until nicely browned and bubbly. Serve warm or at room temperature.

Sam's Cooking Tip

To make up for the more-than-usual amount of fat, this recipe uses heart-healthy canola oil instead of shortening or butter. You could also cut the fat somewhat by using 1% milk instead of whole milk in the crust.

Turkey Waldorf with Fennel

This is a great dish for the day after big holidays such as Thanksgiving, Christmas, or Easter.

Makes 4 to 6 servings

2 cups cooked turkey (smoked or roasted), cubed

2 cups crisp apples such as Fuji, Stayman, or Granny Smith, cored (but not peeled) and cut into ¹/₂-inch dice

1 cup coarsely chopped fennel

¹/₄ cup dried cranberries or dried cherries, soaked 20 minutes in warm water and drained

¹/₄ cup minced scallions

¹/₃ cup low-fat mayonnaise

¹/₃ cup low- or nonfat sour cream

1 tablespoon grated ginger

1 teaspoon lemon or lime juice

Kosher salt and freshly ground black pepper to taste

1. Combine turkey, apples, fennel, cranberries, and scallions in a mixing bowl.

2. In a small bowl, combine remaining ingredients. Pour dressing over turkey et al. Mix well and refrigerate a few hours before serving.

apricots

It seems appropriate that the delicate

apricot with its gentle sweetness would usher

in the summer fruit season. In May and early

June, apricots give us a subtle harbinger of the

bounty that awaits us in the coming months.

Unfortunately, that harbinger can be a bit too

subtle. Since apricots bruise easily in transit, like tomatoes, what we often see in the markets outside California (where most of them are grown) is a sturdier and less flavorful apricot like the Patterson and the Katy varieties, not the sweet and succulent ones like the Blenheim. Unfortunately, we can't all grow apricots in our backyards like we can tomatoes.

If only everyone living outside the Santa Clara Valley in California, where the Blenheim is king, knew the flavor of a Blenheim at its peak, they would never look at another apricot in the same way again. They'd demand that growers and shippers not send us tasteless apricots and find a way to get us better-tasting varieties instead of sacrificing flavor and sweetness on the altar of packaging and transportation expediency. If we can send a man to the moon and develop a frying pan that won't stick, can't we find a way to ship the best apricots America has to offer?

WHERE GROWN

Leading producing countries are Turkey, Italy, Spain, and Greece. The United States ranks sixth in world production. Almost 95 percent of the domestic crop is grown in California, with the remainder coming from Utah and Washington. Imported fresh apricots generally come from Chile.

VARIETIES

Ever wonder why the liqueur amaretto tastes like almonds, even though it's not made with almonds but with apricot pits? It's because apricots and almonds (as well as peaches, cherries, and other fruits) are all members of the rose family or the genus *Prunus*. The apricot branch of the family tree has quite a few members. The leading varieties shipped out of California are, in order of appearance on the market,

Castlebrite, Katy, Improved Flaming Gold, Patterson, and Tilton.

The generally bright orange Castlebrite has good flavor when fully ripe. But as we've said, that doesn't happen often outside local California markets. The large Katy is a relatively new variety, in production since 1978. It's yellow-orange with some blush and excellent flavor when fully ripe. Improved Flaming Gold has an orange-yellow to an occasional yellow color and is not as flavorful as the Katy or Castlebrite. Second to the Castlebrite in volume shipped is the Patterson, which is known more for its yield than for its flavor. The most flavorful of the bunch is the oval and slightly flat Tilton, noted for its "suture" line that goes halfway around the fruit. This longtime favorite, which used to be the dominant California variety, is tender and juicy with a sweet-tart flavor.

Despite the fact that it is usually dried to preserve its distinctive sweet-tart flavor and intense color, we urge you to seek out the fresh Blenheim apricot (see Seasons, below). Though it is sometimes called the Blenheim Royal, the Blenheim and the Royal are two different varieties. But experts consider them so similar that they are commonly referred to as one variety.

SEASONS

Apricots need specific climatic conditions to achieve their full potential. Since they bloom early, they are particularly susceptible to heavy or late frosts. Moderate summers are also preferred over blazing heat.

The domestic season usually begins the first week in May with the Castlebrite variety, which matures around May 7. The following week it's the Katy variety, and Improved Flaming Gold the week after that. The Derby arrives the last week in May followed by the Pomo and

Modesto at the beginning of June. The Blenheim starts about June 7, the Patterson June 12, and the Tracy a few days later. The Tilton appears about June 18 and the Westley around June 25.

If you see these varieties hanging around through August they most likely come from Washington or other parts of the Northwest. Chile begins shipping in mid-November when the first hints of summer appear in the southern hemisphere. The varieties shipped, in order of importance, are the Katy, Modesto, and Castlebrite.

SELECTION, HANDLING & STORAGE

Apricots are notable for their delicate flavor, velvety smooth surface, and wonderfully sweet aroma. But outside California it's difficult to find this tree-ripened fruit when fully ripe. Once ripened, apricots do not ship well.

Look for fairly firm, smooth, plump, well-formed fruit that has an orange-yellow to orange color. If fruit is hard and tinged with green it won't develop full flavor. Fully ripe fruit is soft to the touch, full of juice, and should be eaten as soon as possible.

Store unripe apricots in a paper bag at room temperature away from heat and direct sunlight. Once ripe, usually two to four days, apricots will keep for a day, maybe two, if stored in a plastic bag in the refrigerator. But let the fruit come to room temperature before eating. Don't wash the fruit until you are ready to use it and remember to handle ripe apricots gently, being especially careful not to break the skin.

NUTRITION

A serving of three apricots (114g, about 4 ounces) contains 60 calories, 11g of carbohydrates, 1g of dietary fiber and fat, 45% of the DV for vitamin A, 20% for vitamin C, and 2% each for calcium and iron. Apricots are also a good source of potassium.

Levels of potassium and fiber more than double and vitamin A increases (though vitamin C decreases) with a comparable serving of dried apricots.

As with apples, the pectin in fresh apricots can be helpful in warding off colon cancer.

YIELD

A pound of eight to twelve apricots will yield about $2\frac{1}{2}$ to 3 cups of sliced fruit.

Tony's Tip

> When buying dried apricots, look for sun-dried apricots. They have a much finer flavor than those dried using other techniques.

PREPARATION

Because of the delicate nature of apricots and their small size, it's not advisable (or necessary) to peel them or to use them in any severe cooking method. A spicy chutney, for example, would obliterate the subtle flavor of fresh apricots (though dried apricots would fare well). And since perfectly ripe, flavorful, fresh apricots are not always easy to get, canned apricots are often an adequate substitute in many dishes.

Apricots can be employed in many recipes that call for nectarines or peaches. They can be used in tarts, cobblers, and crisps, in jams, chutneys, and compotes. They can be grilled, sautéed, broiled, or baked. They go particularly well with poultry and pork. Cinnamon, nutmeg, ginger, almonds, rum, brandy, amaretto, and sherry are good flavorings.

Apricot and Strawberry Cobbler

Instead of the usual dollop of ice cream or frozen yogurt, try a drizzle of cool, thick buttermilk on top of this warm cobbler. The buttermilk makes a nice counterpoint to the sweet fruit.

Makes 6 servings

2 pounds ripe apricots, pitted and sliced
1 pint fresh strawberries, hulled, halved if large and whole if small
$^3/_4$ cup plus 2 tablespoons sugar
2 tablespoons cornstarch
$^1/_2$ teaspoon ground nutmeg
3 tablespoons rum or brandy (optional)
1 tablespoon fresh lemon juice

Butter-flavored cooking spray
1 cup all-purpose flour
1 teaspoon baking powder
$^1/_4$ teaspoon salt
3 tablespoons chilled butter, cut into small pieces
1 cup low-fat buttermilk, approximately

1. Combine apricots and strawberries in a large mixing bowl. Sprinkle with $^3/_4$ cup sugar, cornstarch, and nutmeg. Toss. Sprinkle with rum and lemon juice. Toss. Spray a 2-quart baking dish with butter-flavored spray and spread the fruit evenly inside.

2. Preheat oven to 375°F. Put flour, baking powder, salt, and remaining granulated sugar in a mixing bowl. Cut in the butter with a large fork or pastry blender until the mixture resembles coarse meal. Add just enough buttermilk to get a thick batter.

3. Spread batter over fruit. Spray with butter-flavored spray. Bake 30 to 35 minutes or until top is nicely browned and fruit is bubbly. Serve warm or at room temperature.

Sam's Cooking Tip

Since apricots, like peaches and other stone fruit, can vary in sweetness, the amount of sugar should be varied accordingly. The amount above is for perfectly ripe fruit. Less ripe, and thus less sweet, fruit will need a bit more sugar.

Sautéed Apricots with Ginger

Cooked fruit doesn't have to be a dessert. Try this dish as a condiment for roasted meats, especially pork.

Makes 4 servings

1 tablespoon butter	3 tablespoons brown sugar
1 tablespoon fresh ginger, chopped	1 tablespoon balsamic vinegar
1 shallot, chopped	Juice of 1 lime
2 cups halved and pitted apricots	

1. Melt butter in a skillet over medium heat. Add ginger and shallot and cook just until shallot softens, a few minutes.

2. Add apricots, cut side down, brown sugar, balsamic vinegar, and lime juice. Cover and cook, stirring a few times, until fruit softens but still keeps its shape, about 5 minutes.

Apricot Fool

The amount of sugar you use in this old-fashioned dessert will depend on the ripeness and quality of the apricots and on your sweet tooth.

Makes 4 servings

1 pound ripe apricots	Pinch Kosher salt
$1/2$ to $2/3$ cup sugar	Ground cinnamon plus 4 cinnamon sticks
$3/4$ teaspoon almond extract	for garnish
3 egg whites	

1. Puree apricots with half the sugar and the almond extract. Set aside.

2. Beat egg whites with salt and remaining sugar until peaks are stiff by not dry. Fold apricot puree into egg whites.

3. Pour into 4 goblets or parfait glasses. Chill for an hour and serve dusted with cinnamon and with a cinnamon stick stuck into each.

Apricot and Smoked Chicken Salad

A perfect main-course luncheon salad for the peak of apricot season.
If the apricots are especially sweet, you can cut back a little on the honey.

Makes 4 servings

4 cups red leaf, butterhead, or Bibb or mesclun salad mix, cleaned and broken into bite-size pieces

One 8-ounce can sliced water chestnuts, drained

10 to 12 ounces smoked chicken or turkey breast, cut into thin strips

4 to 6 ripe apricots, each cut into 8 to 10 lengthwise strips

2 tablespoons raspberry vinegar

2 tablespoons walnut oil

1 tablespoon lemon juice

1 tablespoon honey

2 tablespoons chopped chives

Kosher salt and freshly ground black pepper to taste

1. Put greens in a bowl, add water chestnuts, chicken, and apricots.

2. In a cup or small bowl, combine other ingredients. Add to salad mixture and toss.

avocados

What fruit is shaped like a pear but has the

skin of an alligator? Why, the alligator pear, of

course. You probably know the alligator pear by its

more common name: the avocado. Because of its

leathery skin, smooth buttery flavor, and pear

shape, the avocado is sometimes referred to as an

"alligator pear" or just "butter pear." You may also think of the avocado as a vegetable instead of a fruit. It's not terribly sweet and it's much creamier than most fruit without that backbone of acidity that many fruits have. But nope, it's a fruit.

Though there are many varieties of avocado, the one that most people know is the Hass avocado, which is the one with the pebbly skin and silky rich texture inside. It's the only variety used in the Latin culture to make guacamole dip, because it has the highest oil content of all avocados with a rich, creamy texture and nutty, full-bodied flavor everyone expects to stand up to salty tortilla chips.

The popularity of guacamole, incidentally, coincides with that of America's most-watched sporting event. A few years ago, the California Avocado Commission estimated that on Super Bowl Sunday in 1995, eight million pounds of guacamole were consumed, using more avocados than at any other time of the year.

But according to the California Avocado Commission, Americans are relatively conventional in their use of avocados. Brazilians add them to ice cream. Indonesians mix them with milk, coffee, and rum for a cold drink. And Chileans put them on hot dogs.

WHERE GROWN

Avocados are grown in most tropical and subtropical countries of the world including Israel, Cuba, South Africa, and Australia, with limited quantities grown in Martinique, Cameroon, Morocco, Swaziland, the Canary Islands, Angola, Kenya, and New Zealand. But the largest commercial production occurs in Mexico, with approximately one-fifth of the world's 1.5 million metric tons. Most of the 4,500 metric tons the United States imports comes from Mexico, and that number

may increase in the next few years as trade restrictions between the United States and Mexico ease.

Commercial production in the United States, the world's second-largest producer, is almost entirely limited to Florida and California. California, with 6,000 avocado growers (mostly between San Luis Obispo and the Mexican border), produces 95 percent, about 600 million avocados, of the domestic crop. If there is an avocado capital, it's San Diego. San Diego County produces 60 percent of all California avocados. There are also small amounts of avocados grown in Texas and Hawaii.

VARIETIES

Avocados come in three basic categories: Mexican, Guatemalan, and West Indian. The Mexican type is the hardiest variety and is the one most often found in California. Florida's crops are usually of the West Indian category with a little of the Guatemalan cultivated in California and Florida.

California avocados are usually smaller and creamier with a rougher skin surface than the avocados of Florida. The Hass (rhymes with "pass") avocado accounts for 80 to 90 percent of California's production. Six other varieties— Fuerte, Bacon, Zutano, Pinkerton, Gwen, and Reed—make up the remainder of the California production. The Florida varieties are Booth, Lula, Hill, and Hickson. They usually have a lighter green, shiny skin and a higher water content. The higher water content means they are larger, less rich, and less creamy (meaning less fat) than the California varieties. But it's not always as simple as that (see Nutrition, page 297).

SEASONS

You can usually find avocados in the markets year-round, with the Hass the most reliably available variety. The other California avocado varieties are staggered during the year, such as the Zutano in early winter and the Fuerte and Pinkerton in winter and spring. California avocados peak in spring and summer, while Florida's season peaks in October. Prices for avocados are often the lowest in the summer so they can be competitive with all the other fruits in the market.

SELECTION, HANDLING & STORAGE

Ripe avocados are like police officers: They never seem to be around when you need them. Most avocados you see in the market are anywhere from firm to rock hard, requiring from a few days up to six days at room temperature to soften. That's because avocados don't ripen until after they're picked. Growers leave avocados on the tree to delay the ripening process. But once picked, avocados immediately begin to ripen.

Ideally, a gentle squeeze with the avocado in the palm of your hand will tell you when it's ready; it should give just slightly to pressure. Most people, however, use the thumb technique. Here, too, the avocado should yield to gentle pressure. If your thumb leaves a heavy dent, though, it's overripe and probably only good for mashing. A good avocado will feel heavy for its size, meaning it has a lot of moisture. It should also be unblemished with no broken skin. While the Hass avocado turns dark green or black when ripe, some other varieties, such as the Fuerte, Zutano, and Reed, retain their green color even when ripe.

Once at the appropriate stage of ripeness avocados will keep in the refrigerator for up to one week at temperatures between 36°F and 40°F. But if you leave them at cold temperatures too long, they become discolored and the flavor changes. They can also easily pick up the odors from foods around them.

If you purchase unripened fruit, don't refrigerate it before the ripening process is complete. Refrigeration stops the ripening process. (Cutting the fruit also stops the ripening process.) You can speed up ripening by putting avocados in a paper bag with an apple, banana, tomato, or pear, all of which give off ethylene gas, which hastens ripening. Leave the bag out at room temperature, folded over at the top.

NUTRITION

Very often people say no to avocados because of their high fat content. But while an average avocado (4 ounces flesh) has 25g of fat, most of the fat in avocados (about 60 percent, higher in avocado oil) is monounsaturated fat, one of the cornerstones of the heart-healthy Mediterranean diet because it lowers the "bad" or LDL cholesterol but not the "good" or HDL cholesterol. And some studies indicate that regular consumption of avocados may actually lower overall cholesterol.

And the fat content of avocados varies depending on the time of year, says Charlene Rainey, CEO of Nutrition Network, which does nutrition research for food companies. Rainey says that in the early part of the harvest season, California avocados have a fat content of close to 2 grams per ounce, while later in the year they can reach their peak of 6 grams per ounce. The same is true for Florida avocados, which start around 1 gram of fat per ounce and go up to 4 or 5 grams per ounce. So technically, you'll get less fat from a California avocado eaten in February (when California avocados are not at their peak) than if you consumed an equal amount of a Florida avocado in October, when it is at its peak.

Rainey also points out that if you eat California avocados year-round, the fat content averages out to closer to 4 grams per ounce rather than 6 grams per ounce. (In its labeling, the Food and Drug Administration uses the highest number during the year.)

The FDA lists a serving of avocados as 30g or 1.1 ounces (about ¹/₅ of a medium avocado). This serving contains 55 calories, 3g of carbohydrates, 1g of protein, 5g of fat, and 4% of the DV for vitamin C. Avocados have the highest dietary fiber, by weight, of any fruit, about 3g of fiber (mostly insoluble) per ounce and a similarly large amount of potassium. Though a serving contains only 170mg of potassium, a whole avocado contains about 850mg. Avocados are also good sources of folic acid and magnesium.

And we're not done yet. Avocados are one of the best sources of glutathione, a major antioxidant that has been shown to retard a number of cancers as well as showing promise against the AIDS virus.

YIELD

One medium avocado will produce about 1 cup of mashed fruit.

PREPARATION

To halve and pit a ripe avocado, cut it in half lengthwise until you reach the pit. Then twist the two halves in opposite directions to separate them. The safest way to remove the pit is with a spoon. A less safe method, though not hazardous if you're careful, is tapping the seed with the blade of a chef's knife. When the knife sticks, twist and lift out the seed.

Once the pit is removed, the halves can be used for stuffing, or they can be peeled and sliced. To peel, put the avocado half on a cutting surface, cut side down. Peel back the skin with a paring knife or with your fingers. Then slice as desired. You can also scoop out the flesh with a spoon. Williams-Sonoma (kitchen store and mail-order company) carries a special avocado scooper that looks a little like a tongue depressor with a handle.

Tony's Tip

Most everyone knows that once an avocado has been cut, a sprinkle of lemon or lime juice (actually any citrus juice) will keep it from turning color. A corollary to that is the old saw about burying the avocado pit—technically called the seed—in the middle of guacamole dip to keep the guacamole from turning brown. We've done some tests and have found the pit routine to be unnecessary. What is important, however, is to keep air away from the surface of the cut avocado. So whether by tradition or habit you put the pit in the guacamole, make sure you cover your guacamole or any exposed avocado flesh by putting plastic wrap directly on the surface of the fruit before you store it in the refrigerator.

Avocados are equally versatile when cubed, sliced, or mashed. Cubed avocado can be used in cold chicken or turkey salads, or combined with walnuts, sun-dried tomatoes, basil, and green onions over fettuccine for a hot dish. Smaller cubes can be put in sushi rolls with crab meat.

Cut in ¹/₂-inch-thick slices (with the skin on), they can be put on the grill for a few minutes. Thinner slices can be put on a California-style pizza or hamburger along with sprouts. In either of these last two dishes, cut back on the cheese to keep the fat from getting out of control.

Grilled Chicken Taco with Avocado Salsa

We prefer the soft flour tortillas to the brittle "exploding" ones—those U-shaped corn tortillas that go flying all over your shirt at the first bite. Now most markets carry lower-fat flour tortillas, which taste just as good as the regular ones.

Makes 4 servings

1 tablespoon balsamic vinegar

1 tablespoon extra-virgin olive oil

1 teaspoon kosher salt

2 boneless chicken breast halves

3 jalapeño or serrano chiles, roasted, peeled, seeded, and finely chopped (page 205)

$^1/_4$ cup finely minced scallions, white and 1 inch of green

$^1/_4$ cup chopped cilantro

1 medium ripe tomato, chopped

1 ripe avocado, diced

1 teaspoon lime juice

2 cups shredded romaine lettuce

Four 8-inch, low-fat flour tortillas

1. Preheat broiler. Mix the vinegar, oil, and half the salt. Rub chicken breast halves with the mixture and grill breast halves about 5 minutes on each side or until no pink remains but meat is still quite juicy.

2. Meanwhile, combine remaining salt with chiles, scallions, cilantro, tomato, avocado, and lime juice. When chicken is done, remove skin and cut the chicken into thin strips or chunks.

3. Lay out all 4 tortillas and divide lettuce, chicken, and salsa equally among each. Fold up tacos and serve.

Sam's Cooking Tip

For the famous fish tacos of San Diego and Baja California, shredded cabbage is used instead of lettuce because it doesn't wilt as easily in the summer heat. You may want to give it a try here too (see Mango Taco, page 385).

Guacamole

The usual guacamole recipe gets slimmed down quite a bit here with the aid of salsa and nonfat sour cream. There is just enough of both to retain the avocado's subtle silky qualities.

Makes 4 servings

1 jalapeño pepper

2 shallots

2 ripe avocados, peeled and pitted (see Preparation, page 298)

3 tablespoons nonfat sour cream

2 tablespoons chopped cilantro

4 teaspoons fresh lime juice

3/4 teaspoon toasted cumin seeds, ground (see tip below)

1 teaspoon Kosher salt

3 tablespoons medium-hot commercial or homemade salsa

1. Roast jalapeño and shallots in a 500°F oven until soft and nicely charred, 15 to 20 minutes. Cool to room temperature.

2. Meanwhile, puree remaining ingredients in a food processor until smooth. Peel, seed, and finely chop jalapeño. Peel and chop shallots. Fold both into avocado mixture.

Sam's Cooking Tip

To toast cumin seeds or other whole spices, put them in a cast-iron or other heavy skillet over low heat and shake them periodically. When their aroma begins to be noticeable, after about 5 minutes, remove the skillet from heat. Cool the seeds, then grind them in a spice grinder (like a coffee grinder not used for coffee), or by hand with a mortar and pestle.

Shrimp and Pasta Salad with Avocado Mayonnaise

Shrimp and avocados are a natural. Here the avocado's fattiness is minimized by using low- or nonfat mayonnaise and yogurt and stretching things out with pasta.

Makes 6 servings

10 whole black peppercorns
1/2 cup chopped celery or celery tops
1/2 lemon, juice and all
2 teaspoons salt
1 1/4 pounds medium shrimp in shells
1 ripe avocado, peeled and pitted
  (see Preparation, page 298)
1/4 cup low-fat mayonnaise
1/4 cup nonfat yogurt
1/4 teaspoon freshly ground black pepper

3/4 pound short pasta such as fusilli,
  rotini, or penne, cooked, drained, and
  cooled under cold running water
1 red bell pepper, roasted, skinned, and
  seeded (page 205), and cut into very
  thin strips
2 tablespoons chopped fresh basil
3 cups coarsely chopped arugula
1 tablespoon chopped fresh chives

1. Preheat oven broiler. Put peppercorns, celery, lemon, and half the salt in a saucepan with 2 quarts of water. Bring to a boil and simmer 10 minutes. Add shrimp and cook about 3 minutes or until just firm and opaque. Drain and chill.

2. Mash avocado in a mixing bowl (or use a food processor). Add mayonnaise and yogurt. Season with remaining salt and black pepper. Peel shrimp and add to mayonnaise mixture along with pasta, red bell pepper, and basil. Toss well and adjust for salt. Pour onto a serving platter lined with arugula. Sprinkle with chives.

Stuffed Avocado with Ceviche

Please feel free to substitute your favorite crab or shrimp salad recipe for the ceviche.

Makes 4 servings as a first course

Butterhead or garden lettuce leaves, cleaned
2 ripe but firm avocados
Double recipe for Ceviche (page 377), about 2 cups

1. Line 4 plates with lettuce leaves.

2. Halve avocados lengthwise and remove pits. Cut a small slice from the bottom of each half to make it stable. Put a half on each plate cut side up and fill each with ¼ of the Ceviche.

Avocado Soup

Though this soup can be eaten hot or cold, we prefer it cold accompanied by some baked, not fried, tortilla chips.

Makes 6 servings

2 ripe medium avocados
2 cups defatted Chicken Stock (page 9)
2 cups 1% low-fat milk
2 teaspoons lemon juice
1 tablespoon dry vermouth

1 teaspoon Kosher salt
Pinch cayenne pepper
1 tablespoon chopped fresh chives or
  cilantro for garnish

1. Halve avocados and scoop out flesh into a blender or food processor. Add stock and blend until smooth. Put into a mixing bowl (or heavy-bottomed saucepan if serving hot) with remaining ingredients. Blend well.

2. If serving hot, heat gently to a simmer while stirring. Taste for seasonings and adjust.

3. If serving cold, chill several hours, then taste for seasonings. Sprinkle with chives or cilantro.

Sam's Cooking Tip

As strange as it may seem, 1% milk is actually creamier than 2% milk, which has more fat. The reason is that 1% milk has more milk solids. So save the fat and use 1% when you can.

bananas

(including plantains)

Giovanni Tantillo (Tony's dad) would always say, "You treat bananas like a baby; too warm they'll get mad, too cold they'll get mad, too. You want to put them to bed at nice, sleepy temperatures, somewhere between 58°F and 65°F."

Handling bananas isn't everyone's cup of tea, even within the produce business. As a matter of fact, for every one hundred people working in produce, maybe two are in bananas. Very few people know how to gas, ripen, and process bananas properly.

Bananas are harvested green. Unlike vine-ripened tomatoes, vine-ripened bananas don't taste very good. If bananas turn yellow on the plant, the starch in the banana never turns to sugar and they become bland with a cottony texture.

After they are picked, boxed, and put on ships, bananas are kept at 57°F to 58°F at low humidity so that the ripening process is slowed to a crawl. The temperature is taken every hour during the voyage. Once at their destination, bananas can be ripened in their containers or, more often, in special warehouses.

When it is time to ripen the bananas, ripening rooms are heated to 65°F to 67°F, depending on how fast the bananas are scheduled to ripen. At the same time, liquid ethylene gas, a natural gas emitted from some ripening produce such as tomatoes and apples, is distributed throughout the sealed ripening rooms. This process allows the bananas to ripen evenly without affecting the color or texture of the fruit.

The ripening process takes from three to seven days, depending on how the temperature, humidity, and amount of ethylene gas are controlled. When the bananas reach a temperature of 60°F, they are ready to ship to market. The time from harvest to your supermarket produce section takes between fourteen to twenty days in the United States, twenty to thirty days in Europe.

WHERE GROWN

Bananas grow best in volcanic alluvial soil where the climate is warm and moist, with average temperatures of 80°F and annual rainfall that can approach a hundred inches—usually within 20° on either side of the equator. Like money, bananas don't grow on trees. They grow on plants that are giant herbs, members of the same family that includes lilies and orchids. These plants reach as high as 25 feet, producing a flowering stem with a huge bud at the end. The bud contains lots of purple leaves or petals, called bracts, and as the stem gets longer the bracts roll back, showing rows of small flowers that become small green bananas.

Bananas grow on these stems in clusters called hands. Each stem has seven to nine hands. And each hand contains twelve to fourteen bananas. (At the retail level, four to six bananas is called a cluster.) Each individual banana is called, not surprisingly, a finger. It takes nine to twelve months for a new planting of bananas from bulblike rhizomes to harvest.

India is the world's leading banana producer, with 6.2 million metric tons. But Americans never see Indian bananas because India consumes virtually all it produces. The same is true of Brazil, the second leading producer, with 5.5 million metric tons. Ecuador, the Philippines (which sends most of its bananas to Japan), Colombia, and China (which consumes all of its crop) round out the major banana-producing nations. The most important commercial banana-producing region for the U.S. supply is Latin America with Costa Rica the leading supplier. Ecuador, Colombia, Honduras, Panama, Guatemala, and Mexico also supply bananas to the United States.

For plantains, the "vegetable bananas," Uganda, Colombia, Rwanda, and Zaire are the top four producers.

VARIETIES

Although there are some one thousand varieties in the world today, the main commercial banana is the Cavendish or Giant Cavendish. For years before World War II the main export variety was the Gros Michel, a big yellow, flavorful banana with a thick skin that protected it during shipping. But a disease called Black Sigatoka virtually wiped out the world's supply, and Gros Michel is no longer a factor in worldwide production.

The shorter, more blunt **Cavendish** is less brightly colored than the Gros Michel and bruises easily because of a thinner skin. But it's more disease resistant and has a deeper root system that makes it more resistant to wind storms. The **Dwarf Cavendish**, named for the shortness of the stem on which it grows, can tolerate a cooler climate than most bananas. In the trade, Dwarf Cavendish bananas are called Petites.

The standard size of shipping bananas is 7 to 7½ inches, though they may go above 8 inches. Petites have become popular in food service where larger bananas tend to take up too much room on cafeteria trays and because one good-size banana is often too much for one individual to eat at one sitting. Occasionally, baby bananas are sold as a special variety. In reality, they are Cavendish bananas that are picked from the bottom of the stalk. These bananas are also sometimes called finger bananas.

Specialty bananas are a tiny portion of the millions of boxes of bananas that come into the United States each year, and then mostly seen only on the coasts. In addition, they're often expensive and spoil quickly.

The **Burro** banana from Mexico looks like a squarish, stubbier version of the Cavendish, which is why it is sometimes called the chunky banana. It is somewhat tangier than the Cavendish with a lemonlike flavor. When ripe, the yellow skin shows dark spots like the normal banana and the soft flesh will have a slight firmness toward the center.

The **Manzano** banana is also called the Apple banana because it has an applelike flavor (as well as some hints of strawberry). The light golden color turns totally black when ripe.

The **Red** banana looks nothing like the Cavendish, though it grows on a similar bush. It is stubby, like the Burro, but round, not squarish. The dull red skin turns to a reddish-purple or maroon when fully ripe. The Red banana is sweeter than the Cavendish with a heartier flavor, though the texture of the pinkish-orange flesh is softer.

The **Saba** banana does double duty as a cooking and eating banana. Starchier than the Cavendish, it has a faint resemblance to the flavor of a sweet potato when cooked. It is shorter and thicker than the Cavendish and turns dark yellow when ripe.

With the tremendous increase in the Hispanic population in the United States, **plantains** are becoming more available at mainstream markets. Plantains are the starchy members of the banana family. They're similar in shape to bananas but larger with thicker skins. Plantains are often called "cooking bananas" or "Mexican potatoes" because they are prepared and served as a vegetable in Latin American cuisines, mostly fried, but also used in soups, stews, and desserts.

SEASONS

Bananas are a year-round fruit with some peaks in May and June.

SELECTION, STORAGE & HANDLING

Bananas go through a ten-color spectrum that produce professionals refer to when ordering or storing the fruit. At one end is Number 1, the bright green color of just-picked fruit. At the other end are Numbers 9 and 10, brown bananas good only for banana cake. Most retail markets order Number 4, which is a greenish yellow. Number 5 is green-tipped yellow. And Number 7 shows some of the brown specks, known as sugar specks, that indicate ripeness.

The best time to buy bananas is at Number 5 when they are about 75 percent yellow with a small amount of green at both ends. They should be firm, plump, and brightly colored without blemishes. Depressed, moist, and dark areas on the skin usually mean the fruit inside is bruised. Occasional brown specks are an indication of ripeness. Bananas with a dull yellow or grayish cast have probably been subjected to chilling and won't ripen properly.

Bananas should be stored at room temperature, ideally between 55°F and 75°F. However, in the summertime bananas can ripen quickly at home unless the house is kept below 75°F. In wintertime, you might want to speed up the ripening process. In that case, put the bananas in a plastic or paper bag with an apple.

Once ripened, they'll keep a maximum of two days before decay begins. If you wish to keep bananas from ripening any further, store them in the refrigerator. Expect the skin to turn dark brown. The flesh will remain firm and white for a couple of days, though the flavor may be affected somewhat.

When keeping bananas at room temperature, be sure they aren't stored too closely to other fruits. The ethylene gas released by bananas could alter the ripening of the other fruits. For the best flavor and aroma, eat the bananas when they are fully yellow with little brown specks. To avoid having the flesh turn brown once the banana is peeled, dip the fruit in a citrus juice such as orange, lemon, or lime juice.

For red bananas, the riper the fruit the more purple its skin becomes. A deep purple skin indicates a very soft flesh. Other varieties should be true to their color and unblemished.

As with bananas, plantains turn yellow and develop dark spots or specks—actually, more like streaks—as they ripen, though some dark spots even appear on green plantains. Plantains become black when totally ripe. However, even when jet black, they will not be as sweet as fully ripe bananas. Inside the plantain you will find an orange- or peach-hued flesh (reminiscent of sweet potatoes) instead of the creamy white or pale yellow color of bananas. The ripened flesh may develop some dark spots similar to those of ripe bananas.

Sometimes though, a plantain will just refuse to ripen. It will start to turn black but never really yellow or get sweet. Because plantains take so long to ripen—at least a week and sometimes two—it's best to buy an extra one or two, just in case.

NUTRITION

A medium banana (126g, about 4.5 ounces), contains 110 calories, 29g of carbohydrates, 1g of protein, 4g of dietary fiber, 15% of the DV for vitamin C, and 2% for iron.

Bananas have the highest ready-to-eat source of vitamin B_6 you can get, with a serving providing 20% of the DV. Bananas are also a decent source for folic acid and riboflavin, magnesium, and copper.

A banana has more potassium by weight (400mg) than any other single fruit except an avocado. (A serving of kiwifruit has more but includes two kiwifruit.)

Plantains are comparable to bananas in most categories except the following: They have more than twenty times the amount of vitamin A, about three times the vitamin C, almost twice the potassium, and double the amount of magnesium.

YIELD

Three medium bananas weigh about 1 pound. One medium banana makes about $^2/_3$ cup of sliced fruit. Two medium bananas make 1 cup of diced fruit. Three medium bananas make 1 cup of mashed fruit.

A plantain will yield about 1 to $1^1/_4$ cups of sliced fruit because it is usually larger than a regular banana.

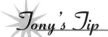

Tony's Tip

Athletes trying to naturally replace spent nutrients should consider eating a few bananas before and after strenuous workouts.

PREPARATION

Bananas that are fully yellow are best for cooking because they will hold their shape. Speckled bananas are best for eating out of hand or for topping cereal. Overripe bananas should be used for breads, muffins, puddings, or pureed in smoothies. Smoothies are even better with frozen bananas. Just toss a sliced one, still frozen, into a blender with some orange juice and some strawberries if you like, and puree.

Frozen bananas can be fun, too. Freezing is a good way to store bananas that have ripened too quickly. Peel a ripe banana, wrap it tightly with plastic or freezer wrap, and freeze it. Later, you can put it on a wooden stick and give it to the kids for a low-fat snack, or dip it into melted chocolate or caramel and roll in nuts for a delicious dessert.

And speaking of fun for kids, try bananas on the grill. Start with bananas that have few or no brown specks (but no green). Put them whole and unpeeled on the grill over medium heat and cook until black all over. They should be soft but not mushy. This will take about 5 to 7 minutes. Slit the banana lengthwise along the curved side. Peel off one side of the skin, then flip the fruit over and peel off the other. Sprinkle with chopped peanuts or almonds.

When making a fruit salad, add the bananas at the last minute so they won't turn brown. Or soak them in orange juice for an hour or so first.

Cinnamon is probably the best seasoning for bananas. Orange flavorings, whether in the form of juice or liqueur, are also good with bananas, as is rum. And next time you're doing an Indian curry, drop in some banana slices at the end.

Pork Medallions and Plantains

This festive dish can be put together in a flash, making it a good candidate for a weeknight meal. Try it with some Nectarine Chutney (page 406) for an added kick.

Makes 3 servings

1 pork tenderloin, about 12 ounces
2 tablespoons all-purpose flour
Kosher salt and freshly ground black
  pepper to taste
1 tablespoon butter

1 ripe plantain, cut into 15 slices about
  $^1/_2$ inch thick
$^1/_3$ cup rum or bourbon, or double the
  defatted Chicken Stock
$^1/_3$ cup defatted Chicken Stock (page 9)

1. Cut pork tenderloin in 3 equal pieces, crosswise. Put pieces, one at a time, between 2 sheets of foil, cut side down. Pound to a thickness of $^3/_8$ to $^1/_2$ inch. Combine flour, salt, and pepper in a shallow dish or pie plate.

2. Put butter in a skillet over medium heat. Dredge medallions in seasoned flour mixture and shake off excess. Cook pork 3 to 4 minutes on each side until slightly pink inside. (They should be gently firm when pressed with a finger.)

3. Remove pork and keep warm on a serving platter. Add plantain slices and cook until they start to caramelize on each side, 3 or 4 minutes total. Add rum and stock and raise heat, scraping any bits of meat off the bottom. Reduce liquid by half and pour liquid and plantain over pork medallions.

Sam's Cooking Tip

Pork tenderloin should not be confused with much fattier pork cuts, even though pork is much leaner than it's ever been. Pork tenderloins contain about the same amount of fat and calories as skinless white meat chicken.

Bananas Foster

This is our version of the classic dessert created at Brennan's restaurant in New Orleans.

Makes 2 servings

1 tablespoon butter
2 tablespoons brown sugar
Juice of 1 orange
Healthy pinch cinnamon
2 ripe but firm bananas, peeled and cut
  crosswise into $1/2$-inch slices

2 tablespoons rum
2 scoops nonfat vanilla yogurt or ice
  cream

1. Put butter in a skillet over medium heat. When butter sizzles, add brown sugar and stir 1 minute. Add orange juice and cinnamon and mix to smooth.

2. Add bananas, coat well, and cook 1 minute. Add rum, raise heat to medium high, and carefully ignite the mixture; cook, swirling mixture until flames subside and mixture begins to thicken. Spoon over frozen yogurt or ice cream in a goblet or cut-glass dessert dish.

Sam's Cooking Tip

Flambéing isn't hard or dangerous as long as you follow a few simple rules: (1) Use only the amount of alcohol called for in the dish; (2) don't wear loose clothing or have hair dangling; and (3) have a large cover close by to snuff out the flames if they get out of hand.

Plantain and Lentil Stew
*This dish was inspired by a recipe by Diane Kennedy,
the queen of Mexican cookery.*

Makes 4 servings

1 cup lentils
1 tablespoon olive oil
1 small onion, chopped
2 cloves garlic, chopped
1 large tomato, cored and chopped

1½ cups pineapple cut into ½-inch cubes
2 plantains, peeled and cut into 3/8-inch slices
1 teaspoon Kosher salt
Cooked rice

1. In a large saucepan, cook lentils in 2 quarts water until just barely tender, about 45 minutes. Drain, reserving liquid.

2. Wipe out saucepan. Heat oil over moderate heat. Add onion and garlic and cook until onion is soft, about 4 or 5 minutes. Add tomato and cook a few minutes. Add lentils, about 1 cup of lentil broth, pineapple, plantains, and salt.

3. Cook about 20 minutes until the stew thickens slightly. Check for salt and serve over rice.

Banana Ice Cream with Bourbon
*We first got the idea of making "ice cream" with frozen fruit from
Jacques Pepin's Cuisine Economique (William Morrow and Co., 1992).
Try it with other fruits as well.*

Makes 4 servings

4 ripe bananas, peeled
4 pitted prunes, chopped
2 tablespoons bourbon
¼ cup superfine sugar

1½ cups nonfat vanilla yogurt
2 tablespoons sliced almonds, toasted (optional)

1. Freeze bananas for several hours or overnight. Put prunes and bourbon in a small shallow dish to soak until bananas are frozen, then drain well.

2. Cut bananas into ½-inch slices and put in a food processor with sugar. Pulse a few times. Add yogurt and pulse just until bananas are chopped and well integrated with yogurt. Don't puree until entirely smooth; leave a little chunky. Pour into a bowl and fold in prunes. Eat immediately or freeze until ready to eat; top with almonds if desired.

berries

The phrase "as American as apple pie"

should probably be changed to "as American as

blueberries and cranberries," because blueberries

and cranberries are two of the three fruits that

are native to North America (along with Concord

grapes). As the Ocean Spray cranberry people say,

"They didn't come over on the Mayflower, they were already here."

Blueberries have been a big part of early American culinary culture since Colonial times when they were used in numerous desserts from buckles and grunts to fools.

Even strawberries, not a native American fruit, were grown by North American Indians in pre-Pilgrim times. And what do we eat on Independence Day, apple pie or strawberry shortcake?

WHERE GROWN

With approximately twenty-three thousand acres planted, California produces 80 percent of the nation's strawberry crop. The coastal regions of San Diego, Oxnard, Orange County, Santa Maria, and Watsonville-Salinas provide the ideal conditions for growing strawberries: warm sunny days and cool foggy nights. Strawberries grown in the San Joaquin Valley of Central California are used mainly for processing. Florida accounts for virtually all of the remaining domestic strawberry production.

Most of the imported strawberries come from Mexico. Smaller amounts come from New Zealand, Canada, Colombia, and Guatemala.

Contrary to popular belief, cranberries are not grown in water. They grow on vines in beds called bogs or marshes, layered with sand, peat, gravel, and clay. Though cranberries require a special set of growing conditions—acid soil, plenty of fresh water, and a long growing season—vines are hearty and have been known to last as long as 150 years.

Most of the world's cranberries are grown on thirty thousand acres of wetlands and coastal uplands in five states and another four thousand acres in Canada, mainly British Columbia. The leading cranberry-producing states, in descending order of size of production are Massachusetts, Wisconsin, New Jersey, Oregon, and Washington.

Blueberries thrive in conditions similar to those of cranberries. The United States and Canada are the largest producers (and consumers) of blueberries, with New Jersey, Michigan, North Carolina, Oregon, and British Columbia the primary growing areas. Wild blueberries are grown commercially in only two areas of North America: eastern Canada and Maine. Maine produces approximately 98 percent of the wild blueberries in the United States.

Though wild raspberries are still a common sight almost everywhere in the United States, commercial production comes primarily from California and Washington. Oregon, Texas, California, and Washington provide the bulk of blackberries.

Pale green, pin-striped gooseberries come primarily from New Zealand, though small amounts are grown in Oregon and California. Oregon is also where most of the brilliantly red, tiny fresh currants come from.

VARIETIES

Strawberries are by far the most popular berries on the market. There are about seventy varie-ties produced. The more significant varieties include Pajaro, Chandler, Selva, Oso Grande, Seascape, Camarosa, and proprietary varieties from Driscoll Strawberry Associates, a major grower in Watsonville, California.

Bluecrop is the major **blueberry** variety. Other varieties include the Jersey, Tifblue, Blueray, Bluetta, Weymuth, Duke, and Elliott. The blueberry is closely related to the European bilberry.

Wild blueberries are smaller, more compact, and have a brighter blue color than cultivated blueberries. And for many, wild blueberries have a more intense blueberry flavor.

There are more than one hundred different **cranberry** varieties, but there are four major commercial varieties: Early Black, Howes, McFarlin, and Searles. Ben Lear and Stevens are two other varieties grown primarily in Wisconsin.

Though now available in purple and golden hues as well as black, red **raspberries** remain the favorite with five varieties dominating commercially: Willamette, Meeker, Heritage, Amity, and Sweet Briar.

Blackberry varieties include the sweet-tart Olallie, the tangy Marion, the sweet Cherokee, the mild Chester, and the tangy and sweet Kotata.

The slightly acidic, dark red **loganberry** is thought to be a hybrid of the raspberry and blackberry. The large and red-black boysenberry is a cross between blackberry, loganberry, and raspberry.

There are two kinds of **currants,** which are often thought of as tiny dried grapes. The one that is more of a berry is a member of the Ribes family, which also includes gooseberries. The most common currant is bright red with a tart flavor that requires a good deal of sugar to bring out its goodness. There are also less common white and black varieties.

SEASONS

Strawberries are available year-round, with the California varieties peaking from April through June and significant supplies available until October. The Florida season begins in late November and peaks in March. Mexican, Central American, and New Zealand strawberries run from November through April, with peak supplies from December through March.

Blueberries are available from the United States from April to October, with July and August being the peak months. The Canadian crop begins in July and ends in October. Chile, which has grown rapidly as a blueberry exporter, sends more than 90 percent of its exports to the United States beginning in November and continuing until February.

The California raspberry crop begins in May and peaks from June through September, with some supplies in October and November. A significant Canadian crop peaks in July. Chilean raspberries begin in December and continue into May. Olallie blackberries are the earliest blackberry arrivals in May. Most others peak in July and August.

Cranberries begin to hit the market in late September and continue into early December. Every once in a while there is a fresh cranberry shortage. So to avoid scrambling around for that essential addition to a holiday dinner, stock up early and freeze several bags.

Red currants from California are available from May to June; from New Zealand, from late December to early February along with black currants (not the dried grapes). Domestic gooseberries run from May to August. New Zealand supplies go from October through June, depending on the variety, but most come in November, December, and January.

SELECTION, HANDLING & STORAGE

For best flavor, purchase whatever berry you're looking for in the peak of the season or as close to it as you can. And always seek out local berries when possible, since they are invariably the most flavorful.

Choose berries carefully, being sure to stay away from fruits that are not true in color, or berries that are soft, wet, sticky to the touch or appear moldy. Plump, dry, firm, well-shaped, and uniformly colored fruit indicates it is ready to take home. Avoid strawberries with green or white tips, for example. Blackberries should be entirely deep purple or black.

If boxed in cardboard or other paper product, pay particular attention to the dampness and/or staining, especially at the bottom of the container. This may be evidence of significantly overripe, even decaying fruit.

There should be no twigs or other debris in the packaging. With the exception of strawberries and their "caps," don't buy the fruit if it still has stems or leaves attached.

Cranberries, usually found sealed in plastic, should be checked for size, deep red color, and as little debris or withered fruit as possible.

Choose firm gooseberries with a lustrous sheen. Currants should have rich, red berries. Be on the lookout for too many smashed or bruised berries.

In less than a day, berries can become mush. Once home, remove the fruit from any container, check all pieces, and remove soft, overripe fruit for immediate consumption or to be thrown away if mushy or moldy. The remaining fruit should be blotted to remove excess water or juices and placed in a shallow plate or pan, covered with a paper towel, and the whole container covered with plastic wrap and placed in the refrigerator.

Blueberries will last up to ten days if stored this way, while cranberries will be okay for up to two weeks. Cranberries take extremely well to freezing and can be used right from the freezer in almost any recipe that calls for fresh cranberries except a few kinds of relish that require fresh fruit. Raspberries should be used immediately, while the rest of the varieties will last a couple of days in refrigeration.

Raspberries are usually the most expensive berries, due to their fragile nature and limited supply. Under normal circumstances they'll last only a few days once put up for sale.

Don't wash any berries until you're ready to eat them or use them in a recipe. They'll turn moldy and mushy.

NUTRITION

A cup of blueberries (140g, about 5 ounces) contains 100 calories, 27g of carbohydrates, 3g of dietary fiber, and 1g each of fat and protein. A serving of blueberries also contains 15% of the DV for vitamin C and 2% for iron. In Sweden, blueberries have been used as an antidote for diarrhea for years. Though cranberries have gotten more publicity for it, blueberries can help prevent or relieve the symptoms of bladder infections. Blueberries act as a natural aspirin and an antibacterial agent, and studies show they can help slow vision loss.

A cup of raw cranberries weighs about 100g (3.5 ounces) and contains 46 calories. However, that figure triples when sugar is added to make them palatable. That raw serving amount also contains about 11g of carbohydrates, just under 1g of fat, about .5g of protein, about 1.5g of dietary fiber, and 18% of the DV for vitamin C. In addition to their antibiotic properties, particularly as they pertain to urinary and bladder infections, cranberries also act as an antiviral agent.

A serving of eight medium strawberries (147g, about 5.3 ounces) contains 45 calories, 12g of carbohydrates, 4g of dietary fiber, 1g of protein, 160% of the DV for vitamin C, 2% for calcium, and 4% for iron. Strawberries are also a pretty good source of potassium (270mg) and folic acid. The high concentration of vitamin C in strawberries has been shown to be effective in minimizing LDL, or the so-called bad component of cholesterol. Strawberries are also an effective cancer fighter.

A cup of raspberries (125g, about 4.5 ounces) contains 50 calories, 17g of carbohydrates, 8g of dietary fiber, 1g of protein, 40% of the DV for vitamin C, and 2% each for calcium and iron. Like blueberries, raspberries act as a natural aspirin. And like strawberries, raspberries are a strong anticancer agent and a good source of folic acid.

YIELDS

One pint of blueberries weighs about 12 ounces and yields about 2$\frac{1}{2}$ cups of fruit.

The standard 12-ounce bag of fresh cranberries yields about 3 cups whole berries, 2$\frac{1}{2}$ cups chopped.

One pint of strawberries (from twelve to thirty-six berries depending on size) yields 3$\frac{1}{2}$ cups of whole, 2$\frac{1}{2}$ cups sliced, and 1$\frac{2}{3}$ cups pureed fruit.

A half pint of raspberries (the standard marketing size) yields 1 cup of fruit.

Tony's Tip

Most berries freeze nicely, keeping up to ten months in the freezer. To freeze berries (except for cranberries, which don't require this method), rinse them gently and dry in a colander or on paper towels. Put them on a sheet pan or tray in a single layer and put the tray in the freezer. When frozen, put the berries in a bag. This way they won't stick to each other and you can measure out as much as you want for your morning cereal, for ice cream topping, and for pies, cobblers, cakes, and pastries.

PREPARATION

If selected and stored properly, most berries need little additional preparation. Stems and tops of gooseberries can be snipped with scissors. To prevent the absorption of water, wash strawberries before they are hulled (removing the stems). The simplest tool for hulling is a sharp paring knife. But a teaspoon, especially the serrated kind for grapefruit, is also good.

Blueberries need to be picked through to ferret out any rotted or unformed berries as well as the tiny stems.

The cranberry is perhaps the most accommodating when it comes to seasonings. It almost craves to be tossed one way or the other with whatever spices, liqueurs, or sweeteners suit your fancy. Though the traditional sweetener is sugar, there's no reason why you can't use honey or brown sugar. By using preserves such as marmalade, you add flavoring and sweetening at the same time.

Citrus in general, but orange and lemon in particular, goes well with cranberries. So do nuts such as pecans, walnuts, and almonds. Ginger in all its forms, but especially candied or crystallized, is superb with cranberries. As for liquids, try bourbon, rum, orange juice, and orange liqueurs. For a special kick, try some hot peppers in your cranberry sauce, especially if it is going to be used with some Southwestern dish.

Other berries also go well with citrus whether in the form of juices or fruit. Berries also match nicely with melons and tropical fruits such as mangoes, papaya, pineapple, kiwifruit, and banana. There is nothing finer than a simple fruit salad at the height of summer embellished simply with a squeeze of lemon and a few drops of Triple Sec or other orange liqueur.

Cinnamon, nutmeg, ginger, and mace are good seasonings for these other berries. So are cherry liqueurs and cassis, the currant liqueur. A topping of some dairy product, whether yogurt, sour cream, whipped cream, or crème fraîche gives berries a nice final touch. Blueberries in particular are very much at home in combination with buttermilk in pancakes and muffins.

Strawberries with Balsamic Vinegar and Black Pepper

It may sound weird, but the piquancy of balsamic vinegar and freshly ground pepper adds a marvelous counterpoint to the sweet berries and makes for an interesting dessert.

Makes 4 servings

1 quart strawberries, washed and hulled

4 tablespoons or more cane or brown sugar, depending on the sweetness of the berries

2 teaspoons balsamic vinegar

$1/8$ teaspoon freshly ground black pepper

1. Halve strawberries if large. Cut in thirds or quarters if very large. Put in a mixing bowl and sprinkle with sugar. Toss and set aside for 30 minutes.

2. Sprinkle vinegar and pepper on berries and toss again. Serve immediately.

Cranberry-Pear Cobbler

In addition to its affinity for so many flavorings, the cranberry blends well with most fall fruits.

Makes 6 servings

2 pounds firm but ripe pears, peeled, cored, and cut into $3/8$-inch slices

2 cups fresh or frozen cranberries

1 tablespoon raspberry vinegar

$1/3$ cup plus $1/4$ cup granulated sugar

$1/3$ cup brown sugar

1 tablespoon grated fresh ginger

2 tablespoons cornstarch

Butter-flavored cooking spray

1 cup all-purpose flour

1 teaspoon baking powder

$1/4$ teaspoon kosher salt

3 tablespoons chilled butter, cut into small pieces

7 to 8 tablespoons low-fat buttermilk

Low-fat vanilla ice cream or frozen yogurt for serving (optional)

1. Combine pears, cranberries, vinegar, $1/3$ cup of granulated sugar, brown sugar, ginger, and cornstarch in a bowl. Spray a 2-quart baking dish with butter-flavored spray and spread the fruit mixture evenly inside. Preheat oven to 375°F.

2. Put flour, baking powder, salt, and remaining granulated sugar in a mixing bowl. Cut in the butter with a large fork or pastry blender until the mixture resembles coarse meal. Add the buttermilk and mix just until the dough comes together in a ball.

3. Put the dough between 2 pieces of lightly floured waxed paper and roll out to a size just large enough to cover the baking dish. Peel off the waxed paper and top fruit with dough. Seal the edges with a scalloped shape if desired. Cut 4 or 5 vents into the dough.

4. Bake 35 to 45 minutes or until the top is golden brown and juices bubble up freely. Serve warm with low-fat vanilla ice cream or frozen yogurt if desired.

Mixed Berries with Zabaglione

This is a perfect way to enjoy the explosion of berries in midsummer.
Use any combination of berries or just one kind. In a pinch you
can substitute sweet sherry for Marsala.

Makes 8 servings

5 large eggs, separated (see tip)
$1/2$ cup sugar
$1/2$ cup Marsala
1 pint each blackberries, raspberries, and blueberries

1. In the top of a double boiler or in a heat-proof mixing bowl, whisk yolks and sugar until well combined. Mix in Marsala.

2. Put top of double boiler or mixing bowl over a pan of water so that it barely touches water. Bring water to boil and reduce to simmer, all the while stirring the egg mixture with a whisk. Cook about 10 minutes, stirring constantly, until zabaglione is thick and fluffy. Remove from heat. Stir occasionally until cooled. Cover and refrigerate.

3. Wash berries just before using. Put into 8 cut-glass dishes or goblets. Spoon out a few tablespoons of zabaglione on top of each.

Sam's Cooking Tip

For some, the flavor of zabaglione may be too intense. In that case, whip the separated egg whites with 2 tablespoons sugar until stiff peaks form. Then fold into the zabaglione, about $1/3$ at a time, until you achieve the taste you want.

Madge's Blueberry Pie

Sam's mother-in-law, Madge, bakes a great apple pie, but her blueberry pie (which Madge got from her mother) is even better. It uses the same crust as the Apple Pie (page 286).

Makes 6 to 8 servings

Filling

2 pints blueberries, washed, drained, and picked over

1¹/₂ tablespoons fresh lemon juice

1 cup (or more if you like a sweeter filling) sugar

3 tablespoons quick-cooking tapioca

¹/₈ teaspoon kosher salt

Crust

See Madge's Apple Pie, page 286

A few tablespoons of milk

1 teaspoon sugar

1. Toss blueberries with lemon juice in a mixing bowl. Combine 1 cup sugar, tapioca, and salt in a small bowl. Pour over blueberries and mix well. Preheat oven to 450°F.

2. Roll out just over half the crust and line a 9-inch pie plate. Pour in filling. Roll out remaining crust and top pie, securing all around by fluting the dough in any way you prefer, or pressing down the edges with the tines of a fork. Make a half dozen slits on top for steam to escape. Brush top with milk and sprinkle with the remaining teaspoon of sugar.

3. Put the pie on a sheet or baking pan (to catch any overflowing juices) and bake in the middle of the oven for 20 minutes. Lower heat to 350°F and bake 20 to 25 minutes or until nicely browned and bubbly. Cover the edges of the crust with foil if they darken too soon.

4. Cool to room temperature and serve.

Sam's Cooking Tip

When making pastry crust, I've always used two sheets of waxed paper to sandwich the dough to facilitate rolling. Madge uses plastic wrap, which works even better. First tightly cover a cutting board with the bottom half, then stretch out the top half over the slightly flattened dough and roll.

Cranberry Sauce with Amaretto

Consider this unusual cranberry sauce as part of an Italian-style Thanksgiving dinner with Turkey Breast with Pomegranate Glaze (see page 470) and Squash Ravioli with Parmesan-Sage Cream (see page 264).

Makes 4 servings

$2/3$ cup sugar
$2/3$ cup water
$1/3$ cup Amaretto
12-ounce package fresh or frozen
  cranberries

Juice of 1 orange, about $1/4$ cup
1 tablespoon orange zest, cut julienne
3 tablespoons toasted sliced almonds
  (see page 28)

1. Bring sugar, water, and Amaretto to a boil in a heavy-bottomed saucepan. Add cranberries, stir, and return to a boil. Reduce heat and boil gently, stirring occasionally, for about 8 to 10 minutes or until cranberries pop.

2. Remove from heat, add orange juice and zest, and cool. Just before serving, fold in almonds.

A line from the Joni Mitchell song "Big

Yellow Taxi" says: "Paved paradise and put up a

parking lot." That seems to describe what's hap-

pening to the habitat of one of our favorite fruits,

the Santa Clara Valley in Northern California, home

of the Bing cherry.

We think the Bing, particularly as it is grown in the Santa Clara Valley, is the world's finest cherry: rich, juicy, and full of flavor. The problem is that the valley's orchards are quickly disappearing, being replaced by high-tech industry, condos, and all the other trappings of "progress" (including parking lots).

So enjoy the Santa Clara Bing while you can because it may not be around much longer. If we ever develop an endangered species program for fruits and vegetables like the one for animals, we'd like to put the Santa Clara Valley Bing cherry at the top of the list.

WHERE GROWN

The United States is the world's biggest producer, consumer, and exporter of cherries. Other major producing nations, in order of production, are Germany, Italy, Switzerland, and France.

Sweet cherries are grown on the West Coast with Washington being the largest producer. California is a solid number two, with Oregon third, and small amounts coming from Utah and Idaho. British Columbia in Canada contributes to the market as well. Chile is the major supplier in winter.

Tart cherries (the tart cherry industry is not wild about the term *sour cherries*) are grown primarily in Michigan, where the Grand Traverse Bay area provides perfect conditions: good elevation, dependable rainfall, high humidity, and sandy soil with good drainage. Tart cherries are also grown commercially in New York, Pennsylvania, Utah, and Wisconsin. Smaller amounts are grown in Colorado, Ohio, and Oregon.

VARIETIES

The favorite sweet cherry varieties in the eastern United States are the Windsor, Schmidt, Victor, Napoleon, and Black Tartarian. In the West it's the Bing, Lambert, and Ranier.

Named for a Chinese worker, Bing cherries are usually very firm with glossy deep red to black or mahogany skin, a white heart (the area immediately around the pit), and a bit of a crunch when you bite into them. Heart-shaped Lamberts are smaller, more tender, dark red, and soft, with somewhat watery flesh producing deep, almost blackish-red juice.

Ranier cherries, despite what many think, are not related to Royal Anns (also known as Napoleons). They are yellow to amber with a pink to red blush. They are more fragile than Bings or Lamberts and have a very sweet and mild flavor, juicy flesh, and a white heart. The Royal Anns are used in the production of maraschino cherries, those beautiful bright red and green cherries we use on sundaes.

The sweet Burlat is an early variety arriving in May.

Less common varieties include the Van, Stella, Black Republican, Chinook, Burbank, Chapman, Garnet, Brooks, Ruby, Tulare, Early Garnet, and Lapins.

Though there are 270 varieties of tart cherries, only a few are grown commercially. Tart cherries are classified in two groups, distinguished from each other by the color of the fruit's juice. Clear-juice tart cherries are known as Amarelles or Kentish in Britain. They have less acid and a less pronounced sour taste than the darker varieties. The Early Richmond (or Richmond) and the Montmorency varieties are the best known of the Amarelles. The Montmorency, which originated in the Montmorency Valley of France, is by far the most cultivated of all tart cherries.

Morellos, or as the French call them, Griottes, have darker fruit with colored juice. The English Morellos are the most common of the darker tart cherries.

SEASONS

The sweet cherry season begins in May with Burlats that, when available, don't last very long. Bings begin to arrive in mid-June, Lamberts and Rainiers later in the month. The California crop peaks in June; the Santa Clara Valley crop usually begins by mid-May and is gone by the end of June. The Washington crop peaks in July. Rainers end in early August, Lamberts and Bings a few weeks later.

Small amounts of Canadian imports, from British Columbia, come mostly in June and July. Imports from Chile, mostly Bings, may begin arriving as early as October, peak from the end of November to the end of December, and finish in January.

July is the prime time for tart cherries, with the third week of the month often the peak of the harvest. However, outside the growing areas, tart cherries can be scarce because they do not travel well.

SELECTION, HANDLING & STORAGE

A ripe sweet cherry is heavy for its size, meaning it has plenty of juice, and is meatier and sweeter than an immature cherry. Cherries that are hard, small, and lighter in color were probably picked too soon. Overripe fruit is soft with a dull cast and shriveled skin. Avoid fruit that is sticky or shows signs of decay. Tart cherries should be firm, plump, and bright scarlet in color. All fresh cherries should still have their stems attached and be clean and dry.

Keeping cherries as cool as possible protects the texture and flavor from the effects of warm summer temperatures. Cherries can decay more in one hour at room temperature than they can in twenty-four hours at 32°F.

Though the rule of thumb with cherries, as with berries, is not to wash the fruit until you are ready to use it, we've successfully kept rinsed and thoroughly drained (or towel-dried) fruit in the refrigerator for several days up to almost a week. Freeze them if you don't plan to use them within six days. Wash and drain them dry, then spread them evenly over a cookie sheet or flat tray and freeze them. When frozen solid, transfer the cherries to a plastic bag. They'll keep up to a year this way.

NUTRITION

One cup of pitted sweet cherries (140g, about 5 ounces) contains 90 calories, 22g of carbohydrates, 3g of dietary fiber, 2g of protein, and .5g of fat. A serving of sweet cherries provides 15% of the DV for vitamin C and 2% each for vitamin A, calcium, and iron. Tart cherries are a good source of vitamin A, with more than 10% of the DV, almost five times that of sweet cherries. Sweet and tart cherries have good amounts of potassium as well (300mg).

YIELD

Cherries are sized by rows, which dates from when the cherry industry packed the top layer of cherries in neat rows. If ten cherries fit into a row snugly, that size became a ten row, and so on. A nine-row cherry is considered the largest (probably too large for best flavor, actually) and twelve-row the smallest. There are fifty-four $10^1/_2$-row cherries in a pound. A pound of sweet cherries will yield about $2^1/_2$ cups of pitted and sliced fruit, depending on the size of the cherries.

Tony's Tip

Don't be put off if Rainer cherries have some skin discoloration in the form of scuffing or brown spots. That's often a sign of high sugar content.

PREPARATION

While cherry pitting can be a bit tedious, we consider cherry pitters unnecessary unless you're preparing large quantities for canning or jam. We prefer to simply make a slit, north to south, around the circumference of the cherry and pull it apart. Then pop out the pit with the tip of a paring knife or fingers. Food maven Barbara Kafka suggests pushing the pit through the stem end after the stem is removed. This does work but it's pretty messy.

By using our method, the cherries are not only pitted but halved as well, which is the way most recipes want them.

Cinnamon and nutmeg are two prime cherry seasonings. So are almonds and almond flavorings such as almond extracts and almond liqueurs.

Chocolate and cherries are a natural, which is why chocolate-covered cherries have been around so long. Vanilla also goes quite well with cherries.

Kirsch, the clear cherry brandy, can intensify the cherry flavor in many cherry dishes. However, since most kirsch is harsh to the taste (an exception being St. George Spirits brand from Alameda, California), we prefer maraschino liqueur. Unfortunately, maraschino liqueur is a little more difficult to obtain than kirsch. Such are life's dilemmas.

Pork Loin with Brandied Cherries

This recipe was originally supposed to be pork loin stuffed with figs, but there were no figs in the market that week. Try it either way and with apricots too. A great summer buffet dish.

Makes 6 to 8 servings

1^1/$_2$ cups pitted and halved sweet
 cherries, about 10 ounces
3 tablespoons brandy
3 pounds, approximately, very lean,
 center-cut pork loin
Kosher salt and freshly ground black
 pepper to taste

1. Soak cherries in brandy 1 hour. Drain and reserve juice.

2. Preheat oven to 350°F. Butterfly pork loin (there is a natural seam that will make it easy). With the loin laid out flat, season with salt and pepper and lay the cherries evenly down the center. Roll up and tie with butcher's string.

3. Put the pork on a rack in a shallow roasting pan, fatty side up. Season with salt and pepper and pour cherry juices over. Bake 70 minutes or until internal temperature reaches 155°F in the center.

4. Cool pork to warm or room temperature and cut into ¹/₂-inch slices.

Sam's Cooking Tip

Pork loin is a little fattier than most other meats used in this book but still quite lean. So lean in fact, it easily dries out from overcooking. Make sure you get the center cut, which is the leanest section of the loin.

Tart Cherry Sauce

It may seem silly to sweeten tart cherries to make them taste like sweet cherries, but even when sweetened, tart cherries have a slight tartness reminiscent of cranberries. And, in fact, tart cherries can be used much like cranberries — in crisps, relishes, and sauces like this one, which is terrific over vanilla ice cream.

Makes about 3 cups

3 cups tart cherries (about 1^1/$_4$ pounds), pitted and halved
^{2}/$_3$ cup sugar
1 tablespoon orange rind, cut in julienne strips
2 tablespoons bourbon or brandy
^{1}/$_4$ cup toasted, sliced almonds (see page 28)

1. Combine tart cherries, sugar, orange rind, and bourbon in a saucepan. Set aside for 30 minutes.

2. Bring to a boil over moderate heat. Simmer about 8 to 10 minutes. Cool, then stir in almonds.

Cherry Clafouti

This is an old-fashioned French custard or pudding. So old-fashioned, in fact, that the French don't normally pit their cherries. Ouch!

Makes 6 servings

2 1/2 cups sweet cherries (about 1 pound), pitted and halved

3 tablespoons kirsch

4 large eggs

1/2 cup sugar

1/2 cup sifted all-purpose flour

1 cup milk

3/4 teaspoon almond extract

Butter-flavored cooking spray

Powdered sugar

1. Toss cherries in kirsch and marinate 30 minutes or more. Drain and reserve 1 tablespoon liquid. Preheat oven to 400°F.

2. Meanwhile, combine eggs and sugar in a mixing bowl and mix well by hand or with an electric mixer. Then add flour, then milk, almond extract, and the tablespoon of cherry marinade.

3. Spray an 8-cup baking or gratin dish or deep pie plate with butter-flavored spray. Spread cherries evenly in the pan and pour batter over.

4. Bake in the middle of the oven for 25 to 30 minutes. It will be puffy around the edges but slightly runny in the center. Cool to warm and serve sprinkled with powdered sugar.

Pan-Roasted Duck Breast with Cherry Sauce

Fresh cherries and duck have been a natural combination since the creation of the classic French dish, Duck à la Montmorency, which was initially made with a tart type of cherry.

Makes 4 servings

2 boneless duck breast halves, each about 12 ounces with skin

1 tablespoon butter

2 tablespoons minced shallots

1 tablespoon minced fresh ginger

$1/2$ cup port

1 cup pitted sweet cherries (about $6^1/2$ ounces), quartered if larger, halved if small

$1/2$ teaspoon arrowroot mixed with 2 tablespoons Chicken Stock (page 9)

Kosher salt and freshly ground black pepper to taste

1. Cut duck breasts in half to form 4 pieces. Set aside.

2. Melt butter in a saucepan or skillet over medium heat. Add shallots and ginger and cook until shallots soften, about 3 minutes. Add port, cherries, arrowroot solution, and a pinch of salt. Cook about 5 minutes, until cherries soften but are not falling apart and mixture thickens slightly. Set aside.

3. Heat a large skillet over high heat until a drop of water instantly evaporates on its surface. Add duck breasts skin side down and lower heat to medium low. Cook 5 minutes.

4. Remove duck breasts from the skillet, take off skin, and season both sides with salt and pepper. Pour off all but a thin haze of duck fat from the skillet (not much more than a teaspoon of fat) and put over medium-high heat. When fat smokes add duck breasts. Cook 5 minutes and turn over. Cook 1 minute more for medium-rare doneness.

5. Meanwhile, warm the cherry sauce and spread thinly on 4 plates. Cut each duck breast into 6 or 7 slices on the diagonal. Fan slices on the sauce.

Sam's Cooking Tip

Most good butcher shops have duck breasts. If you don't have such a butcher shop close by, you have three alternatives: (1) Bone out the breast from a duck (and use the rest for another purpose such as cassoulet); (2) order from a company such as D'Artagnan (800/327-8246); or (3) use an equivalent size of turkey cutlets.

Cherry Rice Pudding with Pine Nuts

Since cherries are a warm-weather fruit, and no one wants to turn on the oven in July, this dish is a perfect solution: rice pudding on top of the stove.

Makes 4 to 6 servings

2 cups evaporated skim milk

2 cups skim milk

1 tablespoon butter

3 tablespoons pine nuts

1 cup arborio rice

3 tablespoons kirsch (optional)

1 teaspoon vanilla

1 teaspoon orange zest

$^1/_2$ cup sugar

1 cup sweet cherries (about $6^1/_2$ ounces), pitted and halved

$^1/_2$ teaspoon cinnamon

1. In a heavy-bottomed saucepan over low heat, warm both types of milk.

2. In a large, heavy-bottomed saucepan, heat butter and toast pine nuts over low heat until nicely browned, about 5 minutes. Add rice and stir.

3. Add kirsch and cook a minute. Then add half of the warmed skim milk mixture, the vanilla, and the orange zest. Cook gently, stirring occasionally, until almost all of the liquid is absorbed.

4. Add remaining warm skim milk, sugar, and cherries. Cook, stirring occasionally, until the rice is tender, about 15 to 20 minutes. The mixture should be a little on the soupy side, slightly more runny than a regular risotto. Cool to warm and transfer to a serving bowl or spoon out into individual dishes. Sprinkle with cinnamon.

CHAPTER 37

dates

If you were blindfolded and dropped by parachute into Indio, California, in late February, you'd swear you were transported back to ancient Baghdad. You'd see camel races, Queen Scheherazade swathed in Arabian Nights splendor, and a Middle Eastern bazaar where artisans hawk their wares. All this is part of the ten-day annual National Date Festival.

But this isn't a trumped-up festival like the local zucchini festival. The Coachella Valley, where Indio is located, is desert with deep soil much like Algeria and Iraq from which early date palm transplants were brought. Today, the Coachella Valley is the only area in the Western Hemisphere where dates are grown commercially.

WHERE GROWN

High temperature and low humidity are the ideal conditions for dates along with deep soil. So it's not surprising that 75 percent of the world's date crop is grown in the Middle East, with Iraq the leading regional and world producer. Iran and Saudi Arabia are also among the top producers worldwide. California's Coachella Valley produces 95 percent of the domestic crop. The remaining 5 percent is grown in Bard Valley, which straddles California and Arizona.

In the past few years Israel has been challenging Algeria and Tunisia, traditional exporters to the United States, with dates many believe are of superior quality.

VARIETIES

Because the date palm tree can reach a height of a hundred feet, it is said to grow with its "feet in the water and head in the fires of heaven." Dates grow in rich red to golden brown clusters that weigh about 20 pounds, each containing up to two hundred dates. (Each date is about 1 inch long and contains a single seed.) There are twelve to fifteen clusters or bunches per tree. And a healthy tree can produce as much as three hundred pounds of dates.

There are about thirty varieties of dates grown in California and they are divided into two broad categories: soft and semisoft or semidry. The soft varieties, harvested when still soft and ripe, have a high moisture content, lots of sugar, and a mild flavor. They are mainly grown to be used fresh, as snacks and in cooking. Chefs like to use them in sauces because they break down and caramelize. Soft dates are more delicate so they are harvested by hand. They are also more perishable. Their production in the United States is more limited than that of the semidry type.

There are three main varieties in the soft group. The Halawy is an oblong date from Iraq with a golden to light amber color. It is rich and sweet. Khadrawy is a green date from Iraq with a pleasantly rich flavor and smooth texture. The Medjool was originally imported from Morocco but is now grown in the United States. In fact, because of the bayud disease in Morocco, U.S. growers have been sending Medjool trees to Morocco. The Medjool has become a more important variety in California in recent years and is the largest variety (in size) grown. It is very soft with a rich, sweet flavor.

Semidry dates are the more common type grown in the United States. They are firmer and have a lower moisture content than soft dates. As a result they can be mechanically harvested and last considerably longer.

Although the total sugar content in semidry dates is about the same as for soft dates, the composition of the sugars is different. Soft dates have invert or fruit sugars in the form of dextrose and glucose. Only about 50 percent of the sugars in semidry dates are invert sugars. The remaining sugars are in the form of sucrose.

The most widely available semidry variety is the Deglet Noor, also known as "The Date of Light." It has a dark amber color, firm flesh, high sugar content, and caramellike flavor.

Two other semidry dates are the Zahidi, which is small to medium in size with a reddish-brown color and rich, sweet taste, and the Barhee (sometimes spelled Barhi), a lesser-grown variety that is nonetheless prized by Middle Eastern émigrés. It is green and sweet.

The Chinese Date or jujube is not really a variety of date. It is not even from the same botanical family even though it strongly resembles a true date.

SEASON

Fresh dates are available year-round, with peak supplies from October through December. Some of the more obscure varieties such as Khadrawy and Halawy ripen earlier than others.

SELECTION, HANDLING & STORAGE

Dates are sold several different ways: with and without pits, fresh, dried, or cured. Whole and pitted dates are normally sold in plastic cups or tubs in 8-ounce, 12-ounce, 24-ounce, or 32-ounce sizes. In specialty stores, particularly Middle Eastern markets, and with less common varieties such as Medjool, they may be sold loose.

It's not easy to properly select dates when they are packaged in plastic or cellophane. Both fresh and dried dates should be glossy and plump with smooth skins and a little wrinkling. Skins should not be broken, cracked, or shriveled. Avoid fruit with an aroma of sour milk or crystallized sugar on the surface. Dried dates should be firm but not hard.

If packaged in an airtight container, fresh dates will last from one to eight months without refrigeration, three to twelve months if refrigerated, and up to several years if frozen. Refrigeration should be at temperatures of 30°F to 40°F. Dried dates have been pasteurized to inhibit the growth of mold and will keep more than a year under refrigeration and up to five years in the freezer.

Dates should also be kept away from strong smelling foods because they will absorb odors easily.

NUTRITION

A serving of five to six dates (40g, about 1.5 ounces) contains 120 calories, 31g of carbohydrates, 3g of dietary fiber, 1g of protein, and 2% of the DV for iron and calcium. Dates are also a good source of potassium.

Dates are rich in boron, which can help prevent osteoporosis and increase estrogen levels in postmenopausal women. Along with other dried fruits, dates can be effective against certain forms of cancer, particularly pancreatic cancer. Also like some dried fruits, dates act as a laxative. With regard to headaches, dates are a double-edged sword. They act as a natural aspirin but in some people they may actually cause headaches.

Since dates are 75 percent carbohydrates, the bulk of which are made of naturally occurring sugars such as fructose, glucose, and sucrose, they are assimilated into the body quickly and provide a quick burst of energy.

YIELD

A pound of pitted dates yields about 3 cups chopped.

Tony's Tips

Because they lose so much moisture when they fly, airline pilots routinely eat dried dates to replace potassium. So bring along some dates if you're planning a long plane ride.

PREPARATION

For ease in slicing, separate the dates and put them in the freezer for about an hour to firm up. If your dates are more dried than you'd like, soak them briefly in warm water.

Dates are a wonderful accent to savory dishes such as stews. To cut some of the sweetness it is sometimes a good idea to add some form of acidity such as citrus juice or something spicy such as hot pepper.

Dates are delicious with pork and lamb and they enhance poultry stuffing. Chopped dates add a nice flavor accent to vegetables such as carrots, to chicken salads, and to other cold composed salads like Waldorf salad. Try them in bean or lentil dishes and use them to liven up plain old rice. (Dates are especially good with more aromatic rices such as basmati.)

Dates and other dried fruits are also good companions to fresh fruit as in a mixed fruit salad, perhaps with some chopped walnuts or almonds as well. Wrap dates with prosciutto for a simple hors d'oeuvre or stuff them with pistachio nuts.

Stuffed Medjool Dates

This recipe was inspired by a dish at a wonderful restaurant in Albany, California, called Enoteca Mastro. Our version is much lower in fat.

Makes 4 servings

8 Medjool dates

$^1/_4$ cup low-fat cream cheese

2 teaspoons honey

1 teaspoon orange flower water (available at Middle Eastern markets) or grated orange zest

$^1/_2$ cup Warmed Rum Sauce from Bread Pudding recipe on page 449

About 3 tablespoons pistachio nuts, coarsely chopped

2 blood oranges, cut into 8 sections each

1. If the dates are particularly dry, soak in warm water about 20 minutes and drain well. Pit by making a slit $^3/_4$ of the way down one side of each date and removing pits.

2. Combine cream cheese, honey, and orange flower water. Stuff each date with $^1/_2$ tablespoon of the mixture. Put 2 dates on each of 4 plates. Drizzle 2 tablespoons of rum sauce on each plate and top with about 2 teaspoons of pistachios. Garnish with orange sections.

Lamb Tagine with Rutabaga, Sweet Potatoes, and Dates

Lamb isn't normally thought of as a lean meat. But if you choose the foreshank, shank, or leg and trim the fat judiciously, a 4-ounce serving of meat is between 6.8 and 8.8 grams of fat.

Makes 8 servings

2 pounds lean boneless lamb, cut into
  $3/4$-inch pieces

Kosher salt and freshly ground black
  pepper to taste

1 tablespoon extra-virgin olive oil

1 medium onion, chopped

2 cloves garlic, chopped

2 teaspoons Ras El Hanout
  (page 337)

$1/2$ teaspoon ground cinnamon

$1/2$ teaspoon ground allspice

$1/4$ teaspoon cayenne pepper, or more to
  taste

3 cups Chicken Stock (page 9)

2 pounds rutabaga, cut into 1-inch cubes

2 pounds sweet potatoes, cut into 1-inch
  cubes

2 cups pitted dates, 5 to 6 ounces,
  halved or quartered if large (about
  6 ounces with pits)

2 tablespoons chopped cilantro

1. Preheat oven to 350°F. Season lamb well with salt and pepper. Heat oil in a large skillet over medium flame. In 2 or 3 batches (it's important not to crowd the pan or the lamb will "steam"), brown lamb well, 5 to 7 minutes per batch. Add browned lamb to a casserole or Dutch oven.

2. Add onion to the skillet and lower heat. Cook onion until soft, about 3 or 4 minutes, then add garlic and spices. Cook a few minutes, stirring well. Add stock, raise heat to high, and bring to a simmer, scraping bottom of the pot with a wooden spoon to scoop up any crusted bits. Add to the casserole. Bring to a boil on the stove, cover, then put in the oven for 1 hour.

3. Add rutabaga, then sweet potatoes 10 minutes later. Cook 30 minutes more or until vegetables are tender. Add dates and cook 15 minutes more. Adjust seasonings as desired. Sprinkle with cilantro.

Sam's Cooking Tip

If you use shanks (four meaty shanks will yield about 2 pounds of usable meat), scrape the large muscles of meat off the bone, then trim them of fat and remove as much gristle and sinew as possible. You don't have to get rid of all the connecting tissue; much of it will dissolve in cooking. If you like, make a lamb stock from the bones and scraps, for this dish (which will make it a bit heavier), for steaming couscous, or for the Bulgur Pilaf with Fava Beans (page 31).

Ras El Hanout

This all-purpose spice mix is as common in Morocco as garam masala is in India.

Makes about 4 teaspoons

$1/2$ teaspoon coriander seeds
$1/2$ teaspoon fennel seeds
1-inch piece of cinnamon stick
1 teaspoon black peppercorns
$1/2$ teaspoon each ground nutmeg
  and cardamom

$1/8$ teaspoon ground mace
1 teaspoon ground ginger
1 bay leaf, crumbled
Pinch hot pepper flakes

Put all ingredients in a spice mill and grind to a fine powder.

Date and Cranberry Relish

The sweetness of the dates contrasts nicely with the tart cranberries, giving this dish a North African holiday twist. Serve as you would any cranberry sauce, as a condiment for turkey, but also for other roasted meats such as lamb, game, and beef.

Makes 4 servings

$^1/_2$ pound cranberries, fresh or frozen

12 medium dates, coarsely chopped

$^1/_2$ lemon, peeled, seeded, and diced

$^1/_3$ cup sugar

1 tablespoon cider vinegar

Pinch cayenne pepper

1. Put cranberries, dates, and lemon in a food processor and process until well combined but not totally smooth.

2. Combine sugar, vinegar, and cayenne pepper. Add to mixture and pulse a few times. Chill an hour before serving.

Carrots with Dates and Lemon

The natural sweetness of the carrots blends perfectly with the sweet dates in this dish. The lemon lends some acidity to prevent it from getting too cloying. Serve as a side dish with a simple meat or poultry entrée or as part of a vegetarian mélange.

Makes 4 servings

1 teaspoon grated lemon rind

1 tablespoon fresh lemon juice

1 tablespoon brown sugar

Pinch cayenne pepper

1 teaspoon kosher salt

1 pound carrots, trimmed and scrubbed or peeled, cut into $^1/_4$-inch-thick slices

$^1/_2$ cup chopped dates

1 tablespoon softened butter

1. Put lemon rind, juice, brown sugar, cayenne pepper, and salt in a skillet with 1 cup water. Bring to a boil.

2. Add carrots, return to a boil, and cook, covered, until carrots are tender, about 10 to 12 minutes. Remove carrots to a serving bowl and keep warm.

3. Add dates to the skillet and increase heat to high. Reduce liquid to a syrup, about 2 or 3 minutes. Swirl in butter, pour over carrots, and gently toss.

When it comes to figs, Americans are of two minds. On one hand, one of America's favorite cookies, the Fig Newton, is made with dried figs. On the other hand, comparatively few people have ever tasted fresh figs.

Somehow the popularity of fresh figs in the Mediterranean didn't make its way to the United Sates with the wave of immigrants. For example, for the holidays Sam's mother always made *cuccidati,* traditional Sicilian cookies filled with dried figs, which she learned how to make from her mother, who was born in Sicily. But Sam never ate, or even saw, a fresh fig until he left home and got into the restaurant business.

Tony grew up in Sicily where figs were on every plate during the fig season. But when Tony ate fresh figs in the United States, people thought he was a little weird.

Who knows why? Perhaps it's because those squishy ripe figs aren't so attractive when swarms of flies, attracted by the fig's intense sweetness, hover around them on sultry summer days. Or maybe people are taking the phrase "don't care a fig" literally. Whatever the reason, we think people will be glad if they "give a fig" about fresh figs.

WHERE GROWN

Fresh figs are still produced in great quantities all along the Mediterranean basin. California's hot and dry central valleys produce the largest amount of figs in the United States.

VARIETIES

Though there are more than a hundred varieties of figs, only a few are produced commercially. The Black Mission fig is the best-known variety grown in California. Despite the name it is more of a deep purple than black, with a pear or tear-drop shape and a crimson flesh that, like all fresh figs, is loaded with tiny, edible seeds.

The Kadota fig is rounder with a firmer, thicker, yellow-green skin and a pale interior that has a reddish-brown center. The Brown

Turkey has brownish-purple skin and a rich red flesh. The large, dark brown Brunswick has a mild flavor. The violet-skinned Celeste has a rose-colored, tasty flesh. Large and squat, Calimyrna figs are yellow-green when partially ripe and pale yellow when fully ripe with an amber flesh that drips with syrup from the eye (at the bottom or stem end of the fruit) when totally ripe. They have a sweet, slightly nutty flavor but are rarely seen fresh, particularly outside of California, because they are so perishable. ("Three days from tree to trash" is how the fig industry refers to it.)

SEASONS

The fresh fig season goes through two phases. The first begins in mid-June and goes through the first week in July. This is the smaller of the two crops, about 10 percent of Black Mission figs, even less for Kadota. The season resumes in the beginning of August and goes through September. Depending on the harvest and weather, the season may go well into October, perhaps even to November.

SELECTION, HANDLING & STORAGE

Fresh figs are extremely fragile and bruise or split easily. Handle them carefully and patronize retailers who do the same. Choose plump, fragrant figs that have a little give to them. Avoid those that are hard or dry, or figs that are split, mushy, or show signs of mold. Occasionally figs will have some scarring as a result of the fruit brushing against the leaves of the tree. But this does not damage the quality of the fruit.

Figs that are not fully ripe when purchased can be ripened at home at room temperature. Ripe figs are quite perishable and should be used as soon as possible. They can be refrigerated for up to three days, put in a single layer on a plate or tray lined with paper towels and covered with plastic wrap. Figs can also be frozen for up to six months.

NUTRITION

A serving of three medium figs (153g, about 5 ounces) contains 120 calories, 28g of carbohydrates, 4g of dietary fiber, 1g of protein, 4% of the DV for vitamin A, 6% for vitamin C, 6% for calcium, and 2% for iron. Figs are also a decent source of folic acid (about 5% of the DV) and a good source of potassium. Levels of potassium and dietary fiber more than triple for a similar amount of dried figs.

Benzaldehyde, a compound found in figs, has been shown to help shrink tumors in some tests. Figs are also considered a good laxative as well as an antiulcer and antibacterial food. In some people figs may cause headaches.

YIELD

Eight large or twelve to sixteen small figs will equal a pound.

PREPARATION

Not much is needed in the way of preparing figs. One of the best ways to eat them, after a good washing, is out of hand, skin and all.

A favorite appetizer is figs wrapped in prosciutto, eaten as a first course or an hors d'oeuvre. Another hors d'oeuvre possibility is to stuff figs with nuts or mascarpone, the luxurious Italian sweetened cream cheese.

Tony's Tip

Black Mission figs should have slight cracking or shriveling, particularly near the stem end. This is not a sign of age but merely a reaction to the sun.

Because they are summer fruits, figs have found their way onto the grill, but they must be handled gently, brushed with a little butter or oil and lightly charred, then perhaps drizzled with a little honey. This is a great accompaniment for grilled poultry, game birds, lamb, or pork. Figs can also be wrapped in thin sheets of pancetta, the Italian unsmoked bacon, cooked until the bacon just crisps and served as you would raw figs and prosciutto.

Figs take well to poaching or stewing, by themselves, with other summer fruits, or with dried fruits. They also bake well; bake them just until they soften and concentrate their sugars even further.

Fragrant honey tends to go well with figs, though not much is needed if the figs are ripe. Walnuts are also a good accompaniment. Brandy or rum are good basters for grilled figs and go well in stewed fig preparations. Citrus fruit, particularly oranges, gives a refreshing contrast to the unctuous quality of figs, as in a fig and orange salad. And because figs are so much associated with Arabic cultures, yogurt is a good companion to figs.

Though it's not well known, fresh figs, like fresh pineapple, contain enzymes that prevent gelatin from setting.

Cornish Hens Stuffed with Brandied Figs

As a stuffing, figs add a wonderful, exotic flavor to small birds. Poussin are baby chickens that weigh about a pound. They're quite delicious but expensive. Cornish hens are a worthy substitute but run a little larger. If using Cornish hens, adjust cooking time accordingly.

Makes 4 servings

4 to 6 medium to large fresh figs
$1/2$ teaspoon ground allspice
1 cup port
4 cups rock salt or other coarse salt

Four 1-pound poussin or Cornish hens, giblets removed and rinsed
Kosher salt and freshly ground black pepper to taste

1. Cut figs in quarters. In a small bowl mix allspice with port. Put figs in a resealable plastic bag, add marinade, close, shake back and forth a few times, and marinate 1 hour.

2. Preheat oven to 500°F. Spread rock salt evenly in a shallow roasting pan just large enough to hold all the hens without crowding. (Salt should be to a depth of about $1/2$ inch.)

3. Loosen the skin of the hens and season with kosher salt and black pepper. Season cavity with salt and pepper and stuff with drained figs. (If using small hens, you may have a few figs left over. Don't overstuff the hens, however.) Brush the flesh of the hens with fig marinade and truss hens. Brush any remaining marinade over hens.

4. Place the hens on the salt in the roasting pan (see tip). Put hens in the oven 30 to 35 minutes or until internal temperature reaches 160°F in the deep thigh of the hens. Remove and let rest 10 minutes, covered with foil. Untruss and serve.

Sam's Cooking Tip

Roasting poultry, from Cornish hens to turkeys, on rock salt (or other salt) minimizes grease splattering. Just scrape off any salt that may have attached to the bottom of the birds and discard the grease-soaked salt from the roasting pan.

Basmati Rice with Figs, Mustard Seeds, and Ginger

Serve this with a simple roasted chicken or butterflied and grilled leg of lamb.

Makes 6 servings

1 tablespoon butter
1 tablespoon mustard seeds
1/2 cup minced onion
1 tablespoon minced or grated ginger
1 jalapeño or other hot, small pepper,
  seeded and minced

2 cups basmati rice
Kosher salt to taste
4 small, firm figs, preferably Kadota,
  diced

1. Put butter in a heavy-bottomed saucepan over medium heat. Add mustard seeds, onion, ginger, and jalapeño. Cook until onion softens, about 4 to 5 minutes.

2. Add rice and stir. Add salt, figs, and 3½ cups water. Bring to a boil and reduce heat to low. Cover and cook 10 minutes. Turn off heat and allow to steam another 10 minutes.

Figs Poached in Campari with Oranges

Campari is the red Italian aperitif that looks, and some people say tastes, like cough syrup. But it adds a nice bitter, herbal edge to the sweetness of this dish, which is wonderful for breakfast or brunch.

Makes 6 servings

1 cup Campari
1 cup orange juice
1 cup water
1 cup sugar
12 medium or 8 to 10 large Kadota figs,
  stemmed

2 oranges, each peeled and cut into
  6 sections
Mint sprigs for garnish (optional)

1. Combine Campari, orange juice, water, and sugar in a saucepan. Bring to a boil, lower heat, and simmer about 10 minutes.

2. If using medium figs, cut in half; if large, quarter. Add figs and oranges to pot. Cook gently until figs are softened but not falling apart, about 10 minutes.

3. Remove oranges and figs to a bowl with a slotted spoon. Put pan over high heat and cook until volume is reduced by about half (it should take 10 minutes or so). Pour liquid over figs and oranges and allow mixture to cool to room temperature.

4. For each serving, put 4 fig halves or 5 or 6 quarters in a shallow bowl with 2 orange wedges. Spoon liquid over fruit and garnish with mint sprigs, if desired.

Sam's Cooking Tip

When you want to reduce a liquid, use a pan with as broad a surface as possible, such as a wide pot or deep skillet, to cut down on the amount of time needed to complete the task.

Figs Stuffed with Tapenade

These are two Provençal favorites, though they're not necessarily served together.
But the tangy quality of the tapenade nicely balances the sweet unctuousness of the figs.

Makes 4 servings

15 oil-cured black olives, pitted

2 teaspoons capers

1 anchovy fillet

1 teaspoon fresh thyme or $1/4$ teaspoon
  dried

2 teaspoons olive oil

12 ripe, small Black Mission figs

1. Puree olives, capers, anchovy, thyme, and olive oil together in a food processor or chop by hand.

2. Make a slit in the side of each fig and spoon about $1/2$ teaspoon of tapenade into the fig. Pinch opening closed.

Baked Figs with Honey and Whiskey

Any whiskey will do in this dish, although Scotch seems to lose some of its flavor under intense heat.

Makes 4 servings

¹/₄ cup hazelnuts
¹/₄ cup honey
¹/₄ cup whiskey
8 large or 12 small Black Mission figs, stemmed

Butter-flavored cooking spray
Mint sprigs for garnish (optional)

1. Toast hazelnuts in a preheated 350°F oven for 10 minutes. Put them in a tea towel and rub them against each other to remove skins. Chop and set aside. Raise oven temperature to 500°F.

2. Combine honey and whiskey in a small saucepan and bring to a boil, stirring. Turn off heat.

3. Meanwhile, cut figs in half lengthwise. Spray a gratin dish large enough to hold all the figs in 1 layer with butter-flavored spray. Put in figs, cut side up. Drizzle with honey-whiskey mixture. Sprinkle with hazelnuts.

4. Bake 7 to 10 minutes, depending on size, or just until figs soften but are not falling apart. Cool to warm and put 4 to 6 fig halves on each of 4 serving plates. Spoon pan juices over figs. If desired, put a mint sprig in the middle of each.

grapefruit

By all rights the grapefruit should have been called the shaddock, even though the term *shaddock* is sometimes used interchangeably with the term *pummelo*, often spelled *pumelo* or *pomelo*, the fruit that is the precursor of the grapefruit. Are you still with us?

You see, a certain Captain Shaddock brought the seeds of the pummelo from the Malay Archipelago to the West Indies in 1693. The seeds produced fruit somewhat smaller than the current grapefruit, more like an orange. The size of the fruit and the fact that it grew in bunches or clusters like grapes prompted a nineteenth-century naturalist to liken the new fruit to grapes, with which it has no botanical relationship whatsoever.

But the name stuck and for nearly two centuries, people have been asking, "How come a grapefruit is called a grapefruit?"

WHERE GROWN

The United States is the major producer of grapefruit with 41 percent of the world's share. It's also the biggest grapefruit consumer. Florida grows about 75 percent of the U.S. grapefruit crop in two areas of the state, central Florida and the Indian River. Texas is a distant second, then come California and Arizona. The Indian River area of Florida is such a good spot because it runs parallel to the Gulf Stream and the warm currents protect the groves from the killing frosts that may occur during Florida winters.

California is also the major supplier of pummelos. Jamaica provides Ugli fruit, which is a trade name for a tangelo. Most imported grapefruit comes from the Bahamas.

VARIETIES

Growers have consistently improved the flavor and sweetness of grapefruit and have worked to reduce the number of seeds. Most varieties found in the market today are seedless. Each grapefruit tree produces between 1,300 and 1,500 pounds of fruit annually. About 60 percent of the grapefruit commercial crop today is processed into juice and segments.

There are two main grapefruit varieties: white and red. The white Marsh or Marsh Seedless, a Florida grapefruit that superseded the Duncan, has no seeds but is less flavorful than the seedier Duncan. (What little Duncan there is left is used for processing.) The Redblush or Ruby Red is a red or pink variety that was developed from the Marsh and is primarily grown in Texas.

Marsh Seedless is also called white or golden because it has a bright yellow skin and honey-colored meat that is firm and tart. Ruby Red or Redblush grapefruit has yellow skin with a pronounced red blush and flavorful, pink meat. The color of the meat can range from very pale to deeper reddish tones, depending on the time of year, variety, and growing conditions.

In the past few years "superred" varieties such as the Star Ruby and Rio Red have become more popular. The Star Ruby has a yellow skin and a deeper red color than the Ruby Red. The Rio Red (also called Rio Star) is similar to the Star Ruby but has an even deeper red interior color as well as a red blush on the skin. Other red varieties are the Ruby Sweet (also called a Henderson or Ray), which is seedless with very dark red flesh, and the Flame.

Grapefruit quality depends largely on the time of year it is harvested (see Seasons) and where the fruit is grown. In general, Florida grapefruit is considered to have superior quality because grapefruit requires high heat for sweet flavor. (Though hot areas of California, Texas, and Arizona also produce good fruit.) The Indian River Valley is one of the premier areas for Florida grapefruit, particularly for fruit labeled Orchid, the name of an island in the area. Florida grapefruit has thinner rinds and is juicier than California grapefruit, which is easier to peel.

Because Americans have shown a preference for sweet grapefruit over tart or bitter fruit, the less acidic Melogold and Oroblanco varieties, both crosses between the pummelo and the grapefruit, are becoming more popular. Each has yellow skin and white meat.

The pummelo, also known as the Chinese grapefruit or Shaddock, is popular in Asia but is new to California and rarely seen in the eastern United States. The largest of citrus fruits—it can be as big as a basketball—the pummelo has a very thick skin and white to deep pink flesh. The aromatic and sweet flesh has no trace of bitterness and is easily segmented.

Jamaicans grow the fragrant Ugli (pronounced *OO-gli*), a cross between a grapefruit and a mandarin or tangerine. (That technically makes the Ugli part of the tangelo family, which is discussed in the chapter on oranges. The Ugli is dealt with here because it tastes more like a grapefruit than other tangelos.) Ranging in size from an orange to a large grapefruit, the Ugli gets its name from the somewhat unattractive, russet and yellow-green skin that fits loosely over the fruit. Not surprisingly, this ill-fitting cloak comes off easily, revealing yellow-orange fruit that is moderately sweet, tasting of grapefruit with hints of orange or mandarin. You may also see the Ugli fruit sold as the Uniq fruit.

SEASONS

Although this is a year-round fruit, the peak period for grapefruit runs from January to April, when Florida's grapefruit harvest is in full swing. As the Florida harvest slows to a trickle in late June and July, the California harvest picks up. Overall supplies of grapefruit are at their lowest from July through September.

Some red varieties such as Ruby Sweet, Rio Star, and Flame are available from October through May. Oroblanco and Melogolds are harvested from December through April. Summer is a bad time for citrus in general and especially grapefruit, which is often inferior but still pricey.

Pummelo season is mid-January through mid-February. The Ugli is also a winter fruit, but its season usually extends into the spring.

SELECTION, HANDLING & STORAGE

Look for grapefruit that is smooth, thin-skinned, and round or slightly flattened at each end. These will have the best flavor and the most juice. They should be firm, shiny, and heavy in the hand for their size, an indication of abundant juice.

Avoid coarse, rough-looking, puffy fruit or any with puffy protruding ends, which is an indication that the fruit is dry and flavorless. Good fruit should be springy to touch, not soft, wilted, or flabby. Defects on the surface of the rind such as scale, scars, torn scratches, and discoloration don't affect the eating quality.

Grapefruit is ripe when picked and will not ripen further once off the tree. Store at room temperature for several days. Otherwise refrigerate in a plastic bag or in the high-humidity crisper section of the refrigerator where it will keep for several weeks.

NUTRITION

A serving of $1/2$ a medium grapefruit (154g, about 5.4 ounces) contains 60 calories, 16g of carbohydrates, 1g of protein, 6g of dietary fiber, 15% of the DV for vitamin A, 110% for vitamin C, and 2% for calcium. Grapefruit is also a decent source of potassium (230mg).

Some studies indicate that the pectin in grapefruit pulp (not the juice) helps lower blood cholesterol and may even help to dissolve the plaque that already clogs arteries. Grape-fruit appears to have protective effects against certain forms of cancer, namely stomach and pancreatic cancer. And grapefruit, particularly the redder varieties, is also high in disease-fighting antioxidants.

Freshly squeezed juice stored at 40°F retains 98% of its vitamin C for up to a week. Eight ounces of fresh-squeezed juice supplies 139% to 157% of the DV for vitamin C, while canned juice supplies 112% of DV. Grapefruit juice has antiviral properties though its acidic qualities may aggravate heartburn in some people.

YIELD

Each medium grapefruit has ten to twelve sec-tions, ²/₃ of a cup juice, and 3 to 4 tablespoons of grated peel.

PREPARATION

Most people halve a grapefruit and eat it by scooping out the sections with a teaspoon, often one with a serrated edge specifically for this purpose. But try eating a grapefruit like an orange by pulling off the skin and separating the fruit into sections.

You can also cut grapefruit into wedges for snacks. Cut the fruit in half crosswise. With the halves cut side up, cut each into four or five wedges. For slices and segments free of pith, see Preparation in the Oranges chapter, page 411.

Tony's Tip

> Juice a grapefruit just as you would an orange. Use a juicer and have the fruit at room temperature to extract the maximum amount of juice.

For a change from lemon zest, try grapefruit grated or peeled and julienned in the same manner as a lemon. Or make a grapefruit twist for martinis. Use fresh juice for cocktails with rum, gin, or vodka.

Avocado-Citrus Salad

This salad can be made with any variety of citrus or all one kind if you so choose. In addition, you can slice the fruit or separate it into sections.

Makes 4 servings

3 tablespoons mild rice vinegar or light
  fruit vinegar (see tip)

1 tablespoon extra-virgin olive oil

1 tablespoon chopped cilantro

Kosher salt and freshly ground black
  pepper to taste

1 seedless red grapefruit

1 tangelo

1 navel orange

1 avocado, ripe but still firm

1. Mix vinegar, oil, cilantro, and salt and pepper to taste. Set aside.

2. Peel and cut grapefruit, tangelo, and orange into sections or slices. Halve and peel avocado, then cut into thin slices crosswise.

3. Arrange citrus and avocado alternately (1 avocado slice for every 2 or 3 citrus sections) in a ring on the outside of a platter. Then form a smaller ring inside the larger ring. Pour dressing over and serve.

Sam's Cooking Tip

I first made this salad with mango vinegar and it was terrific. The reason was that the vinegar is very low in acid (about 3 percent) with an intense fruit flavor. Mango vinegar is made by Consorzio and is available at Williams-Sonoma and better food stores. In its place use a low-acid vinegar such as rice wine or another fruit vinegar.

Sautéed Sole with Grapefruit

Though this dish was originally conceived for sole, any mild white-fleshed fish will do. In fact the sauce would also stand up to a more robust fish as well.

Makes 2 servings

1 grapefruit

1 tablespoon butter

2 sole fillets, about 5 or 6 ounces each

Kosher salt, freshly ground black pepper,
  and cayenne pepper to taste

2 tablespoons shallots, minced

3 tablespoons chopped red bell pepper

2 tablespoons grapefruit juice

2 tablespoons orange juice

1 tablespoon chopped cilantro

1. Peel and section grapefruit as in Drunken Oranges, page 413. Save the juice that accumulates and add to the orange and grapefruit juice.

2. Put butter in a nonstick skillet over medium heat. Season sole with salt, black pepper, and cayenne pepper to taste. Add sole and cook about 3 minutes on each side, turning carefully. Remove when springy to the touch and keep warm.

3. Add shallots and bell pepper and cook until shallots soften, about 3 minutes. Add grapefruit sections and both juices. Bring to a boil and let reduce for a minute or two. Pour over fish and sprinkle with cilantro.

Broiled Grapefruit Halves

Grapefruit halves are as traditional for breakfast as cornflakes, and just as boring. Here are a few ways to perk up this standby. Try not to fight with your spouse over the breakfast table to see who gets which one.

Makes 2 servings

1 grapefruit, halved and sectioned

1 tablespoon Grand Marnier or other
  orange liqueur

2 teaspoons minced candied ginger

1 tablespoon rum

1 tablespoon brown sugar

1. Preheat broiler. If necessary, cut a small slice from the bottom of each grapefruit half to make sure it sits evenly.

2. Put halves in ovenproof dishes. Mix Grand Marnier with ginger in a small bowl and spoon over one of the grapefruit halves. Mix rum and brown sugar in another small bowl and spoon over the other half.

3. Run halves under the broiler for about 5 minutes, until they brown lightly. Spoon any excess liquid over the halves, and serve.

Sam's Cooking Tip

Also try a combination of bourbon and maple syrup.

Grapefruit Ambrosia

This is a double twist on the standard ambrosia, which is usually made only with oranges or mandarins and never broiled.

Makes 4 to 6 servings

2 grapefruit

1 navel orange

2 tablespoons Marsala or sweet sherry

$1/3$ cup plus 2 tablespoons sugar

3 egg whites

$1/8$ teaspoon Kosher salt

$1/4$ cup shredded coconut

1. Peel grapefruit and orange and cut into sections as in Drunken Oranges, page 413. Halve the sections crosswise, put in a shallow bowl, and toss with Marsala or sherry and 2 tablespoons of sugar. Set aside for 30 minutes.

2. Turn on broiler. To make meringue, beat egg whites with salt and remaining $1/3$ cup sugar until peaks form. Drain fruit, put into a 9-inch pie plate in one layer, and toss with half the coconut. Spread meringue over fruit and sprinkle with remaining coconut.

3. Put pie plate under the broiler as far away from the heat source as possible. Broil 1 to 2 minutes or until lightly browned. Turn if necessary to brown evenly.

CHAPTER

40

A snapshot of the history of grapes

in America would surely include these three men:

William Wolfskill, Agoston Haraszthy, and William

Thompson. In 1839, William Wolfskill, a former

trapper from Kentucky, planted the first vineyard

of table grapes in California, near what is today

Los Angeles. Like Levi Strauss, who made a fortune selling blue jeans to miners, Wolfskill saw more than gold in them thar hills. He was the first person to ship grapes to Northern California, providing foodstuffs to forty-niners who were flush with profits from the Gold Rush.

Agoston Haraszthy was an immigrant from Hungary who is often referred to as the father of California viticulture (the cultivation of grapes). In the mid-nineteenth century, Haraszthy brought some one hundred thousand vine cuttings from Europe to California. Unlike Wolfskill, his interest was in wine, so these vine cuttings were for three hundred varieties of wine grapes. In addition to planting them at his own winery, Buena Vista, he sold them to growers around the state, giving the wine grape industry a major boost. He also wrote the book *Grape Culture, Wines and Wine Making,* which was used as an important reference tool in the wine grape industry.

William Thompson was born in England in 1839 but emigrated to the United States in 1863, purchasing a farm near Yuba City, California. He ordered three vine cuttings of a grape variety called Lady de Coverly from a nursery catalogue and grafted them to California grapevines. Four years and some additional grafting later, the grapes he produced were awarded a prize at the district fair in Marysville. And the local horticultural society gave Thompson's grapes a new varietal name: Thompson seedless. Today the Thompson seedless grape is the most popular table grape as well as one of the most versatile. It is also used for juice and wine and accounts for 95 percent of the raisins produced in California.

WHERE GROWN

Essentially a plant of temperate zones, the grape grows particularly well in regions where the climate is like that of the Mediterranean. Viticulture is still done primarily by hand on six continents.

California produces 97 percent of all European varieties grown commercially in the United States. Arizona produces the remainder. California is third in the world in table grape production, after number-one Italy and number-two Chile. The vast majority of the grapes imported into the United States come from Chile, with Mexico a distant second.

VARIETIES

There are two types or species of grapes grown in the United States. The native American is called *Vitis labrusca,* and the European, *V. vinifera.* Though early Americans grafted European varieties to the hardier native American rootstocks, the table grapes we see today are direct descendants of European varieties. There are an estimated ten thousand varieties of *Vitis vinifera,* but only a dozen or so are important as table grapes.

Seedless Varieties

The Thompson seedless represents more than a third of the table grapes now grown in California. Light green and oval, it is juicy, crisp, and sweet. Despite being considered a new variety for many years, it is now thought the Thompson seedless has its origins in southern Iran. The Black Beauty, often called the Beauty, is the only seedless black variety. Its flavor resembles that of Concord grapes, spicy and sweet.

The Flame seedless, a cross between the Thompson, Cardinal, and a few other varieties, has grown rapidly in popularity to become the second most popular table grape after the Thompson seedless. It is round and deep red, with a sweet-tart flavor and a pleasant crunch.

The Tokay (Flame Tokay) is a sweeter version of the Flame seedless. Its fruit is large and elongated with orange-red color and crisp texture.

The Perlette is a round, crisp green grape with a frosty white "bloom" on its surface. It is the first grape of the California season and one of the hardiest varieties. Ruby seedless are deep red, oval grapes with a sweet flavor and juicy flesh.

The Black Corinth, often marketed as the Champagne grape, is a tiny, purple fruit with a delicious winelike sweetness and crunchy texture. It is usually available at gourmet markets when fresh, but is more common in dried form as the Zante currant.

The elongated, bright green Superior is a fairly recent variety but has become popular for its sweet flavor and distinctive crunch.

Seeded Varieties

The Emperor was once a major variety, representing a quarter of California's table production, but now it is less than 5 percent. Bunched in reddish to purplish clusters, this grape has a mild, somewhat cherrylike flavor and a lower sugar content than many table grapes. Thick skins make it a good shipper and more tolerant of consumer handling. Its large size and full, round shape make Emperor a popular variety for holiday tables. The Red Globe variety is a very large red grape, with crisp texture, large seeds, and good flavor. It's becoming increasingly important for export, pushing out the Emperor.

The Calmeria is a pale green oval shape with a mildly sweet flavor, comparatively thick skinned, containing a few small seeds. An elongated shape is the reason for its nickname, the "Lady Finger" grape. The Exotic is a blue-black grape with firm flesh and a close resemblance to the Ribier. The Ribier is a large, blue-black grape that grows in generous bunches. It has tender, slightly bitter skins and a sweeter flavor than the Exotic.

Taking the place of the older Muscat varieties is the Italia or Italia Muscat, used today primarily for winemaking. The Italia's flavor is milder than the original Muscats but the winelike sweetness still exists and so does the wonderful fruit fragrance.

The Christmas Rose is a newer variety, a cross of four older varieties. It has large, bright red berries and a tart-sweet flavor.

Native American Varieties

Native American *Vitus labrusca* grapes are sometimes referred to as "slip skin grapes" because their skins easily separate from the flesh. Another characteristic of this group is that their seeds remain tightly imbedded in the flesh.

The most familiar American variety is the Concord. Commercial production is still concentrated in the East, with New York the major grower. Pennsylvania, Michigan, Arkansas, and Washington also produce American grapes. In addition to the Concord, the varieties most often seen in the market are Catawba, Delaware, Niagara, Steuben, and Scuppernong.

The Concord's thick skin holds in a heady, sweet aroma and delicious, medium-sweet flavor with a little zing. This variety originated in the 1840s near Concord, Massachusetts, and is a large, round, blue-black grape with powdery bloom. It is more commonly used in making preserves and juices.

Discovered in the 1820s in Maryland, the Catawba is used primarily for making wine.

The more tender-skinned Delaware is a small pinkish-red grape with sweet flavor and a juicy flesh. A less sweet variety is the Niagara.

The Steuben's blue-black color will remind you of the Concord but its flavor is less winelike.

The Scuppernong is an old native variety that remains popular as a fresh fruit and in the making of homemade preserves and wine.

SEASONS

European varieties are available at different times of the year. The California season begins around May 1 in the southern Coachella Valley then shifts to the San Joaquin Valley farther north in July.

The Perlette seedless is the first variety to arrive in early May and runs into July; Black Beauty, late May to mid-June; Superior May to August; Thompson seedless, June through April; Exotic, June through August; Flame seedless, mid-June through September; Champagne (Black Corinth), mid-July through mid-August; Italia (Italia Muscat), August through November; Tokay (Flame Tokay) and Christmas Rose, August through December; Ribier, August through February; Ruby seedless, August to February; Emperor, August through March; Red Globe and Calmeria, September through January. The season for labrusca grapes is a rather short period in September and October.

The Chilean season begins with a November trickle, picks up steam in December, and is in full throttle from January through April. Of the nineteen varieties grown, Thompson seedless, Flame seedless, Ribier, Ruby seedless, Red Globe, Black seedless, Red seedless, and Perlette account for 90 percent of Chile's exports.

SELECTION, HANDLING & STORAGE

Grapes are harvested only when ripe so they should always be ready to eat when you buy them. Use color as a guide to sweetness of the fruit. Green grapes should have a yellow cast or straw color with a touch of amber when at their peak instead of an opaque grassy green color. Red grapes should be a deep crimson, not a milky or pale red. Blue grapes should be darkly hued, almost black, not pale or tinged with green.

Grapes should be plump. Pass over any bunch that has lots of underdeveloped, very green fruit. Remove any spoiled fruit—grapes with broken skins or browning—from the bunch. You can always judge the freshness of grapes by the stem. The greener the stem, the fresher the grapes. And grapes should always be firmly attached to their stems.

If you want to rinse the sticky juice from the bunch, pass the bunch under the faucet with cool water and wrap in a paper towel to absorb excess water. Air dry for a while, then store in the refrigerator. They should keep a week to ten days. Each day you nibble from the bunch, check it and remove any spoilage.

Because of their relatively thin, easily damaged skins, grapes should be stored no more than two bunches deep. Grapes can last up to three months in the freezer (see tip, page 359).

NUTRITION

A serving of 1½ cups of grapes (138g, just under 5 ounces) contains 90 calories, 24g of carbohydrates, 1g each of dietary fiber, fat, and protein, 25% of the DV for vitamin C, and 2% each for vitamin A, iron, and calcium.

Because fruits with deep color have more antioxidants than those with paler colors, red grapes are more nutritious than white or green grapes. In particular, red grapes are high in the antioxidant quercetin. Like vitamins C and E and beta-carotene, quercetin is an antioxidant. Antioxidants protect the body's cells by warding off destructive oxygen molecules that can render the body more vulnerable to diseases. And to ward off cancer, nutrition writer Jean Carper says, "you should eat red grapes with a passion." Grapes in general are a good source of boron, which may be beneficial for mental acuity (especially as we age) and osteoporosis.

YIELD

A pound of seedless grapes will yield about 3 cups.

Tony's Tip

> Frozen grapes are a great, nutritious snack for kids. Put Red Flame or other seedless grapes on a tray in the freezer. When frozen, put them in a resealable plastic bag and return them to the freezer. Then kids can have sweet, frozen snacks anytime.

PREPARATION

Washing and removing them from their stems is about all one needs to do with grapes if they are to be used in a particular dish. If bunches are left whole for fruit or fruit and cheese platters, rinse the bunches briefly under cool water and drain to refresh them about 30 minutes before serving.

Cold salads, especially chicken, turkey, or tuna salads, get a nice perking up with grapes. So do grain dishes with bulgur, rice, and wild rice, especially those with a Middle Eastern touch.

But grapes can also be added to hot preparations such as the classic sole Veronique, poached fish in a white wine sauce with seedless green grapes.

Cinnamon is probably the most accommodating spice for grapes. Also try curry and nuts, especially walnuts and almonds.

Spiced Concord Grape Jelly

Sam's mom would make grape jelly using fruit from the grape arbor in their backyard in Buffalo, New York. This is a spicy version of what she made. In some circles this type of jelly is called venison jelly because it was served with venison meat.

Makes 4 half pints

3 to 3¹⁄₂ pounds (2 quarts) Concord grapes
2 cinnamon sticks
10 allspice berries
3 cups sugar
4 sterilized ¹⁄₂ pint canning jars with lids and rings

1. Stem and wash grapes, discarding any that are withered or blemished. Put them in a 4- to 6-quart stainless steel pot; mash them with a potato masher, extracting as much juice as possible. Put mixture over medium heat until it comes to a boil. Simmer, stirring, 10 minutes.

2. Strain through strainer. You should have 4 cups. Return juice to the same kettle. Add cinnamon sticks and allspice berries. Bring to a boil over medium-high heat and add sugar. Boil, stirring, for 20 minutes. To test for jelling, put a teaspoonful in a dish and put the dish in the freezer for a minute. If the jelly wrinkles when gently pushed with a finger, it's ready.

3. Strain to remove cinnamon sticks and allspice berries. Pack into hot sterilized jars. Label and date. Store in the refrigerator up to 6 months.

Sam's Cooking Tip

You'll notice that unlike some jelly recipes, this one has no added pectin, the substance that helps to create jelling. That's because Concord grapes are naturally high in pectin.

Wild Rice Salad with Grapes and Toasted Almonds

This is a fine side dish for an alfresco lunch with barbecued chicken or leftover roasted chicken or turkey from the night before.

Makes 6 servings

1 cup wild rice	1 tablespoon Dijon mustard
Kosher salt	1 tablespoon honey
1¹/₂ cups red and green seedless grapes	¹/₂ teaspoon cardamom
1 rib celery	Freshly ground black pepper to taste
1 tablespoon fresh lemon juice	2 cups cooked white rice
1 tablespoon rice wine or cider vinegar	¹/₃ cup toasted sliced almonds
1 tablespoon walnut or almond oil	(page 28)

1. Put wild rice in a saucepan with 3 cups water and ¹/₂ teaspoon salt. Bring to a boil, reduce heat, and simmer, covered, 45 minutes or until just tender but still chewy. Drain any water and cool.

2. Meanwhile halve grapes, and cut celery into very thin crescents.

3. In a small bowl combine lemon juice, vinegar, oil, mustard, honey, cardamom, and salt and pepper to taste.

4. Put wild and cooked white rice in a mixing bowl with celery, almonds, and grapes. Pour dressing over and mix well.

Sautéed Sea Bass with Grapes and Pistachios

This is a variation on sole Veronique. You can substitute any relatively mild fish.

Makes 2 servings

1 tablespoon clarified butter or whole
  butter (page 284)
2 tablespoons flour
Kosher salt and freshly ground black
  pepper to taste
Two 5-ounce fillets of sea bass

2 tablespoons shelled pistachios
$1/3$ to $1/2$ cup dry vermouth or dry white
  wine
$1/2$ cup seedless green and red grapes,
  halved

1. Put butter in a skillet over medium-high heat.

2. Combine flour, salt, and pepper. Dredge fillets in flour mixture, shake off excess, and add to the skillet. Cook fish 3 minutes on one side. Turn gently with a wide spatula and cook about 2 minutes on the other side or until fillets spring back when pressed with a finger.

3. Remove fillets to a warm platter, skin side down. Add pistachios to skillet and cook 1 minute, shaking the pan. Add wine and grapes. Scrape up any bits on the bottom of the pan with a wooden spoon. Reduce just until sauce thickens, a few minutes. Pour sauce over fish fillets.

Grape and Bulgur Stuffing

This is a delicious, low-fat stuffing for poultry of any kind. It will fill the cavity of a 6½-pound roasting chicken with about a cup left over.

Makes 6 servings

¼ cup sultana raisins

3 tablespoons brandy

1 cup coarse-grained bulgur

1 tablespoon butter

2 ribs celery, cut into thin crescents

½ cup minced scallions, whites and
  1 inch of greens

1 cup mixed green and red grapes, halved

⅓ cup chopped fresh mint

Kosher salt and freshly ground black
  pepper to taste

1. Put raisins in a small bowl with brandy to soak for 20 minutes or more. Drain.

2. Meanwhile, pour ¾ cup boiling water over bulgur, fluff with a fork, and set aside for 10 minutes. Taste. If too hard and chewy, add more water, 2 tablespoons at a time; fluff and let sit.

3. Melt butter in a skillet over medium heat and add celery and scallions. Cook, stirring, until scallions soften, 3 or 4 minutes. Add to bulgur along with grapes, raisins, and mint. Season with salt and pepper. If not put into the cavity of a bird, the stuffing should be put into a casserole that has been greased with butter-flavored cooking spray, moistened with about ¼ cup Chicken Stock, and baked at 350°F about 30 minutes or until heated through.

Frosted Grapes

*This is a simple snack or garnish for dessert that's easy to make.
Kids might like to join in the fun.*

Makes 6 adult servings, 10 kid servings

1 cup sugar
1 teaspoon cinnamon
About 60 seedless red and green grapes, stemmed

1. Mix sugar with cinnamon in a small bowl.

2. Wash grapes, but do not dry. Roll individually in the sugar mixture and place on a 12 × 17-inch sheet pan so they do not touch. Put the pan in the freezer for about an hour or until grapes are frozen. Remove and eat as a snack or use as a garnish for desserts.

Sam's Cooking Tip

You can substitute powdered ginger, mace, or nutmeg for cinnamon, or divide the grapes into groups and season each group with a different spice.

CHAPTER

41

Few people are more synonymous with a single fruit or vegetable than Frieda Caplan is with kiwifruit. Before it became the culinary rage, kiwifruit was called the Chinese gooseberry. It was not a name that Madison Avenue would have dreamed up. On top of that, the Chinese gooseberry wasn't terribly attractive; it looked like a large, brown egg with a two-day-old beard.

But at a customer's request, Caplan's company, Produce Specialties (now called Frieda's), began importing the kiwifruit in 1962, a year after kiwifruit had its U.S. restaurant debut Trader Vic's in San Francisco. It took Caplan four months to sell a thousand kiwifruit. Luckily, the fruit's long shelf life allowed it to hold up splendidly. A fellow food broker suggested she might sell fruit faster if the name were changed to that of the flightless New Zealand bird whose fuzzy brown coat looked a lot like a kiwifruit skin. Caplan suggested it to the growers in New Zealand and they loved it. (Unbeknownst to Caplan at the time, Australian food authority Graham Kerr had suggested the name Golden Berry. It didn't fly.)

Caplan championed the fruit wherever she could. She got a local bakery to make kiwifruit tarts, which were sold for little more than cost. In 1970, she bought the entire first California crop (which yielded a mere 1,200 pounds). And she convinced a major supermarket chain to sell kiwifruit for ten cents apiece.

By 1980 kiwifruit had taken off. Famous chefs like Wolfgang Puck were putting them on menus. By the end of the decade, it seemed you couldn't walk into a restaurant that didn't have kiwifruit in some form. "We call it the eighteen-year overnight success," Caplan now says with a combination of amusement and satisfaction.

Today, thanks to Frieda Caplan, kiwifruit is considered a commodity just like apples and oranges. As a matter of fact, it's doing better than those two fruits, or any other fruit, in terms of growth. According to the California Kiwifruit Commission, kiwifruit was the fastest-growing fruit from 1987 to 1995.

WHERE GROWN

California produces about 99 percent of the kiwifruit consumed in the United States. A tiny amount is grown in South Carolina.

Surprisingly, the bulk of the fruit from April through October is supplied not by New Zealand but by Chile, where kiwifruit is the third most-planted fruit, after apples and grapes. Chile supplies the United States with 93 percent of the kiwifruit during this second kiwifruit season, New Zealand only 7 percent. (Imports of New Zealand kiwifruit have decreased in recent years because of an anti-dumping suit brought against the New Zealanders by California Kiwifruit Growers.)

In terms of worldwide kiwifruit production, Italy is number one, followed by New Zealand, Chile, France, Japan, Greece, the United States, Portugal, Korea, Spain, and Australia.

VARIETIES

Though it looks like a tree fruit, kiwifruit is actually a berry that grows on treelike shrubs that can reach as high as 25 feet. The shrubs are trellised much like grape vines. The Hayward, named after nurseryman Hayward Wright, is the principal kiwifruit variety grown in New Zealand, Chile, and California. Each fruit is egg-shaped and about 3 inches long with a thin, fuzzy, brown skin. The flesh is a bright green studded with tiny edible black seeds in a beautiful sunburst pattern.

SEASONS

Since Chile and New Zealand have opposite growing seasons from California, there is virtually a year-round supply of kiwifruit. Chilean imports begin in April, peak from May through June, and continue until mid-October. New Zealand's season is the same. The California season begins in late October and goes through April and into May. The term *peak season* for kiwifruit is a relative one, since much of the fruit is harvested at the same time and kept in storage, where it is metered out over the course of the season. Kiwifruit can last ten months without resorting to a controlled atmosphere, and up to a year if the storage atmosphere is under tight control.

SELECTION, HANDLING & STORAGE

When kiwifruit was still considered an uncommon fruit, author Elizabeth Schneider referred to it in her *Uncommon Fruits and Vegetables* (Harper and Row, 1986) as a fruit handler's dream. Why? Because it can be picked early and hard, stored up to ten months in cold storage, and protected from bruises and breaks by its thin but durable fuzzy, brown skin.

Fruit with the sweetest, fullest flavor should be plump, fragrant, and yield to gentle pressure. Reject shriveled or mushy fruit or fruit with bruises or wet spots. Unripe fruit has a hard core and tart, almost astringent, taste. Much like bananas, kiwifruit are ripened with ethylene gas when they are ready for retail sale. As with bananas, hard fruit can be ripened at home by letting it sit at room temperature. You can speed up the process by putting the fruit in a bag with an apple, pear, or banana. To prevent further ripening, keep kiwifruit away from other fruits that emit ethylene gas.

Ripe kiwifruit will keep in the refrigerator up to ten days. Unripe kiwifruit will last in the refrigerator for up to a month.

NUTRITION

Kiwifruit doesn't get the nutritional hoopla it deserves. A serving of two kiwifruit (148g, about 5.3 ounces) has almost twice the vitamin C of an orange (240% of the DV) and more potassium than a comparable serving of bananas. It is also high in fiber (4g) and has 2% of the DV for vitamin A, 6% for calcium, and 4% for iron. Kiwifruit is also a good source of vitamin E.

Credit goes to those numerous poppylike seeds that kiwifruit have. They act much like grains, providing a powerhouse of nutrition.

A serving of kiwifruit contains 100 calories, 24g of carbohydrates, 1g of fat, and 2g of protein.

Tony's Tip

Kids might like the "soft-boiled-egg" approach to eating kiwifruit as a snack. Halve the fruit crosswise and scoop out the fruit from each half with a spoon, preferably a grapefruit spoon that has a serrated edge on one side. Save the skins if you want to use kiwifruit as a meat tenderizer (see Preparation).

PREPARATION

Though the skin is edible, most people peel kiwifruit before eating or using in dishes. To peel, lop off both ends, then peel off skin with a sharp stainless-steel paring knife or vegetable peeler. Then cut the fruit into thin slices or halve lengthwise and cut into half-moon slices.

Kiwifruit contains an enzyme that makes it a decent meat tenderizer. (But don't expect miracles.) Use kiwi slices or peels with some flesh on them, place the slices or peels directly on the meat, and marinate 30 minutes for each inch of the meat's thickness. As with fresh pineapple, this enzyme also prevents gelatin from setting. So if you want to use kiwi in a gelatin mold, you'll have to poach it, though you'll risk some loss of texture and color.

Kiwifruit combines well with both tropical and semitropical or subtropical fruit, meaning it goes well with bananas and mangoes as well as oranges and strawberries. It adds a lively burst of color and tart-sweet flavor.

Kiwifruit Salad

Since kiwifruit is often described as having elements of citrus, strawberry, and melon, we decided to put them all together for an intense kiwi experience.

Makes 4 to 6 servings

1 teaspoon minced fresh ginger

2 tablespoons honey

2 tablespoons fresh lemon juice

1 tablespoon mild vinegar such as rice or cider vinegar

1 tablespoon almond oil or walnut oil

Kosher salt to taste

$1/2$ small cantaloupe, peeled and seeds removed

1 pint strawberries, washed and stemmed

1 navel orange, peeled with all white pith removed

4 kiwifruit, peeled and cut into thin rounds

Small head of radicchio for lining a platter

2 tablespoons toasted, sliced almonds (page 28)

1. Combine ginger, honey, lemon juice, vinegar, oil, and salt in a small bowl. Set aside.

2. With cut side of cantaloupe down on a work surface, cut into very thin slices crosswise. Then cut slices in half crosswise. Halve strawberries lengthwise. Cut oranges into thin slices.

3. Put radicchio on a platter, flattening it out to make as even a surface as possible. Arrange fruit in concentric rings around the platter; first the cantaloupe on the outside, then half the strawberries inside that. Then arrange kiwi, remaining strawberries, and orange slices in the center.

4. Stir up dressing again and pour over fruit. Sprinkle with almonds.

Sam's Cooking Tip

By using sliced almonds, which are cut much thinner than you can do at home, you can get the same almond flavor in many dishes while using fewer nuts. This keeps the cost and the fat down.

Spicy Kiwi Salsa

Serve this with a meaty grilled fish such as swordfish, grilled poultry, or roasted pork.

Makes 4 servings

4 kiwifruit, peeled and cut into 3/8-inch dice

1 teaspoon minced red jalapeño or other fresh hot red pepper

1 tablespoon tequila (optional)

1 tablespoon freshly squeezed orange juice

1 tablespoon chopped mint

Pinch kosher salt

Combine ingredients and chill 30 minutes to 1 hour.

Kiwi Daiquiri

By switching the rum to tequila and adding a little Triple Sec,
this drink becomes a margarita.

Makes 4 servings

12 very ripe kiwifruit, peeled and diced

Juice of 2 limes

1/2 cup superfine sugar

1 1/4 cups water

6 ounces rum

4 unpeeled kiwifruit slices for garnish

1. Put kiwifruit in a food processor with lime juice. Pulse only a few times until fruit is just pureed. Mix sugar and water and combine with puree, pulsing a few times until smooth.

2. Put kiwifruit mixture in a metal or glass pan and mix with a whisk or wooden spoon. Freeze until solid.

3. Scoop up frozen mixture and put into a food processor or blender. Add the rum and puree just until a slushy drink is formed. Pour into goblets. Make a slit halfway into the kiwifruit slices and put a slice on the rim of each glass.

Sam's Cooking Tip

When pureeing kiwi it's important to avoid overprocessing, which can break the seeds and cause bitterness.

Lamb Kebabs with Kiwifruit Salad

This dish uses kiwifruit in two ways: as a meat tenderizer and as a salad ingredient.

Makes 4 servings

6 kiwifruit

1 pound lean lamb shoulder, cut into
  $3/4$-inch cubes

1 small to medium red onion

1 small to medium red bell pepper

2 teaspoons walnut oil or peanut oil

1 tablespoon fresh lemon juice

1 tablespoon cider or rice vinegar

1 teaspoon honey

Kosher salt to taste

1. Soak 4 wooden skewers in water for 30 minutes (or use thin metal skewers).

2. Meanwhile, peel kiwi so that the peels come off in strips as large as possible. Set peeled kiwi aside.

3. Lay half the peels, flesh side up, in a small, flat dish. Prick the skin of the lamb all over and put on the kiwi skins. Put remaining skins on the other side of the lamb, flesh side against the meat. Wrap with foil, weigh down with a plate and some cans, and set aside at room temperature for 1 hour.

4. While lamb marinates, halve peeled kiwi lengthwise. Then cut into half-moon slices. Do the same with half the onion, making slices as thin as possible. You should have $3/4$ to 1 cup. Coarsely chop half the bell pepper. You should have about $1/2$ cup. Set aside the rest of the onion and bell pepper.

5. Put cut-up kiwi, onion, and bell pepper in a small bowl. Combine remaining ingredients in a cup. Add to kiwi, onion, and bell pepper and toss. Preheat broiler.

6. Cut remaining onion and bell pepper into 1 × 1-inch squares. Remove lamb from marinade. Put on 4 skewers, alternating with bell pepper and onion. Broil kebabs about 3 or 4 minutes on each side for medium rare. Serve with kiwifruit salad.

lemons *and* limes

It's a shame that we call something a lemon when it doesn't work, like the car we bought from the guy who now doesn't recognize us or the kitchen appliance we got from that Sunday morning infomercial. It's a shame because the lemon is one of the world's great flavor enhancers.

Think of what the cocktail would be without lemons. No Bloody Marys, Singapore slings, whiskey sours, mint juleps, or martinis with a twist. Or seafood, from grilled swordfish to oysters and clams on the half shell. Or desserts from sorbets, where lemons perk up the flavor of just about every other fruit, to lemon meringue pie to fruit pies and tarts. Or grilled and sautéed chicken dishes. And don't forget marinades, dressings, and salads.

Lemons make great preservatives, too. Their acid slows the oxidation on fresh-cut fruits and vegetables.

With the increased influence of Asian and Hispanic cooking in our culture, limes are also becoming a valuable seasoning tool in our kitchen arsenal. We use truckloads on guacamole and margaritas alone.

So if someone sells you a lemon, thank them. Then make some lemonade.

WHERE GROWN

The top-five lemon/lime-producing countries are the United States, Mexico, Italy, Spain, and India.

Lemons are more partial to the subtropics in part because they are quite susceptible to disease if grown in wet climates. California, with 30 percent of the world market, produces almost all the lemons consumed domestically. Arizona is a distant second.

Lemon trees produce year-round with blossoms, buds, and mature fruit appearing all at once on the tree. If not picked when mature, the fruit may grow to 12 to 17 inches in diameter, and the peel colors can sometimes get quite freakish blends of green, yellow, and brown. Lemons are usually hand picked when they are about 2½ inches in diameter and still relatively green. About half the domestic crop is shipped for use as fresh

lemons, while the rest is made into a variety of products.

Limes flourish best in the tropics. Mexico is the world's leader, while Florida is the principal provider (85 percent) for domestic markets. California produces a very small lime crop.

VARIETIES

Though there are two types of lemons, acidic and sweet, only the acidic types are grown commercially. The **sweet lemon or limetta** is a hybrid of the Mexican lime, sweet lemon, and citron. It is grown on small scale in India and around the Mediterranean as well as by home gardeners in the United States. Lance Walheim, co-author with Richard Ray of *Citrus: How to Select, Grow and Enjoy* (HP Books, 1980) points out that sweet is a misnomer. "They're actually flat and insipid because they have no acidity," he says.

There are two main acidic lemons. The **Eureka** is distinguished by a short neck at the stem end, while the Lisbon has no distinct neck. Its blossom end tapers to a pointed nipple. The Eureka has a pitted skin and contains few seeds. The **Lisbon** has a smoother skin and is usually seedless. Both have a medium-thick peel and are abundantly juicy. The Lisbon type lemon is grown in some parts of Florida.

Slightly sweeter than acidic lemons but with sufficient acidity for good flavor is the **Meyer or Improved Meyer lemon,** popular in home gardens in California but not widely available commercially, though it's a favorite of many chefs because of its fragrance and flavor. The Meyer is generally thought to be a cross between a lemon and an orange, so not surprisingly it has a noticeable orange accent.

There are essentially two species of limes in common use. The large-fruited Tahitian type is called the **Bearss lime** in California and the

Persian lime in Florida. The smaller **Mexican** or bartender's lime is more widely known as the Key lime of Florida.

The **Persian lime** is the main lime found in markets in the United States. Though technically it is fully ripe when the skin is pale yellow, the Persian lime is generally sold only when it is green. It is larger than the Key lime, has virtually no seeds (unlike the Key lime), but it is less aromatic and less flavorful than the Key lime.

The **Key lime** is more sensitive to cold and needs more heat to fully develop its flavor. But when conditions are right, the fruit becomes highly aromatic and more intensely flavorful than Tahitian-type limes. It is smaller and rounder with a thinner, more leathery skin that ranges from light green to yellow. The flesh is straw yellow. Because Key limes are in much shorter supply than Persian limes, and because they don't store as well (they dry out quickly), their juice is most often bottled and found in gourmet shops or sold by mail.

The **citron** resembles a lemon but is larger and has coarser, thicker skin. You won't find it fresh in the United States very often, but the candied peel is commonly used in baking for things such as fruitcake.

Hybridizers are experimenting with a sweet lime that's a cross between a kumquat and a lime that is sometimes found in Hispanic markets and often used in the preparation of such Hispanic recipes as menudo, the spicy Mexican tripe soup.

SEASONS

Lemons and limes are harvested year-round. Slight seasonal peaks for lemons occur from April through July, for limes from late spring through summer.

SELECTION, HANDLING & STORAGE

Fruits should be firm, glossy, and bright in color. Lemons should be bright yellow. Persian limes should be dark green. Key limes should be pale green to yellow.

Larger lemons tend to have thicker skin and therefore less flesh and juice. Fruit that is heavy in the hand with fine-grained skin is the juiciest. Avoid fruit that is hard or spongy and soft, though it should have some give. Lemons will keep on the counter at room temperature for a maximum of two weeks, depending on the temperature and humidity. Limes will need to be refrigerated. Both will keep in the refrigerator in plastic up to six weeks.

If you have extras, squeeze and freeze the juice in ice trays and transfer cubes to plastic bags for long-term storage. It's a much better alternative than bottled lemon juice.

NUTRITION

Though scurvy isn't the problem it once was with the British navy, lemons and limes are still a good source of vitamin C. One medium lemon (58g, about 2 ounces) contains about 40% of the DV for vitamin C, limes 35%. A lemon also contains 15 calories, 5g of carbohydrates, 1g of dietary fiber, no protein, and 2% of the DV for calcium.

One medium lime (67g, about 2.4 ounces) has 20 calories, 7g of carbohydrates, 2g of dietary fiber, and no protein.

Because of its vitamin C, lemon juice is an antioxidant, the multitalented disease fighter. But some studies indicate that lemon peel may also act as an antioxidant. If you ate enough lemon pulp, the pectin therein might also be beneficial in lowering blood cholesterol.

YIELD

One medium lemon will produce about 3 tablespoons of juice and 3 teaspoons of grated zest. A pound of lemons (six medium) will yield about 1 cup of juice. One medium lime will produce about 1½ tablespoons of juice and about 1½ teaspoons grated zest. A pound of limes (six to eight) will yield about ½ to ⅔ cup of juice.

Tony's Tip

If your cooking ventures result in ugly stains on fingers and nails, just whip out a cut lemon and rub. This is also effective in removing fish and onion odors from hands and work surfaces. And a squeezed lemon thrown down the garbage disposal will give it a fresh smell.

PREPARATION

The zest is the outermost skin of the lemon or lime, yellow and green respectively. It is a valuable culinary resource for a number of dishes. Most often the zest is grated. This can be done with the smallest holes of a four-sided grater. Either fruit grates more easily once frozen.

The zest can also be cut into strips and used to flavor poaching liquid for fruit. Or it can be cut into julienne strips (matchstick size) or minced. To remove the zest for any of these purposes, use a vegetable peeler. Try to avoid getting too much of the bitter white pith (the inner skin). If you use a lot of julienne strips of citrus zest, there is a hand zester tool available at good cookware stores.

Because lemons and other citrus products are usually sprayed with chemicals, it's important to wash them and dry them well before using the peel.

There are numerous ways to juice lemons and limes without using an electrical appliance. The most effective and least expensive way is to use various forms of citrus juice reamers. These are most often ridged cones set atop dishes that catch juice or allow juice to filter into a container below. They can be made of plastic, porcelain, or earthenware. There is also a wooden, hand-held reamer that upscale cookware stores like Williams-Sonoma carry. In a pinch, squeezing the juice through an upturned hand, with fingers split just enough to let juice through, but catch pits, will do.

If you don't need all the juice from a lemon, there are metal and plastic extractors that look something like duck callers. One end is inserted into the fruit, the fruit is squeezed to produce just enough juice, then the fruit is put into the refrigerator for later use. A similar but more homespun method is to pierce the fruit with a toothpick, squeeze out the juice, and reinsert the toothpick.

To get maximum juice, up to 30 percent more, from lemons or limes, make sure the fruit is at room temperature. Then roll it around on a countertop with the heel of your hand until it softens before juicing. Immerse shriveled lemons in hot water for a half hour to restore freshness and increase the amount of juice extracted.

Catfish Piccata

Makes 2 servings

2 tablespoons flour
Kosher salt and freshly ground black
  pepper to taste
1 tablespoon clarified butter or whole
  butter (page 284)
2 catfish fillets, each 5 ounces

Juice of $1/2$ lemon
$1/3$ cup dry white wine
2 teaspoons small capers, well drained
2 teaspoons chopped parsley
Lemon slices for garnish

1. Mix flour with seasonings. Put butter in a large, nonstick skillet over medium heat.

2. Dredge catfish fillets in seasoned flour and shake off excess. When butter in the pan is hot, add fillets, and raise heat to medium high. Cook fish 3 minutes on one side. Turn gently with a wide spatula and cook about 3 minutes on the other side or until fillets spring back when pressed with a finger.

3. Remove fillets to a warm platter. Add lemon juice, wine, and capers to the skillet. Raise heat to medium high and scrape up any bits on the bottom of the pan with a wooden spoon. Reduce just until sauce thickens, a minute or two.

4. Pour sauce and capers over fish fillets. Sprinkle with parsley and serve with lemon slices as garnish.

Sam's Cooking Tip

Because of their acidity, lemons and lemon juice should not come in contact with cooking utensils made with metals that would adversely react to it such as cast iron or aluminum. Instead, use nonreactive materials such as stainless steel, glass, ceramic, and porcelain.

Steamed Carrots with Lemon and Garlic

The lemon and garlic, always a great combination, play off nicely here against the sweetness of the carrots. Serve this as a side dish with almost any type of roasted or grilled entrée.

Makes 4 servings

1 pound carrots, trimmed, scrubbed or peeled, and cut into $3/8$-inch slices
$1^1/_2$ tablespoons butter
2 cloves garlic, minced

2 teaspoons fresh lemon juice
1 teaspoon grated lemon zest
Kosher salt and freshly ground black pepper to taste

1. Steam carrots in a steamer basket over an inch of water in covered saucepan for about 10 minutes or until tender.

2. Put butter in a nonstick skillet over medium heat. Cook garlic about a minute. Add lemon juice and rind and stir. Add carrots, salt, and pepper. Cook until carrots are nicely coated.

Ceviche

In ceviche (sometimes spelled seviche), the acids in citrus juices actually "cook" the seafood when left in contact with the seafood for a period of several hours or more.

Makes 2 servings as a first course

¹/₂ pound bay scallops
Juice of 2 to 3 limes
2 tablespoons minced red bell pepper
2 tablespoons minced scallions
2 tablespoons cilantro, minced

¹/₂ teaspoon kosher salt
¹/₂ teaspoon minced jalapeño pepper
Lettuce for garnish
6 to 8 tomato wedges for garnish

1. Remove thin white strip of muscle or "hinge" from scallops, the small strip that becomes tough and rather indigestible when cooked. Marinate scallops in lime juice about 3 hours.

2. Remove to a bowl with slotted spoon and add 1 tablespoon of the lime juice and all the remaining ingredients except lettuce and tomato wedges. Taste and adjust seasonings. Divide between 2 small plates lined with lettuce leaves. Garnish with tomato wedges.

Frozen Lemon Soufflé

This is a low-fat adaptation of a recipe from our all-time favorite dessert maker, Maida Heatter. Serve with cookies.

Makes 4 servings

1 teaspoon unflavored gelatin
¹/₄ cup cold water
4 eggs, separated
1 teaspoon grated lemon zest

¹/₂ cup fresh lemon juice
1 cup sugar
Pinch Kosher salt

1. Sprinkle gelatin over water. Set aside. Put egg yolks and grated lemon zest in the top of double boiler and stir. Gradually mix in lemon juice and half the sugar.

2. Put the double broiler over simmering water, stirring constantly with a rubber spatula, until the mixture thickens enough to coat the back of a spoon, about 15 to 20 minutes. Remove from heat, add gelatin, and stir to dissolve. Let cool, stirring occasionally.

3. When lemon mixture is cool, beat egg whites and salt until whites start to thicken. Gradually add the remaining sugar and beat until peaks form. Do not overbeat or the whites will become dry.

4. Fold lemon mixture into the meringue and pour into a 1-quart soufflé dish. Cover with plastic wrap, then foil. Freeze several hours or more.

mangoes

Today's produce question is: What's the number-one consumed fruit in the world? Apples? Good guess, but no. Bananas? Even better, but still wrong. Nope, it's mangoes, consumed worldwide by a factor of three to one over bananas and ten to one over apples.

Next question: If mangoes are so popular, how come we aren't seeing more in the United States? Actually we are. With the increased "globalization" of cooking in the United States, mangoes are being used in everything from sorbets to salsas.

But most varieties, including our favorite, the Manila mango, never make it into the United States because their thin, delicate skin will not survive the heat treatment required by the U.S. Department of Agriculture to remove potential larvae.

Still, there are plenty from Mexico, Brazil, and Haiti. Maybe someday the mango will be number one in the United States, too.

WHERE GROWN

Mangoes are a staple in India, Southeast Asia, and Latin America. Mexico is far and away the biggest U.S. supplier followed by Peru, Haiti, Venezuela, Guatemala, and Brazil.

Since Hurricane Andrew wiped out most of Florida's production (mostly Tommy Atkins and Haden varieties), mango production has been reduced to backyard growers selling their "crop" to retailers and wholesalers mostly for statewide distribution. In California, Sun World, a grower of specialty produce, has done a remarkable job with Kiett mangoes in the Coachella Valley. While the quality is good, production is minuscule by Mexican standards. And though the quantity will reach five hundred thousand boxes by 1998, it's unlikely to grow significantly beyond that according to company officials.

VARIETIES

There are hundreds of varieties of mangoes— no one seems to know exactly how many— varying in size from a few inches to ones that weigh as much as 5 pounds! Most varieties turn yellow as they ripen except the Kiett and Kent, which can be ripe while still green. The flesh is a comparable yellow-orange.

Haden is the number-one mango in production, distinguished by smooth skin and an oval, slight kidney shape. It weighs just under a pound, has a flat, oval pit, bright yellow-orange flesh, and firm texture. The large and plump (about $1\frac{1}{4}$ pounds) Kent is full of juice and meat with little fiber or string. The flesh is sweet with good tropical flavor.

Tommy Atkins is the brightest mango, distinguished by its red, hard skin. It's shaped like a Haden, but is not as flavorful.

Kiett is a large mango whose weight can reach 3 pounds, though it averages slightly more than half of that. It is only moderately sweet with juicy, yellow flesh.

The Francisque is a medium-size, flat mango from Haiti with deeper orange flesh and apricotlike flavor qualities. The Van Dyke is a small mango with a distinctive protruding nipple and a pineapplelike flavor. Another small mango is the Atalufo.

SEASONS

Not long ago, the mango season lasted only from April to August. Now we can get mangoes virtually year-round. From February to October, mangoes come from Mexico, and from November to January from Brazil, Peru, and Ecuador. Francisque mangoes run from November to August. The Atalufo is available from March through June, the Van Dyke in June and July.

Mangoes from Mexico are at their peak of production, and thus their lowest price, from May to August. Kietts from Sun World come in during October and November when mangoes are normally least available.

SELECTION, HANDLING & STORAGE

With the exception of the Kiett and Kent, the less green a mango skin has the better. Look for bright yellow and red hues instead. The Kiett may occasionally have a yellow or orange blush. Smell the stem end for good fragrance.

To check a mango for ripeness, hold it in the palm of your hand and give it a gentle squeeze. It should give slightly.

Mangoes that are allowed into the United States have a thick skin that protects the flesh from most damage. The skin should be taut, not shriveled.

Mangoes should be stored at temperatures between 55°F and 65°F in a dry place. As with all tropical fruit, whole unripe mangoes should never be stored in the refrigerator. Unripe mangoes will ripen in two to three days when left on a countertop. The Tommy Atkins variety may take up to five or six days. Once ripened, mangoes can be stored in the refrigerator, but should be consumed within a few days.

Tony's Tip

> Don't worry if your mango has a few surface blemishes. Some mangoes have black spots that frighten away some consumers. But they're just a sign that the sugar content is high. In fact, we look for mangoes with some black spots.

NUTRITION

A serving size is listed by the FDA as ½ of a mango, but we can never eat less than one. For a serving of ½ mango, about 104g, you'll get 70 calories, 17g of carbohydrates, .5g of fat, 1g of dietary fiber, 40% of the DV for vitamin A, and 15% for vitamin C. Mangoes are also a fair source of potassium.

YIELD

An average mango yields between ¾ and 1 cup of usable flesh.

PREPARATION

Mangoes are known to be a messy fruit because they have a large, flat pit and lots of juice. The best way to cut out the flesh, or just eat mangoes out of hand, is to use the "pop up" method. Place the mango, narrow side facing you, on a cutting surface. Slice through the mango as close to the pit as possible on one side. Then repeat on the other. You now have two thick mango slices and the pit, surrounded by a small amount of mango flesh.

Take one of the two thick slices and place, skin side down, on a cutting surface. Make vertical and horizontal slashes through the flesh (but not through the skin), as if you were going to play ticktacktoe. The actual number of cuts will be determined by how big the mango is and how small you want the cut pieces to be.

Hold the sides of the mango slice with each hand and pop up the fruit by turning the skin in an inside-out manner. Then eat the fleshy cubes or cut them away for whatever dish you're preparing. Peel the skin that remains around the pit and cut away whatever flesh remains attached to the pit, or eat it over the sink. (Indian cookbook author Madhur Jaffrey calls this your reward for having struggled with the mango.)

Mango Sorbet

Sorbets are great low-fat desserts. You can minimize the sugar by making sure the mango is dead ripe when you use it. But don't skimp on the sugar in any event. It's the fat that puts on the majority of our calories, not the sweet stuff.

Makes 4 to 6 servings

1 tablespoon chopped candied ginger

4 ripe mangoes, peeled and cut into chunks using the pop-up method (see Preparation, page 381)

1 recipe Sugar Syrup (recipe follows)

Juice of 1 lemon

2 egg whites, whipped until foamy

1. With the motor of a food processor running, add the candied ginger through the feed tube. When the ginger is finely minced, scrape down the sides of the bowl and add the mango flesh. Puree, stopping several times to scrape down the sides of the bowl, until the puree is very smooth.

2. Sweeten mango puree with Sugar Syrup to taste, about $2/3$ cup. It should be quite sweet because when frozen the sorbet will lose some of its sweetness. Add lemon juice, a tablespoon at a time, until you achieve the flavor you desire.

3. Freeze according to your ice cream maker's instructions. Or, put into a shallow pan. When doing the latter, or if making well ahead of time, fold in the egg whites, then freeze until solid. Immediately before serving, break up the sorbet and puree in a food processor.

Sam's Cooking Tip

There are a number of ice cream makers on the market today. We recommend the Donvier because of its simplicity: It requires no electricity or salt.

Sugar Syrup
Makes 1 cup

$1/2$ cup water

1 cup sugar

Combine water and sugar in saucepan and bring to boil over medium-high heat. Boil 30 to 45 seconds until syrup is clear, stirring to make sure sugar is dissolved. Cool and store in the refrigerator.

Mango Shrimp

The yin and yang of sweet mangoes and hot peppers is delightful in this dish.
Seed the peppers to lessen the heat, or use fewer peppers.

Makes 4 servings

Salsa

1 large ripe tomato, cut in $1/4$-inch dice

2 medium mangoes, peeled and cut in $1/2$-inch dice

2 to 3 roasted jalapeño peppers, stemmed, seeded, and chopped (page 205)

$1/2$ cup chopped cilantro leaves, approximately

3 tablespoons fresh lime juice

1 small red bell pepper, diced

1 small red onion, diced

Kosher salt and freshly ground black pepper to taste

To Complete the Dish

1 pound shrimp, peeled and deveined, tails left on if desired

$1/2$ cup tequila

Kosher salt and freshly ground black pepper to taste

1 tablespoon olive oil

2 cloves garlic, chopped

4 cups cooked basmati rice (about $1^1/3$ cups uncooked)

1. Make salsa by combining all salsa ingredients. Adjust seasonings to taste by adding more jalapeño peppers (or leaving seeds on), cilantro, salt, and pepper. Cover and set aside at room temperature 30 to 60 minutes.

2. Meanwhile, in a shallow dish, marinate shrimp in tequila 30 minutes. Drain well, reserving tequila. Pat shrimp dry and season well with salt and pepper.

3. In a large, nonstick skillet, heat oil over medium-high heat. Add shrimp and garlic. Shake pan and turn shrimp to cook evenly, about 1 minute on each side. Add tequila and cook 2 minutes longer. Remove from heat.

4. To serve you can either fold in salsa or put the shrimp in a circle with the salsa in the middle. Put over rice with the former method. Serve rice on the side with the latter.

Mango-Pork Stir-Fry

This is a light, quick midweek meal for a hard-working couple.

Makes 2 servings

1 pork tenderloin, about ¹/₂ pound, trimmed of excess fat

1 teaspoon sesame oil

2 tablespoons light soy sauce

2 tablespoons rice wine or dry sherry

¹/₂ red bell pepper

1 large clove garlic

2 teaspoons fresh ginger

1 medium mango

1 teaspoon cornstarch

2 teaspoons peanut oil

2 cups cooked basmati rice

1. Cut pork across the grain into pieces ¹/₄ inch thick and about 2 inches long. Mix sesame oil, soy sauce, and rice wine or sherry in a shallow bowl and marinate pork in that mixture 20 to 30 minutes at room temperature.

2. Meanwhile, cut bell pepper into ¹/₄-inch-wide strips. Mince garlic and ginger and peel and cut mango using pop up method (see Preparation, page 381). Mango cubes should be about ³/₄ inch square. Drain pork, reserving liquid in a cup or small bowl. Add ¹/₄ cup water to the liquid and mix in cornstarch.

3. Put peanut oil in a large skillet or wok over high heat. When hot, add pork and cook, stirring, 1 minute. Add bell pepper and cook 1 minute more. Add garlic and ginger and cook 1 minute more. Add marinating liquid and stir until mixture just begins to thicken. Add mango and stir gently. Add more water if mixture thickens too quickly. When mango is heated through but still holds its shape, remove from heat and serve over basmati rice.

Mango Taco

This is a fun dish, especially for kids, and a great way to stretch the remains of last night's roast chicken. Don't like playing with tortillas? Try the ingredients mixed together as a salad.

Makes 8 tacos

Eight 6-inch or 8-inch low-fat flour tortillas
1/2 cup low-fat sour cream
1 pound shredded, cooked chicken meat

Kosher salt to taste
1 recipe mango salsa (page 383)
2 cups shredded red cabbage

1. Spread each tortilla with 1 tablespoon sour cream. Spread with 2 ounces chicken. Season with salt to taste. Add 2 tablespoons mango salsa and 1/4 cup cabbage. Fold up.

2. Repeat with remaining tortillas.

Mango Avocado Salad

Since mangoes are part of the cashew family, a salad garnished with cashews seems entirely appropriate. Peanuts or macadamia nuts would also suffice.

Makes 3 to 4 servings

Juice of 1 lime
1 tablespoon sherry vinegar
1 tablespoon light soy sauce
1 tablespoon peanut oil
$1/2$ teaspoon minced chile pepper
1 teaspoon ground coriander
$1/3$ cup chopped tomato
2 tablespoons chopped cilantro
2 tablespoons chopped basil or
 flat-leaf parsley

Kosher salt and freshly ground black
 pepper to taste
1 mango
1 avocado
3 cups frisée or curly endive lettuce,
 cleaned and chopped into bite-size
 pieces
1 ounce toasted cashews, chopped
 (toast at 350°F for 15 minutes)

1. Mix lime juice, sherry vinegar, soy sauce, peanut oil, chile, coriander, tomato, cilantro, basil, salt, and pepper in a small bowl. Set aside.

2. Peel and cut mangoes into $1/4$-inch slices. Do the same with the avocado. Put the lettuce on an oval platter. Lay the mango and avocado slices on top, alternating. Pour dressing over and top with chopped cashews.

melons

You see it almost every day of the summer in supermarket produce sections, farmer's markets, roadside stands, and anywhere melons are sold. Consumers look, shake, sniff, feel, weigh, tap, in fact, do everything except hold a divining rod over the melons in an effort to find a perfect one.

Eventually they shrug their shoulders, toss the melon into their shopping cart, and say a little prayer, hoping they made the right choice.

Someone once said that finding a good melon is like finding a good wife or husband. You have to go through a lot before you get a good one. Sounds like the success rate in picking melons and spouses is running neck and neck.

There are two reasons why people are melon challenged. One is that the rules for all melons are not the same. Some will ripen further when brought home, others will not. Another problem is that consumers get conflicting advice. Should it be creamy or white? Does the netting make a difference? Are hard ones going to soften? And, unfortunately, not enough retailers are there with the right answers.

Fortunately, one melon dilemma has been solved in recent years. Imported melons that were previously shipped in a less than ripe condition are now allowed to ripen and develop more sugar before being harvested. Better postharvest techniques, primarily the ability to cool the fruit quickly and retard any deterioration, enable consumers to get an improved product.

We'll talk about specifics in a minute. But two things are universal for melons as they are for most fruits. The first is to follow your nose. If it smells fragrant, a melon will probably taste good. The second universal truth is weight. If you have two melons of equal size, the heavier one is almost assuredly going to be better.

Now you can put away your divining rod and start enjoying some melons.

WHERE GROWN

California is the number-one domestic melon supplier. In the peak of the melon season from June through October, for example, the San Joaquin Valley in central California supplies 95 percent of the cantaloupes bought in North America. Florida and Texas are first and second in watermelon production. Most imports come from Mexico and Central America, particularly Costa Rica, Guatemala, and Honduras.

VARIETIES

The big three of the melon world in descending order of total production are the watermelon, cantaloupe, and honeydew. Americans consume 13 pounds of watermelon per person per year. That's down from 17 pounds in 1960, a fault less of watermelon and more of the increased competition from other fruits. (For example, who ate mangoes thirty-five years ago?)

The **watermelon** is one of the most varied of all melons, with some two hundred varieties grown in forty-four states. Even the seeds can be white, spotted, brown, striped, black, pink, or red, and range in size from 5 to 15 millimeters.

Among the more popular watermelon varieties, and one of the largest with weights up to 45 pounds, is the Jubilee. It is long with a light green rind that has dark green stripes. The flesh can range from pink to red. Similar in shape and only slightly smaller is the Allsweet. It is dark green with light green mottling and deep red flesh. Smaller still but up to 35 pounds is another oblong watermelon, the Charleston Grey. It has a pale green rind and crimson flesh.

The Crimson Sweet ranges from 16 to 35 pounds and may be round or oval with a color that is dark green with light green stripes or the reverse, depending on how you look at it. The flesh is deep red. The Peacock or Calsweet is oval and dark green with red flesh. It ranges from 15 to 25 pounds.

Icebox watermelons are so-called because they are small enough to fit whole in the refrigerator. They are round with a dark or light rind and range in size from 5 to 15 pounds. The flesh may be yellow or red. Varieties include the Sugar Baby, Mickeylee, Minilee, Petite Sweet, Yellow Doll, and Tiger Baby.

Yellow flesh watermelons come in a variety of shapes and rind colors and weigh from 10 to 30 pounds. Varieties include Desert King, Tender Sweet, Orangeglo, Tenderfold, and Honeyhart.

Seedless watermelons not only come in a variety of shapes and skin colors, they come with red or yellow flesh as well. Sizes range from 10 to 25 pounds and varieties include Sun World Seedless, King of Hearts, Jack of Hearts, Queen of Hearts, Crimson Trio, Nova, Laurel, Farmers Wonderful, Tiffany, and Honey Heart.

The **cantaloupe** is one of the main types of muskmelon though it differs considerably from other muskmelons like the honeydew and casaba. It is characterized by an oval shape and raised, sand-colored netting over a green background. (Legendary produce expert Joe Carcione once said cantaloupes were called megs because they looked like large nutmegs.) The flesh is orange. California cantaloupe varieties include Top Mark, PMR 45, Hymark, and Mission.

Somewhat larger and more oval than a cantaloupe, the **honeydew** has a skin that turns from stark white to creamy yellow as it matures. Most honeydew has a pale, lime-colored flesh but some varieties show an orange flesh and have a flavor similar to cantaloupe. The best honeydews tend to be in the 5-pound range.

After the big three we have what might be called specialty melons. The roundish **casaba** has a ridged skin that is bright yellow with a greenish cast. The flesh is green, juicy, and lightly sweet. Somewhat more ridged—actually it looks wrinkled—is the yellow Crenshaw (sometimes spelled Cranshaw). These fragile melons yield an aromatic flesh that is sweet, juicy, and lightly spiced.

The **Juan Canary** is another yellow melon that is oval and smooth, almost like a yellow honeydew. The pale green flesh is sweet and fragrant. The dark green and yellow-striped Santa Claus, so named because it comes on the market in December (it's also called a Christmas melon), has a flesh similar to casaba, but it is not quite as sweet as many of the other varieties.

The **Persian melon** looks like a rounder, larger cousin of the cantaloupe with fine netting over a dark background. The pink-orange flesh is firmer than that of a cantaloupe and described by some as buttery.

You'll have to look harder for the following:

- Sharlyn: tan variegated skin and pale flesh similar in some respects to the Crenshaw.
- Crane: a hybrid of three melons with a tangy, deep orange flesh and skin that changes from creamy to light orange when ripe.
- Galia: a sweet and juicy winter melon often imported from Israel but also from the Caribbean.

SEASONS

Peak months for most melons are June through September, particularly August and September. With production all over the country and in Latin America, the watermelon, cantaloupe, and honeydew are virtually year-round products. About 75 percent of watermelon is sold from June through August. Specialty melons such as the Santa Claus and Galia have shorter seasons.

SELECTION, HANDLING & STORAGE

While most people rely on the "thump" method, the National Watermelon Promotion

Board suggests this as a more reliable way to choose watermelons: Turn the melon over; if the underside is yellow and the rind overall has a healthy sheen, the watermelon is probably ripe. The Georgia Department of Agriculture adds that if the melon is hard, white, or very pale green on the underside, it's probably immature. Since many people purchase watermelon already cut, one should look for sections that have deep red, firm flesh that is not broken.

For cantaloupes, the netting, that raised surface all around the melon, should cover the melon completely. A large bald or smooth spot is a bad sign, though it's all right for one side of the netting to be bleached from where the melon touched the ground. And cantaloupes should have a "full slip." This means the melon has detached from the stem of the plant with little effort resulting in a smooth stem end. An unacceptable "half-slip" condition will have some stem fibers at the end. Avoid very small cantaloupes; they should be no less than 5 inches in diameter.

Honeydews change from stark white or white with a greenish tinge to creamy white or creamy yellow as they mature. They will also have a textural change in the skin from cue-ball hard and smooth to somewhat giving with a velvety feel and perhaps a light stickiness when ripe. Best quality honeydews weigh about 5 pounds.

Beyond these specifics, here are some general melon-choosing rules.

- Melons should be fragrant, particularly at the stem end. This is less true for watermelons, however.
- Melons should be firm but have some give, which should not be confused with softness, which means the melon is overripe. This is particularly true of the stem

end, which should yield to pressure but not be soft or mushy.
- Shake the melon. If you hear liquid sloshing inside, the melon is probably overripe.
- Melons should have good color and shape for their variety.
- Good moisture content means that the melon will be heavy for its size.
- As with most fruit, avoid melons that show cracks, shriveling, or other obvious signs of poor quality.

Melons will ripen after they are picked but their sugar content won't increase. To ripen, keep melons at room temperature until they achieve the above characteristics. It should take no more than a few days, four at the most. Since melons are ethylene sensitive, they will ripen more rapidly in the presence of ethylene-producing fruit such as bananas and pears.

Don't refrigerate melons unless they become too ripe or have been cut. Whole watermelons can be stored at room temperature for two weeks, longer if the room temperature is between 50°F and 60°F. However, after two weeks the quality will begin to deteriorate.

Whole ripe or cut melons should be stored at between 40°F and 45°F. A whole ripe melon will last in the refrigerator about five days, cut melon about three days. To keep the melon moist, leave the seeds inside until it's ready to be eaten. While most cut melons should be tightly wrapped, cut watermelon should be loosely covered in plastic wrap before refrigerating.

With the exception of watermelons that almost always taste better the colder they are, melons are best appreciated at room temperature; we've never understood why restaurants make a big thing about "chilled melon." Melons don't freeze well.

NUTRITION

A 134g serving of cantaloupe (about 4.8 ounces, $1/4$ of a medium melon) contains 50 calories, 12g of carbohydrates, 1g each of dietary fiber and protein, 100% of the DV for vitamin A, 80% for vitamin C, and 2% each for calcium and iron.

A similar weight of honeydew (albeit from $1/10$ of a melon) has the same number of calories and contains 13g of carbohydrates, 1g each of dietary fiber and protein, 45% of the DV for vitamin C, and 2% each for iron and vitamin A.

A serving of watermelon is defined as $1/18$ of a medium melon or 2 cups of diced pieces (280g, just under 10 ounces). Since this is double the serving amount for cantaloupe and honeydew, the nutrition numbers should be viewed accordingly. A serving of watermelon has 80 calories, 27g of carbohydrates, 2g of dietary fiber, 1g of protein, 25% of the DV for vitamin C, 20% for vitamin A, 2% for calcium, and 4% for iron.

As far as potassium is concerned, honeydew leads the melon parade with 310mg per serving, followed by cantaloupe (280mg) and watermelon (230mg).

Cantaloupe and other orange melons contain the antioxidant beta-carotene, a powerful weapon against blood and circulatory diseases, certain cancers, and a laundry list of other diseases. Both honeydew and cantaloupe help to keep blood thin and avoid clotting that leads to strokes and heart attacks.

YIELD

A 2-pound cantaloupe will yield about 3 cups cut into $1/2$-inch dice. A $1 1/4$-pound piece of honeydew will yield about $2 1/2$ cups cut into $1/2$-inch dice. A $1 1/2$-pound piece of watermelon (with rind) will yield about 3 cups cut into $1/2$-inch dice. Smaller watermelons will not yield as much usable fruit as larger ones.

Tony's Tip

> If the flesh of cut melon has a clear or watery look, it's probably overripe.

PREPARATION

Though it's not typically done with other melons, the National Watermelon Promotion Board suggests washing whole watermelons with clean water before slicing to remove any potential bacteria.

The easiest way to enjoy a melon (other than a watermelon) is to halve it, scoop out the seeds with a tablespoon and eat a half or quarter (depending on size), scooping out the flesh with a teaspoon.

To get cubes you have two choices. Take a melon that has been quartered lengthwise and slice off the usable fruit from the rind with a sharp knife, then cube as desired. Or, put half a melon cut side down on a cutting board. Then slice off the skin with a sharp chef's knife, slice lengthwise (to the desired width), and cut crosswise into cubes. The latter method works best when you have a lot of melon cubes to do.

Melon balls can be scooped right from a melon half without removing the rind. Melon ballers come in various sizes and are handy not just for melons but for other fruit as well. A twist of the wrist and a little twirl will give you pretty round shapes.

This easy method for removing watermelon seeds comes from the National Watermelon Promotion Board: Cut the melon lengthwise in half, then cut each half crosswise into quarters. Cut each quarter into three or four lengthwise wedges. With the flesh of each wedge on top and the rind sitting on the counter, notice a row of seeds along the flesh of each wedge, about two-thirds up from the countertop. Using a long paring or utility knife, cut along this seed line and remove the strip of flesh above it. Scrape the seeds from the remaining flesh that still remains attached to the rind.

Prosciutto and melon is a classic hors d'oeuvre or first course. As an hors d'oeuvre, cube melon, wrap in a thin slice of prosciutto, and secure with a toothpick. For a first course, lay a few thin slices of melon across a plate, then drape or lightly wrap sheer slices of prosciutto over them.

Melon that is discovered to be not quite ripe after you've cut it open can be rescued with some liqueur such as an orange liqueur (there is a melon liqueur), orange or other citrus juice, a little sugar, and maybe some minced candied ginger for added flavor. Overripe melon can be used for a cold melon soup or a smoothie with some yogurt, honey, and orange juice.

Hollowed melon cavities can be used for summer fruit salads or dips. (But if that salad has gelatin, don't use honeydew because it has enzymes that prevent gelatin from setting.) And, of course, watermelons can be carved into baskets and a menagerie of animals to house fruit salad for a crowd. And when the crowd goes home, pickled watermelon rind!

Cantaloupe Soup

This is a good way to use that overripe cantaloupe. If you don't use a very ripe cantaloupe, you may need a touch of sweetener such as honey.

Makes 4 servings

1 large ripe cantaloupe
2 teaspoons candied ginger, finely
 chopped
Pinch Kosher salt

1 cup evaporated skim milk
Honey (optional)
Cinnamon or freshly ground nutmeg for
 garnish

1. Cut cantaloupe in half and scoop out the seeds. Put the halves on a cutting board, cut side down. Slice off the skin of the melon with a sharp chef's or utility knife. Then cut into 1-inch chunks. You should have about 5 cups.

2. Puree cantaloupe in a food processor with ginger and salt. With the motor running, pour milk down the feed tube of the food processor and puree until a smooth consistency is achieved. Taste and add honey if not sweet enough.

3. Refrigerate a few hours before serving. To serve, dust with cinnamon or freshly ground nutmeg.

Melon and Sweet Potato Salad

This is a good way to use up that leftover barbecued chicken and melon from yesterday's picnic. It's also a good way to think of sweet potatoes for something other than Thanksgiving.

Makes 4 servings

1 cup cooked sweet potatoes, cut into
  ¹/₂-inch cubes

1 cup cubed melon (other than watermelon)

1 cup cooked, skinless chicken breast
  meat, cut into ¹/₂-inch cubes

¹/₂ cup celery crescents, cut ¹/₄-inch thick

¹/₄ cup toasted, sliced almonds
  (page 28)

1 teaspoon grated ginger

2 tablespoons fresh lemon juice

1 tablespoon rice vinegar or other mild
  vinegar

1 tablespoon honey

Kosher salt to taste

Lettuce leaves

1. Combine potatoes, melon, chicken, celery, and almonds in a mixing bowl.

2. In a smaller bowl, combine remaining ingredients except lettuce. Add to chicken mixture and toss well. Serve on lettuce leaves.

Agua Fresca

This is a marvelously refreshing drink, especially when you don't sweeten it too much. However, have extra sugar ready for people who may not find it sweet enough.

Makes about 4 servings

2 cups watermelon pulp
2 cups water
$1/4$ cup sugar plus additional sugar to pass
1 tablespoon fresh lime juice
Lime slices for garnish

1. Puree watermelon in a food processor, food mill, or blender.

2. Whisk water with $1/4$ cup sugar in a mixing bowl until sugar dissolves. Add lime juice and watermelon puree and stir well.

3. Refrigerate or serve over ice, garnished with lime slices that have been slit so they can hang on the edge of the glasses. Pass additional sugar for sweetening to taste.

Watermelon Granita

The difference between a sorbet and a granita is texture.
Sorbets are smooth, whereas granitas are coarse.

Makes 4 servings

4 cups watermelon pulp
1 cup Sugar Syrup (page 382)
2 tablespoons fresh lemon juice
Mint sprigs for garnish

1. Puree watermelon in a food processor.

2. Put melon, syrup, and lemon juice in a baking pan such as a 9 × 13-inch pan. Stir well and freeze about 4 hours or until frozen solid.

3. To serve, scrape up granita with a spoon or fork into goblets or clear, cut-glass dishes. Garnish with mint sprigs.

Sam's Cooking Tip

Because granitas are coarse they are less in need of an ice cream maker than sorbets are. A baking pan works just fine.

Melon Kebabs with Honey and Curry
This is a perfect, light summer dessert that can be made ahead.

Makes 4 servings

1 teaspoon curry powder
Juice of 3 limes, about $1/3$ cup
3 tablespoons honey
Few dashes Angostura bitters
Sixteen 1-inch cubes of firm but ripe
 cantaloupe or other orange-flesh melon

Sixteen 1-inch cubes of firm but ripe
 honeydew or other green-flesh melon
4 mint sprigs for garnish

1. Put curry powder in a small, heavy skillet over medium-low heat and stir a few minutes until it becomes fragrant and darker brown in color. Remove from heat and combine with lime juice, honey, and bitters. Set aside.

2. Put 4 melon cubes, alternating cantaloupe and honeydew, on each of 8 small (about 6 inches) wooden or metal skewers. (If only 12-inch wooden skewers are available, they can easily be cut in half with a sturdy scissors.) Put kebabs in a shallow pan or dish in 1 layer. Add curry marinade, basting the kebabs a few times. Cover and refrigerate 1 to 2 hours, basting a few times. Remove from refrigeration about 20 minutes before serving.

3. Put 2 kebabs on each of 4 dessert plates, spoon about $1^1/2$ tablespoons of the marinade over each serving, and garnish with a mint sprig.

Sam's Cooking Tip
Angostura bitters is the little bottle with the yellow cap and oversized label that every bar in America carries, though you can find it in most supermarkets. It's a blend of herbs and spices that adds just the right accent for this sauce as well as other fruit dishes such as fruit salads.

nectarines

Most people go through life assuming that the nectarine is the love child of a peach and plum. No, we haven't heard rumors. But just look at the kid. It's got that peach size and shape. The coloring is about the same, redder, yes, and a bit more brightly yellow. But you can see the resemblance to daddy peach. It must have been mommy plum that donated that smooth skin to the nectarine. She also probably gave little "necky" some of her red and purple tones too. Ah yes, the lovely child of two attractive parents.

But about half the books we've seen question the nectarine's birth certificate. They say the nectarine isn't a cross between a peach and a plum at all—give back the dowry, pop. Instead, they say it's a variety of a peach, created from the peach's rib (botanically, you understand), like Adam's better half.

Wrong again. The nectarine was not created from a peach's rib, arm, or toenail. Though the peach and the nectarine are technically from the same family, it's a very big family, the rose family, and they haven't seen each other for years. (Remember the War of the Roses?) In fact, some botanists such as Luther Burbank believe the nectarine is older than the peach. So for all practical purposes, the nectarine is from nothing except the magical dust from which everything else was created. It is what it always was: a wonderfully independent, juicy, and delicious nectarine.

WHERE GROWN

The nectarine is susceptible to disease when grown in hot, humid climates, so it's not surprising that California is responsible for almost 98 percent of the domestic crop, with Washington a distant second. However, small amounts from southern and eastern states (Georgia, Virginia, South Carolina, and New Jersey) normally have excellent quality.

Limited quantities are imported from the Middle East and South America. Chile is the biggest exporter to the United States. About 60 percent of its total nectarine crop comes here. But imports aren't normally as sweet as domestic nectarines because they are usually picked at an earlier stage, before they are mature and full of sugar.

VARIETIES

As with the peach, there are two categories of nectarines: freestone and clingstone. The freestone is easily separated from the center stone or pit of the fruit, while the clingstone varieties usually leave flesh attached to the pit. There is an in-between type as well, referred to as the semifreestone. As you might guess, the pit on this one isn't quite as hard to remove as the clingstone's, but is harder than the freestone. Generally, as the fruit ripens, the pit comes off more easily with the semifreestone.

Also like peaches, nectarine varieties are constantly being improved with better flavor, more attractive appearance, and longer shelf life. So don't get too attached to the new kids on the block. Many new varieties you see today may not be around in ten years.

The approximately 150 varieties of nectarines differ only slightly in size, shape, taste, texture, and color. May Glo is an early, smallish, clingstone variety. It is followed on the market by the semifreestone May Grand, the best-tasting early variety. The semifreestone Firebrite and the freestone Spring Red are early June varieties. The almost fully red Red Diamond is a mid-June freestone, as is the sweet-tart Flavortop.

The most popular variety (at least for the moment) is the Summer Grand. This nectarine has good size, travels well, and is perfect for eating out of hand. Summer Bright comes in at about the same time, the end of June or early July. The eye-appealing Summer Diamond shows up next. Royal Giant, August Red, Flamekist, Red Jim, and September Red, all clingstone varieties, bring up the rear of the season with fairly new September Red extending nectarine availability into October.

White nectarines, once a fragile and not terribly attractive fruit, are becoming increasingly popular, with two or three new varieties showing up each year. New strains have longer shelf life than previous whites and because of the way the acid breaks down in the fruit, these new white varieties taste sweeter than their yellow-fleshed cousins. In addition to their white flesh, white nectarines also have a paler background to their reddish skin.

SEASONS

Nectarines start arriving in early May with the May Glo. The season peaks in July and August and trails off into October. As the season progresses, nectarine sizes become larger, reaching peak size in August.

Chilean fruit starts arriving in mid-November—primarily May Grand, Early Sun Grand, Fantasia, Flavortop, Flamekist, and Fairlane—and concludes in early March.

SELECTION, HANDLING & STORAGE

Select bright, well-rounded fruit with shades of deep yellow or orange-yellow under a red blush. Ripe fruit should yield to gentle pressure, particularly along the seam, though it should be somewhat firmer than a ripe peach. A ripe nectarine has a sweet fragrance, and smell as much as feel should be used to determine good, ripe fruit. Once picked, nectarines will not get sweeter but will become softer and juicier. Avoid fruit that is rock-hard, green, mushy, or has shriveled skin.

Usually if the fruit is brightly colored but firm to moderately hard it will ripen in two to three days at room temperature, 51°F to 77°F.

(Above 78°F ripening actually slows down, negatively affecting flavor and texture.) A paper bag will speed up ripening, especially when nectarines are put in with apples, bananas, or pears, fruits that produce ethylene gas.

Store nectarines at room temperature until fully ripe. Refrigerate if fully ripe but for no more than a couple of days. Otherwise, the chill may rob the fruit of its juice and flavor.

NUTRITION

One medium nectarine (140g, just under 5 ounces) contains 70 calories, 16g of carbohydrates, 2g of dietary fiber, 1g of protein, .5g of fat, 4% of the DV for vitamin A, 15% for vitamin C, and 2% for iron.

YIELD

One pound of nectarines (about 3 medium) yields about 2 cups of sliced fruit, 1³/₄ cups diced, or 1¹/₂ cups pureed.

Tony's Tip
Nectarines can be used in almost any recipe that calls for peaches. For a real change of pace, try nectarine halves grilled with a splash of amaretto, or sliced on cereal instead of bananas.

PREPARATION

Unlike peaches, there is really no need to peel nectarines. The skin doesn't get in the way of cooked or raw presentations.

The easiest way to pit freestone nectarines is to make a cut on the seam all the way around and through the fruit down to the pit. Then twist each half in opposite directions. Clingstones are a bit stickier. It's best to cut the sections (slices, quarters, etc.) right from the whole fruit by slicing down to the pit and removing the desired amount. As with apples, pears, and peaches, lemon or other citrus juice retards browning on cut areas.

If you got a good deal on nectarines only to find out you have more ripe fruit than you can handle, freeze some of it. Halve or slice the fruit and put on sheet trays in the freezer. When solid, put the frozen pieces in a plastic freezer bag.

Spices and seasonings that go well with peaches go well with nectarines. They include almonds, cinnamon, nutmeg, ginger, coriander, mace, sherry, Marsala, rum, and amaretto.

Roasted Chicken Breasts Stuffed with Nectarines

Don't let the number of steps on this recipe throw you. This is a remarkably simple dish and a good way to combine fruit and meat in a presentation that isn't overly sweet. Keeping the skin on the chicken retains the moisture of the fruit and meat, though we recommend removing the skin before eating.

Makes 4 servings

2 medium to large nectarines, ripe but firm

1½ cups dessert wine such as later harvest Riesling or gewürztraminer

4 chicken breast halves, on the bone with skin

Kosher salt and freshly ground black pepper to taste

1. Halve nectarines by cutting a slit along the seam all the way to the pit. Give a twist, releasing the halves. Pop out the pit with the tip of a paring knife. With the cut side down, cut each half into 5 slices lengthwise. (If halves don't twist off easily, you can cut wedges from the whole nectarine by cutting down to the pit and lifting off wedges.)

2. Put slices in a shallow bowl and add wine. Allow to marinate 30 minutes.

3. Preheat oven to 500°F. Loosen the skin on the chicken breasts, taking care not to tear it. Season flesh with salt and pepper.

4. Place 4 nectarine slices between the skin and breast, covering the slices with the skin and securing the skin, nectarines, and flesh together with toothpicks. (You will have some nectarine slices left over.) Reserve marinade.

5. Put breasts on a sheet pan lined with foil, drizzle a tablespoon of wine marinade over each, and bake 25 to 30 minutes or until temperature in the deepest part of the flesh reads 160°F. Remove to a platter or individual plates.

6. Meanwhile, put marinade with remaining slices in a saucepan over medium heat. Cook until reduced to a light, syrupy glaze, about 15 minutes. Pour over breasts.

Sam's Cooking Tip

Having worked in hospital food service, I'm a stickler for avoiding cross contamination after handling poultry. One way to avoid this is to combine the amount of salt and pepper you'll need in a small dish. Then take what you'll need to season each breast from the dish with your fingers and rub onto the flesh of the breast. This eliminates handling the salt shaker and pepper mill with unclean hands.

Nectarine-Berry Cobbler with Hazelnut-Polenta Topping

Polenta provides a flavorful topping for cobblers without lots of butter.

Makes 6 to 8 servings

Butter-flavored cooking spray

2 pounds firm but ripe nectarines, pitted and sliced about $3/8$ to $1/2$ inch thick

$1^1/_2$ to 2 pints blackberries or raspberries, washed and picked over

2 tablespoons fresh lemon juice

$1/_3$ cup plus $1/_4$ cup sugar

$1/_4$ teaspoon each ground cinnamon and nutmeg

2 tablespoons cornstarch

$1/_2$ cup cornmeal

$1/_4$ cup flour

$1/_8$ teaspoon kosher salt

1 teaspoon baking powder

$1/_2$ cup 1% low-fat milk

$1/_4$ cup toasted and skinned hazelnuts, chopped (page 28)

1. Spray a 2-quart gratin or baking dish with butter-flavored cooking spray. Preheat oven to 400°F.

2. In a mixing bowl, toss nectarine slices and berries with lemon juice. In a smaller bowl, combine $1/_3$ cup sugar, cinnamon, nutmeg, and cornstarch. Add to fruit and toss. Add fruit to gratin dish and level out.

3. In a mixing bowl, combine cornmeal, flour, salt, baking powder, milk, hazelnuts, and $1/_4$ cup sugar. Spoon or spread over fruit. Spray with butter-flavored spray.

4. Bake about 30 minutes or until top begins to brown and fruit bubbles up. Cool and serve warm or at room temperature.

Baked Nectarines Stuffed with Amaretti Cookies

A variation of a classic Italian recipe from the Piedmont region that uses peaches. Amaretti are Italian macaroons flavored with amaretto, the bitter almond liqueur.

Makes 6 servings

6 medium to large ripe nectarines
1 cup amaretti cookies
1 egg, beaten

Butter-flavored cooking spray
1 pint low-fat or nonfat frozen vanilla
 yogurt or ice cream

1. Preheat oven to 350°F. Halve nectarines along the seam and separate two halves by twisting each half. Remove pits.

2. Crush amaretti in a food processor or by putting them in a tea towel and mashing them with the bottom of a wine bottle or meat pounder. Combine crumbs with beaten egg.

3. Stuff each nectarine half with a tablespoon of the amaretti mixture. Spray top with butter-flavored spray and put on a small baking pan which has also been sprayed.

4. Bake nectarines about 30 to 35 minutes or until tender but not falling apart. Cool to warm. Allow frozen yogurt to melt about 80 percent of the way. Whisk smooth with a fork or small whisk. Spoon about 2 tablespoons each onto 6 plates. Top with 2 nectarine halves.

Nectarine Chutney

This recipe is from Preserving Today by Jeanne Lesem (Knopf, 1992). The hardcover version of Jeanne's book is out of print, but there are plans for a paperback edition.

Makes 3 pints

1¹/₂ to 1³/₄ pounds firm, ripe, unpeeled nectarines

¹/₂ pound red onions, diced (about 2 cups)

3 tablespoons (about 2 ounces) grated or finely chopped crystallized ginger or ¹/₂ teaspoon ground ginger

2 cups fresh orange juice

¹/₂ cup white wine vinegar or white vinegar

2¹/₂ cups (15-ounce box) packed golden raisins

One 2- to 2¹/₂-inch cinnamon stick

¹/₄ teaspoon dried crushed red pepper

1 teaspoon Kosher salt

¹/₂ teaspoon ground mace

¹/₂ cup blanched almonds halves or slivers

3 hot, sterilized pint jars and lids

1. Wash, dry, and pit nectarines and slice them thinly. Put in a heavy-bottomed, 4-quart saucepan.

2. Add remaining ingredients except almonds. Bring to a boil over medium heat. Reduce heat and boil slowly about 40 minutes. Stir occasionally, then more frequently during the last 15 minutes to prevent sticking.

3. Stir in almonds and boil, stirring, 5 minutes more. Spoon at once into the jars. Seal, cool, and label with the date. Refrigerate at least 1 month before using.

⭐ Sam's Cooking Tip

Actually, it's Jeanne Lesem's cooking tip and the basis for her book. Her premise is that despite the current conventional wisdom, you don't have to can large quantities of food at one time and you don't have to process the ingredients by boiling or pressure cooking the filled cans or jars. Small quantities of certain canned foods, such as the chutney above, can be made without lengthy processing methods if stored in the refrigerator, or at temperatures in the mid-fifties, such as in a wine cellar. And they can stay perfectly safe for several months. However, if you feel the need to use a water-processing method, 15 minutes in a boiling-water canner should do it.

oranges

(including mandarins and tangerines)

Oranges are the most important citrus

crop in the world. They are so abundant and ubiq-

uitous we usually take them for granted. But

Americans couldn't always open the refrigerator

and grab a glass of orange juice or walk by the

corner fruit stand and pick up a navel orange.

According to Richard Ray and Lance Walheim, authors of *Citrus: How to Select, Grow and Enjoy* (HP Books, 1980), the story of oranges in America is a kind of a citrus version of how the West was won.

In 1841, William Wolfskill—remember him, the guy who planted the first table grape arbor?—planted the first orange tree in Los Angeles. Though he was almost laughed out of town for even thinking of selling oranges, he persevered. He sold oranges to gold rush miners and, with the completion of the transcontinental railroad, shipped them to St. Louis in 1877. The California citrus business was off and running.

In 1873, Eliza Tibbets was given three branches of an orange variety from Brazil by an official of the U.S. Department of Agriculture. By 1878 she had three fruit-bearing trees and had started the navel orange industry in Riverside, California. Today, we're all eating descendants of the Washington navel she developed. And one of the three original trees she started with is still alive and bearing fruit.

WHERE GROWN
In general, oranges in their various forms, like other citrus, thrive in semitropical regions such as Florida and subtropical regions such as California and the Mediterranean. Florida produces about three times the amount of oranges as California, according to 1995 figures from the U.S. Department of Agriculture. Texas and Arizona are the only other U.S. orange-producing states of note.

In world orange production, Brazil is the leader followed by the United States. Actually, Florida is second by itself to Brazil in orange production. (Brazil is also the leader in overall citrus production with the United States again number two.) Because of its huge production,

the United States imports comparatively little citrus. Mandarin oranges come primarily from Spain and to a lesser extent from Mexico and Morocco. And oranges are imported primarily from Australia with lesser amounts from the Dominican Republic, Jamaica, Mexico, and Israel.

Oranges also grow in tropical areas, mainly parts of South and Central America as well as some areas of Southeast Asia. However, tropical fruit is less predictable than fruit from semitropical areas because the hot weather matures fruit so quickly. In addition, citrus fruit from tropical areas will often still have a green rind because it takes cool nights for the bright color to set. All this is moot for most consumers since most tropical oranges and other citrus is consumed locally.

However, it does explain why most Florida oranges are turned into juice. That state's climate is warmer and more humid than that of California, where cooler evenings and lower humidity produce more attractive fruit with higher acid levels, though Florida fruit is generally sweeter.

The Mediterranean rim produces a variety of oranges, from the bitter or Seville orange of Spain to the Clementine of Morocco, the blood orange of Italy, and the Jaffa orange of Israel.

Mandarins are widely grown in China and the United States. The Satsuma is the pride of Japan, though it is also produced in Florida.

VARIETIES
If oranges were royalty—the House of Orange perhaps—then Valencias and navels would be this dynasty's king and queen.

The thin-skinned **Valencia orange,** which originated on the Iberian peninsula, is the world's most important commercial variety. Valencias are nearly seedless and are excellent juicers. And the juice doesn't lose its vitamin C overnight in the refrigerator.

Probably the best eating orange in the world is the **navel orange** of California. The most important navel variety is the Washington. As with Valencias, newer varieties of navels are constantly being introduced but without being labeled for consumers. Such varieties include Becks, Tule Gold, Atwood, Fukumoto, and Lane Late as well as the older Skaggs Bonanza. The navel is a seedless orange, oval with a thick, easy-to-remove peel and segments that separate cleanly. Though not normally used as a juice orange, the navel can be juiced, but the juice must be used immediately or it will become bitter. The word *navel* comes from the development of a secondary fruit at the end of the main fruit, which causes a belly-button look.

The nearly seedless **Hamlin** and the seedy **Pineapple** are both excellent juice oranges though they also double as eating oranges.

Seville oranges are exported from Spain to Britain where they are used almost exclusively for making marmalade. Some Seville oranges are grown in Florida. The fragrant and pleasantly sweet **Jaffas,** also known as Shamouti oranges, are an important Mediterranean orange mostly associated with Israel. **Blood oranges,** so called because of a pigment that gives the flesh a deep red color reminiscent of blood, have a rich orange flavor with strawberry and raspberry notes. The Moro blood orange has a rounded shape and the Tarocco is more elongated. Both are slightly less acidic than other varieties.

You might call the mandarin the crowned prince of the House of Orange. Actually, the mandarin has its own large and varied family. Mandarins as a whole are a smaller, slightly flattened variety with loose or puffy skin that is easily separated from the pulp of the fruit. Hence, the reference as "slip-skin oranges."

Segments are easily separated and the juice has less acid than a normal orange.

Mandarins generally fall into four main groups, some of which (but not all) may be considered tangerines. They include Satsumas, Mediterranean mandarins, the King mandarins of Indonesia, and the common mandarins that include Clementines and Dancys. Many of the newer varieties are hybrids of members of these groups.

A word about **tangerines:** Most consumers and far too many retailers casually use the word *tangerine* to refer to what is actually a mandarin. This is done in much the same way that butchers call cuts of beef "London Broil" when there is no such cut, but a dish that, ironically, uses a totally different cut. Tangerines have no botanical standing. They originally referred to the Dancy mandarin and stuck when that variety caught on. Now the term *tangerine* most often refers to any brightly colored mandarin.

The mild and sweet-tasting **Satsuma** is a popular seedless mandarin because it comes in time for the holidays. The Dancy tangerine, introduced to Florida from Morocco, was once the leading commercial variety but is not now widely planted. It is small to medium in size, with an easily peeled, dark orange skin and lively, rich flavor. The aromatic **Honey mandarin** (not to be confused, as it often is, with the Murcott) has a slightly flattened shape with a smooth, glossy orange, thin skin that peels easily. The good news is that the flesh is rich, juicy, and very sweet. The bad news: lots of seeds.

The **Clementine** is a cross between the mandarin and Seville orange. It is small with an intense flavor. The **Fairchild** is a cross between the Clementine and the Orlando tangelo. The skin is a deep orange, somewhat pebbly, and peels easily. It is juicy with a rich and sweet flavor.

The **Tangor** is most often called a Temple orange in stores and less frequently a Royal Mandarin. This cross between an orange and a mandarin is larger than a tangerine but smaller than an orange with a red-orange color and easy-to-peel skin. It has a rich, spicy flavor and a Sevillelike fragrance.

The **tangelo** is a hybrid of the mandarin and grapefruit and has five varieties, only two of which are widely available. The Orlando is a medium to large, flat-round fruit that is juicy and has a mild flavor. More popular is the Mineola, which looks like an orange with a stubby neck or large nipple at the stem end. It has a deep red-orange color and pebbly feel. There are few seeds and the skin peels easily, revealing flesh that has a rich, sharp flavor.

SEASONS

Seasons for orange varieties overlap so you can almost guarantee some kind of orange all year long.

The bulk of the naval orange harvest is from November through May, with peak supplies from January through March and some early availability in October from Texas. Valencias are sometimes called summer oranges because they peak in May, June, and July, though they begin arriving in February and run through October. Some form of mandarin orange is available from November through April though supplies can begin as early as mid-October (usually the Satsuma) and run into May.

Blood oranges from California run mid-December through mid-April. Jaffa oranges from Israel arrive in midwinter. Australian imports are bunched almost entirely in July and August.

SELECTION, HANDLING & STORAGE

All citrus fruits should be heavy for their size indicating they are full of juice. Lighter fruit has more skin and drier pulp. As Valencias ripen on the tree they go from green to yellow-orange and then regain a little green tinge starting at the stem end as a result of chlorophyll returning to the peel. Don't confuse this "regreening," as it is called, with immaturity.

In general, look for fruit with unblemished skin, absent of wrinkles, soft areas, or mold. Florida and Texas sometimes use a dye to enhance the appearance of their fruit for the marketplace and therefore, must be stamped "color added." People with allergies to certain food dyes should be aware of this treatment. Make sure the skin of the oranges you select is nice and shiny. The shinier the skin, the fresher the fruit. (All citrus is waxed to replace natural wax that is removed during the washing process.)

Store oranges in a cool place outside the refrigerator and try to use them within a few days. If keeping longer, refrigerate them in a plastic bag or in the vegetable crisper section of the refrigerator.

NUTRITION

Oranges have been well known for their high vitamin C, 130% of the DV for one medium orange (154g or 5.5 ounces of edible pulp). But few recognize their high fiber content, 7g per serving, more than any other major fruit. An orange also contains 70 calories, 21g of carbohydrates, 1g of protein, 6% of the DV for calcium, 2% each for iron and vitamin A, and 260mg of potassium.

A serving of one medium mandarin orange or tangerine weighing 109g, about 3.9 ounces, contains 50 calories, 15g of carbohydrates, 3g of dietary fiber, 1g of protein, and .5g of fat. Vitamin C is lower than that of oranges at 50% of the DV. (Though note that serving size is about 2/3 of an orange in weight.) Calcium is 4% of the DV.

Oranges, along with other citrus, contain substances such as carotenoids, flavonoids, and coumarins that are considered powerful anti-carcinogens. Oranges also have high levels of the powerful antioxidant glutathione and cancer-inhibitor glucarate.

YIELD

Three medium oranges make a pound. It takes two to four medium oranges to get 1 cup of juice. For 1 cup of bite-size pieces you'll need two medium oranges with each orange yielding ten to twelve sections. One medium orange provides 4 teaspoons of grated zest or peel.

Four or five average-size mandarins or tangerines (about 2¼ inches in diameter) make a pound. One tangerine yields 3 tablespoons of juice, 1 teaspoon of grated zest or peel, and ten to twelve segments (eighteen to twenty-one segments per cup).

PREPARATION

When a dish calls for sliced oranges, you have your choice of Valencia, navel, or blood, depending on the dish. Blood oranges make a particularly dramatic look. To avoid getting the unsightly white pith, use this method: Cut a slice off both ends so you have a flat, stable surface. Then, with one of the flat surfaces on a cutting board, run a sharp paring knife down from the north to the south poles, slicing off strips of skin and pith as you do. In the beginning, you'll probably take off a little bit more flesh than you'd like. But after a few attempts, you'll be getting only skin and pith. When you've gone all around the orange, turn it upside down and slice off the small amount that was hard to get on the bottom. Then you can cut the orange into sections or slices.

Tony's Tip

The Otaheite orange (also called the Chinese New Year and Tahiti orange) is one of several dwarf citrus trees that grow remarkably well outside normal citrus regions. The key is to keep the tree indoors during cold weather and move it outdoors when the weather turns warm. Check mail-order nursery catalogues for other varieties.

Some flavorings for oranges include cinnamon, mint, sherry vinegar, orange liqueurs from Triple Sec to Grand Marnier, chocolate, and almonds.

Orange Salad with Olives and Mint

This kind of salad you can imagine eating anywhere along the Mediterranean, from Morocco to Sicily to Greece.

Makes 4 servings

1 small red onion, peeled and thinly sliced

4 navel oranges, peeled

3 tablespoons olive oil

1 tablespoon fresh lemon juice

1 tablespoon orange juice

2 tablespoons fresh mint, chopped

Kosher salt to taste

12 black olives (preferably oil-cured), pitted and halved

1. Soak onion in ice water for 30 minutes. (This takes out some of the bite.) Drain.

2. Meanwhile, peel oranges as directed above, making sure as much of the white pith as possible is removed. Slice crosswise, as thinly as possible, and save any juice that accumulates from the slicing. Lay the oranges in a spiral on a platter.

3. Combine the oil and lemon and orange juices with mint, salt, and any of the accumulated orange juice. Strew the onion slices over the oranges. Spread the dressing over both evenly. Then sprinkle with olives.

Drunken Oranges

This dish was inspired from a dessert we had at a restaurant in New York called Il Giglio. They wouldn't give the recipe so we had to guess at the ingredients and the proportions.

Makes 4 servings

4 navel oranges	2 tablespoons amaretto
1^1/$_2$ cups sugar	^{1}/$_4$ cup Grand Marnier
1 cup Triple Sec or other orange liqueur	4 mint sprigs
^{1}/$_4$ cup brandy	4 almond or chocolate biscotti

1. Peel 2 of the oranges with a vegetable peeler so you get strips about 2 to 2^1/$_2$ inches long and about ^{1}/$_2$ inch wide. Stack peels. Then cut them into julienne strips.

2. Put peels in a saucepan with cold water just to cover. Bring to a boil and simmer 15 minutes. Drain. Put sugar and 1^1/$_2$ cups water and drained orange strips into a heavy-bottomed saucepan over medium heat. Bring to a boil, stirring, and simmer gently about 20 minutes. Let cool in the pan.

3. Meanwhile, peel oranges entirely, removing all the white pith with a sharp paring knife. Then section the oranges by cutting wedges in between the membranes and discarding the membranes. Put sections in a shallow dish. Mix orange liqueur with brandy and amaretto. Pour over the sections, cover with plastic, and refrigerate until ready to serve, at least several hours.

4. To serve, arrange sections in a ring on a plate. Put candied orange peel in the center and sprinkle all with Grand Marnier. Garnish with fresh mint and serve with almond or chocolate biscotti.

Blood Orange Sorbet

The juice of blood oranges makes a dramatic presentation in this dish.
Its intense (some might even say ghoulish) color provides a wonderful contrast
when paired with pale, thin, butter cookies.

Makes 4 servings

7 or 8 blood oranges
3/4 cup Sugar Syrup, approximately
  (page 382)
2 egg whites
1 tablespoon Grand Marnier

1. Juice oranges leaving some of the pulp for texture. You'll need a total of 1 1/2 cups juice and pulp combined.

2. In a mixing bowl, combine juice and pulp with 1/2 cup of Sugar Syrup. Add more syrup in 1/4-cup increments until you have the sweetness you desire. Remember, when frozen the sorbet will lose some of its sweetness.

3. Whip the egg whites in a clean bowl until foamy but with no peaks showing. Swish into the juice mixture with a wire whip.

4. Pour into an ice cream maker such as a Donvier or other hand crank model that requires no electricity or salt. Follow manufacturer's directions. Just before the sorbet totally solidifies, add the Grand Marnier. (Alcohol raises the freezing temperature, so you shouldn't put it in until the mixture is almost frozen.) Serve immediately or put into the freezer until you're ready to serve. Allow to soften slightly before serving.

5. If you don't have an ice cream maker, put the juice mixture into a shallow pan and freeze. When ready to serve, put in a food processor to puree until smooth and serve immediately.

Spicy Cabbage with Mandarin Oranges

The concept of fruit with hearty vegetables like cabbage is something we think should be done more often. Experiment with other combinations.

Makes 4 servings

3 mandarin oranges

1 tablespoon chile oil or 1 chile pepper sautéed a few minutes in 1 tablespoon canola oil

1 pound red cabbage, shredded

2 tablespoons sherry vinegar or 1 tablespoon each sherry and red wine vinegar

2 tablespoons sugar

Kosher salt to taste

Cayenne pepper to taste

1. Peel and section oranges, remove membranes, and cut in half crosswise. Set aside.

2. Put oil in a wok over medium-high heat and add cabbage. Stir a few times, lower heat and cook, covered, 5 minutes.

3. Combine vinegar and sugar in a cup. Add salt and cayenne pepper to taste. Add to cabbage and toss well. Cook 1 minute. Add mandarin orange segments. Toss and cook 1 minute more.

paPaYas

Did you ever play the "desert island" game? It goes this way: If you were stranded on a desert island, what one—and here you can fill in the blank—book, wine, man, woman, CD, aftershave, etc., would you like to have with you? If you were considering a fruit, it might well be the papaya.

Why? Aside from the fact that you'd more likely find a papaya on a desert island than an apple, the papaya is among the most nutritious fruits. Maybe *the* most nutritious fruit.

In 1992, the Center for Science in the Public Interest (CSPI), a Washington-based consumer group that studies nutrition, compared forty fruits for their overall healthfulness. Papaya, with 252 points, was number one, followed by cantaloupe, strawberries, oranges, and tangerines.

The way CSPI (as it is affectionately known) did the study was to take the percentage of the recommended daily allowance (now called the daily value) for each fruit in nine categories plus estimations for potassium and fiber (for which there was no RDA). So, for example, since papaya got 61 percent of the RDA for vitamin A, it got 61 points for that category. Papaya hit the jackpot with vitamin C with 157 percent of the RDA or 157 points. Additional points were given for calcium (4 percent of the RDA), niacin, riboflavin, and thiamin (3 percent each), iron (1 percent), and potassium and fiber (11 percent each).

That comes to 254 points, but when rounded off the total was 252. So it looks like we should be eating a papaya a day instead of an apple. Apples, incidentally, finished thirteenth in the survey with fifty-eight points.

WHERE GROWN

Brazil is the largest papaya producer, with about 43 percent of world production. Mexico is second, followed by India, Indonesia, and Zaire. Virtually all the papayas consumed in the United States come from Hawaii, and more than 95 percent of that state's papayas are grown in the volcanic soil of the eastern end of the island of Hawaii. Florida produces a small quantity. Imports come mainly from Mexico but also from the Dominican Republic, Belize, Jamaica, and Costa Rica.

VARIETIES

The papaya grows directly on the stalk of a branchless tree that can reach a height of 30 feet. Botanically a berry, the papaya is a member of a very small family of fruits that includes the passion fruit, but not, as some mistakenly believe, the papaw, a wild American fruit that has some of the papaya's flavor characteristics.

Papayas range in shape from that of a good-size pear weighing about $1/2$ pound to an oblong watermelon weighing up to 20 pounds (though there are some obscure varieties that are only a few inches long). The Solo variety is the most common available in the United States and is the variety grown in Hawaii. Pear-shaped and weighing about a pound it comes in two types, the Kapoho and Sunrise. Both have a medium green skin when picked and mature to yellow or yellow-orange when ripe. Inside, the flesh of the Kapoho is a golden yellow, whereas the Sunrise is a pinkish orange or light salmon.

A less common Hawaiian variety called the Waimanalo is grown on the island of Oahu. It is larger than the Solo with yellow-orange flesh.

The Mexican papaya is becoming more available in the United States as our Latin population increases. This papaya is long and cylindrical with a flesh similar to the Sunrise but a bit deeper in color.

All papayas have glistening black seeds that look a little like caviar.

The flesh of papayas is somewhat melonlike in texture. The flavor has elements of banana, peach, and mango.

SEASONS

Because papayas are tropical fruits they are available year-round with little or no interruption. However, mid-April through June and mid-October through mid-December offer greater quantities that may result in somewhat lower prices. (Solo papayas don't usually sell for much less than $2 each and can cost as much as $3 or more.)

SELECTION, HANDLING & STORAGE

Papayas are normally picked at the mature green stage because when ripe they bruise too easily during transit. From this point the fruit will pass through three additional stages with increasing amounts of yellow appearing on the exterior, beginning at the bottom or blossom end of the fruit and working its way to the top or stem end.

The second or quarter-ripe stage will begin to show some yellowing. The third or half-ripe stage will be equally green and yellow. And the fourth or three-quarters to fully ripe stage will show mostly yellow. A ripe papaya should have a light fragrance and yield slightly to pressure, much like an avocado.

Ideally you want to buy the fruit in the third stage when it's almost ripe but has not gotten damaged (which happens all too often) during the final stage of ripening. However, don't be daunted by less than smooth skin unless there are obvious soft or sunken spots. The stem end will be a good indicator of any decay. At this point you can consume the fruit or ripen it further at home under room temperature conditions. Green papayas will take five to seven days to ripen, stage two about two to four days, and stage three about one to two days.

Since papayas are ethylene sensitive, they can ripen more quickly when put in a paper bag along with ethylene-producing fruit such as apples or bananas. But keep those fruits away when the papaya is fully ripe. Ripe papayas will keep in the refrigerator for up to a week. Papayas do not take well to freezing.

NUTRITION

In addition to those impressive nutrition numbers mentioned previously, the papaya has other health benefits. Since it is high in vitamin A, the precursor of beta-carotene, the papaya is high in antioxidants, which have an arsenal of disease fighters. According to *Staying Healthy with Nutrition* by Elson M. Haas, MD (Celestial Arts, 1992), the enzyme papain (see tip below) may also contribute to better digestion. Haas also says papayas may have a disinfectant property when used to clean wounds and skin or mouth sores.

YIELD

One Solo papaya will serve two people. When peeled and sliced it will yield about $1\frac{1}{4}$ to $1\frac{1}{2}$ cups.

Tony's Tip

Papain is a milky latex collected from unripe papayas, then dried and sold as a disinfectant, digestive aid, beer clarifier, and meat tenderizer. But don't try making your own tenderizer with papayas. The Solo variety contains very little papain.

PREPARATION

In many ways, papayas can be prepared like melons. Halve them, then scoop out the seeds and eat the flesh with a spoon, perhaps with a squeeze of fresh lime juice. The cavities can be filled with fruit, salads, yogurt, sherbet, or ice cream. And also like melons, papayas won't darken when exposed to air.

Unlike melons, the seeds of papayas are worth saving. Rinse them and add them to dishes as a garnish. They're nutty and slightly peppery.

Depending on how ripe the papaya is, use a sharp paring knife or vegetable peeler to peel the papaya if the meat is going to be cubed or sliced. Then halve, scoop out the seeds, and cut as desired. In salads or fruit kebabs, papayas go naturally with other tropical fruit such as mangoes, bananas, pineapples, and coconuts. But don't put them in gelatin salads. Like fresh pineapples, papayas have an enzyme that prevents gelatin from setting.

Dead-ripe papayas can be pureed for sauces or smoothies with honey and fruit juices and perhaps some yogurt.

In addition to slices and halves, you can cut papayas into rings: Cut off the stem end and scoop out the seeds. Then cut into rings. Or you can stuff the hollowed-out papaya (packed nice and tightly) and have filled rings. Much like melons, you can also create a decorative fruit basket by slicing papaya from each end one quarter of the way to the center and out, leaving a "handle." To serve, remove the seeds and fill the basket with fresh fruit.

Pork meats, especially ham, and poultry go well with papaya. Because seafood cooks so quickly, you can grill fish or other seafood on skewers with papaya cubes. And try papayas with prosciutto instead of melon. Ginger is a logical seasoning choice, along with cinnamon, nutmeg, curry, lime, and macadamia nuts.

Sautéed Papaya with Macadamia Nuts

This quick dessert can easily be doubled with a large skillet.

Makes 2 servings

1 papaya, 1 to 1¼ pounds
Butter-flavored cooking spray
3 tablespoons brown sugar

3 tablespoons rum
2 tablespoons fresh lime juice
4 teaspoons chopped macadamia nuts

1. Peel papaya, halve lengthwise, and scoop out seeds. Cut each half into 4 lengthwise slices.

2. Spray a large, nonstick skillet with butter-flavored spray and put over medium heat. Add papaya and sauté until lightly browned all over, about 7 minutes.

3. Sprinkle with brown sugar. Add rum and lime juice and swirl pan. Turn papaya quarters to coat evenly. Put quarters on each of 2 plates. Sprinkle with nuts.

Sautéed Chicken Breasts with Papaya

Many people are familiar with fruit and chicken in cold salads, but fruit such as papaya can combine for a hot entrée as well.

Makes 4 servings

1 small Hawaiian papaya, about $3/4$ pound
1 to 2 teaspoons sugar (optional)
Four 4-ounce boneless and skinless
  chicken breasts
2 tablespoons all-purpose flour
1 teaspoon ground coriander
$1/2$ teaspoon each ground nutmeg and
  cinnamon

1 teaspoon kosher salt
$1/8$ teaspoon freshly ground black pepper
Butter-flavored cooking spray
2 tablespoons minced shallots
1 tablespoon fresh lime juice
$1/2$ cup Chicken Stock (page 9)

1. Peel papaya, halve lengthwise, and scoop out seeds. Reserve about $1^1/2$ teaspoons of seeds, removing any clinging flesh. Rinse seeds and pat dry. Cut papaya into $3/4$-inch cubes and, if the fruit is neither sweet nor very ripe, toss with sugar. You should have about $1^1/4$ cups. Set papaya and seeds aside.

2. Put chicken breasts between 2 sheets of foil, plastic wrap, or butcher paper and pound with the side of a cleaver or meat pounder until about $3/8$ inch thick.

3. Combine flour, coriander, nutmeg, cinnamon, salt, and pepper in a pie plate. Grease a large, nonstick skillet with butter-flavored spray and put over medium heat. Dredge chicken in seasoned flour, shake off excess, and sauté in skillet until well browned and just cooked through, about 5 minutes on each side. Remove chicken from skillet and keep warm.

4. Add shallots to the pan and cook 2 minutes or until shallots soften and brown slightly. Add lime juice, stock, and papaya. Raise heat to medium high and cook just until sauce thickens, about 3 minutes.

5. Pour papaya and sauce over chicken and sprinkle with reserved seeds.

Sam's Cooking Tip

The meat on chicken breasts (more accurately breast halves, one side of the full breast) usually weighs more than four ounces, but you can get down to that weight easily by removing the tenders, an inch-wide strip under the breast. Freeze the tenders and use them in a future stir-fry dish with lots of vegetables.

Date and Papaya Salad

*This is something a little different for your breakfast fruit cup.
If you can't find fresh dates, dried dates will do but you may want
to cut back a little on the honey.*

Makes 4 servings

1 small Sunrise papaya

6 fresh dates, pitted and quartered
lengthwise

1 navel orange, peeled and cut into
sections

2 tablespoons raspberry vinegar

1 tablespoon honey

2 teaspoons minced candied ginger

Pinch kosher salt

1. Halve papaya lengthwise, remove seeds, peel, and cut into slices crosswise. Put in a mixing bowl.

2. Add dates and orange sections to papaya.

3. Combine remaining ingredients in a cup. Add to fruit and toss. Let sit 30 minutes, toss, and serve.

Papaya–Sweet Potato Bake

This dish wins the Superbowl of nutrition. The papaya and sweet potato have been judged to be the most nutritious fruit and vegetable respectively.

Makes 6 to 8 servings

Butter-flavored cooking spray

2 pounds sweet potatoes, peeled and thinly sliced

Kosher salt

3 to 4 tablespoons brown sugar

1 ripe papaya, halved lengthwise, seeded, peeled, and sliced

3 tablespoons chopped macadamia nuts

1. Preheat oven to 400°F.

2. Spray a gratin dish with butter-flavored spray. Layer ⅓ of the sweet potatoes on the dish. Season with salt to taste and a heaping tablespoon of brown sugar. Then layer half of the papaya on top. Repeat and then add a final layer of sweet potatoes.

3. Cover and bake 35 to 40 minutes or until sweet potatoes are tender. Uncover, sprinkle with macadamia nuts, and bake 5 to 10 minutes more or until nuts are lightly browned.

CHAPTER

48

peaches

That glorious quest that Don Quixote

sang about in *Man of La Mancha* could very well

have been to find a ripe peach instead of following

that star. Actually, the issue is one of maturity,

not ripeness. For several years too many growers,

particularly in California where most peaches

come from, picked fruit too early. Peaches were too often not fully mature, meaning the background color was greenish yellow instead of a deep yellow. These immature peaches looked okay but they didn't taste very sweet or flavorful, even when they softened up.

Retailers deserve some blame too. They frequently stored peaches at closer to 34°F than the more desirable 50°F. Colder temperatures mean that peaches will deteriorate by first losing flavor. Then they will be unable to ripen. And after prolonged exposure to cold, peaches develop a mealy texture.

This isn't the first time the public has been in a peach pickle. In 1980, consumers told California growers that they were disappointed with the quality of peaches they were getting. Growers shaped up nicely, but in 1992 there was a setback when, at the insistence of a few large growers, the standard was lowered for maturity from what is called California Well Mature to U.S. Mature. It's taken several years for overall fruit to get back to that post-1980 period. Now 90 percent of California peach growers ship fruit that is California Well Mature. (Shipping boxes will say "Cal Well Mat." A more recent designation, "tree ripened," also means that the fruit is California Well Mature.)

But that was only half the battle because even when consumers did get mature fruit, they often didn't know how to ripen it. So since 1990, the California Tree Fruit Agreement, which represents the California peach growers, has been campaigning to get retailers to teach customers how to ripen fruit properly in paper bags with programs such as "Do the Ripe Thing."

Since the summer of 1996 we've seen a definite improvement in peaches at local produce markets. And we're using our paper bags.

Still, you always have to be on the lookout. If the peaches at your market aren't fully mature,

pass them by and tell the produce manager. And if the fruit feels as if it was just taken out of the deep freeze, ask the produce manager why he's not taking better care of those delicate peaches.

If you live in an area where peaches are grown commercially, buy the local stuff at roadside stands and farmer's markets. This will encourage growers to grow more. Because shipping and handling are less of a problem when farmers sell their own peaches, your chances of fulfilling that glorious quest will be that much greater.

WHERE GROWN

The peach is more at home in areas of the world where climates are similar to that of the Mediterranean basin. American growers, especially those in California, have done the most to shape the pattern of world production in the twentieth century. So, not surprisingly, the United States is the largest peach producer in the world, and California the leading producing state, with about 60 percent of all peaches grown commercially.

However, peaches are grown commercially in almost every region of the country. After California, the leading producers are South Carolina, Georgia, New Jersey, and Pennsylvania.

The vast majority of imported peaches come from Chile, which sells almost 60 percent of its crop to the United States.

VARIETIES

There are two categories of peaches: freestone and clingstone. The freestone is easily separated from the center stone or pit of the fruit, while the clingstone varieties usually leave flesh attached to the pit. Fewer and fewer clingstone varieties can be seen in retail markets these days. Most are freestone or semifreestone, the latter not as clinging as clingstone nor as free as freestone, and smaller in size than the freestone varieties.

The season begins with the Crest family. Queen Crest, May Crest, and Ray Crest all arrive in the first week of May, followed by Springcrest a week or so later. May Crest in particular has exceptional flavor and color. Spring Lady in mid-May is the first significant variety in the Lady family, noted for their good red color. It is followed by Rich Lady and June Lady. Flavorcrest begins in June. All of the above are semifreestone.

The popular Redtop ushers in the major freestone varieties. This variety is an excellent shipper with consistently good flavor. Elegant Lady is the number-one variety for its good eye appeal, good flavor, and long shelf life. The large O'Henry ranks second in popularity. Its yellow flesh is streaked with red, especially near the pit. Coming in-between Elegant Lady and O'Henry is a newer variety (a combination of those two actually) called Summer Lady. Though the August-arriving Fairtime has good flavor, it is now used more in processing (mostly frozen) than for eating fresh. Carnival is similar to Fairtime and is a late freestone that may be around into October.

There are also many local varieties that have their following such as the Eastern variety Red Haven, a top cooking and canning peach, and Rio Oso Gem, a favorite for eating out of hand in years past but now relegated to backyard plantings because of its unattractive appearance.

White peaches are becoming more popular and at a faster rate than white nectarines. The primary white peach for many years has been the Babcock, which has ten or twelve subvarieties. Newer white peaches to look out for include the White Lady and Sugar Giant.

The primary varieties from Chile are Springcrest, Merrill Gemfree, Flavorcrest, Elegant Lady, and O'Henry.

SEASONS

Domestically grown peaches are available from May to mid-October. Peak season is in July and August. Chilean peaches begin arriving in November, peak in January and February, and are gone by April.

SELECTION, HANDLING & STORAGE

Select bright, well-rounded fruit with shades of deep yellow under a red blush. If ripe, the fruit should yield to gentle pressure, particularly along the seam. Ripe fruit has a sweet fragrance. Usually if the fruit is brightly colored but firm to moderately hard, it will ripen in two to three days at room temperature. Avoid fruit that is rock-hard, green or mushy, or fruit that has shriveled skin.

Store peaches at room temperature until ripe. Putting them in a paper bag will hasten ripening. Refrigerate when ripe, but not for more than a couple of days since extended chilling may rob the fruit of its juice and flavor.

Before using peaches, simply wash in cool water and dry with a paper towel or soft cloth to remove the fuzz, most of which is already removed by commercial washing before you get it.

NUTRITION

One medium peach (98g, just under 3.5 ounces) contains about 40 calories, 10g of carbohydrates, 1g of protein, 2g of dietary fiber, 10% of the DV for vitamin C, and 2% for vitamin A.

Peaches are also a good source of boron, which has been shown to boost estrogen levels in postmenopausal women, help prevent osteo-porosis, and stimulate brain activity.

YIELD

One pound of peaches, three medium or two large, yields 2 cups of sliced fruit, $1^2/_3$ cups diced, and $1^1/_2$ cups pureed.

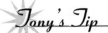

Tony's Tip

The white Babcock peach is my favorite. I like to slice one and put the slices in a glass of red wine before dinner. Then after dinner both the red wine and the peach taste even better. This is one classic Sicilian dessert.

PREPARATION

The easiest way to pit freestone peaches is to make a cut on the seam all the way around and through the fruit down to the pit. Then twist each half in opposite directions. Clingstones are a bit stickier. It's best to cut the sections (slices, quarters, etc.) right from the whole fruit by slicing down to the pit and removing the desired amount. As with apples, pears, and peaches, lemon or other citrus juice retards browning on cut areas.

If you got a good deal on peaches only to find out you have more ripe fruit than you can handle, freeze some of it. Halve or slice the fruit, remove pits, and put halves on sheet trays in the freezer. When solid, put the frozen pieces in a plastic freezer bag.

To peel peaches easily, place fruit in strainer and dip it into boiling water for 30 to 60 seconds, or drop them in gently and remove them with a slotted spoon or skimmer. Put into cold water to cool. Then, using a sharp paring knife, peel off the skin.

Spices and seasonings that go well with peaches include almonds, cinnamon, nutmeg, ginger, coriander, mace, sherry, Marsala, rum, and amaretto.

Don't think of peaches only as a fresh snack or dessert fruit. Peaches are a good match with poultry, including quail, Cornish hen, squab, or just plain old chicken. Peaches with pork or veal are also good combinations.

Peach-Amaretto Skillet Upside-Down Cake

This variation on the familiar pineapple upside-down cake is a snap using an old-fashioned cast-iron skillet.

Makes 6 servings

1¹/₂ cups all-purpose flour
1 teaspoon baking powder
Pinch kosher salt
¹/₂ cup sugar
¹/₂ cup low-fat buttermilk
1 egg, beaten

4 tablespoons butter (¹/₂ stick)
¹/₂ cup brown sugar
¹/₄ cup amaretto
4¹/₂ cups peeled and sliced (¹/₂ inch thick) peaches

1. In a mixing bowl combine flour, baking powder, salt, and sugar. In a mixing cup, combine buttermilk and egg. Preheat oven to 375°F.

2. In a cast-iron skillet or other 9-inch ovenproof skillet, melt butter on top of the stove. Pour half the butter into the buttermilk mixture and add brown sugar to the skillet. Stir and cook brown sugar and remaining butter over low heat until sugar dissolves. Add amaretto and stir well. Remove from heat.

3. Layer peaches in the skillet, overlapping. Add buttermilk mixture to flour mixture and pour over peaches. Bake about 35 minutes or until a toothpick tester comes out clean. Let cool and invert onto a plate.

Mom's Canned Peaches

Along with pears, peaches are the fruit that holds up best to canning, especially when processed the way Sam's mother does them. Whichever variety you choose, make sure they are freestone peaches or you'll spend all day trying to remove the pits from the flesh. Sam's mom always puts a peach pit in the bottom of the jar because she says it adds something "extra" to the flavor.

Makes 3 quarts

6 pounds ripe, but still firm, freestone peaches
2 cups sugar
5 cups water
Three 1-quart canning jars with new lids
A kettle for processing jars with a wire rack insert

1. Bring a kettle (such as the one in which you'll later process the peaches) filled with a few quarts of water to a boil. Drop in peaches (in two batches) for a minute or so and remove. When cool enough to handle, cut peaches in half along the seam, remove pits, then peel and drop in a basin of cold water. Save 3 of the peach pits.

2. In a bowl or plastic bucket, combine sugar and water until sugar dissolves.

3. Put a peach pit in the bottom of each of the 3 jars and add peach halves, hollow side down, until each jar is filled to within ½ inch of the top. Add sugar water.

4. Screw on the tops of the jars tightly, then release tops about ¼ inch (to allow rubber lid to expand during cooking). Put jars in a kettle fitted with wire racks for canning jars. Fill kettle with tepid water to cover jars; cover kettle.

5. Bring water to a boil. Boil gently for 15 minutes. Remove jars and seal tightly with the aid of a dish towel. Let cool on a ½-inch stack of newspapers (or a similar absorbent cushion) for 48 hours.

Sam's Cooking Tip

To do this right you should buy a kettle specifically for canning, one that has a wire insert to hold jars in place. As an alternative, you can separate the jars with towels to prevent them from smashing against each other. While you can reuse jars, you should not use previously used lids. Rings or bands should only be reused if not dented or rusted.

Gugino Bellini

The Bellini was created at Harry's Bar in Venice. It's normally made with peach nectar, but this version with Mom's Canned Peaches is equally good—maybe better. You can also use commercial canned peaches.

Makes 4 servings

4 or 5 peach halves (depending on size)
  from Mom's Canned Peaches (page 430)
1 cup syrup from Mom's Canned Peaches (page 430)
1 bottle extra-dry champagne
Grenadine (optional)

1. Combine peach halves and syrup in a blender until thoroughly mixed. You'll have about 1 cup.

2. Pour ¼ of the peach mixture into each of 4 champagne glasses. Fill each with 4 to 6 ounces of champagne, pouring down the side of the glass. Mix briefly so as not to break up too many bubbles. Add a drop or two of grenadine if desired.

Sam's Cooking Tip

A bone-dry champagne gets lost in this drink, which is why I don't recommend most brut types of champagne. Also, it's important that the champagne (any sparkling wine, really) have enough acidity to cut through the sweetness of the peach puree.

Peach Salad

Sam got this idea from the Greek pavilion at the Fancy Food show in New York a few years ago. The Greeks used canned peaches, which isn't so awful since, more than any other fruit, canned peaches, especially if home canned, approximate and possibly exceed the quality of fresh peaches. Serve as a condiment with grilled fish, poultry, or lamb.

Makes 2 to 3 servings

2 large, ripe, freestone peaches, peeled
2 tablespoons chopped pimiento or
  roasted red bell peppers
1/2 teaspoon fennel seeds
Large pinch sugar

1 tablespoon fruity, mild vinegar such as
  pineapple, raspberry, or mango
1 tablespoon canola oil
Kosher salt to taste

1. Cut peaches into wedges and put into a mixing bowl with pimiento.

2. Put remaining ingredients in a large cup and mix well. Add to peaches and toss gently. Let sit about 30 minutes before serving.

Veal Chops with Spiced Peaches

You could also use center-cut loin pork chops for this dish, but in smaller portions if you want the fat and calories to be comparable. Add more sugar if the peaches aren't especially sweet.

Makes 4 servings

$^1/_2$ teaspoon ground allspice
$^1/_8$ teaspoon ground cayenne
$^1/_4$ teaspoon ground mace
2 teaspoons sugar
Kosher salt
4 firm but ripe small peaches, peeled
  (see Preparation, page 428) and quartered, or 2 large peaches cut in eighths

4 loin veal chops on the bone,
  each about 9 ounces
Freshly ground black pepper to taste
Vegetable oil spray
3 tablespoons balsamic vinegar
$^1/_4$ cup orange juice
$^3/_4$ teaspoon almond extract
2 tablespoons chopped chives (optional)

1. Preheat oven to 350°F. Mix allspice, cayenne, mace, and sugar with $^1/_2$ teaspoon salt. Put peaches in a small bowl. Add seasoning mixture and toss a few times. Set aside.

2. Season chops well with salt and pepper. Coat a nonstick skillet with vegetable oil spray and put over medium-high heat. Brown chops 3 minutes on each side. Transfer to a shallow baking dish.

3. Reduce heat in the skillet to medium, add peaches, and cook 2 minutes, stirring a few times. Meanwhile, mix balsamic vinegar, orange juice, and almond extract in a small cup. Add to the pan and raise heat to high, stirring 2 minutes.

4. Pour peaches and sauce on the chops. Cover and bake 30 minutes. Remove and keep chops and peaches warm. Put liquid in the same skillet over high heat, stirring until just syrupy, about 3 or 4 minutes. (You can add a bit more sugar here if you want a little sweeter sauce.) Top each chop with 4 peach wedges and pour sauce over. Sprinkle on chives if desired.

pears

Maybe it's coincidence, and maybe it's the fruit itself, but some of our fondest fruit memories involve pears.

Tony says, "One of my favorite fruits in the whole world is soft pears, especially the Comice. When my dad brought these pears home from the market, we'd rush to eat them, the sweet juice rolling down our cheeks after the first bite. The pear was so smooth and rich it was like biting into sweet butter. Sometimes, we'd spoon out the flesh, just like a cantaloupe. Who needs anything else for a perfect dessert?"

Sam adds, "I have two memories of pears, both involving Bartletts. The first is the smell of the bushels of perfectly ripe pears my mother bought at the farmer's market. It was part of her canning ritual each late August as the weather was beginning to turn cool and football season was about to start. The whole house was perfumed with the intoxicating smell of pears as Mom put up over a hundred quarts. To this day, the end of summer and the start of football makes me think of Mom's canned pears.

"The second memory is of my wife, Mary, and me having an alfresco lunch in a small park just off St. Mark's Square in Venice. Schoolchildren were playing around a pond filled with fish exclaiming 'Pesce! Pesce!' as we munched on ripe Barletts, a torta layered with mascarpone and Gorgonzola cheeses, and whole wheat bread, all washed down with a bottle of Lacryma Christi. It's hard to imagine a simpler but more satisfying meal. Gorgonzola and Bartlett pears remain one of my favorite food combinations."

WHERE GROWN

The primary pear producers today are China, the United States, and Italy. There is some production in areas of Russia, Japan, Spain, Turkey, Germany, France, and Argentina.

California, Oregon, and Washington account for 98 percent of the pears grown commercially in the United States. Minor growing regions include New York and Pennsylvania.

VARIETIES

The eight most common pear varieties are the Anjou, Bartlett, Bosc, Comice, Hardy, Seckel, Wilder, and Winter Nellis. The Anjou has its origins in France and was introduced to the United States in about 1842. It is a medium-size fruit with a roundish shape with a short neck. It remains green when ripe and is quite juicy and sweet with a somewhat tannic bite. The red Anjou is similar in taste and texture and remains red when ripe.

The **Bartlett** is the result of a chance seedling introduced to the United States in 1797 from Europe, where it is called the Williams pear and from which the famous Poire William *eau de vie* or clear pear brandy is made. It is usually a medium to large fruit with a classic pear shape. It ripens to bright yellow and gives off a lovely perfume. Sweet and juicy, the Bartlett is perfect for eating out of hand but is also an excellent canning pear. The red Bartlett has bright red skin when ripe but otherwise has the same characteristics as the yellow Bartlett.

The **Bosc** pear has its origin in Belgium and was introduced to the United States in 1832. It is a rather large variety with a long, tapering neck and long stem. Color ranges from deep yellow to dark tan, and the skin often has a russet look. The Bosc is sweet, but not particularly juicy, with dense flesh that makes it ideal for cooking, especially baking or poaching.

The **Comice** is a French variety developed about 1849. It has a stubby, almost round shape with green skin and often a significant red blush on one cheek. Considered the king of the pears because of its extreme juiciness and sweetness, the Comice is the variety most often found in holiday gift boxes. Because of its delicate nature, it is the least likely candidate for cooking, though the favorite for pairing raw with cheese as a dessert.

The **Seckel,** developed in about 1800, is a small variety with a dull green cast and often red highlights. It is very sweet with a somewhat grainy texture since it is a hybrid of European and Asian pears. Seckel pears are the variety most often found in home orchards.

The **Nellis or Winter Nellis** (sometimes spelled Nelis) originated in Belgium, and came to the United States in 1823. Though it is a good all-purpose pear for eating out of hand and cooking, it suffers from a rather unattractive appearance. Small to medium in size, it has a dull yellow-green russeted, almost mottled, skin.

The **Forelle** is another good holiday pear in part because of its attractive golden yellow color with a bright red blush and characteristic red freckles. Rather small, it is sweet and quite juicy.

The **Packham** is a fairly new strain, developed in Australia and similar to the Bartlett in color and flavor but it has a rougher shape. Also like the Bartlett, it can be used for eating out of hand and cooking, though it should be on the firm side when used for the latter purpose.

The **Clapp or Clapp's Favorite** was found by chance in Massachusetts in 1850. It is a large, oval, greenish-yellow pear with a little bit of a red blush. It resembles the Bartlett in size, shape, color, and flavor, though it may be grainy and gritty. The Red Clapp's Favorite may be marketed as the Stark Crimson and Red Bartlett by unknowing (or uncaring) retailers. It has good flavor but storage life is very short.

Asian pears are sometimes called apple-pears or pear-apples because they have the juiciness of pears and the roundness and crispness of apples. But despite the popular notion, they are not a hybrid of the two but a true pear. Asian pears are not quite as flavorful as European pears, but unlike pears (or apples), the flesh will not brown when exposed to the air.

Though there are about ten Asian pear varieties marketed, you won't see more than one or two in your market, unless your market happens to cater to Asian clientele. Colors can range from green to yellow-green to russet brown. The most popular variety is the Twentieth Century or the Nijisseiki. Others include the Kosui, Kikusui, Hosui, Shinseiki, Shinko, and Niitaka.

SEASONS

For practical purposes, the California pear season begins in July with the Stark Crimson. Bartletts and Red Bartletts begin in the third week of July. Bartletts usually run through December. The Bosc, Comice, and Seckel pears become available in August with Seckels ending in February, Comice in March, and Bosc in April.

Both the Nellis and Forelle begin in September with the Forelle ending in February and the Nellis a few months later. The Anjou is considered a winter pear whose season does not begin until October but lasts through May and occasionally into June.

The season for Asian pears begins in late July with Hosui and Shinseiki. In mid-August come the Twentieth Century, Kosui, and Kikusui. Shinko arrives in early September and Niitaka in late September.

Chile is by far the largest exporter of pears to the United States, with sixteen varieties cultivated, including the Packham, Bosc, Red Sensation, and Bartlett. The peak is February and March, with decent supplies in April, May, and June. Chile also exports Asian pears.

SELECTION, HANDLING & STORAGE

When selecting the perfect pear, keep in mind author Edward Bunyard's observation: "As it is, in my view, the duty of an apple to be crisp and crunchable, a pear should have such a texture as leads to silent consumption."

Pears are among the few fruits that improve after they're picked as long as they are picked fully mature, but not ripe. If left to ripen fully on the tree, pears can become mealy. Generally, mature pears are picked and then held in controlled-atmosphere environments until ready for retail sale. Pears that are harvested before they are fully mature can develop a grittiness, mainly around the core.

Select green pears that are firm, not soft, and free of blemishes or bruises. The stems should be intact. Leave them out at room temperature and they will ripen in a few days to a week, depending on the maturity when purchased. Most pears show subtle changes in color as they ripen and some will develop a sweet fragrance. To be sure the one you select is ready to eat, apply gentle pressure to the stem end of the pear with your thumb and if it yields slightly it is ready.

If you choose to hold off the ripening process, the fruit should be refrigerated and will hold three to four weeks there until ready to ripen. Once ripe, a pear will not last much more than a couple of days, even in the refrigerator. If you find the pear's texture excessively coarse, woody, or gritty, it has been left too long on the tree.

Like apples, Asian pears are ready to eat when picked. Green-skinned varieties should have turned somewhat yellow before they are ready to eat. Russet varieties should have a nice, deep golden color. Though they will last a week at room temperature, it's best to refrigerate them in plastic so they'll keep up to three months.

NUTRITION

One medium pear weighing about 166g (just under 5.9 ounces) contains 100 calories, 25g of carbohydrates, 1g each of fat and protein, 4g of dietary fiber, 10% of the DV for vitamin C, and 2% for calcium.

Pears also contain high levels of pectin and boron. Studies have shown pectin helps inhibit certain cancers such as colon cancer. Boron promotes the stimulation of electrical activity in the brain as well as helping the body to retain calcium to prevent or retard osteoporosis.

YIELD

A pound of European pears (about three medium) yields approximately 3 cups of sliced fruit. A pound of Asian pears (about four or five) provides about 2 cups of sliced fruit.

Tony's Tip

Scars or blemishes, if only on the skin, will not affect the flavor. Some russeting will occur on even the best pears.

PREPARATION

The best way to eat pears is out of hand. A sharp pocket knife is helpful to cut slivers off for picnicking or enjoying on the front porch.

A standard apple corer and vegetable peeler will suffice for dishes that require clean halves or chunks. But for whole-pear presentations, try to keep the stem on. It gives the pear a regal look. This is particularly true for Bosc pears, which are best for poaching because they maintain their shape better than other pears. Pear flavor can be intensified by pear brandy. Pears are also amenable to ginger, vanilla, nutmeg, cinnamon, lemon, off-dry (slightly sweet) and late harvest white wines, blue cheese, almonds, hazelnuts, walnuts, and pecans.

Pears Poached in Zinfandel and Orange Zest

Bosc pears hold up well to this spicy poaching liquid. Serve this with a dollop or two of fat-free vanilla ice cream or frozen yogurt, or some almond biscotti.

Makes 6 servings

1 teaspoon allspice berries

1 bottle fruity red zinfandel

1 cup water

Zest from 1 large orange, julienned

2^1/$_2$ cups sugar

1 cinnamon stick

6 Bosc pears with stems

1. Put allspice in a tea ball or cheesecloth. In a nonreactive saucepan large enough to hold all the pears, mix allspice with all other ingredients except pears. Bring to a boil, then lower heat, and simmer, stirring a few minutes until the sugar is dissolved, a few minutes.

2. Meanwhile, peel and core pears, leaving them whole with stems attached. Put them in the wine mixture and cover with a plate so that pears remained submerged. Gently boil until they are easily pierced by a paring knife, about 20 to 25 minutes.

3. Remove pears and stand them up in a deep platter. (Cut a small slice from the bottoms, if necessary, to allow pears to stand easily). Discard cinnamon stick and allspice, and reduce liquid to about 2 cups or until it becomes slightly syrupy. (It will thicken more as it cools.)

4. Spoon poaching liquid over pears every 5 minutes for a half hour or more until pears get a nice deep sheen. Let strands of orange zest drape decoratively over the sides and tops of the pears. Serve each cooled pear in a shallow dish in a small pool of wine glaze.

Pear Compote with Hard Cider

Compotes with pears, dried fruit, nuts, and cider are very evocative of cool weather. If you can't find hard (alcoholic) cider, sweet (nonalcoholic) cider will do, but you will probably need less sugar.

Makes 4 servings

2 Bosc pears, peeled, cored, and cut into ¹/₂-inch dice

1 cup pitted prunes

1 cup dried apricots, halved if large

1¹/₂ cups hard cider

1 tablespoon chopped candied ginger

¹/₂ cup dried cherries or cranberries

Sugar to taste

1. Combine all ingredients except dried cherries or cranberries and sugar in a nonreactive saucepan and bring to a boil. Reduce to a simmer and cook, covered, 5 minutes.

2. Add cherries or cranberries and cook, covered, 10 minutes more. Taste and add a few tablespoons of sugar, if desired, then heat a few more minutes, gently stirring to incorporate the sugar. Cool and serve warm or at room temperature as a dessert or breakfast dish.

Duck Breast with Oven-Roasted Pear Sauce

Roasting pears brings out marvelous flavors. You should look for fruit that is barely ripe and still quite firm.

Makes 4 servings

2 Bartlett or Anjou pears, peeled, cored, and halved

$^1/_2$ teaspoon cinnamon

1 tablespoon sugar

Kosher salt

Butter-flavored cooking spray

1 boneless duck breast (2 halves), about 30 ounces, with skin

$^1/_2$ teaspoon aromatic pepper (see tip)

2 tablespoons minced shallots

$^1/_4$ cup pear brandy or a richly flavored chardonnay

$^2/_3$ cup Chicken Stock (page 9)

$^1/_4$ teaspoon arrowroot or cornstarch mixed with 2 tablespoons Chicken Stock (page 9)

1. Preheat oven to 500°F. Cut pear halves crosswise into $^1/_4$-inch-thick slices. Combine cinnamon, sugar, and 1 teaspoon of salt in a mixing bowl. Add pear slices and toss well. Spray an ovenproof skillet with cooking spray. Add pear slices and spray with cooking spray. Cook in the oven 20 minutes, turning once, or until tender.

2. Meanwhile, remove skin from duck, reserving half of the skin. Cut breast halves into 4 equal pieces total, about 4 to 5 ounces for each piece. Put breast pieces between sheets of foil, butcher paper, or plastic wrap. Pound with a meat pounder or the side of a cleaver to half of their original thickness. Season both sides with salt and aromatic pepper.

3. Heat a large skillet over high heat until a drop of water instantly evaporates on its surface. Add duck skin and lower heat to medium low. Cook, covered, 5 minutes. Discard skin, pour off all but a thin haze of duck fat and put pan over medium-high heat. When pan smokes add duck breast pieces. Cook 3 minutes on each side for medium rare. Remove and keep warm.

4. Add shallots to the same skillet and lower heat to medium. Cook until shallots soften, about 2 minutes. Add pear brandy and stir a minute. Add pears, Chicken Stock, and arrowroot mixture. Cook a few minutes, until sauce thickens slightly.

5. Cut each duck breast piece into 5 or 6 slices on the diagonal. Fan slices on the each of 4 plates. Put pear sauce on the side.

Sam's Cooking Tip

Aromatic pepper is equal amounts of freshly ground allspice berries and black peppercorns.

Pears Stuffed with Blue Cheese

With a sweet dressing this could be a dessert or perhaps a cheese and dessert course combined. By using a more savory dressing with Dijon mustard, minced shallots, and olive oil, it could be a first course. Here, it's the former.

Makes 4 servings

3 tablespoons fresh lemon juice

1½ tablespoons honey

3 tablespoons port wine

2 ounces quality blue cheese at room temperature

3 tablespoons low-fat cream cheese (5g of fat per ounce) at room temperature

2 large ripe Comice pears

Mint sprigs for garnish

1. Combine lemon juice, honey, and port. Set aside. Put blue and cream cheeses in a small bowl and mix until completely combined.

2. Core pears, leaving them whole. With a paring knife or small melon baller, scoop out a little more from the center of the pears, being careful not to crack or split them. The cavities should be about ³/₄ inch wide through the center of the pears.

3. With a butter knife, fill the hole in each pear with the blue cheese mixture, packing it tightly, but again being careful not to crack the pears. Peel pears, then slice pears in half lengthwise. Put a half, cut side down, on each of 4 small plates.

4. Drizzle about 1½ tablespoons of port dressing over each pear half. Garnish each plate with a mint sprig.

Sam's Cooking Tip

Even though it sounds strange, the pears in this recipe are stuffed, then peeled, because Comice pears are so juicy, they're harder to handle when peeled.

CHAPTER

50

persimmons

It's important that you know there are two kinds of persimmons: the Fuyu, the kind you can eat right away, and the Hachiya, the kind you can't. Why is this important? Take a bite out of an Hachiya persimmon and you'll find out. Your mouth will feel as if it just drank six cups of extrastrength tea or a bottle of Barolo wine that needs ten more years of aging.

What all three of those things have in common is tannin, that mouth-puckering acid that in small doses, particularly in wine, is fine. But it's not so welcoming when you're expecting a persimmon to be ripe and sweet.

Capt. John Smith was said to have described his experience with a native American persimmon this way: "if it is not ripe, it will drive a mans [sic] mouth awrie [sic] with much torment; but when it is ripe, it is as delicious as an apricock [sic]."

We weren't aware of the importance of distinguishing between the Hachiya and Fuyu until we started talking persimmons with a produce manager in Manhattan. He said he was glad we were doing a produce book that included persimmons. "A lot of people come in here who have never tasted a persimmon," he said. "They buy Hachiya persimmons that aren't ripe and take a bite out of one. Then they throw the rest out and decide they don't like persimmons."

Maybe that's the big reason why Fuyu persimmons are now outselling Hachiya persimmons. In fact, the California Fuyu Growers Association prefers to drop the persimmon label entirely and just call their product the Fuyu. You can eat Fuyu persimmons right away, like an apple. And if you feel like some tannin, you can drink a few cups of tea.

WHERE GROWN

China is the largest producer of persimmons, followed by Brazil, Japan, and Korea. After those four, production drops off considerably. Italy, Israel, and the United States, the next three in order, grow comparatively few persimmons. Virtually all the domestic crop of persimmons comes from California, with Fresno and Tulare Counties the biggest growing regions.

Chile has increased plantings of persimmons over the past several decades and now sends about 75 percent of its exports to the United States.

VARIETIES

At one time 90 percent of the persimmons sold in the United States were the Hachiya variety. This beautiful fruit is about the size of a medium peach, acorn-shaped with a shiny, bright orange skin and pale green papery calyx, or leafy cap. Produce specialist Elizabeth Schneider once described it as "a gleaming, lacquered bud vase." So attractive are they that many people, some of whom have never tasted the fruit, merely use persimmons as holiday table decorations, since they are at their peak in late fall and early winter.

As the fruit ripens, the skin dulls and takes on the texture of a water balloon. The astringent tannin evaporates and the fruit becomes sweeter with an apricotlike flavor, though some liken the flavor to plums, even pumpkin.

The Fuyu persimmon, which now represents almost 80 percent of the persimmon market, is squatter and rounder than the Hachiya. The color is a yellow-orange and not as brilliant as the Hachiya. In some ways, it almost looks like a minipumpkin or perhaps a slightly flattened tomato. But unlike the Hachiya, the Fuyu can be consumed immediately. It is crisp, lightly sweet (not quite as sweet as a ripe Hachiya), and crunchy, like a Fuji apple.

According to Jim Bathgate, president of the California Fuyu Growers Association, most Fuyu persimmons grown in the United States are actually Jiro persimmons because the original Fuyus were not compatible with the root stock (*Diospyros lotus*) to which they were grafted. However, it's unlikely that a name change is in the offing because the Fuyu name has already been established and Fuyu growers have a big enough job trying to convince non-Asians that the Fuyu is not astringent like the Hachiya.

If you're wondering why you don't see more Fuyus, it's probably because many are funneled into ethnic markets (primarily Asian) where the demand is high.

There are more obscure persimmon varieties that you are only likely to see in California or specialty markets elsewhere. One is the reddish orange Giant Fuyu, which is related to the regular Fuyu in name only and isn't as tasty. *Chocolate* is a term applied to several varieties of persimmon because of their dark flesh and faint chocolate flavor. One is the attractive red-orange Maru. Another is the Hyakume, whose skin color ranges from pale yellow to orange.

SEASONS

The domestic persimmon runs from late September through December, with peak supplies in October and November. Chilean persimmons arrive in the second half of March and continue into May.

SELECTION, HANDLING & STORAGE

Hachiyas should be deep orange with no green (except at the stem) and no yellow showing. They may occasionally have dark spots caused by sunburn, but you can disregard this unless the flesh is sunken at those spots. There should be no breaks in the skin, but there may be some harmless scarring caused by rubbing against tree branches during harvesting. When ripe, they should feel squishy, like a water balloon. Fuyus should be firm and yellow-orange.

Soft, ripe Hachiyas should be handled carefully to avoid breaking the skin. They should be refrigerated and used as soon as possible, within a few days at most. Unripe Hachiyas can be ripened by keeping them at room temperature for a week or more. To hasten ripening, put them in a bag with a banana or an apple. If you can't use ripe Hachiyas right away, it's best to freeze them whole or pureed (see Preparation). The whole fruit or pulp, well wrapped, will last about six months.

Fuyu persimmons will stay firm for two or three weeks at room temperature (ideally 55°F). Eventually, after about three weeks, they will soften somewhat like the Hachiya, though, depending on the specific strain they may get more pasty than squishy. Some people feel the Fuyu's sweetness increases at this stage.

Some also believe that the crispness can be prolonged by refrigeration. And indeed this is true only if the temperature remains close to freezing (32°F). But once the fruit is returned to room temperature, it will soften. And persimmons stored at normal refrigerator temperature, about 40°F, will actually deteriorate faster than if stored at 55°F.

Though Fuyus look heartier than Hachiyas, they can bruise easily and those bruises will not show externally. So they should be handled with care. Fuyus are ethylene sensitive and should not be stored near ethylene-producing fruit such as apples or bananas.

NUTRITION

A 100g or 3.5-ounce serving of persimmon contains about 77 calories, about 20g of carbohydrates, 1g of protein, and less than .5g of fat. A good source of vitamin A, a serving of persimmons contains about 20% of the DV. It also contains 18% of the DV for vitamin C, and a decent amount of potassium.

YIELD

One large Hachiya will yield about ³/₄ to 1 cup of pureed fruit. One large Fuyu will yield about ³/₄ to 1 cup of sliced fruit.

Tony's Tip

> To speed up ripening of Hachiya persimmons and eliminate the tannin, put them in the freezer for twenty-four hours. Then defrost and use as you would a perfectly ripe persimmon.

PREPARATION

Hachiya skins are somewhat like tomato skins, though less intrusive. We've never felt the need to remove them. But if you want an absolutely pristine persimmon pulp, you can puree the ripe fruit in a food mill or strain the puree through a sieve. There is no need to peel the Fuyu. Occasionally a persimmon will have a few dark seeds.

The nature of the Hachiya persimmon is such that it is almost always used as a puree, in cookies, cakes, brownies, breads, puddings, flans, and sauces. However, since baking with ripe Hachiyas can sometimes reintroduce tannin, it's best to add baking soda to the recipe to counteract that possibility. Citrus juice will help prevent persimmons from darkening during baking.

For fruit leather, spread a thin layer of persimmon puree on aluminum foil and dry in the oven. To dry slices, slice like tomatoes and put on a tray in one layer. Put in the oven at 140°F to 150°F, leaving the door slightly ajar. Drying will take about 12 hours. For a quick dessert, persimmon halves can also be brushed with butter and sprinkled with brown sugar and run under the broiler for a few minutes.

To make an easy persimmon sorbet, just freeze the whole fruit, then allow it to defrost slightly in the refrigerator. Peel back the skin and spoon out the flesh. You can add a few drops of rum, bourbon, or brandy, all of which go well in persimmon preparations. Appropriate persimmon seasonings include ginger, vanilla, nutmeg, ground coriander, cinnamon, and allspice. Ann Beldon, a San Francisco chef, recommends toasted fennel seeds and cayenne because "good persimmons have their own subtle spiciness. A dash of cayenne brings out that sweet, hot flavor."

Since persimmons are a fall/winter fruit, nuts such as hazelnuts, almonds, and walnuts go well with them as do dried fruits such as raisins and prunes. Orange juice, orange liqueurs, and brown sugar also match up nicely with persimmons.

Unlike Hachiyas, Fuyu persimmons can be eaten out of hand like an apple or pear. In fact, the California Fuyu Growers describe them as crisp like an apple, sweet like a pear. A squeeze of lime perks up the flavor.

Fuyus can also be used like apples and pears in fruit salads, cobblers, or crisps. But they are sturdy enough to be used in stir-fries as well. And because they do not darken when cut, Fuyu persimmons can be sliced and made part of a vegetable or fruit tray.

Persimmon Smoothie

You won't have the excuse of not having enough time for breakfast with this quick and fortifying concoction.

Makes 2 cups, about 2 servings

1 ripe Hachiya persimmon
1 cup nonfat vanilla yogurt
$^1/_2$ cup orange juice
1 tablespoon honey
$^1/_4$ to $^1/_2$ teaspoon powdered ginger

1. Remove stem and calyx from persimmon and puree in a blender or food processor.

2. Add remaining ingredients and mix until smooth. Adjust honey if more sweetness is desired. Makes 1 good-size serving or 2 small servings.

Persimmon and Carrot Cake

This cake is so moist and delicious you'll swear it's loaded with fat, but it's not.

Makes 12 servings

Butter-flavored cooking spray
2¹⁄₂ cups all-purpose flour
1³⁄₄ cups sugar
1 teaspoon kosher salt
2 teaspoons baking powder
2 teaspoons baking soda
1 teaspoon each cinnamon and allspice
¹⁄₂ teaspoon ground nutmeg
3 cups packed shredded carrots,
  about 5 carrots
¹⁄₂ cup toasted walnuts, chopped
¹⁄₂ cup raisins, soaked in warm water
  20 minutes and drained

²⁄₃ cup nonfat sour cream
¹⁄₂ cup egg substitute or 2 whole eggs
2 ripe medium Hachiya persimmons,
  cored and pureed, about 2 cups
¹⁄₄ cup canola oil
1 cup confectioners' sugar
1 teaspoon vanilla
1 tablespoon orange liqueur such as
  Triple Sec (optional)
1 to 2 tablespoons orange juice

1. Preheat oven to 350°F. Spray a 10-inch bundt cake pan with cooking spray.

2. Sift flour, sugar, salt, baking powder, baking soda, cinnamon, allspice, and nutmeg together in a mixing bowl. Add carrots, walnuts, and raisins. Toss until ingredients are well mixed.

3. In another bowl, thoroughly combine sour cream, egg substitute, persimmon puree, and oil. Add to the carrot mixture and stir well. Pour into bundt cake pan.

4. Bake about 70 to 75 minutes or until toothpick tester comes out clean. Cool 10 minutes, then invert onto a rack to cool completely.

5. When cake is cooled, make a glaze by combining confectioners' sugar, vanilla, orange liqueur, and 1 tablespoon of orange juice. Add remaining orange juice if you want a thinner glaze. Drizzle over cake.

Sam's Cooking Tip

To get the most out of your food processor without having to wash it, first grate the carrots. Then change to the blade and coarsely chop the nuts, then puree the persimmons.

Persimmon Bread Pudding with Rum Sauce

When Sam worked at Chestnut Hill Hospital in Philadelphia
he used stale Danish, doughnuts, and other breakfast pastry items for bread pudding.
Sounds weird but tastes great.

Makes 8 servings

4 eggs
Pinch kosher salt
1 cup sugar
2 cups skim milk
1 teaspoon vanilla
$^1/_2$ teaspoon each ground nutmeg
 and cinnamon
2 ripe Hachiya persimmons, stemmed,
 seeded, and pureed, about 2 cups

6 cups crustless country French
 sourdough bread, cut into 1-inch cubes
Butter-flavored cooking spray
$^2/_3$ cup orange juice
$^1/_2$ cup rum
1 tablespoon butter
$^1/_3$ cup light brown sugar
$^1/_4$ teaspoon ground allspice
1 tablespoon cornstarch

1. Combine eggs, salt, and sugar in a large mixing bowl. Stir in milk, then add vanilla, nutmeg, cinnamon, and persimmon purée. Add bread, mix well, and let stand at room temperature 30 to 60 minutes. Preheat oven to 400°F.

2. Spray a 9 × 13-inch baking pan or similar-sized pan with cooking spray. Distribute bread pudding mixture evenly. Put pan into a larger pan that contains enough hot water to come halfway up the sides of the bread pudding pan.

3. Bake about 40 minutes or until a knife comes out clean. Cool to warm.

4. While pudding cools to warm, combine orange juice, rum, butter, brown sugar, and allspice in a small saucepan. Bring to a boil then reduce to a simmer. Combine cornstarch with $^1/_2$ cup water. Add to the orange-juice mixture. Stir until thickened. Serve bread pudding warm, cut into 8 even portions. Drizzle each with about 2 tablespoons of warm sauce.

Persimmon and Fennel Salad

This clean, crisp, and lightly sweet fall salad is a perfect contrast to heavier cold-weather dishes. It would go particularly well with a pork roast.

Makes 6 servings

2 Fuyu persimmons

1 small to medium fennel bulb

2 cups frisée lettuce or a mesclun mix of salad greens

3 tablespoons walnut oil

1 tablespoon each rice vinegar and balsamic vinegar

Kosher salt and freshly ground white pepper to taste

3 tablespoons walnut pieces, toasted

1. Core, seed, and halve persimmons vertically. With the cut side down, thinly slice and put in a salad bowl. Trim top green part and slice off about ¼ inch from the bottom of the fennel bulb. Remove any bruised parts from the outer layer. Halve lengthwise, then, with the cut side down, slice into thin crescents. Add to bowl. Clean lettuce and break into bite-size pieces. Add to bowl.

2. Put walnut oil, vinegars, salt, and pepper in a screw-top jar. Shake well to mix. Add dressing to salad and toss. Add walnuts and toss again.

Sam's Cooking Tip

Frisée, the pale inner part of curly endive or chicory, is not always available in mainstream markets. An alternative is to use a mesclun salad mix, or gourmet salad mix as it may be called, now available in most good supermarkets. It normally contains some frisée.

pineapples

The next time you visit a Colonial building (or a more modern one with Colonial-American influences) that has a wrought-iron fence, take a look at the design on the fence and see if you can distinguish a particular fruit in the design work. Chances are you'll see pineapples, probably on top of the posts of the fence. Pineapples might also adorn doorways or other means of entrance. The reason is that since Columbus first came upon pineapples in the Caribbean, they have symbolized welcome to Europeans and European settlers of the Americas. (Because he was under the delusion that he was somewhere in or close to India, Columbus referred to these spiky fruits as "pines of the Indies.")

West Indians put pineapples or pineapple tops at the entrance of their huts as a sign of welcome. The Spanish, who took an immediate liking to pineapples as a fruit, adopted this custom as well. The English and English colonists followed suit.

Inside the home, pineapple designs might also be on furniture or place mats, again as a sign of welcome. A variation of this sign of hospitality was the fact that pineapples were also a symbol of wealth and social standing. Thus, pineapples were a way of showing off your best, particularly on special occasions.

So the next time you're invited for dinner at a friend's house, consider bringing a pineapple instead of a bottle of wine. Or, if you're the host and want to impress your guests or make them feel particularly welcome, serve pineapple for dinner.

WHERE GROWN

Hawaii, particularly the island of Lanai, is the largest producer of domestically consumed pineapples. The only other state that grows pineapples is Florida, but production there is negligible.

Since pineapples lack a starch reserve like some other fruit, they don't ripen or get any sweeter after they are picked. So they must be picked ripe. This created a logistical problem because by the time ripe pineapples arrived at markets on the mainland, they had deteriorated or spoiled. But this dilemma has been eliminated by jetting ripe pineapples to major markets all over the United States. Most arrive within thirty-six hours of harvesting.

Though Hawaii has always been associated with pineapples in consumers' minds, a great number of pineapples are grown in their native habitat, Central America and the Caribbean. In fact, Del Monte, which dominates the market along with Dole, grows slightly more than half of its pineapples in Latin America, primarily Costa Rica. Other pineapples consumed domestically come from Mexico, Honduras, the Dominican Republic, and Puerto Rico. Pineapples also grow in South Africa, Madagascar, India, China, and the Philippines.

VARIETIES

The primary variety is the Smooth Cayenne noted for its high acid and sugar content. This variety weighs between 3 and 5½ pounds. It is the main variety grown in Hawaii and considered the premier pineapple variety in the world. In the past decade or so it has been transplanted successfully in Central America.

The difference between the Hawaiian Smooth Cayenne and the Central American Smooth Cayenne is the skin or shell color. When ripe, the Hawaiian pineapple is a golden tan or reddish orange color. The Central American varieties are still green when ripe, which causes confusion to consumers who assume they are not ready to eat.

The name Smooth Cayenne is sometimes used interchangeably with Champaka, which is a variety of Smooth Cayenne. Other pineapple varieties are the Spanish or Red Spanish, spicy but less sweet than the Cayenne; Queen, less acidic than the Cayenne; Pernambuco, also less acidic than the Cayenne; Sugarloaf; and Cabaiani.

One of the best pineapples we've ever eaten is a hybrid of the Hawaiian Smooth Cayenne pineapple and the Sugarloaf. It is grown organically in Puerto Rico and jetted to the mainland by a small company called Eco Fruit. Unfortunately, at this writing, the company only distributes to the East Coast because it cannot compete with Dole for the West Coast market.

In 1996 Del Monte introduced Del Monte Gold, its brand name for a new hybrid with the unsexy official name of MD-2. This variety has a sweet, deep yellow flesh that has a hint of coconut flavor.

SEASONS

Pineapples are available year-round, peaking from March through June.

SELECTION, HANDLING & STORAGE

Look for pineapple that is plump and firm, not soft. It should be fresh looking with deep green leaves that show no yellowing, browning, or dryness. Since pineapples are, or should be, fully ripe when picked, it's futile to tug at the inner leaves of the crown to see if one comes out easily as an indicator of ripeness. So is thumping.

What is important is smell. Good pineapples should give off a good, fresh tropical smell. Any off or unpleasant odor is an indicator of unacceptable fruit. In addition, avoid any fruit that has discoloration or soft spots, and dark or watery eyes. The eyes are those thorny studs within the puffy squares on the skin.

As noted above, the Central American pineapple is still green when ripe and Hawaiian pineapples may also be green when ripe. So

Nick Vanee, owner of Eco Fruit has this suggestion: If the pineapple is green, look at the bottom of the fruit. If there is some yellow breaking through, it is an indication that the sugar has developed in the fruit. If no yellow exists, the sugar isn't there and the pineapple will not be sweet.

Ripe pineapples should be refrigerated, but not too cold, around 45°F. Covered in a plastic bag to prevent moisture loss, pineapples will last several days in the refrigerator.

In addition to whole pineapples, large supermarkets and produce stores sell pineapple cylinders that are already cored and peeled. You may also be able to find slices and chunks or tidbits. Cut pineapple should be tightly wrapped or put in a well-sealed container and consumed within a few days.

NUTRITION

A 112g serving of pineapple, just under 4 ounces (two slices about 3 inches in diameter and $3/4$ inch thick) contains 60 calories, 16g of carbohydrates, 1g each of dietary fiber and protein, 25% of the DV for vitamin C, and 2% each for calcium and iron.

The enzyme in pineapple that prevents gelatin from gelling (see tip, page 454), as well as the fruit itself, work as antibacterial, antiviral, and anti-inflammatory agents. Much like papaya, pineapple aids in digestion as well. Because of its high level of manganese, pineapple helps to strengthen bones, thus helping to prevent osteoporosis. Pineapple aids in dissolving blood clots and provides small amounts of estrogen.

YIELD

One medium pineapple, peeled and cored, will yield about 3 cups of chunked fruit.

Tony's Tip

Fresh pineapple should not be used in recipes with gelatin. It contains the enzyme bromelain that digests and softens gelatin. Use only canned pineapple in molded gelatin salads. For the same reason, fresh pineapple should not be mixed with dairy products such as cottage cheese or sour cream until the dish is ready to be served.

PREPARATION

Preparing a pineapple involves peeling, removing the eyes, and removing or cutting around the fibrous center core. First trim the top and bottom to the flesh. Then, with the pineapple upright, slice down, removing the shell or skin in sheets. With a sharp paring knife, remove the eyes by making diagonal cuts across the flesh on either side of the eyes just deep enough to lift out the section that contains the eyes.

At this point, you have several choices. First, you can work around the center core by cutting lengthwise wedges off the cylinder that come to point at the core. Second, you can cut crosswise slices of varying thickness and remove the cores individually with a 1-inch cookie cutter.

If you eat a lot of pineapple, you might consider gadgets that core and peel pineapple simultaneously. And at the other end of the spectrum is slicing the pineapple without peeling or coring, which is a good idea if you're grilling the fruit.

Another method is to quarter the pineapple lengthwise, right through the leaves. The core will be sitting on top of the wedge of each quarter. Run a sharp paring knife under this top part (down about $1/2$ inch or so; where the core ends will be readily visible). Remove the core. With a somewhat longer knife, cut under the fruit as close to the skin as possible, much the same way you would cut a wedge of melon. Then cut down, making thin or thick slices. One, two, or three lengthwise cuts will create cubes of various sizes. The pineapple can be consumed in this fashion (with the cubes reassembled on the pineapple shell, again, like a melon) for a simple dessert or for breakfast. The attached leaves give a little decoration.

Cubed pineapple can be used in kebabs with other fruit, or alternating with fish or other seafood for the broiler or grill. It can also be used as part of a fruit salad with other tropical fruit such as bananas, papayas, and mangoes with perhaps some strawberries and kiwifruit for added color.

A hollowed-out shell makes an attractive cavity for fruit salads or chicken or seafood salads. To hollow out a shell, choose a rather small pineapple and cut it in half lengthwise, right through the crown or leaves. Remove the inner core by making a **V** cut underneath it, then lifting it out. With a short, sharp knife, cut all around the inside of the fruit leaving a $1/2$-inch-thick rim all around. Lift out the fruit inside the cavity and cut into chunks or cubes of desired size. Or, scoop out with a melon baller. Prepare the salad with the cubes or balls of pineapple and fill the cavity. Again, the attached leaves add to the decoration. To keep the boat from rocking it may be necessary to cut a thin slice from the bottom of each half.

Broiled Pineapple

Try this as a breakfast alternative to that bowl of prunes.

Makes 4 servings

4 center-cut slices of pineapple, ¹/₂ inch thick, peeled and with eyes removed
¹/₄ cup rum
8 teaspoons brown sugar, preferably the
    free-pouring variety

1. Put pineapple slices on a deep platter large enough to hold all in 1 layer. Sprinkle half the rum on one side. Turn slices over and sprinkle remaining rum on the other side. Marinate at room temperature 30 minutes, turning a few times, while you preheat broiler.

2. Put pineapple slices on a baking pan all in 1 layer. Sprinkle half the brown sugar on the slices and put under the broiler, about 5 inches from the flame, for 3 minutes. Turn slices, sprinkle with remaining sugar, and broil another 3 minutes or until surface of the slices turns a nice golden, bubbly brown. Put on a platter and pour any juices from the pan over the slices.

Sam's Cooking Tip

I think rum and pineapple are a natural tropical combination. But you could also use bourbon, brandy, or amaretto. The amaretto will give the pineapple a sweeter flavor.

Stuffed Pineapple Boats

A friend said this dish sounded very fifties. Anyone got a Hula-Hoop?

Makes 4 servings

2 small to medium pineapples

12 to 16 ounces roasted chicken breast meat, cut into $1/2$-inch cubes

$3/4$ cup pitted prunes, halved

1 cup diced celery

2 tablespoons sliced, toasted almonds

1 to 2 teaspoons minced jalapeño pepper

1 teaspoon freshly grated ginger

2 tablespoons cider vinegar

2 tablespoons orange liqueur (optional)

1 tablespoon almond or walnut oil

Kosher salt to taste

2 tablespoons shredded coconut

1. Prepare pineapple halves for stuffing as in Preparation (page 454). Cut pineapple into $1/2$-inch chunks or melon ball shapes. You should have about 6 cups. Save any juice for the dressing as you work. Squeeze out juice from any bits of extra pineapple meat to extract more juice. You should have about $1/4$ cup juice.

2. Combine pineapple with chicken, prunes, celery, almonds, and jalapeño in a mixing bowl. Combine ginger, vinegar, orange liqueur, oil, salt, and reserved pineapple juice in a separate bowl. Pour over salad mixture and mix well.

3. Put boats on large plates. Stuff each boat with $1/4$ of the salad mixture and sprinkle with coconut.

Sam's Cooking Tip

This dish can be made ahead only if you don't add the chicken until the last minute. The acids and enzymes in the pineapple turn the meat to mush after a few hours. Instead of chicken you can use turkey or pork tenderloin.

Grilled Pineapple Salsa

This is a delicious, nonfat accompaniment to grilled poultry, pork, or fish.
It should be eaten the same day it is made.

Makes 4 to 6 servings, about 2 cups

$^1/_2$ pineapple

$^1/_2$ red bell pepper, chopped

2 tablespoons minced red onion

1 or 2 jalapeño peppers, minced

$^1/_4$ cup chopped cilantro

1 tablespoon ground cumin

1 tablespoon fresh lime juice

Kosher salt to taste

1. Cut pineapple into $^1/_2$-inch-thick slices, leaving skin on. Put on a well-oiled grill over medium heat and cook until nicely brown on both sides, about 10 minutes.

2. Remove skin and eyes and cut pineapple into $^1/_4$-inch dice. Combine with remaining ingredients and refrigerate a few hours.

Sam's Cooking Tip

As with so many dishes that involve chile peppers, add the smaller quantity to begin with. Then let the dish sit for 20 to 30 minutes. Taste again to determine if you can tolerate more heat.

Tropical Salad with Yogurt Dressing

Feel free to mix and match with other tropical fruits if you like or to increase or decrease the amounts of particular fruit. Though they're not a tropical fruit, strawberries would add some color.

Makes 6 servings

1 cup nonfat vanilla yogurt or plain yogurt with 1 teaspoon vanilla

2 teaspoons grated ginger

1 tablespoon honey

1 tablespoon lime juice

2 bananas, cut into $^1/_2$-inch slices and tossed with $^1/_2$ cup orange juice

2 cups fresh pineapple cut into $^1/_2$-inch chunks

2 cups papaya (or mango) cut into $^1/_2$-inch chunks

3 kiwifruit, peeled, halved lengthwise, and cut into half-moon slices

6 mint sprigs for garnish

1. Combine yogurt, ginger, honey, and lime juice. Set aside.

2. Drain bananas and put into a bowl with pineapple, papaya, and kiwifruit. Mix well but do not bruise.

3. Fill 6 wine goblets with equal amounts of the fruit mixture, about 1 cup each. Top with a few tablespoons of the dressing and a mint sprig.

For centuries the plum has been associated with things that are choice or desirable or perhaps a reward whether expected or unexpected. We congratulate someone who got a "plum" job, which the dictionary says is "a well-paying job requiring little work." For many, however, a plum job, role (for an actor), or assignment may require considerable work but carries with it prestige or financial rewards or both.

A "political plum" may be a reward bestowed on an important supporter by a grateful, recently elected politician. And the British colloquial description of something as "plummy" means that something is coveted.

The connection between plum and goodness can be traced to the Mother Goose nursery rhyme of Little Jack Horner who sat in the corner and pulled a plum out of a Christmas pie, exclaiming, "What a good boy am I!"

This rhyme has some basis in history, according to *Eatioms* by John D. Jacobson (Laurel, 1993). Legend has it that there was a real Jack Horner whose name was actually Thomas. In the sixteenth century, the bishop of Glastonbury Cathedral gave Horner twelve deeds to valuable properties to present to King Henry VIII. The deeds, a gift from the bishop to the king, were placed in a large Christmas pie for safekeeping. On his way to London, the greedy and curious Horner opened the crust and removed one of the deeds, the "plum" he kept for himself.

WHERE GROWN

About 90 percent of the plums consumed in the United States are grown in California, much of them in the San Joaquin Valley in the central part of the state. Most of these are of the Japanese variety. Plums are also grown in Washington, Oregon, Idaho, Michigan, and New York.

Chile produces both European- and Japanese-style plums with the latter about twice as prominent. About 40 percent of its exports go to the United States. Other large plum-producing countries include Germany, Turkey, and Japan as well as the former Yugoslavia, noted for its fiery plum brandy called *slivovitz*.

VARIETIES

Plums are divided into two broad categories: Japanese plums and European plums, or prunes. The Japanese plum is eaten fresh, canned, and put into jams and jellies. If dried with the pit intact, it will ferment rather than dry like a prune.

European plums are often called prunes because they can be dried without their pits being removed. In fact, that's the way most people see these plums. But prunes can also be eaten fresh or used fresh in cooking. In an effort to avoid some of the confusion, the produce industry has tried to label these fresh prunes as purple plums, but you may also see them as prune plums and prunes as well as European plums.

Twelve varieties of Japanese plums account for three-fourths of California's plum production. The Red Beaut and Black Beaut are two of the earliest varieties. The Red Beaut has bright red skin and mild yellow flesh. The fairly round shape of the Black Beaut closely resembles that of the Red Beaut but the skin is darker, running to purplish black, and the mild flesh is sweet and juicy.

The Rosa family of plums has several commercially productive members. The popular Santa Rosa has a purple-crimson exterior with light freckles. (Freckling is characteristic of the Rosa family.) The flesh goes from sweet and yellow at the exterior to tart and red in the center. The Queen Rosa is similar to the Santa Rosa on the outside except for its greenish yellow shoulders. The mild and very juicy amber flesh becomes tangy when cooked, though sweeter if the skin is left on. Another member of the Rosa family is the heart-shaped Simka. It has red to reddish purple skin and firm, pleasantly sweet, golden flesh. The Casselman is bright red to crimson with firm flesh that is tangy and sweet when ripe.

The smooth-skinned black or deep purple Blackamber is noted for its firmness. The El Dorado has a bright red to reddish black skin with purple highlights. It has amber flesh that is mellow and sweet and stays firm during cooking, making it a prime candidate for canning. One of the better plums for eating out of hand is the Laroda. It has a dark red to purple, thin skin with a golden flesh that is sweet and richly flavored.

The Friar has a black or deep blue or purple-colored skin with amber flesh that is sweet when ripe. Green-skinned Kelsey turns yellow with red highlights when ripe. The green-tinged yellow flesh is sweet. The Angeleno is dark red, turning to purple and blue. The amber flesh has a gentle sweetness when ripe.

European plums (prunes or prune plums) are always freestone, meaning the flesh does not adhere to the pit. They are also always blue or purple in color. European plums are smaller and firmer than the Japanese plums, as well as sweeter and less juicy. The most familiar type is labeled the Italian prune plum, which is grown in Washington. It is reddish blue when unripe, purple-blue with a powdery white bloom when ripe. This hardy plum is good for cooking and preserving. Unfortunately, due to decreased demand, Italian prune plum production in Washington is one-third of what it once was.

Other main types of prune plums are the Stanley, which is dark blue-black with a firm, greenish yellow flesh and the Blufre (or Blue Free) which is somewhat larger. Both are grown primarily in Michigan. The small, blue Damson prune plum has excellent flavor and is used most often in preserves.

A good deal of experimentation is being done (much of it at Cornell University in New York) to create new, higher quality prune plums that may be more appealing to consumers. In the coming years, look for new varieties such as Valor, Longjohn, Victory, and Castleton.

Chilean varieties include Santa Rosa, Angeleno, Laroda, Friar, Roysum, Black Beaut, Autumn Giant, Larry Ann, Blackamber, Harry Pickstone, and Red Beaut.

SEASONS

Plums begin arriving in May with the Black Beaut and Red Beaut varieties. Santa Rosas are available the first week of June and run through Independence Day. Then come the Blackamber, Queen Rosa, El Dorado, Laroda, Simka, Friar, Kelsey, and Casselman. The Angeleno brings up the rear, beginning in August and continuing through Thanksgiving. The peak period for plums is mid-June through mid-August with heaviest supplies in mid-July.

Prunes from Michigan and Washington begin arriving in August and go through September, sometimes early October. The later Italian prune plum in Washington (called Late Italian) is considered to have more flavor. Chilean fruit starts arriving in November and continues into April.

SELECTION, HANDLING & STORAGE

Plums should show good color for their variety with a slight firmness to light softness. Avoid fruit that is hard or very soft, poorly colored, or with shriveling, bruises, or breaks in the skin.

Plums are generally picked mature but not fully ripe. Ripen them at room temperature, between 51°F and 77°F (ideally 64°F), speeded up by being placed in a paper bag with ethylene-producing fruit such as a banana, apple, or pear. They are ready when they give off a gentle, sweet plum aroma, and they are soft to the touch.

Store ripe plums at very cool temperatures, as low as 32°F, in the refrigerator, away from ethylene-producing foods that may ripen them further.

NUTRITION

A serving of two medium plums (132g, about 4.7 ounces) contains 80 calories, 19g of carbohydrates, 2g of dietary fiber, 1g each of protein and fat, 6% of the DV for vitamin A, and 20% for vitamin C.

Though not as potent as dried prunes, fresh plums work well as a laxative. Plums also contain antibacterial and antiviral compounds.

YIELD

About six medium-size Japanese plums (twelve to fifteen European) will equal a pound. A pound of fresh plums yields about 2¹/₂ cups sliced, 2 cups diced, or 1³/₄ cups pureed.

Tony's Tip

The best way to remember the distinction between the prune and the plum is with this saying: "A prune is always a plum, but a plum is not always a prune."

PREPARATION

You can separate the two halves of a freestone plum by cutting along the seam to the pit, then twisting each half in opposite directions. Clingstone plums (those whose flesh clings to the pit) are best prepared by cutting wedges from the skin to the pit until the whole plum has been cut up.

Plums take reasonably well to freezing. Halve and pit, put on trays, and freeze until solid. Then put into freezer-safe bags.

Plums are generally not peeled because the skins add a contrasting tartness to the usually sweet flesh. However, you can peel plums by dropping them in boiling water for 30 seconds or so (depending on the number of plums you're doing at one time) and then chilling the fruit in ice water. The skins will slip off like those of peaches or tomatoes done in a similar fashion.

Aside from canning, most people don't cook with plums. But plums can be delicious with, for example, poultry and pork, either sautéed or baked. They're delicious poached, for dessert or breakfast. And they go well in stuffings and cakes. Plums match up well with cinnamon, nutmeg, cloves, lemon, orange, orange liqueurs, brandy, and port.

Crepes with Spicy Plum Jam

Crepes are a great vehicle for many forms of fruit, whether cooked slices, purees, butters, or jams. A nice change of pace for dessert or Sunday brunch.

Makes 6 servings

4 cups pitted and diced purple- or red-skinned plums

3 cups sugar

1 tablespoon fresh lemon juice

$1/2$ teaspoon ground allspice

2 tablespoons brandy

2 eggs

1 teaspoon sugar

Pinch kosher salt

$3/4$ cup flour

$3/4$ cup skim milk

1 tablespoon canola oil

Butter-flavored cooking spray

Powdered sugar

1. Put plums, sugar, lemon juice, allspice, and brandy in a heavy-bottomed saucepan and bring to a boil over medium-high heat, stirring frequently. Lower heat to medium and cook 20 to 25 minutes or until thickened. (It will thicken more as it cools to room temperature.)

2. While jam cools, combine eggs, sugar, and salt with a whisk in a mixing bowl. Stir in flour, $1/4$ cup at a time. Then stir in skim milk and oil.

3. Spray a well-seasoned 7- or 8-inch cast-iron skillet or omelet pan with butter-flavored spray. Put over medium heat. When hot, ladle in just enough batter to cover the bottom of the pan, about 3 tablespoons. Then tilt the pan and swirl to cover the entire surface. (If you pour too much in, you can pour out the excess.) Cook about 45 seconds on 1 side and flip over using a spatula to help loosen. Cook about 30 seconds on the other side.

4. Stack crepes on a platter, separating them with sheets of waxed paper. Crepes can be refrigerated or frozen if not used immediately. You should have about 12 crepes.

5. To serve, warm crepes if necessary and spread a tablespoon of jam in the center of each crepe. Fold over once and sprinkle with powdered sugar. Allow 2 crepes per person. (There will be extra jam.)

Sam's Cooking Tip

Don't be discouraged if the first few crepes stick or get torn and have to be discarded. Spray the pan again as needed and keep on plugging. As you get good at this, you'll be able to turn the crepes in the pan with your fingers.

Pan-Roasted Cornish Hens with Italian Plums

This is not the sickeningly sweet kind of plum sauce you might find in cheap Chinese restaurants. In fact, it's remarkably unsweet, though delicious.

Makes 4 servings

2 Cornish hens, each about 1¼ to 1½ pounds

Kosher salt and freshly ground black pepper to taste

2 tablespoons clarified butter (page 284) or whole butter

¼ cup minced shallots

12 Italian plums, halved lengthwise and pitted

¼ teaspoon cinnamon

¼ teaspoon ground nutmeg

⅓ cup brandy (optional, substitute extra Chicken Stock, page 9)

½ cup Chicken Stock (page 9) mixed with 1 teaspoon arrowroot or cornstarch

1. Cut hens in half at the breast bone. Remove skin and wing tips. Flatten by covering with foil, butcher paper, or plastic wrap and pounding a few times with the side of a large cleaver or bottom of a skillet. Season with salt and pepper.

2. Put butter in a large cast-iron skillet (or 2 smaller ones) over medium heat. When fat is hot, put hen halves in, meaty side down. Brown well, about 10 to 12 minutes.

3. Turn over, add shallots and plums. Sprinkle with cinnamon, nutmeg, and additional salt and pepper. Cook, covered, 10 to 12 minutes. (Thigh meat should be firm and juices run clear when pricked.) Uncover and add brandy. Cook a few minutes watching for any flames.

4. Remove hens to a platter. Add chicken stock mixed with arrowroot. Reduce until lightly thickened, scraping the bottom of the pan with a wooden spoon. Pour sauce and plums over Cornish hens.

Sam's Cooking Tip

Most people probably don't have a skillet large enough to hold both the Cornish hens. But this recipe works easily with two smaller skillets. It's important not to crowd the meat into the pan, otherwise it will steam and not brown properly.

Plum Kuchen

Kuchen is an old-fashioned dessert that also doubles as a coffee cake. This one is more the former than the latter. But it would go nicely with afternoon tea.

Makes 6 servings

1 cup all-purpose flour

1 teaspoon baking powder

Pinch kosher salt

$^1/_4$ cup plus 1 tablespoon sugar

2 tablespoons cold butter, cut into pieces

1 egg

$^1/_2$ cup buttermilk or skim milk

$^3/_4$ teaspoon vanilla extract

Butter-flavored cooking spray

$^1/_4$ cup sliced almonds

4 medium to large plums, about 1 pound total

$^1/_2$ teaspoon cinnamon

$^1/_3$ cup spicy plum jam from Crepes with Spicy Plum Jam, page 463, or purchased plum jam

1. Preheat oven to 400°F. In a mixing bowl, combine flour, baking powder, salt, and sugar. Add butter with a pastry blender or large fork until texture resembles coarse meal.

2. Combine egg with buttermilk and vanilla extract. Stir into flour mixture and mix just until combined. Spread into the bottom of an 8 × 8 × 2-inch pan sprayed with butter-flavored spray. Sprinkle with sliced almonds.

3. Halve plums lengthwise and cut each half into 4 slices. Arrange plum slices on batter in rows. Spray with butter-flavored spray. Mix cinnamon with remaining tablespoon of sugar and sprinkle onto plums. Bake in the middle of the oven 30 minutes or until plums are tender.

4. Meanwhile, prepare glaze by heating plum jam in a small pan or in a microwave oven until it begins to boil. Brush on top of kuchen when comes out of the oven. Serve warm or at room temperature.

Sam's Cooking Tip

This dish can also be made in an equivalent size round cake pan. If using a round pan you can make a ring or circle pattern with the plums. Peaches and nectarines would also make a good kuchen.

Plums Poached in Port

*Plums take well to poaching and make a marvelous fat-free breakfast dish.
Or try them as a simple dessert by themselves or over fat-free frozen yogurt.*

Makes 4 servings

¹/₂ cup sugar
¹/₂ cup port
1 cinnamon stick
12 whole black peppercorns

3 quarter-size slices fresh ginger
2 cups water
1 pound small, ripe but firm European
   purple plums

1. In a large saucepan, combine sugar, port, cinnamon stick, peppercorns, ginger, and water. Bring to a boil, stir, and reduce to a simmer.

2. Prick the plums a few times with the sharp tip of a paring knife. Add to the saucepan and cook gently about 10 minutes or until plums are very tender but not falling apart.

3. Remove plums to a shallow bowl. Return saucepan to stove and reduce cooking liquid by half over medium-high heat, about 10 minutes. Pour strained liquid over plums and cool to room temperature.

Sam's Cooking Tip

Pricking the skin of plums helps to prevent bursting during the cooking process.

Pomegranates

If there is a more exotic fruit than the

pomegranate—at least one that is readily avail-

able to people in the United States—we don't

know of it. The mango pales in comparison. Even

the spiky pineapple becomes familiar once you cut

into it. But the pomegranate, with its glistening

ruby seeds and blood-red juice makes everything it touches tantalizing and unusual.

We are not alone in our belief in the mysterious nature of the pomegranate. According to Greek legend, when Hades, god of the underworld, kidnapped Persephone, the daughter of Demeter, goddess of the harvest, he agreed to set her free if she ate nothing during her stay. But Hades knew Persephone would be unable to resist the pomegranate. And so for each of the six seeds she ate, she had to spend a month with him in the underworld for eternity. The saddened Demeter could grow nothing while her daughter was away. And this is how the barrenness of winter came to be.

In Chinese and Hebrew lore pomegranates are a symbol of fertility. For Jews, the pomegranate is used in the Succoth, the eight-day harvest celebration. When Moses described the abundance of the promised land, he included pomegranates. And pomegranates are used during Rosh Hashanah to bring good luck for the new year.

It's not a great leap from fertility to love. And, in fact, pomegranates were alleged to have been first planted by Aphrodite, the goddess of love. Solomon sang of an orchard of pomegranates when he wooed Sheba. And Juliet was serenaded by Romeo's nightingale under a pomegranate tree.

And if love and fertility aren't enough, how about spiritual cleansing? The prophet Mohammed believed that pomegranates could purge the human system of envy and hatred.

WHERE GROWN

The San Joaquin Valley in California is the only serious growing area for pomegranates in the United States. Pomegranates are also grown in Spain and Italy as well as Central and South America and the Middle East.

VARIETIES

The pomegranate is about the size of an apple with a red, leathery skin. In some ways it also looks like a Christmas tree ornament—the small calyx looks like the place where the hook goes for hanging on the tree. Inside, there is a honeycomb of bright red seeds in clusters, separated by white inedible pith.

The Wonderful or Red Wonderful is the most common variety. There are smaller plantings of Early Foothill.

SEASONS

Pomegranates are available from late August through December, with peak supplies in October and November.

SELECTION, HANDLING & STORAGE

Pomegranates are shipped ripe and ready to eat. Look for fruit that is heavy with juice and has a thin but tough skin that is not broken. The pithy membrane that surrounds the seeds should not be too prominent, meaning that the seeds should be abundant as well as full of juice. The seeds should also be tender.

Store pomegranates out of direct sunlight and in a cool place and they'll last a few weeks. In the refrigerator they will last two months or more. The seeds will last a week or more in the refrigerator and can be frozen for up to a year. Pomegranate juice will last about five days under refrigeration, up to six months frozen (see Preparation, page 469).

NUTRITION

One hundred grams of pomegranate seeds (about 3.5 ounces) contains 63 calories, 16g of carbohydrates, .5g or less of protein, fiber, and fat, and about 6% of the DV for vitamin C. Pomegranates are also a decent source of potassium.

YIELD

A medium pomegranate yields about ³/₄ cup of seeds and ¹/₂ cup of juice.

Tony's Tip

To give kids a real treat, roll pomegranates around to loosen seeds, then make a slit in the skin and let them suck out the sweet-tart juice. (You can stick in a straw if you like.) But make sure they wear old clothes and stay away from the nice furniture because pomegranate stains are hard to get out.

PREPARATION

When it comes to stripping away the bad and the ugly to get to the good, the artichoke has nothing on the pomegranate. In *The Food Lover's Tiptionary* (Hearst Books, 1994), Sharon Tyler Herbst calls the pomegranate nature's most labor-intensive fruit.

The seeds are everything in this fruit. And the key is to extract them without bringing along the bitter pith. The method suggested by the Simonian Fruit Company as well as by highly regarded food writers like Paula Wolfert goes like this: Cut the crown or calyx off the top and lightly score the rind in several places. Submerge the fruit in a large bowl of water for five minutes. Then, while holding the fruit under water, break the sections apart, separating the seeds from the membranes. The membranes and rind will float to the top and the seeds will sink to the bottom. Skim away the former and drain the seeds in a colander.

We prefer to follow the above except for submerging in water, which doesn't seem to make things any easier and dulls the sheen on the seeds. We separate the seeds on top of a counter.

If all you want is the juice, you can squeeze the seeds over the sieve and discard them once all their juice has been rendered. If you use the submersion method, the seeds can be run through a blender or food processor to liquefy, then strained over a cheesecloth-lined sieve.

Because pomegranate juice stains like the dickens, it can be used to color other foods, especially fruits like pears. The juice can also be used in marinades and sauces. For example, make a pan sauce for sautéed chicken or turkey breast or pork medallions by deglazing the pan with pomegranate juice along with a little chicken stock. Sometimes you can combine red wine or port with pomegranate juice for a more complex flavor.

Pomegranate Syrup (page 472) has more versatility in marinades, sauces, and dressings because of its thick texture and intense flavor. It can be used in a marinade for lamb, in a salad dressing (see page 471), or in drinks with vodka, champagne, or an old-fashioned Shirley Temple instead of commercial grenadine, which may contain all sorts of things you don't want.

Pomegranate seeds are a wonderful garnish for a wide array of dishes, certainly for any that contain pomegranate juice or syrup, but also anything else that needs perking up such as salads, ice cream dishes, rice, mixed fruit, yogurt, and puddings.

Citrus juices go well with pomegranate syrup or juice in sauces and dressings. Spices that you would use in Middle Eastern dishes would also be appropriate with pomegranate, particularly garlic and cumin.

Turkey Breast with Pomegranate Glaze

If you're strictly a white meat person, or a whole turkey is just too much food for you, a fresh turkey breast or breast half is a good alternative, for Thanksgiving or any other time.

Makes 4 to 6 servings

2 large pomegranates
1/2 cup dry red wine
1/2 cup Chicken Stock (page 9) or
  turkey stock
3 to 3 1/2-pound turkey breast half

Kosher salt and freshly ground black
  pepper to taste
Rock salt (optional)
1 teaspoon arrowroot or 3/4 teaspoon
  cornstarch

1. Roll pomegranates on a hard, level surface pressing down on them with the heel of your hand to loosen the seeds. Don't press too hard or the pomegranates will burst. Cut pomegranates in half and squeeze each half over a strainer into a bowl. Press seeds to extract juice. You should have 3/4 to 1 cup liquid. Reserve 1/4 cup seeds.

2. Preheat oven to 500°F. Combine half the pomegranate juice with red wine and stock in a saucepan. Over medium heat, reduce by half, about 10 minutes. Remove from heat and set sauce aside.

3. Loosen skin of turkey breast. Season flesh with salt and pepper. Brush flesh under skin with some of the remaining pomegranate juice (not the sauce). Put breast on a 1/2-inch layer of rock salt (or on a rack) in a roasting pan. Cook in the oven, basting a few more times with pomegranate juice, for about 50 to 55 minutes, or until the internal temperature reads 165°F.

4. Remove turkey and cover with foil for 10 minutes. Put sauce over medium heat and whisk in arrowroot. Season with salt and pepper and cook a few minutes until smooth and lightly thickened.

5. Remove skin from turkey, slice, and serve with pomegranate sauce. Sprinkle with reserved pomegranate seeds.

Sam's Cooking Tip

The best way to get even slices from a turkey breast (and this can be used when you're dealing with a whole turkey) is to first remove the breast meat in one piece from the bone, beginning at the breast bone. Then, with the boneless breast on a cutting board, cut thin slices on the diagonal.

Green Salad with Pomegranate Vinaigrette

This dish calls for a mesclun mix now available in many supermarkets. Make sure you get a good amount of bitter greens such as mustard and frisée to give a nice contrast to the sweet-tart nature of Pomegranate Syrup.

Makes 4 to 6 servings

3 tablespoons Pomegranate Syrup
  (page 472)
3 tablespoons fresh lemon juice
1 tablespoon walnut oil
Kosher salt and freshly ground black
  pepper to taste

6 cups mixed salad greens, with some
  bitter greens included, washed and
  dried
3 tablespoons toasted walnuts,
  coarsely chopped (page 28)
2 tablespoons pomegranate seeds

1. In a small bowl, combine Pomegranate Syrup, lemon juice, walnut oil, salt, and pepper.

2. Put greens in a salad bowl. Add about ³/₄ of the dressing. Toss. Add walnuts and pomegranate seeds. Toss again and taste. Add more dressing if desired.

Pomegranate Syrup

This is much better than bottled grenadine. Try it over ice cream, drizzled on roasted sweet potatoes, in dressings, or in drinks like the Shirley Temple or the Pomegranate Kir Royale (page 473).

Makes about 2 cups

Juice of 3 pomegranates, about 1⅓ cups
1⅓ cups sugar
1 teaspoon fresh lemon juice

1. Combine pomegranate juice and sugar in a saucepan. Bring to a boil, stirring. Lower heat and simmer about 5 minutes.

2. Remove from heat. Add lemon juice.

Pomegranate Kir Royale

*A Kir Royale is normally made with champagne and crème de cassis
(currant liqueur). This version has a similar color but a slightly more exotic flavor.
Make your friends guess what the secret ingredient is.*

Makes 5 servings

5 tablespoons Pomegranate Syrup (page 472)
1 bottle champagne or other sparkling wine

Put 1 tablespoon of Pomegranate Syrup into each of 5 champagne flutes. Pour 5 ounces of champagne into each flute and serve.

quince

We've heard of clothes going out of style. Cars, hairdos, and football formations too. But can a fruit go out of style?

Yes, it can. Just ask the quince. Once considered a staple in Colonial-American kitchens and for home cooks well into the nineteenth century, the quince fell victim to the industrial revolution and changing lifestyles.

You see, the quince can't be eaten like an apple or a pear, two fruits with which it has physical and sensory commonality. A raw quince has dry, almost cottony flesh and tart, bordering on astringent taste. But when cooked, quince yields a wonderful perfume and a delightfully mellow fall flavor. It also has loads of pectin, which makes it perfect for canning. Quince jams, marmalade, and conserves (as well as quince candy) were as common in eighteenth- and nineteenth-century America as grape jelly is today. There was even something called quince cheese, fruit boiled all day long until it eventually solidified.

But by 1850, the American canning industry was well underway and home canning began to dwindle like home bread baking. And for those who continued to can, quince became less and less of a candidate until it almost reached oblivion in post–World War II America. Quince isn't even mentioned in Joe Carcione's *The Greengrocer,* published in 1972 (Chronicle Books), not because our friend Joe was deficient but because quince was still in limbo a quarter of a century ago.

Now this cuddly fruit (sometimes it has a grayish, woolly coating) has made a comeback of sorts. You'll see it in farmer's markets and specialty stores mostly, but it's there. It will probably never be as "in" as it once was. But in this crazy world of ours, sometimes a thing is so out, it's in.

WHERE GROWN

Quinces are grown in the United States in the same kind of climate in which you find pears and apples. Most major commercial production is in California. Quinces are also grown in France, Greece, Argentina, New Zealand, and Iran.

VARIETIES

There are many varieties of quince but only two of note. The perfumed quince has an oval shape with tapered ends. The skin is smooth and yellow and the tart flesh is white. The larger pineapple quince looks somewhat like a knobby pear with yellow skin when ripe. The white, acidic flesh has a faint flavor of pineapple.

SEASONS

The pineapple quince begins in August and runs through November. The perfumed quince season is October through February.

SELECTION, HANDLING & STORAGE

Choose fruit that is as large as possible because it is the most economical and easiest to handle. Quinces may be pale green like a Granny Smith apple or yellow like a Golden Delicious. Generally, earlier fruit is greener and later fruit more golden. But both are usually ready to cook with when purchased, though a lot of people like to leave quinces out in a fruit bowl for their gentle fragrance. Don't let them remain at room temperature for more than a week, however, or they will start to deteriorate.

Refrigerate as you would apples but wrap them well to avoid bruising, though bruising will not affect the overall quality of the cooked fruit. Under refrigeration, quinces will last about as long as apples.

NUTRITION

Quinces are not going to make a comeback on their nutrition laurels. A 100g (3.5-ounce) serving contains 57 calories, which is misleading because to make the fruit palatable, you'll need quite a few calories more of sugar or other sweeteners. A serving also contains 15g of carbohydrates, about .5g of protein, just under

2g of dietary fiber, 25% of the DV for vitamin C, and about 4% for iron. Quinces are also a fair source of potassium.

YIELD

A pound of quinces (three medium to large) will yield about 1½ cups of chopped or sliced fruit.

Tony's Tip

> In some parts of the world, quince seeds are dried, then cooked in small amounts of water and taken as a relief for coughing.

PREPARATION

There may be some woolly fuzz on quinces, especially on smaller perfumed quinces, which you're more likely to see at farmer's markets. This rubs off easily.

Quinces can be peeled and cored like apples and pears. However, because the seed sack in the center of the quince is somewhat rounder, we find it easier to first halve the quince lengthwise, then scoop out the seeds with a melon baller.

Almost any kind of cooking will improve quinces. They are wonderful poached in syrup with aromatics like cardamom and cinnamon, and with lemon and orange peel and spirits such as orange liqueur and pear or apple brandy. The addition of dried fruits such as prunes and apricots makes for satisfying compotes.

Try them baked as you would apples (although quince pies may take some getting used to). Normally, quinces are accompanied by other fruits, in cobblers for example. Apples or pears are naturals, but so are other fall fruits such as cranberries.

In North African and Middle Eastern cuisines, quinces are frequently used with meat—very often lamb but also poultry, especially duck—in savory stews and tagines (see Chicken and Quince Tagine, page 479).

In addition to cinnamon and nutmeg, flavorings appropriate to quince are nutmeg, mace, allspice, ground coriander, ginger, very floral honeys, aromatic dry and sweet white wines, almonds, and vanilla.

Quince Pandowdy with Apples and Cranberries

Pandowdies are an old New England variation on deep-dish pies and cobblers, originally served for breakfast, which we think is still a good idea. The word pandowdy comes from "dowdying," meaning breaking the crust up into pieces before serving.

Makes 6 servings

4 cups peeled and sliced quinces
3 cups peeled and sliced tart apples
1¹/₂ cups cranberries
¹/₂ cup spicy orange marmalade
¹/₄ cup orange juice
1 cup brown sugar
3 tablespoons quick-cooking tapioca
Butter-flavored cooking spray
1 cup all-purpose flour
2 teaspoons baking powder

¹/₄ teaspoon salt
¹/₄ cup plus 1 tablespoon granulated sugar
3 tablespoons chilled butter, cut into small pieces
¹/₂ cup plus a few tablespoons chilled low-fat buttermilk, approximately
¹/₄ teaspoon cinnamon
Low-fat vanilla ice cream or frozen yogurt (optional)

1. Put quinces, apples, cranberries, and marmalade in a large mixing bowl. Mix orange juice and marmalade in a small bowl. Add to fruit and mix well.

2. Combine brown sugar and tapioca in a small bowl. Pour over fruit and mix well. Preheat oven to 375°F.

3. Spray a 2-quart gratin or baking dish with butter-flavored spray. Pour fruit mixture into the pan and spread out evenly.

4. Put flour, baking powder, salt, and ¹/₄ cup granulated sugar in a mixing bowl. Cut in the butter with a large fork or pastry blender until the mixture resembles coarse meal. Add ¹/₄ cup buttermilk and mix just until the dough comes together in a ball. Chill in freezer 10 minutes.

5. Cover a cutting board with plastic wrap, pulled tightly and tucked under the board. Dust with flour, put the dough in the middle, dust with a little more flour, and flatten slightly. Cover with another sheet of plastic wrap, tightly drawn and tucked under the cutting board. Roll out dough just large enough to fit inside the baking dish. Peel off plastic wrap and top fruit with dough. Cut 4 or 5 vents into the dough. Brush the crust with the remaining buttermilk. Combine 1 tablespoon sugar and cinnamon and sprinkle on top of the crust.

6. Bake 30 minutes or until the top is golden brown and juices bubble up freely. Remove from oven and cut through the crust with a large serving fork or spatula, creating 2-inch pieces (they should be irregular for that homey touch). Then push the pieces of crust into the fruit with the back of the spatula. Bake another 10 minutes. Serve warm with low-fat vanilla ice cream or frozen yogurt if desired.

Chicken and Quince Tagine

Serve this fragrant and warming dish with couscous to soak up some of the delightful broth and an off-dry (slightly sweet) Riesling.

Makes 4 servings

1½ teaspoons ground allspice

2 teaspoons kosher salt

2 chicken breast halves, on the bone, skin and wings removed

2 chicken legs, skin removed

Olive oil cooking spray

1 medium onion, halved and thinly sliced

⅛ teaspoon saffron threads mixed with 1 cup defatted Chicken Stock (page 9)

½ cup apple juice or apple cider mixed with 2 tablespoons honey

2 large quinces, about 1 pound, peeled, cored and cut in eighths

½ cup pitted prunes

1. Mix half the allspice with 1 teaspoon salt and rub all over chicken parts. Spray a non-stick skillet with olive oil spray and put over medium heat. Brown chicken well on all sides and put into a Dutch oven or casserole.

2. Spray skillet again and add onion. Cover and cook over medium-low heat until softened, about 5 minutes. Raise heat to brown onion (about 2 minutes) and add to chicken. Add stock mixed with saffron to the pan, bring to a boil, and add to chicken. Add cider and honey to chicken along with quinces, prunes, remaining allspice, and another teaspoon of salt.

3. Bring casserole to a boil on top of the stove. Lower heat, cover, and continue cooking on the stove or put into a preheated 350°F oven. Cook about 30 minutes or until chicken and quinces are tender.

Sam's Cooking Tip

Rather than spending about twice as much money buying parts, buy a whole chicken and cut it up yourself for the parts needed in this dish. Use leftovers for stock.

Quince Anna

This is made using the same concept as Potatoes Anna, a classic French dish of thinly sliced potatoes baked in a shallow dish or pie plate. Serve it as a simple dessert with low-fat or nonfat frozen vanilla yogurt or ice cream.

Makes 4 to 6 servings

2 tablespoons each granulated and cane sugar
$^1/_2$ teaspoon each ground cinnamon and ground ginger
4 large or 6 small quinces, about 2 pounds
2 tablespoons chilled butter

1. Mix sugars with spices in a small bowl. Set aside. Preheat oven to 350°F.

2. Halve, peel, and core quinces. Cut quinces into thin slices.

3. Cut half the butter into small pieces. Melt the other half in a 7-inch cast-iron skillet over low heat. While the skillet is still over the heat, arrange slices overlapping in 1 layer in concentric circles. Sprinkle with $^1/_4$ of the sugar mixture and $^1/_4$ of the remaining butter. Repeat process with circles going in the opposite direction. Add sugar mixture and butter and repeat, alternating the direction of the circles until all the quince is used up. Fill in the center with odd-shaped pieces. (Don't worry if it mounds in the center. It will collapse when it cooks.)

4. Raise heat to medium and cook 5 minutes on the stove. Cover and put in the oven for 20 minutes or until very tender. Remove and invert onto a plate.

Quince Conserve with Cardamom

This can be used over low-fat ice cream or frozen yogurt for dessert or on waffles and pancakes for breakfast.

Makes about 4 cups

1¹/₂ cups Sugar Syrup (page 382)

¹/₂ cup dessert wine such as a late-harvest Riesling

2 tablespoons honey

1 tablespoon cardamom pods, put in a tea ball or wrapped in cheesecloth

2 cinnamon sticks

1 tablespoon minced orange zest plus juice of 1 orange

2 pounds quinces (about 2 large or 3 medium), peeled, cored, and cut into ³/₈-inch dice

1. Combine all ingredients except quince in a heavy-bottomed saucepan. Bring to a boil and add quinces.

2. Simmer, partially covered, about 40 minutes over low heat, stirring occasionally, until quinces are very soft. Remove from heat, discard cardamom and cinnamon, and allow to cool. Refrigerate up to a month.

bibliography

In addition to the books listed below, our book is indebted to the Produce Marketing Association, the United Fresh Fruit and Vegetable Association, and the numerous associations, boards, and commissions that represent fruits and vegetables, as well as private fruit and vegetable companies throughout the country, including the following:

Fruits

Brooks Tropicals, California Apricot Advisory Board, California Avocado Commission, California Avocado Media Bureau, California Cantaloupe Advisory Board, California Date Administrative Committee, California Fig Advisory Board, California Fuyu Growers Association, California Kiwifruit Commission, California Strawberry Commission, California Table Grape Commission, California Tree Fruit Agreement, Cherry Marketing Institute, Chilean Fresh Fruit Association, Confederation of Mexico Fruit and Vegetable Grower Associations, Del Monte Fresh Produce, Dole Food Co., Florida Department of Citrus, Frieda's, Georgia Department of Agriculture, Georgia Peach Commission, International Apple Institute, International Banana Association, Maine Blueberry Commission, Michigan Blueberry

Growers Association, Michigan Plum Advisory Board, National Peach Council, National Watermelon Promotion Board, New Jersey Blueberry Industry Advisory Council, Northwest Cherry Growers, Ocean Spray Cranberries, Oregon Blueberry Commission, Oregon Raspberry and Blackberry Commission, Oregon Strawberry Commission, Oregon-Washington-California Pear Bureau, Papaya Administrative Committee, Pineapple Growers Association of Hawaii, Simonian Fruit Company, Sunkist Growers, Sun World International, TexaSweet Citrus Marketing, Washington Apple Commission, Washington Blueberry Commission, Washington Red Raspberry Commission, Washington State Fruit Commission, Wild Blueberry Association of North America.

Vegetables

American Celery Council, Belgian Endive Marketing Board, California Artichoke Advisory Board, California Asparagus Commission, California Fresh Carrot Advisory Board, California Tomato Board, Christopher Ranch, D'Arrigo Bros. Co., Florida Tomato Committee, Fresh Garlic Association, Georgia Sweet Potato Commission, Idaho-Eastern Oregon Onion Promotion Committee, Imperial Sweet Onion Commission, Ketchum Public Relations, Leafy Greens Council, Michigan Asparagus Advisory Board, Michigan Celery Promotion Co-operative, Mushroom Council, North American Radish Council, OSO Sweet Onions, The Potato Board, Sweet Potato Council of the United States, Tanimura and Antle, Vidalia Onion Committee, Washington State Potato Commission, Washington Rhubarb Growers Association.

In addition, Jesse Cool's produce columns, which originated in the San Jose Mercury News, were a valuable resource as well as a constant inspiration.

Aikens, Curtis G. *Curtis Aikens' Guide to the Harvest.* Atlanta: Peachtree Publishers, 1993.

Armstrong, Jane. "Squashing Questions about Hard Shell Squash." *IGA Grocergram.* September 1989.

Bailey, Adrian, ed. *Cook's Ingredients.* Pleasantville, N.Y.: The Reader's Digest Association, 1990.

Ball, Frank, and Arlene Feltman, eds. *Trucs of the Trade.* New York: HarperPerennial, 1992.

Beard, James. *James Beard's American Cookery*. Boston: Little, Brown and Co., 1972

Belk Rian, Sarah. "Peas." *The Cook's Magazine*. May/June 1984.

Berkeley, Robert. *Peppers: A Cookbook*. New York: Fireside, 1992.

Bittman, Mark. "Eating Well." *New York Times*. August 31, 1994.

Brennan, Georgeanne, and Charlotte Glenn. *Peppers, Hot and Chile*. Berkeley: Aris Books, 1988.

Carcione, Joe, and Bob Lucas. *The Greengrocer*. San Francisco: Chronicle Books, 1972.

Carper, Jean. *Food: Your Miracle Medicine*. New York: HarperCollins Publishers, 1993.

———. *The Food Pharmacy*. New York: Bantam Books, 1988.

Chalmers, Irena, Milton Glaser and others. *Great American Food Almanac*. New York: Harper and Row, 1986.

Creasy, Rosalind. *Cooking from the Garden*. San Francisco: Sierra Club Books, 1988.

Cunningham, Marion. *The Fanny Farmer Cookbook*. New York: Alfred A. Knopf, 1990.

Czarnecki, Jack. *A Cook's Book of Mushrooms*. New York: Artisan, 1995.

———. *Joe's Book of Mushroom Cookery*. New York: Atheneum, 1988.

Dahlen, Martha, and Karen Phillipps. *A Popular Guide to Chinese Vegetables*. New York: Crown, 1983.

DeVos, Neal E. "Artichoke Production in California." *HortTechnology*, 2(4). October/December 1992.

Elving, Phyllis, ed. *Sunset Fresh Produce*. Menlo Park, Calif.: Lane Publishing Co., 1987.

Ensminger, Audrey H., M. E. Ensminger, James E. Konlande, and John R. K. Robson. *Foods and Nutrition Encyclopedia*. Boca Raton, Fla.: CRC Press, 1994.

Fletcher, Janet. *More Vegetables, Please*. Emeryville, Calif.: Harlow and Ratner, 1992.

Fussell, Betty. *Crazy for Corn*. New York: HarperCollins, 1995.

———. *The Story of Corn*. New York: Alfred A. Knopf, 1992.

Gelb, Barbara Levine, ed. *The Dictionary of Food and What's in It for You.* London: Paddington Press, 1978.

Griffith, Linda, and Fred Griffith. *Onions, Onions, Onions.* Shelburne, Vt.: Chapters, 1994.

Haas, Elson M. *Staying Healthy with Nutrition.* Berkeley: Celestial Arts, 1992.

Heatter, Maida. *Maida Heatter's Book of Great Desserts.* New York: Alfred A. Knopf, 1977.

Herbst, Sharon Tyler. *Food Lover's Companion.* Hauppauge, N.Y.: Barron's Educational Series, 1990.

————. *The Food Lover's Tiptionary.* New York: Hearst Books, 1994.

Hirasuna, Delphine. *Vegetables.* San Francisco: Chronicle Books, 1985.

Hodgson, Moira. *The New York Times Gourmet Shopper.* New York: New York Press, 1983.

Idone, Christopher. *Lemons: A Country Garden Cookbook.* San Francisco: CollinsPublishersSan Francisco, 1993.

Jacobson, John D. *Eatioms.* New York: Dell Publishing, 1993.

Jamieson, Patricia, and Cheryl Dorschner, eds. *Recipe Rescue Cookbook.* Charlotte, Vt.: Camden House Publishing, 1993.

Jones, Evan. *American Food: The Gastronomic Story.* New York: Vintage, 1981.

Kafka, Barbara. *Microwave Gourmet.* New York: William Morrow and Co., 1987.

Kirschmann, John D., and Lavon J. Dunne. *Nutrition Almanac.* New York: McGraw-Hill Book Co., 1984.

Kraus Sibella. *Greens: A Country Garden Cookbook.* San Francisco: CollinsPublishersSan Francisco, 1993.

Leibenstein, Margaret. *The Edible Mushroom.* New York: Fawcett Columbine, 1986.

Lesem, Jeanne. *Preserving Today.* New York: Alfred A. Knopf, 1992.

Logan, Michele, ed. *The Packer 1995 Produce Availability and Merchandising Guide.* Lenexa, Kan.: Vance Publishing Corp., 1995.

Martin, Rux, Patricia Jamieson, and M. S. Hiser, eds. *The Eating Well Cookbook.* Charlotte, Vt.: Camden House Publishing, 1991.

McGee, Harold. *The Curious Cook.* San Francisco: North Point Press, 1990.

Montagne, Prosper. *The New Larousse Gastronomique.* New York: Crown Publishers, 1977.

Morgan, Lane. *Winter Harvest Cookbook.* Seattle: Sasquatch Books, 1990.

Netzer, Corinne T. *The Corinne T. Netzer Encyclopedia of Food Values.* New York: Dell Publishing, 1992.

Olney, Richard. *Provence the Beautiful Cookbook.* San Francisco: CollinsPublishersSan Francisco, 1993.

Owen, Millie, ed. *Lois Burpee's Gardener's Companion and Cookbook.* New York: Harper and Row, 1968.

Payne, Rolce Redard, and Dorrit Speyer Senior. *Cooking with Fruit.* New York: Crown Publishers, 1992

Pennington, Jean A. T. *Bowes and Church's Food Values of Portions Commonly Used.* Philadelphia: J. B. Lippincott Company, 1994.

Pepin, Jacques. *Cuisine Economique.* New York: William Morrow and Co., 1992.

Rain, Patricia. *The Artichoke Cookbook.* Berkeley: Celestial Arts, 1985.

Richard, Ray, and Lance Walheim. *Citrus: How to Select, Grow and Enjoy.* Los Angeles: HP Books, 1980.

Rosenthal, Sylvia, ed. *Fresh Food.* New York: E. P. Dutton, 1978.

Rozin, Elisabeth. *Blue Corn and Chocolate.* New York: Alfred. A Knopf, 1992.

Schneider, Elizabeth. "Citrus Fruit: Part 1." *Food Arts.* September 1990.

———. "Citrus Savvy: Part 2." *Food Arts.* October 1990.

———. "Great Greens!" *Food and Wine.* October 1985.

———. "Greens for the Pot." *Food Arts.* June 1994.

———. "The Truth about Okra." *Beard House.* August 1995.

———. *Uncommon Fruits and Vegetables: A Commonsense Guide.* New York: Harper and Row, 1986.

Schwartz, Leonard. *Salads.* New York: HarperPerennial, 1992.

Sokolov, Raymond. *Why We Eat What We Eat.* New York: Touchstone, 1991.

Stone, Sally, and Martin Stone. *The Essential Root Vegetable Cookbook.* New York: Clarkson Potter Publishers, 1991.

Sunset Books and Sunset Magazine, eds. *Sunset Fresh Produce A to Z.* Menlo Park, Calif: Sunset Publishing Corp., 1987.

Sunset Books and Sunset Magazine, eds. *Sunset Home Canning.* Menlo Park, Calif: Sunset Publishing Corp., 1992.

Whitman, Joan, ed. *Craig Claiborne's The New York Times Food Encyclopedia.* New York: Times Books, 1985.

Yockelson, Lisa. *Fruit Desserts.* New York: HarperCollins Publishers, 1991.

Zimmerman, Linda, and Peggy Mellody. *Cobblers, Crumbles and Crisps.* New York: Clarkson Potter Publishers, 1991.

index